TRANSIT CIRCLE
The Story of William Simms
(1793 to 1860)

Front Cover: William Simms, 1850

Flamstead House, home of the Astronomer Royal, 1850.

Transit Circle
The Story of
WILLIAM SIMMS
(1793 to 1860)

by
Eleanor Mennim, M.B.Ch.

William Sessions Limited
York, England

ISBN 1 85072 101 7

To
Michael

Printed in 10 on 11 point Plantin Typeface
by William Sessions Limited
The Ebor Press
York, England

Contents

List of Illustrations

Preface

WILLIAM SIMMS WAS, WITHOUT DOUBT, a great man – great in intellect, in skills, in generosity and even in physical size. He was also quiet and retiring, so that we hear little of him except second-hand through the achievements of those who used his instruments to bridge the gulf of research between the early astronomers of the 17th and 18th centuries and the complicated astrophysics of the 20th.

William, however, repays study because, starting with a few bare facts, there emerges a comprehensive story owing to five particular attributes. The first of these must be that his life was an eventful one, and in the mainstream of his genre. From his work he came to know a range of eminent people, some like Brunel, household names; others such as George Airy, the energetic Astronomer Royal, on a more lofty plane, but, whilst fascinating to follow, still prone to human failings. The great land surveys of the early 19th century in this country and abroad carried William's instruments across the world, and the accompanying increased attention to astronomy and navigation diverted his thoughts to India, Australia, the Cape, the 'US of America', as well as European destinations. Of all the centres of study, the most influential was however, the Royal Observatory at Greenwich with which he worked for 30 years and created his famous triumvirate of major telescopes, finally adding his swansong, the Great Equatorial, the year before he died. His recognition by the Royal Society and at the Great Exhibition are evidence enough of the regard in which he was held.

The second characteristic associated with William Simms is the unequivocal pattern of his life, almost as if planned from the beginning, and indeed it is clearly noticeable that at every stage he grasped opportunities as they arose, and though 'manipulation' would be too emotive a word, he certainly anticipated events sufficiently to ease himself into their paths. From boyhood training in his father's optical workshop, through tutoring in mathematics after school, to wise apprenticeship at the hub of the instrument trade, he was provided with a flying start in his career. Once a Freeman, he directed his first invention, modest though it was, towards the Society of Arts, following it by his own presence at their lectures and open meetings, where its worth was recognised, his own potential marked, and his progress watched with interest by men who were to influence his life. He came to know Bryan Donkin, an engineer, inventor, and key figure in the future Astronomical Society; Colonel Colby who showed confidence enough in him to give him large orders for surveying equipment; and most importantly the doyen of the optical world, Edward Troughton who ultimately offered him a partnership in his flourishing Fleet Street business. From this stage, increasingly important orders for work and an unsullied reputation – (with the extraordinary exception concerning Sir James South), reached their zenith in 1852 with his Fellowship of the Royal Society, followed by a gradual passing on to his son, James, of his professional mantle. Thus was the transit of his life's circle completed.

The essential base for piecing William's story together needs to be a large pool of archival material. There is no lack of this although time has inevitably played havoc in some areas. The most important, not surprisingly, are those collections belonging to the Royal Greenwich Observatory and the Royal Astronomical Society, to Vickers Instruments (20th century successors of Troughton & Simms), and the Cambridge Observatory where William spent many hours. The Royal Observatory at Edinburgh has yielded much of interest of its predecessor on Calton Hill, and the National Museum of Scotland has a good collection of work by William Simms. There are many other sources, great and small, and as far as his personality is concerned, by far the most illuminating are the large number of his letters written to friends, colleagues and clients, in which the small throwaway phrase, turn of sentence, personal comment by way of postscript, or his clear rolling prose, speak volumes about a man whose main features were simplicity, sense of humour and sheer adroitness with his creations. His forgetfulness over trivia is an aspect which only serves to humanise him.

The third facet which study of William Simms reveals is the influence of his family background, of which a remarkable amount has been discovered. His large family and its inevitable joys and sadnesses are described at length because of their importance to him, and no doubt his effect on them in the normal course of a Regency and early Victorian home life in London, and later the move to the Surrey countryside, which have all been fully explored and placed in their historical context. To this has been added personal aspects such as what William wore, what he ate, the apprenticeship system, with whom he mixed socially, how he came to know his two successive wives, where he went for holidays, how he posted his letters, what he read, his religious persuasion, and lastly his illnesses, all adding colour to the picture. Not least are the descriptions of his various homes, the streets he knew well, the churches where he was married and his 12 children baptised, and finally the family burial places.

To complete this study the period of political and social change in which William lived is described at length throughout the book, since its very nature was integral to his being, and commencing in the first chapters with a detailed picture of how the scene was set in the preceding century. It was one of the most extraordinary times of transition from which the 18th century man with his tricorn hat, powdered wig, embroidered coat, breeches, hose and buckled shoes was replaced by the soberly clad Victorian gentleman in his top hat and dark dress coat and trousers. The transformation in clothes was orchestrated by the mores of the French wars and the agrarian revolution in the country which developed into the industrial upheavals of the towns, for which the invention of steam power was fundamental. The long-distance coach gave way to the railway train, the Napoleonic feud to a long period of peace, candles to gas lamps, and the suburban fields surrounding large cities such as London and Birmingham to an unending sprawl of speculative housing.

This then, is not primarily an account of the development of scientific instruments with which William Simms was involved. All the instruments alluded to in the text are noted in an inventory at the end, but the list does not pretend to be definitive, and only enumerates those mentioned in letters, drawings and memoirs, although naturally the most important figure there. Rather this is the story of a distinguished craftsman of the first half of the 19th century who was typical of his time; how he trained and worked and thought, and of all the factors surrounding him which affected his life in a mutating world which included Trafalgar, Waterloo, the Bread Riots, the formation of the police force, the horrors of the Irish famine and London poverty, and the rise of great prosperity and Empire.

To pull the tale together brings a confusion of names, particularly Williams and James', and resort has therefore been necessary in the interests of clarity to the inclusion in brackets of the year of birth after a name where identity has seemed doubtful. This leads unfortunately to jerky flow of the text, and therefore where the meaning appears obvious it has been omitted. Events also have only been mentioned where there is clear evidence for them, or the inference is overwhelming. Much as one would like to know what Ann Nutting looked like, there is no known picture of her, but her clothing and hairstyle are described as far as possible as they would have been in real life. Similarly the family visits to Crystal Palace after it moved to Sydenham, or to Greenwich on the new railway and back on the river, is only what all Londoners enjoyed at the time, and is most probably true of William of whom there is no lack of evidence as to his fondness for his children.

A list of principal sources is appended, and acknowledgement made here of the selfless help freely given to me in my searches by archivists, librarians and others approached. I am most appreciative of their many kindnesses. As always, my prop has been my husband, who has quietly provided the conditions to assimilate and collate the material gathered.

Research is not definitive, and a study of William's instruments themselves will, I hope, be undertaken by someone more qualified than I to do so. Meanwhile, new facts and evidence will continue to come to light, sometimes contradicting earlier evidence and deduction. However, at some point one must call a halt, close the files and put down one's pen, though tangential paths which have not yet been explored will still beckon, and often belatedly provide clues to the family. The byways are endless, some leading to streams of light, others to darkened skies. 'Transit Circle' is only a lens, a 19th century wheel of fortune, ever travelling round to new galaxies and focussing on the stars.

Acknowledgements

MY MAIN SOURCES HAVE BEEN the archives of the following institutions to which my sincere thanks is offered:

Royal Greenwich Observatory, by permission of the Syndics of Cambridge
    University Library and the Director of the Royal Greenwich Observatory
Vickers Instruments, Borthwick Institute, University of York
Cambridge Observatory
Royal Astronomical Society
India Office
Ordnance Survey
Royal Society
Royal Society of Arts
Harvard University
Institute of Civil Engineers
Worshipful Society of Apothecaries
Guildhall Library, Corporation of London
Camden Local History Library
Birmingham Library Services
Public Record Offices –
    Somerset House
    St Catherine's House
    Chancery Lane
    Greater London
Society of Friends
British Medical Association
South African Astronomical Observatory
New Observatory, Edinburgh and the following museums:
    Whipple Museum, Cambridge
    Science Museum, South Kensington
    Science Museum, Edinburgh
London Borough of Sutton Heritage Department
Museum of History of Science, Oxford

The following have gone out of their way to help me:

A. E. B. Owen, Keeper of Manuscripts, Cambridge University Library
Dr A. Perkins, Archivist, Royal Greenwich Observatory/Cambridge University Library
Dr D. Smith, Borthwick Institute, York
Mrs Alison Brech, Archivist, Vickers Instruments
Dr David Dewhirst, Cambridge Observatory
Miss Mary Chibnell, Royal Astronomical Society
Alan J. Clark, Royal Society
Major Charles O'Leary, Apothecaries Hall
Dr John McConnell, Co Down
Dr Charles Mollan, Royal Dublin Society
Dr John Butler, Armagh Observatory
Dr John Andrews, Trinity College, Dublin
Prof Patrick A. Wayman, Dunsink Observatory
The Earl of Rosse, Birr Castle
Miss A. Morrison-Low, Edinburgh Science Museum
Dr J. A. Caldecott
Miss Joyce Brown, Imperial College
R. Penniston Taylor, Wymondham, Leicester
Miss J. S. Ringrose, Archivist, Pembroke College, Cambridge
Dr J. A. Bennett, Whipple Museum, Cambridge
The staff of York Reference Library
Alison Garnett, who typed the manuscript, and its many alterations
The Royal Astronomical Society with financial assistance

Abbreviations

VIA	Vickers Instrument Archives
RGO	Royal Greenwich Observatory
RAS	Royal Astronomical Society
RS	Royal Society
WB	Workbook
Mem	Memoirs
MN	Monthly Notes
COA	Cambridge Observatory Archives
Phil Trans	Philosophical Transactions
Proc RS	Proceedings of the Royal Society
MEAI	Minutes of Edinburgh Astronomical Institution
AROE	Archives of Royal Observatory at Edinburgh
UAV	Harvard College Archives
UA	Harvard College Archives
HOS	*History of the Ordnance Survey*. Ed. A. Seymour
Phillimore	Historical Records of the Survey of India collected and compiled by Col R. H. Phillimore CIE, DSO
Dreyer	*History of the Royal Astronomical Society 1820-1920*, J. L. E. Dreyer, et. al.
Proc ICE	Proceedings of the Institute of Civil Engineers
Mins	Minutes
WS Tech	William Simms' Technical notes
McCrea	*The Royal Greenwich Observatory*, by W. H. McCrea FRS
SA	Society of Apothecaries
RSA	Royal Society of Arts

Simms' family – Birmingham/London

William
c1640-

William
1670-

James
1710-1795

William
1763-1828

William
1793-1860

CHAPTER 1

Introduction

WILLIAM SIMMS WAS BORN IN December 1793 in Birmingham, but spent most of his life in London. His father, William, was born in 1763 in London, but spent the first half of his adult life in Birmingham. His grandfather, James, was born in Birmingham in 1710, having numerous relatives in the town, but he came to live in London in middle life. James' own father, another William, 'son of William', was born in Birmingham in 1670. William's father must have been born about 1640, but a record of the baptism of this early William has not, however, come to light. Perhaps the Civil War which broke out shortly after his birth provides a reason for this omission. Perhaps it was due to carelessness on the part of the parish clerk at the only church in Birmingham, St Martin's, or perhaps he was born in one of the villages roundabout. Registration was in any case a haphazard system, depending not only on the integrity and literacy of the clerk, but also on the need for someone merely to remember to fill in the actual register after the baptism service. Like much else over these years came the recognition of the need for parish records to be developed, standardised and transformed into a national register. The country ways of previous years were not good enough for the social revolutions to come.

★ ★ ★ ★

Each century as it continues and passes in England leaves its own distinctive mark and characteristics on the country. The 18th century was no exception. Rather it was the opposite, as it bridged the gap to the future from the rural community of the 17th century with its primitive and unhygienic living conditions, its coarse manners, its bitter civil war, and its contentions between Catholics, Protestants and Dissenters. Emerging gradually from feudalism, it also, however, left a heritage of increasingly refined craftsmanship, particularly in timber and building, and in painting. The 19th century in contrast was one of rapidly developing technology and industrialisation, increasing population with all its accompanying poverty of the working classes on the one hand. On the other hand it produced its

1

Victorian grandeur and yet an awareness of its slums and its cruelty in mine and factory and penal institution, whilst in our own 20th century the experience of two world wars and the remarkable inventions in all fields has been a consummation of earlier advances, and revolutionised our homes and way of life. In between the extremes of the pastoral 17th century and the industrial 19th came the century of change and transition.

The 18th century first saw light in the last days of Protestant William of Orange, who launched his bloodless revolution in 1688 by landing in the little Devonshire fishing town of Brixham. With his English consort, Mary, the elder daughter of the reigning Catholic monarch, James II, he was received thankfully by the general populace who in June had heard of the birth of a Prince of Wales to James and Mary of Modena, who would be a future threat as Catholic contender to the throne. William successfully turned the tables against Rome, ousted his predecessor to France, and with increasing tolerance for the Catholic minority, ruled hand-in-hand with Parliament, but without personal attraction, until the new century dawned. In 1702 his sister-in-law, Anne, succeeded him, firm in her Protestant beliefs, but being a grand-daughter of Clarendon as well as second daughter of her Catholic father, James, retained an affection for the Tories, remained an Anglican, and was an upholder of the aristocracy and the squirearchy.

England was a rural community in the first years of the 18th century. Its total population was only five-and-a-half million, and it was a land of villages and hamlets, and a very few country towns. In between each cluster of dwellings were enormous tracts of land, virtually uninhabited, unfarmed, and often without more than a bridlepath to cross them. Each little gathering of cottages was very nearly self-sufficient, lived simply on its own crafts and food production, had its own farriers, butchers, spinners, weavers, tailors and shoemakers, brewed its own beer, and built its own houses. It seldom visited or was visited by outsiders. The villagers lived as a unit, the ploughmen working together, the shepherd guarding the sheep of the whole village. The pasture was mostly common land where grazing rights belonged to everyone. Surrounding each village were a few acres hedged or walled, where strips of territory belonged to individuals, but were attended to varyingly by their owners or by a neighbour. Tools were of the simplest, and methods both of agriculture and of other trades had been virtually unchanged for centuries. Folk tales abounded. Witchcraft was feared. Pastoral amusements and tradition continued, all by word of mouth, though the occasional village dame did her lowly best to instill the three Rs.

The near-complete isolation of each village was the cause of this stagnation. Only very few roads had any pretence of upkeep, let alone clearing and surfacing. In the main they were mere tracks around fields or across commons, often deeply depressed by long usage between opposing land boundaries to form the dark tunnel-like holloways which still survive

2

in places today. The village itself was responsible for the upkeep of the roads nearby, but as these were seldom used by themselves, and only by travellers passing through, there was no incentive to maintain the tracks, which remained mere rutted bridlepaths. In winter the surfaces deteriorated into blancmange-like mud and bog, and were frequently impassable in any degree of comfort, if at all. In summer the ridged ruts baked hard, a hazard for carts and carriages, and even for mounted horses. The pack-horse was the only practical method of transferring goods across the country, and this was a slow and tedious business, but often virtually the only link with the outside world. The journeyman looking for work, and the pedlar with his pack full of goods, even trinkets, were often the only contact with other villages or nearby towns, and their gossip, however they slanted it, would be absorbed with relish by the villagers. Few people could read, so it was only by this dubious word-of-mouth method that any news or information was disseminated. In our days of constant bombardment with opinion, news, comment and contra-opinion, where the written and spoken word, photography and noise are so pervasive, it needs a positive effort to comprehend the quiet, the isolation, the necessary self-sufficiency and the reliance on each other in these little communities both for everyday existence and especially in times of trouble.

No wonder social development remained almost static, and methods of manufacture and agriculture were so stultified. Food was basic, hygiene primitive, houses and workshops and backyards insanitary. Medical treatment was often non-existent except in the larger places, and then it was liable to be based on misconceptions of underlying physical processes, and frequently on quasi-religious beliefs, ills being attributable to 'God's will'. The only back-stop in times of real destitution was 'the Parish', which, especially after 1723 when communities could combine to give relief, meant the workhouse with its impersonal and inhumane treatment, and its basic amenities which often offered merely the chance to be kept alive, if that.

However, in spite of what we would nowadays regard as intolerable conditions, the village communities give every evidence of having been happy places to live, particularly if the Squire at the Great House was a good master and the parson both present and approachable. The village inn provided a meeting point in the winter evenings with its welcoming warmth and ale, its flagged floors and its log fires. In summer the village green with its central position and its maypole was a vantage point for local gossip, and the church a source of music and singing and togetherness on a Sunday. The village fidler played his important part in all these locations, the village idiot the butt of local wit. When a traveller did manage to cross the heaths and woods surrounding each community, avoiding robbery and attack on his journey, he was immediately the focus of attention for the news he brought from neighbouring settlements, and indeed from further afield, however

3

disjointed and embroidered the information had become on its constant retelling. Newspapers seldom were seen in the rural areas until well into the 19th century, so the country folk had only the faintest notion of what was going on in the world outside their own little location, and this had the advantage that on the whole they were unaware of the better things in life, nor therefore did they miss them. Hard work was their accepted lot for survival, and contentment was general because of ignorance.

Townspeople were to some degree better off in that their slums were brought to the notice of the middle and upper classes, and the overcrowded squalor, disease and filth could not so easily be ignored, if only because of the very stench of the poor areas. In London only one child in four survived at the beginning of the century. Few streets, even in the capital, were paved, and in the smaller towns, if not just earth-based, they might be cobbled if they were much used, but generally were deep in refuse of all kinds. Even so the towns also had their sense of community, their fairs and markets, their traditions and trades, even if broken into ghettos by class, street or craft.

In 1700 the population of London was 674,000, but it was the only town in England approaching any size. All the cities we now recognise as huge industrial centres of population such as Manchester, Liverpool, Sheffield, Coventry and Birmingham, had very much smaller numbers, and were merely market towns or even large villages, and even well into the century none of them approached the 50,000 mark. They all suffered from the violence, crime, and desperate poverty which was so widespread, and was a product of the hopeless housing conditions, but also of the gin-drinking which developed in the first part of the century as a panacea to the miserable penury of the tightly-packed verminous dwellings. Country folk, as always tended to believe that the streets of towns were paved in gold which would offer relief from the destitution and privations of their own village. They would hopefully travel townwards, only to swell the numbers living in want, and thereby increasing the problem. Itinerant Irishmen added to the multitude of homeless entering the towns, but disease and early death from the gin-drinking maintained the burial rate which continued to be higher than the rate of baptisms to such an extent that in 1751 the Government, sensing disaster, passed an act which so highly taxed spirits that their retail by distillers and shopkeepers ceased, and tea became the predominant drink of all classes. The death rate began to fall dramatically after this date, due also to the enormously improved medical facilities and training of doctors, the foundation of hospitals, and the revolutionising of midwifery practice. At the same time orphan and bastard children were taken into 'foundling hospitals', such as Coram's and the Greycoat and Bluecoat schools, educated and given a trade. Further aids to health were undoubtedly the widespread use of cotton material which could be washed, and the introduction of pottery for kitchen and dining utensils which could be well scoured.

4

1740-1780 thus saw great improvement in social conditions. It was on the whole a peaceful interlude, which experienced the rule of law, and an upsurge of humanitarianism and creative vigour. It reaped the rewards of the charity school movement which began in the reign of Queen Anne and now resulted in an increased ability of even the lower classes to read. The endowed grammar schools had been in existence for some time, but now there were also schools for Dissenters as well. The number of provincial newspapers increased, nearly all started since 1700, and there was an enlarging number of printed tracts, newsletters and even books of fiction, not to mention diaries and letters of all sorts written privately or circulated. Much of this did not come into the hands of the poorest classes, but some of the newsletters were available in coffee-shops of the period, and even these were within the means of artisans and apprentices, disseminating information and broadening outlooks.

The cultural life of the 18th century was centred on London where a tenth of the population of England resided, and a good half of its trained thinking thrived. In architecture and art, drama and literature, law, the church, the army and navy and parliament all contributed to the elevated and widespread interests in the finer sides of life, for which the great houses of the aristocracy west of Temple Bar were places where thought and fine art could be pooled and displayed, and where the great Whig houses fermented knowledge in the developments of industry, agriculture and the sciences. The Royal Society, founded by Charles II in 1660, flourished now a century later. Men of all levels of society were questioning earlier precepts, arguing previously-held views, creating original new thoughts. It was a century of great contrasts between extreme need, ignorance, and satisfaction with the status quo on the one hand; with exuberant creativity, highly skilled craftsmanship, and intellect exercised in the furtherance of enterprise and culture on the other. The great names of the world of the arts, Vanburgh, Nash, Robert Adam, Sheridan, Swift, Sterne, Goldsmith, Gainsborough, Reynolds, are well-known as only a sample. From the fields of invention and science come the names of James Watt, whose steam-engines invented in 1769, underlay the future mechanisation of industry; Benjamin Franklin in the understanding of the nature of electricity; Henry Cavendish in chemistry; Joseph Priestley in chemistry, physics and philosophy; Hargreaves for his invention of the spinning jenny, so seminal to the cloth trade; and Samuel Crompton and Matthew Boulton with their innovations in the organisation of industry in the production of wool and of hardware. These men of applied science laid the foundation of all that followed in the manufacturing industries of the next century, beginning with the mechanisation of cottage industries, first in the workers' homes, then gradually migrating to the many-floored, purpose-built factories and mills. Full-blooded industrialisation steadily followed, gobbling up large tracts of land, and enveloping the towns in the furnace smoke and grime and the vastly increased population drawn from the country around, with all its problems. Men, women and children were gathered willy-nilly into the tentacles of the new way of life, and the country areas became denuded of people, whilst those who had left the villages were now housed in row-upon-row of back-to-back lookalikes, devoid of inspiration or hope, always over-shadowed by the demands of their foremen, and slaves to the knocker-up and the factory bell. It was a squalid life that such folk lived.

In a less overt manner, the agricultural revolution which gave the backing to the later industrialisation with its need for more and cheaper food, began early in the 18th century. Its basis was the complete alteration of the countryside as a result of the enclosure acts. The previously haphazard open pastures and rolling hills and valleys, the marshes and woodlands, even some of the ancient forests, were gradually divided up into manageable areas. This not only transformed methods of farming, but the appearance of the country itself into what we know today as the vast stretches of square-angled fields, each surrounded by hawthorn hedges or dry-stone walls. Now the farmers were each responsible for their own crops and their own cattle and sheep, and they learned to breed selectively, to fertilise the ground, to marl sandy soil and drain swampy areas, to rotate their crops, and to use horse-power for ploughing and leading. In general each man could be free of his neighbours so that he could improve his yields without waste of effort due to others' dilitoriness. The landowners contributed to this revolution by increasing the length of leases so that each tenant reaped the benefit of his own improvements, and the weight of both crops and of livestock increased vastly within a very few years, fortunately hand-in-hand with the country's increasing population.

The enclosure movement started slowly around 1700, but as the years passed and news of the modern methods circulated, it gathered momentum until between 1751 and 1800 there were almost 3,000 further Acts. Meanwhile, as the area of enclosed fields spread further and further from the village centres, so the farmers began to build their dwellings in more isolated sites near to their land in order to avoid the constant journeying. Thus came about the lonely clusters of farm buildings with a single farmhouse, often surrounding a well-protected foldyard, which were so much a feature of England until recently.

The hopelessly bad road system was now given a boost because of the need for better communications between villages and towns and from one village to the next. Thus came about the Turnpike Trusts which were responsible for defined lengths of road, usually between market towns, and could charge for their use. Gradually over the second half of the 18th century, not only the drainage and surfaces of the roads improved, but also the menace of robbery on the highway was tackled, and goods and people could pass without fear of assault. Toll houses were erected, and stage-

6

coaches became established, staging-inns were built, and finally the mail-coach appeared as well as vast waggons of materials needed for industry or finished products on their way to market.

Rivers had already been used for cheap haulage from time immemorial. Some isolated coastal towns such as Whitby which had only poor and dangerous access landwards, depended almost wholly on communication by water. However, rivers did not always run in the right direction, or were too small or meandering to be viable for transport, and now the extensive development of the canal system commenced, starting in 1761 by the Duke of Bridgewater who ordered the cutting of the Worsley Canal by which the price of coal in Manchester was halved. This was quickly followed by a whole network of canals or cuts across river bends, using as far as possible the contours of the land, but if necessary locks and tunnels. Factories and mills in the Midlands and the north could now be supplied easily from their own canal basins with raw materials, and their finished goods removed for marketing.

This then was the countryside which the ordinary person saw if he ventured from his town or village during the Hanoverian period, varying from the truly pastoral and untouched in the reign of Queen Anne, to the encroachment of the new industries on the countryside with its organised field system in the late Georgian. Using only his own legs or riding a horse, he would be unlikely to penetrate the further parts of his county early in the period, but by the end of it he may well have used the stage-coach to travel on reasonable highways from place to place, and indeed in the case of the Simms family this undoubtedly was so, moving as they did between Birmingham and London, a grim and uncertain undertaking as recently as 1700.

★   ★   ★   ★

Birmingham itself is a good example of a developing industrial town. Centred on an ancient site from which it derived its name in reverse – the home or ham of the tribe (ing) of the Berms – in 1538 it is reported by Leland to have had a population of 1,500 living in 200 houses in half-a-dozen streets. Its original raison d'etre was its puny river, the Rea which gave it cheap access to sources of iron, coal, wood and sand, all to be found nearby. From at least the 16th century Birmingham had a predominance of craftsmen engaged in metal work. It also had tanneries and a 'multitude' of forges. By 1700 the population had risen to 11,300 living in 1,900 houses, which doubled in the first half of the 18th century, and then rapidly mounted to 73,630 in 1801, when the number of houses was estimated at 15,630.

7

Although not on any of the great highways which had mostly retained the old Roman pattern it was near enough to be accessible to what is now the A5, and even the old Great North Road, the A1. It also remained an unincorporated town until 1838, and therefore was free of many restrictions, having no constitution, member of Parliament or town council to compose or enforce regulations. It was consequently a magnet for artisans of every trade, however proficient or ordinary, to set up their own workshops unencumbered by either social, trade or religious repressions. There were, in addition, no trade unions, guilds or companies to order working practices, or indeed to set standards.

Like most industrial towns in the Civil War, Birmingham had been sympathetic towards Parliament. Indeed it provided their forces with 15,000 swords. As a consequence it was sacked and burned by Prince Rupert in 1643. At the Restoration the country as a whole was for both King and Parliament working in unison, and for enforcement of law. Bishops, the Prayer book and Anglican beliefs officially took the place of Puritanism, and the Act of Uniformity whereby attendance at religious meetings other than the Church of England were forbidden, and all positions in national and local government as well as commissions in the army were closed to men of other persuasions, was enforced. Merchants and traders wished, however, to have a say in the country's planning, and some refused to accept the re-established Church of England. Birmingham was a free-thinking city, and welcomed Dissenters, who could take refuge by moving into its tolerant community. Attitudes improved by 1672, when the Declaration of Indulgence allowed Nonconformists to worship publically in chapels of their own, and Roman Catholics to celebrate mass at home. In 1689 William and Mary instituted a further Act of Toleration withdrawing more restrictions. By 1700 there were already two congregations of Presbyterians in Birmingham, and a meeting house for Quakers, and in 1732 the New Meeting House for Unitarians was opened, whilst conditions in the town were favourable for the newcomers. The raw materials for the workshops seemed inexhaustible, and even when supplies of wood for making charcoal were running low, Darby of Coalbrookdale invented coke with which to smelt iron, and as the coal-seams had to be dug ever deeper, Newcomen's steam pumps drew the flooding from the mines. Watermills provided power even before the advent in 1769 of Watts steam engines.

Like everywhere else in England, by the early 18th century there was a trade boom in Birmingham, where the hardware business was predominant. This varied from what were called 'toys' and small domestic ware, jugs, knives, saucepans and the rest, to a burgeoning trade in large metal machinery and equipment which included everything from kitchen cranes and firebacks to factory items, swords, and particularly guns of every description. In 1767, Sketley's Directory of Birmingham listed sixty-two

8

workshops making guns and analogous trades. There were lorimers working metalware for horses, nailers producing goods for all trades, while the 'toy-makers' created small items for the amusement of mainly adults; brooches, watch-chains, bracelets, and (from a fashion started in Charles II's time) shoe-buckles. Later, a vast trade in buttons, metal and otherwise, developed, and in 1755 John Taylor's factory employed five hundred operatives for this alone. Coins, both of the realm and tokens for paying workmen, were made in colossal numbers, particularly in the 1790s. As in other towns, the various trades tended to centre around each other in particular areas, the jewellery quarter being to the north where later St Paul's Church, the 'Jewellery Church' was built. Between that and the important Colmore Row, and bounded by Easy Row and Livery Street, were built rows of workaday streets to house the new labourers. Steelhouse Lane, an eastwards continuation of Colmore Row, was the centre of the gunsmith's workshops, and their housing spread eastwards in uninspiring rows across Snow Hill.

St Martin's-in-the-Bullring, the only church in Birmingham until St Philips's was built further north in the early 18th century, housed the local registers, and outside its south door was the large open-air market. Built in the 13th century, St Martin's replaced a Norman church, and was typically surrounded by a clutter of houses and shops and market booths. In 1690 it was much altered by being cased in brick to support its withering stonework, its windows lengthened to accommodate its new galleries, a balustrade built above the aisles, and a small pedimented south porch added. [*History of Birmingham*, William Hutton 1781]. It was the centre of Birmingham in its early phases, and there all the Simms family were baptised, until St Philip's offered an alternative for the expanding number of cousins. The main streets were cobbled with egg-shaped flints very hard on the feet, particularly those leading to the principal coaching inn, the Swan, near the New Street corner of the High Street, from where the new two-and-a-half day service to London began in May 1731 at a cost of 21 shillings per passenger. Other less-used streets retained their earthy surfaces overlain with the usual mediaeval rubbish. There were several big old estates in the town which later became broken up as trade demanded their sites, but the newer housing in such as Old Square replaced the need for large mansions by select residences near to the centre of the town. The view from the top of the Bullring was still, in 1791, of a 'pretty stretch of country at the end of the High Street'. But not for much longer.

This huge increase in trade and population, with its accompanying mores, was all due to iron. Iron and coal. In unison they underlay the enormous changes. Together they ordained the future of Birmingham. The town of a thousand trades, with its many small workshops, had as its basis the hardware business, the most important facet of which was guns. Here

9

St Martin's Church, 1781. (History of Birmingham – *William Hutton*).

10

Birmingham had unrivalled knowledge of metal-working, even super-seding London in that respect, until between 1804 and 1815, the year of Waterloo, it produced three million gun barrels and three million gun locks. In 1812 alone it manufactured a quarter of a million nails. Every farm had its own forge to work wrought-iron goods when there was nothing to be done on the land. The big coal rush of the 1760s found patches of surface coal being dug up wherever it was discovered. In common with other places, Birmingham also recognised that improved transport was essential, and its first canal was surveyed and built by James Brindley, and the first coal barges arrived from Wolverhampton along its twenty-two mile length in the autumn of 1769. The price of coal dropped from thirteen shillings to seven. Thereafter the other canals were dug until finally Birmingham was connected to London via an extension to the Oxford canal joining with the Grand Union canal, at Napton Junction. The centre of Birmingham must have taken on an unusual appearance when the full total of 550 private canal basins brought commercial traffic into the heart of the town and its districts, to feed the factories. The rattle of the boats loading and unloading began to break the peace of the place. Still there were woody environs, but gradually any view of them became obscured by the thick smoke emerging from the thousands of chimneys, and the bursts of flame from the many forges. The quiet of the past was blasted by fierce explosions from the gun-proofing, the rumbling of wagons over the cobbles and the clank of steam engines as the great town took its place as one of Britain's foremost industrial centres.

Simms × Collins

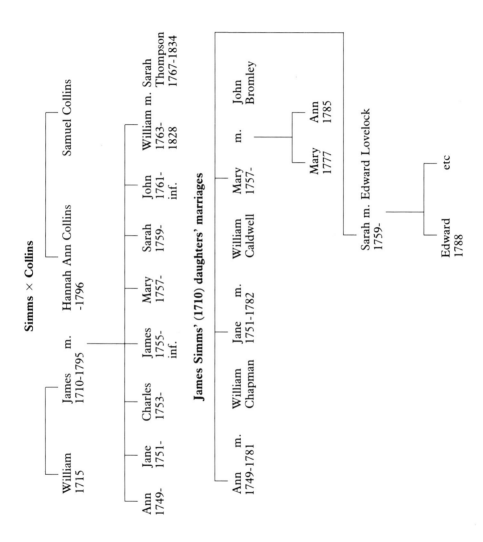

Samuel Collins

Hannah Ann Collins
-1796

James m.
1710-1795

William m. **Sarah Thompson**
1763-1828   1767-1834

John
1761-
inf.

Sarah
1759-

Mary
1757-

James
1755-
inf.

Charles
1753-

Jane
1751-

Ann
1749-

William
1715

James Simms' (1710) daughters' marriages

Mary
1757-   m.   **John Bromley**

William Caldwell   **Jane** m.
1751-1782

William Chapman

Ann m.
1749-1781

Mary   **Ann**
1777   1785

Sarah m. **Edward Lovelock**
1759-

Edward   etc
1788

12

CHAPTER 2

1688-1791

ALTHOUGH BLOODLESS, THE GLORIOUS REVOLUTION of 1688 was not without problems, and families that were loyal to James II, whether or not they were Catholics, did not pass unscathed. The William Simms of the period was 18 years old this year, his father about 48. This latter William must therefore have lived through the excitement of the Civil War as a little boy, in which Cavaliers came not only from the upper classes and squirearchy, but could be artisans or even labourers from either town or country. The war was not completely geographically distributed, because the independence of the small master and his workmen determined their freedom to choose on which side they would be. A particular town would contain adherents from both sides of the conflict, usually one in much greater numbers than the other. A stretch of country similarly would have families of both sides living there, so that there was an intermix of views in any one area regarding the war.

On the whole, however, the industrial towns contained a preponderance of families who supported the Cromwellians. They were composed largely of thrusting manufacturers and merchants interested in reform and technical advance, often Nonconformist in religion, and merging later to form the Whig party. As in London and Birmingham they overruled the smaller number of Royalists who often wanted to maintain the old ways but because they were in a minority did not have a chance to raise their heads. During the Commonwealth the rise of the Puritans with their interference in the daily lives and religious practices of ordinary people so incensed the populace that bigotry paradoxically became allied in their minds with Roman practices, and was one of the reasons for the 1688 revolution. From the Cavaliers, who were mainly Protestants and had a great love of and respect for the Church of England, developed the Tory party, largely though by no means exclusively composed of the upper classes and the more conservative members of the public. As one would expect, they thus often included country folk from villages and market towns.

The 17th century William Simms (born in 1670) was a Tory, probably a Jacobite. He may have been a member of the squirearchy, but certainly was at least a yeoman of some consequence, owning land of his own in the

Birmingham region, and not merely a tenant. He found himself on the 'wrong' side in 1688, thereby losing a considerable amount of property in the process. Threatened by execution, it seems likely that he was rabid in his beliefs, possibly a high churchman, certainly antagonistic to Dutch Williams and thus in a minority. During Queen Anne's reign there was a temporary resurgence of Torysim, and William's son who was born in 1710 was named James, which even if a family name, did not hide his sympathies. His second son, born in 1715, was another William. With the Old Pretender whipping up Jacobite enthusiasms in Scotland and the first Hanoverian on the throne, it was as well not to be provocative that year, and anyway it was normal practice to call children after their parents.

James inherited his father's Toryism, probably his Jacobite leanings, but he sufficiently veiled his views to be able to continue life in Birmingham until middle age. There were a number of cousins in the town, including several William Simms', so he was amongst family. He had his own business as a typical Birmingham 'toy' maker in the Jewellery Quarter along Litchfield Street, where he made all sorts of small metal fancies and adornments on the premises. He worked in gold and in silver, creating watch seals and chains, brooches, rings, bracelets, and the fashionable shoe buckles of the time. Now is the first occasion with a hint of scientific bent, as compasses were included in his repertoire and for these and his other pieces of jewellery he was a proficient engraver.

Here in Birmingham James married a young woman from the opposite end of the religious spectrum from himself. Hannah Ann Collins came from a well-known Quaker family in Stoke-on-Trent, some forty miles to the north, but which in the 18th century migrated to Birmingham, and set up as box-makers in Dale End. Sketchley[1] cites her brother, Samuel, as a gilt and silver box-maker and instrument maker residing at 28 John Street, and so the overlap of family interests is evident. But although James' trade as a gold and silversmith or maker of small instruments was one favoured by the Society of Friends, (the 'Quakers'), trinkets and other pieces of adornment were anathema to the plainly-dressed congregation. Quakers then and until at least 1810 (depending on their 'Monthly Meeting') were forbidden to marry out of their faith, or rather, to marry before a priest. Ann was consequently excluded by the Society of Friends from further membership, and probably thereafter was unwelcome in her family home or her native town of Stoke, although in Birmingham attitudes were less strict. She and James continued to live in Litchfield Street, and when their own first children arrived, they were baptised in St Philip's Church, then about forty years old and rather nearer to their home in the north of the town than St Martin's where all the earlier Simms mentioned above were baptised.

Birmingham was, however, not a comfortable place for a man of James' political views to live, especially one who called his first son (baptised

14

Litchfield Street

Birmingham 1781.

23rd June 1753) Charles, and his next son who arrived two years later James (baptised 23rd May 1755). James died in childhood, and their four daughters (Ann 1749, Jane 1751, Mary 1757 and Sarah 1759) all had acceptable names, as did John (1761) who died in infancy. However whether for political, trading or domestic reasons, or a mixture of all three, James senior handed over his business to his cousin, William Simms, about 1762, and moved his young family to London. There were already family ties in the area of Aldersgate in the City, so that is where he chose to settle, near to fellow jewellers in Fleet Street and Hatton Gardens. He found a house in White Cross Street, north of St Giles without Cripplegate and here he set up business, and except for a move in the 1790s to the neighbouring Doby Court in Monkwell Street, lived out the rest of his long life. Here too his youngest child, William, was born and was baptised on 3rd August 1763 at St Giles. The baby's elder brother, Charles was now ten years old.

London at this time was the most densely populated area in the country, containing as it did one tenth of the inhabitants of England, many of them living in filthy over-crowding, especially towards the eastern end of the City. There the labourers manned the busy docks from where sailed ships loaded with goods to Europe, the Mediterranean, Africa, and the Indies, both East and West. Interspersed between the brick dwellings were the warehouses of merchants, shops with the families living over, refugees from France in the silk factories of Spitalfields, and the Huguenots in Soho. Craftsmen such as James accommodated their workshops in their own homes, with their servants and apprentices living in the attics, and their porters and messengers bedding down in the cellars or under the counter. Bankers' houses mingled with those of inn-keepers' and with coffee shops; professionals with artisans. Though the lanes and alleys were crowded, the river was the most heavily used highway of all in London, not only for boats travelling up and down on the tide, but also for crossing from bank to bank, even though since 1738 Westminster Bridge had taken some of the traffic from London Bridge and the ferry boats. All households burnt coal, with resulting filthy effluent puffing from their chimneys in torrents, filling the air with smuts and grey murkiness which veiled the streets from the light of day, or at night from the gas lamps which began to appear in the 1790s. The London pea-soupers were notorious for obscuring criminals and travellers alike. The dirt formed a veneer over the City, a gaseous film causing illness and disability, and provoking the threat of tuberculosis which continued to the end of the 19th century.

Young William (1763) followed the normal practice for adolescents by being apprenticed to a local craftsman, who in his case was his brother, Charles. Charles belonged to the Butchers Company, and was a working butcher, having his business in the Fleet Market, today Farringdon Street, under the shadow of Smithfield. Apprenticeships normally lasted seven

16

years from the age of fourteen, but by law could be no less than four years and no more than eight. It was on 1st April 1779 that he received his indentures and commenced work, amidst news of the hostilities from America which had begun in earnest three years earlier with the Declaration of Independence and the Revolutionary War.

At home there was widespread discontent over poverty, the horrific punishments for relatively minor offences, and the ever-present threat from Catholic France. The Catholics, in consequence, were blamed for all life's problems, and in 1780 this emerged in riots whipped up by the rabble-rouser, 'Lord' George Gordon, who led the torch-bearing mobs into London, storming four of the prisons, and setting multitudes of houses known to belong to Catholic families on fire. There was no police-force to forestall them except the Bow Street Runners, the army had to be called out, and there followed intense anti-Catholic hatred and ferocious fighting in the streets.

William's brother, Charles, now lived in the Old Bailey, a street running north from Ludgate Street to Newgate, and he remained there all that day, having kept the shutters up over his shop in the Fleet Market, as rumours of the trouble preceded the arrivals of the mobs in the City. The previous evening he and young William had seen the red glow in the sky in the direction of Essex beyond Dagenham to the east, and now in the distance they could hear shouting and confused singing, as the increasingly large crowd of malcontents, anti-Catholic and hangers-on marched from the country, burning property as they went, stealing cheap gin from the inns along their way until they were provoked into a kind of mad frenzy by the charasmatically ranting Lord George. Now the beat of the drums and the creak of falling house timbers accompanied by the sizzling of fire and the sickly smell of burning, together with showers of sparks as the wind aided the rioters in their hatred and lust. Now William was horrified to see the mob hack and heave all together at the great wooden doors of Newgate jail until it was battered to the ground. Then, with a mighty shout of malevolence, the intoxicated yelling mass rushed over the barricades after their leader, over-powering warders, releasing prisoners, and with their burning torches, setting the whole place alight. They took no notice of this frightened youth of seventeen in his apprentice's apron, too intent were they on destruction. Eventually the troops arrived, but too late to prevent the damage or to capture Lord George, who escaped to Birmingham where he laid low in hiding for four months, embracing somewhat startlingly the Jewish faith for protection. He became known as the Birmingham Moses, but was ultimately caught and tried, being found guilty of libelling the Queen of France, for which he was sent to the now restored Newgate Gaol, this time under very different conditions from his former triumphant visit. London returned thankfully to its normal routine, and William to his butchering.

17

William's elder sisters were all married at about this time, first Sarah to a wealthy draper of Smithfield, Mr Edward Lovelock, who was a Procter's Assistant, managing cases in the Eclesiastical Courts. The next daughter, Ann, married in January 1781 at St Giles, William Chapman, a perriwig maker in Moorfields, whose forebear, also a Chapman, had been mentioned in Pepys' Diary for 1663, when for £3 he provided that gentleman with his wig. Another sister, Mary, became Mrs Bromley. Her husband owned a shoe warehouse in Foley Street and a thriving export business. The last sister, Jane, married William Caldwell in September 1782 at St Leonards Church, Shoreditch, but she early became a widow.

Meanwhile William served his apprenticeship, but when he should have completed his 'servitude' in 1786, there is no mention in the Butchers Company archives of his acquiring the Freedom; instead we find him going to Birmingham to assist in the hardware business of his father's cousin, another William Simms, with whom at first he lived. This switch from butchering to jewellery and small instrument making is not as surprising as at first it seems, as he had been brought up in the atmosphere of a workshop making such items. He may well have spent his evenings when Charles did not require his presence, back in his father's premises tinkering with his tools and helping his work. It may be that he was an unsatisfactory pupil to Charles, who received no pay for him ('Cons Nil' the indenture states, meaning 'no consideration' – no fee), and there was a row in which William not only left the shambles but also the City of London. It is also possible that his father could not afford the fee to the Butchers Company, required before freedom was granted, nor the very hefty fee of £34 needed by the Corporation for the bestowal of the Freedom of the City. At any rate, William reverted at this point to his native trade, and remained an instrument maker all his life, using his experience with his father as a base to learn more of the technicalities of the trade.

There were still numerous Simms relations and their families in Birmingham, and he had no chance to be lonely. The town was growing apace, absorbing the wealth it had achieved by supplying guns, knives and other equipment for the British forces fighting the Continental Army in America, as well as in Europe for the protagonists of the Seven Years War against France. Birmingham now had good access for materials and merchandise by water, with more canals to its credit than had Venice. The stage-coach to London took less than two days, the mail-coach only 28 hours. Though without the variety of people, classes and culture William was used to living alongside in London, it had formidable scientific interest, led primarily by the Lunar Society which the young William (1763) must have noted with envy as being intellectually and socially quite out of his reach, but none-the-less a magnet for his ambition. This remarkable association of prominent scientists, philosophers and eccentrics, met each Monday nearest to the full moon, in each others' houses to discuss the

18

burning issues of the day, the timing being so that the members should avail themselves of the light of the moon to see themselves home. Hence the strange title. Many well-known names were included in its membership, and all were true friends, ready to exchange knowledge of their different subjects, all having practical applications to the burgeoning industries of the town. They provided a clearing house of ideas that widely affected the course of the Industrial Revolution.

Not least of the members was the Reverend Joseph Priestley, who had been appointed to the new Unitarian Meeting House in 1780. He attracted criticism from his discoveries in physics and chemistry, exploding long-held myths such as the phlogiston theory. Moreover he was a radical Whig of extreme views, who later approved openly of the victory of the American colonists in 1783, and of the French Revolutionaries. This last opinion equated him in the minds of the populace with the hatred atheism of the Jacobins as well as with republicanism. His name was constantly dragged in the mud until eventually in 1791 violence burst out in Birmingham, intended initially to protect the English Church and State. Priestley's own church, his laboratory and his home, Fair Hill at Sparkbrook, were sacked and burnt by the mob, and his apparatus and the scientific records in his library destroyed as a focus of Tory hatred. He escaped with his life to London, and eventually to the American colonies, where he died in 1804.

William was present at this fracas, the rioters passing near his home on their way north to Sparkbrook. To show his loyalty to the Church of England and the Government of George III, and thus to protect the house from the mob, he copied the convention of standing at his outer doorway with a lighted candle held above his head in each hand. However, this did nothing to abate the fury of the crowds, and when a brick came flying between his two upraised arms, he decided that discretion was required, and hastily withdrew, banging the door shut behind him.

Fires raged around William's home, but though the troops had been called from Nottingham, they took a couple of days to arrive, and another four days to bring the unrest under control. A great many buildings were damaged, including some which had no connection with Priestley; fortunately William's own house escaped in spite of his frightening experience, which was just as well as 1791 was also the year of his marriage.

William's new wife was Sarah Thompson. Her family lived at Stone, some thirty miles away to the north in Staffordshire. Perhaps they were friends of his mother's from Stoke-on-Trent which was only about six miles further on and whom he may well have been visiting when he met her. Certainly Dr Lettsom, a prominent member of the Society of Friends used to visit William in London, so some vestiges of the previous affection for the place must have remained to give William a reason to travel to North Staffordshire.

William was now twenty-eight, and well acquainted with his trade. He had been in Birmingham for five years, watching it grow to a population of well over 53,000 souls living in 10,000 houses. New streets were still being built to house incomers from the country. The jewellers, goldsmiths and silversmiths were thriving so much that Birmingham acquired its own assay office in 1773, using the famous anchor as its mark. Flint glass was being manufactured at Chance Bros' factory, and was superior to that of anywhere else because of its high lead content, giving added lustre and brilliance appropriate to optical uses as well as other glass items. Good order in the town was maintained by the fifty Street Commissioners for the various districts, the last Chairman, Richard Cadbury, being already in office. All seemed well for William, but he was not to remain up in the Midlands of far Warwickshire for much longer.

CHAPTER 3

1792-1815

1793 WAS A YEAR OF PORTENT IN EUROPE. The French Revolution had increased in violence and hatred until the laws of the land were ground underfoot, and the mob raged uncontrollably into the Reign of Terror. Madame Guillotine worked day and night to rid the country of its royalty, its aristocracy, its intelligensia, and indeed anyone who crossed its path, so indiscriminative had it become. Refugees fleeing from the merciless blood-bath had been secretly entering England since 1789, and particularly along the south coast there were emigrées, usually of aristocratic birth, living quite openly having left behind all their worldly wealth in the hands of the French proletariat. Once France declared war on England in February 1793, the entry of refugees became suspect and their welcome shrouded with distrust. The English were horrified at the tales of atrocity which filtered across the Channel, and even if they had had some sympathy previously with the underdogs in France, there was little wish for militant social reform of that scale in this country. Jacobins there were in England, who condoled with the revolutionaries, but the blood-lust of the mobs revolted British men and women, who nevertheless feared that the present unpopularity of their own King and Queen could all too easily escalate into scenes similar to those in France.

However, the causes of the war were multiple and had been building up over the years, finally breaking out when French aggression extended to the Scheldt, thereby threatening British commercial interests and the freedom of the Channel. This early part of the campaign resulted in defeat for England in the Netherlands, and breathing space for the Terror, which took the opportunity to mobilise the total industrial resources and manpower of France with unprecedented thoroughness such as had never occurred before. In 1794 the war moved across the Atlantic to the French Sugar Islands in the West Indies where in the next two years 40,000 British troops died, but which was too remote for the average Briton to assimilate. When in 1796 Napoleon became a familiar name on everyone's lips as he attacked the Austrian army in Italy, the war came nearer home, and people increasingly were afraid of its effect. The focal point of the conflict,

Simms' family – Birmingham/London

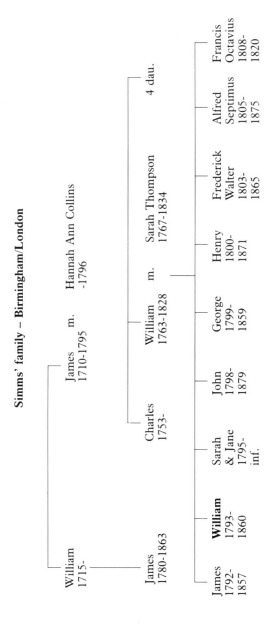

William
1715-

    James   m.   Hannah Ann Collins
    1710-1795   -1796

Charles
1753-

William   m.   Sarah Thompson
1763-1828   1767-1834

James
1780-1863

4 dau.

James
1792-
1857

William
1793-
1860

Sarah
& Jane
1795-
inf.

John
1798-
1879

George
1799-
1859

Henry
1800-
1871

Frederick
Walter
1803-
1865

Alfred
Septimus
1805-
1875

Francis
Octavius
1808-
1820

22

however, for England, transferred to the high seas, and opposite Napoleon was ranged Nelson and his fleet, at first with a trouncing at Toulon, but then great victory at Aboukir Bay off Egypt in August 1798.

As the war proceeded, industry in Britain correspondingly thrived. In Birmingham the hardware trades particularly boomed. William and Sarah lived in the midst of this success, and his uncle's business became less to do with jewellery and more with simple optical items such as compasses, barometers, and dials of all kinds, as scientific interest increased with advancing discoveries. The Church and State riots were only just in the immediate past, and not to be forgotten for their ferocity, but Priestley himself, Wedgewood, Banks, Boulton and Watts, all men of profound scientific enterprise, affected both local and national awareness of scientific advances by their meetings at the Lunar Society. The two Williams, uncle and nephew, were pouring out goods from their workshop to satisfy the onsetting scientific interest of individual amateurs as well as further serious study of physical principles by the more erudite.

Marrying shortly before the riots, Sarah's first baby was born on 2nd February 1792, and was baptised James after his Simms grandfather, at the family church of St Martin's. Less than two years later this baby was joined by a brother, born in December 1793. The new baby was baptised in the New Year of 1794 in his father's name of William, inheriting also his scientific bent. Son of a fervant Whig, there would be no Charles or Edward in this generation, although the Anglican faith of middle stream remained young William's belief, politics a minor feature of his life.

Shortly after his baptism on 9th January 1794, word came from London entreating William senior to return there to take over old James' business in Whitecross Street. He was now well over eighty, and failing in health. Ann was ailing also, and there was no-one else appropriate to see to his affairs. William's elder brother, Charles, had his own butchery business, and his four sisters were all married though still living in London. Although William had numerous cousins in Birmingham, and Sarah's family were in nearby Stone, they decided to uproot themselves to the capital. This would be his own business, to be encouraged into scientific channels at his own direction, and was near to his childhood memories. Although irresistible, this meant giving up his stake in his uncle's firm in Birmingham, which shortly afterwards passed out of the family as there was no-one to take it over, the uncle's only son James having decided that the law offered a more acceptable career than trade. He certainly succeeded in this view as he eventually became Solicitor General for Newfoundland, and from 1846 to 1858 was Puisne Judge there.[2] It was very tempting for William to stay in his place to inherit the Birmingham business.

However, London held all his childhood memories. He was now thirty-one, and in the intervening years the capital must have changed. But still the traffic was enormous and noisy, composed of horses and carts, wagons and barrows, and innumerable people forever moving hither and thither either on foot or in carriages or barouches. The wealthy now tended to reside further west, building fine houses in the squares of Bloomsbury and around Covent Garden, but evermore westwards into Piccadilly and Kensington. The City of London itself was still packed tight with humanity of all grades of society, from the aristocracy and the wealthy Quaker bankers, through the professions, the artisans and apprentices, to the proletariat, the beggars and the whores bidding for custom. The City was a magnet for the poor and the jobless, as well as for the enterprising or the desperate from both town and country. The main streets were by now cobbled with rounded stones the shape of an ostrich egg placed endwise, rattling the vehicles to a slow pace as they trundled over them. Noise and shouting and bustle continued unabated. Fine carriages rumbled to and fro, splashing through the puddles. The clatter of horses' hooves, the thump of barrels being loaded and unloaded into the cellars of the inns, and the street vendors bellowing their wares, continually filled the air with cacophony. Lesser streets still held filth and were often unpaved, and the fetid smells, though improved from mediaeval London with its open sewers, were dominant around the households of the poor. It was an exciting frenetic place, and Sarah had to be introduced to its way of life from the lesser urban tumult of Birmingham.

At first William and Sarah Simms went to join old James in his house at Whitecross Street, where he had his workshop and had lived for over thirty years. He was all too obviously failing, and so was Hannah Ann, so that William immediately took over the business, directing it towards optical instruments and forsaking the jewellery trade.

These last months of the old people's lives whilst Sarah looked after her mother and father-in-law, she had other things on her mind. On 23rd April 1795 she gave birth to twin girls, Sarah and Jane, which must initially have given her and William great joy as they would complement their two little boys. However, as so often, and perhaps after a difficult labour, both babies died, Sarah soon after birth, Jane a year later from convulsions. Now they had two healthy living children, two dead. These were statistics that deserved to be improved even at that period. Few families were unfamiliar with infant deaths, though the official mortality rate had improved in the last century since the lying-in hospitals had been built and midwifery revolutionised by William Smellie, the obstetrician from Lanark who settled in London for twenty years in 1839. The burial registers are full of the names of children who had died of fever, cough, convulsions, or just 'decline'. At St Giles the burial of new babies is not even recorded, their deaths were so frequent an occurrence.

Only three months after Jane's death, Hannah Ann succumbed to old age, on 10th July 1796, and was buried at St Giles without Cripplegate.

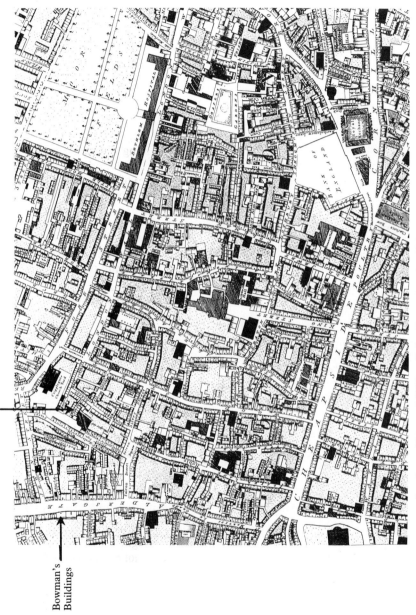

Doby Court

Bowman's
Buildings

London – Horwood 1799 – Doby Court, Monkwell Street and Bowman's Buildings.
BY PERMISSION OF GUILDHALL LIBRARY, CORPORATION OF LONDON

25

Shortly after this series of mournful events, William bought a house in Doby Court, Monkwell Street, just the other side of St Giles, to the south. This area of London is now almost completely unrecognisable, though some of the old names survive. The Museum of London stands high above Aldersgate, at its junction with London Wall. The huge Monkwell Square redevelopment is only dominated by the even larger Barbican Centre, and St Giles without Cripplegate, dwarfed and isolated, has become a quiet sanctuary amongst the commercial din, guarded on its southern boundary by a protective run of the old Roman wall which has been cleared of buildings and traffic. Cripplegate itself is a poor shadow of its forerunner and half obliterated. The name, assumed to refer to the beggars who formerly gathered outside the original entrance to London, more likely derives from the Saxon word 'crepel' meaning a burrow, the deep defensive ditch surrounding the wall. After repair of fire damage in the 16th century, St Giles survived the Great Fire of 1666 only to be badly damaged once more by fire in the 19th centuries, and then again in 1939, and was finally gutted by incendiary bombs between August and December 1940. As in the past, it was once more painstakingly rebuilt, its clustered columns and moulded arches again giving dignity to a church which had witnessed the burial of John Milton in 1674 and his father in 1647, the marriage of Oliver Cromwell to Elizabeth Bourchier in 1620, and later the baptism of Holman Hunt in 1827. Sir Martin Frobisher was buried here in 1594, and Shakespeare attended his nephew's baptism at St Giles in 1607.

Old James Simms, the Jacobite born in the reign of Queen Anne, like her with Tory conviction, must often have entered this church where all his London-born sons and one of his two little daughters were all baptised. In his last years when he had relinquished his business to William, he must have passed his time sitting here with his cronies, leaning on his stick, his back bent from many hours working at his bench, and with calloused fingers and failing eyesight, discussed with them the troubles in France and Ireland, the price of gold, the difficulty of finding suitable apprentices.

It was at Doby Court that old James died before the end of the century, and there also that three more sons were born to William and Sarah; John in 1798, George in 1799 and Henry in 1800. Still no living daughters. William began to realise that one day he would need to depend on the City Livery Companies for his sons' introduction to a craft. More urgently he had come to terms with the fact that before he could legally trade in his own name in the City, it was necessary for him to become a Freeman of one of the Companies, and preferably also a Freeman of the City of London. Without the former distinction he could not trade, nor take on apprentices of his own under official indenture. Without the latter he lacked further privileges, including a say in the running of City affairs. Only a Freeman was able to vote for Alderman and the Common Council, for his Member of Parliament, the Lord Mayor and the Sheriff. A Freeman was excused tolls

26

at fairs, markets and ports throughout the country, and had preferential trading facilities.

William therefore had to remedy this situation, and he applied for his Freedom both to the Butcher's Company and the City Corporation on the strength of his period of servitude many years previously. He was granted both on payment of the fees and submission of his indenture papers together with the signature of Charles Simms, on 19th February 1802. He was now Somebody in the City, and on a par with the best of his contemporaries. He also moved his family round the corner to the west side of Aldersgate Street, to a tenement block known uncompromisingly by the ugly name of Bowman's Buildings. It almost backed onto Bartholomew Close where his sons all ultimately went to school. The Simms' continued to have association with Bowman's Buildings for twenty years, and it served them well. Here the youngest three sons were born, the first being Frederick Walter in 1803, a bright intelligent child like his elder brothers, but also sensitive and introspective. He is said to have been baptised at St Anne's Blackfriers, but this is not so. Like all his brothers and the twin sisters, he was baptised at St Giles.

Now, however, Sarah's luck ran out. The next baby was a dullard, very different from the others, slow to learn, needing extra patience to teach him the ordinary activities of life. He was named Alfred Septimus. And then, lastly in 1808, arrived Francis Octavius who was delicate, and died in childhood when he was twelve.

1802 was not only marked by William's Freedom, important as that was to him personally with his blossoming ambition. To Britain and France it brought an interlude in the war, the year of the Peace of Amiens, and an armistice for a time. It proved to be short-lived, and merely gave Napoleon a chance to re-group and re-arm his men and his boats. As the war resumed in 1803, fear of invasion was foremost in the minds of everyone in England, Old Boney being the centre of many a tale; scare stories of spies landing along the east and south coasts were marketed and embroidered; parole previously granted to French prisoners of officer rank was cancelled; and folk on remote farms and hamlets were on the qui vive for strangers in their area. The Volunteers were formed as a para-military force to protect the country, much as they were during the 20th century wars. The Martello forts were hurriedly but securely built around the East Anglian coast, river mouths and in the Solent; great sturdy thick-walled stone monuments to the Napoleonic threat. The government made plans to move to the centre of Britain in the event of invasion, and the huge stock of munition was housed in specially built stores at Weedon on the River Nene near Northampton, together with barracks for the soldiers who would guard and use them if necessary. So also there was accommodation there for the authorities who would direct the war.

The lives of the ordinary person was little effected by all this activity, except for those living near the coast where gossip was rife, and the press gangs hard at work finding fodder for Nelson's ships. Suspicion also was easily aroused in the areas of the huge prisoner-of-war camps near Peterborough and Norman Cross, and people locked their doors securely at night. The life of the well-to-do altered not at all, and this was probably so for William and Sarah, although for him it meant increasing orders for his navigating equipment as more and more boats were prepared for sea.

By the beginning of the 19th century day-school had become the normal activity for boys of the middle class. Here they received a grounding in the three Rs, religious knowledge, history and geography, much of it by rote, and also possibly the classics depending on the competence of the teacher. The older Simms boys were all in turn sent to Mr Hill's school when they were seven years old. This establishment was in Bartholomew Close, a large open square south-east of Smithfield, only a few minutes walking distance from their home. From here they would walk down Duck Lane to St Paul's Cathedral, or along Paved Alley to watch the comings and goings through the gates of St Bartholomew's Hospital, and Little St Bartholomew's Church. In the opposite direction they could wander up past the old timber-framed building, one of the few to have survived the Great Fire of 1666, which fronted the churchyard of the old Norman church of Great St Bartholomew. Smithfield nearby was still enormously busy with over 100,000 cattle and 1,500,000 sheep estimated to be driven down to the markets in a year at that time. One can imagine the noise created by the confused animals, the drovers, and the purchasers as sales proceeded. The roads used by the herds must have been covered by excrement, turning the area into a huge mire, with the straw which was laid to absorb the mess, flying about on a windy day. The coaching inns of the area, the Bell in Aldersgate, the Belle Sauvage on Ludgate Hill, with its sign of Pocohontas and its stable of 400 horses, and the Bull and Mouth in St Martin's-le-Grand, all added to the bustle and excitement of the world in which these children were brought up.

When he was twelve years old in January 1806, William (1793)[3] was sent to a tutor to be instructed in the ramifications of mathematics. This was a Mr Hayward who lived in Sermon Lane, St Paul's. He had been a scholar in the Mathematical School at Christ's Hospital which then was at Greyfriars, off Newgate. He subsequently joined the navy, becoming an instructor in navigation, and thus was familiar not only with astronomy, geography and meteorology, but very particularly with the instruments handled in their practice. His last commission had been under Nelson in the Battle of the Nile, where he had commanded one of the big guns on the *Orion*. He had retired from the navy thereafter, turning his attention to promising youngsters who needed a thorough grounding in mathematics, and especially who were interested in mathematical instruments and their use.

He had an apt pupil in William Simms (1793), and must have been a considerable influence on his future both for his enthusiasm and knowledge, but also in that he was in touch with the manufacturers of the instruments he demonstrated in his classes – sextants, quadrants, barometers, telescopes, and so on. The historical circumstances of the time were in his favour as a teacher of these subjects, for only three months before William became his pupil, the news of Trafalgar was signalled from Spain in October 1805. Nothing could have excited tutor and pupil more than this great victory, with the same old *Orion* playing its part (though under a different captain), and as the details of the battle emerged, Hayward and William were in a position to analyse the action from their practical knowledge, and no doubt did so as a technical exercise for the boy.

By the end of 1807 William (1793) had completed two years work with Mr Hayward. On 7th December he celebrated his fourteenth birthday, the usual age for a boy of his class to start an apprenticeship. Already he was familiar with the production of small optical instruments with which his father specialised, particularly now marine compasses and other navigating equipment, barometers and lenses of various sorts. He knew something of the cutting and forging of metals, engraving, and the production and use of glass. The Whitefriars glassworks were busily engaged in the production of all sorts of wares, some very beautifully etched, and all processes in its manufacture would be visible from the street to an inquisitive boy, and only a short walk from his home. His father's friends were many of them jewellers or gold- and silversmiths, and doubtless he had visited their workshops, even given a hand at the less skilled jobs on occasion. His father was very anxious that he should become a member of a prominent Livery Company, which would guarantee his success both socially and commercially in the future, and he now turned to one of the top twelve Companies in the City, the Goldsmiths, by-passing his own Butchers Company which ranked only twenty-fourth in the list of importance. He found an apprenticeship for this intelligent son of his with a working goldsmith, Thomas Penstone of White Cross Street, who was a member of the Goldsmiths Company and therefore was a reputable craftsman and Master, and would train William accordingly.

On 6th January 1808 William Simms junior (1793) signed his indenture papers with Thomas Penstone for the usual seven years. There is no mention in the original entry in the Goldsmiths records of any payment to Penstone as there often was, though sometimes this fee was waived between friends and relatives, or if the apprentice was not to be resident in the Master's house. William merely had to walk the short distance several streets to the east of Aldersgate to find Penstone's workshop, and so began his training.

The craft of the goldsmith at first gave him plenty to think about and to learn, and there was also the excitement of leaving school behind. But it all failed to employ his mathematical ability or his already awakened interest in the instruments about which Mr Hayward had taught him and which he had seen in his father's workshop. He had only to walk down Fleet Street and peer in the shop windows there to see the very fine scientific creations which were painstakingly being produced. Before a year of his apprenticeship was up, it was obvious that young William was not going to be satisfied with the goldsmith's art as his life's work, but yearned for the challenge of the highly complicated optics involved in this other field. He was now assured of future Freedom of the Goldsmiths Company if he completed seven years apprenticeship with the agreement of Mr Penstone, and on 7th June 1809, recognising the boy's special aptitude, he was 'turned over' to his father for the remainder of his time. Young William was a quiet-natured person, his father (William, 1763) more firey, and one wonders how much arguing went on before William senior gave way. Mr Hayward perhaps aided and abetted his erstwhile pupil in the choice of an alternative Master.

As was becoming more common in the nineteenth century, the indenture requirements could be switched to another craftsman during a boy's apprenticeship, as long as his named Master approved and continued his nominal responsibility for the youth. William was now ostensibly apprenticed to his father, but in actual fact he began to work for a man who was well known for his highly technical skills. By now the boy had a passion for optics, and it was time to broaden his acquaintance with this craft far beyond what his father could teach him. It was an enthusiasm which continued for the rest of his life with entire dedication and absorbtion, and his appetite for knowledge of the intricacies of this complicated craft demanded satisfying. Of all the Masters who were competent to train this bright young man to the peak of his intellect, the name that came to his father's mind (encouraged by Mr Hayward) was that of one of Ramsden's workmen. Indeed, Mr Hayward probably used one of Ramsden's sextants during his time on the *Orion*.

Jesse Ramsden had been born in Halifax in 1735, where his father kept an inn. After schooling, tutoring in mathematics, and apprenticeship to a local clothworker, he came to London as so many ambitious young men did, and was apprenticed to a mathematical instrument maker named Burton. In 1765 he married Sarah, youngest daughter of John Dolland FRS, a name still well known in the world of optics. Ramsden received, as a wedding dowry, a share in her father's patent for making achromatic lenses, whereupon he opened his own shop in the Haymarket. Later he moved to Piccadilly, where he became well known to the highest in the land for his instruments, many of which were of original design. By 1789 he had constructed over a thousand sextants, and had invented an engine for dividing mathematical instruments, always a tedious labour. He invented a

30

new method of construction of eye-glasses, two new types of micrometer (optical measuring instruments), and made a theodolite in 1787 for General Roy's triangulation of south-east England. His inventions ranged over the whole field of optics, physics, surveying and astronomical investigation, culminating in 1789 with the five-foot vertical circle instead of the familiar quadrant, for Palermo and Dublin Observatories.

Ramsden died in 1800, but he left behind a great number of workmen of extraordinary competence, many of whom had first been apprenticed to him in youth, and stayed on in his workshop all their lives. His house was full of both young lads and older craftsmen living with him, where they were able fully to benefit from the evenings they all spent together discussing designs over a mug of porter and a plate of bread and butter. Apprenticeships were not always the happy arrangement hoped for, and there was either much bullying or alternatively lax supervision, but in Ramsden the system worked to perfection. He was an affable man, whistling and singing over his plans, and if a drawing did not meet his standards, he would exclaim 'Bobs, man. This won't do; we must have it again'. His wife must have been a patient woman, their sole sadness surely that their only son was a sea captain working for the East India Company, where no doubt he used his father's instruments, but would never enter his business.

After Ramsden's death his workmen spread out, many starting their own little businesses. One of these was a man called Bennett, whose premises were in Charles Street, a turning off Hatton Garden. It was with him that William (1793) continued to the end of his seven years. He was now at the very centre of the optical and mathematical world, and for the next few years was consistently surrounded by and breathed, lived and dreamt optics.

William's indenture is interesting. Typical of its kind and date, it is an agreement between Master and apprentice, and covers many items which nowadays are taken for granted or else ignored. In it the Master promised to teach and instruct, or cause to be taught and instruct, the youth, and supply him with 'Meat, Drink, Apparel, Lodging, and all other Necessities according to the Custom'. The apprentice promised for his part to 'serve his Master faithfully and to be obedient'. He must keep the trade secrets of that particular workshop, and do no damage there. Whilst apprenticed to one Master he was not allowed to accept a fee for working elsewhere. He must not commit fornication, nor contract matrimony, nor play cards, dice, tables, or any other unlawful games. He must not haunt taverns or playhouses, nor absent himself from his Master day or night unlawfully. In other words, the accent was on hard work and sobriety.

Today we would say that what a youth does in his free time is no business of his employer as long as he is occupied 'lawfully'. Then it was required

31

that the boy should uphold the moral standards of society, and to fail to do so affected both the thoroughness and skill of his work, and his ability to learn. It also reflected adversely on his Master. To go 'on the tiles' would result in a tired youngster in no good condition to give of his best. Indentures were not always quite so detailed as this one, but on the whole they were similar, and often written on the same type of 'certificate' decorated with a double curve adorning the upper edge. It was always signed by the three parties involved, the Master, the apprentice, and his father.

Meanwhile William senior (1763) continued with his aim to place all his sons with Masters belonging to the more important of the eighty-nine Livery Companies. His eldest son, James (1792), had been apprenticed in 1806 to a jeweller case-maker named Barker who was a Freeman of the Clothworkers Company, and it was from this company that James received his own Freedom when at the age of twenty-one he completed his servitude in 1813. The previous year, on 4th November 1812, John Simms, now fourteen, became indentured to a working goldsmith named Richard Sibley of Red Lion Street, Clerkenwell for the sum of £35 to learn the craft of silversmith. With so many sons to be launched, it took William (1763) a good deal of juggling to place them all at appropriate intervals, but fortunately he could replace one with another. Thus when James won his Freedom in 1813, George being then fourteen, was taken on by him as his own apprentice, and in early 1815 when young William (1793) completed his seven years and became a Freeman of the important Goldsmiths Company on 21st February, Henry was ready for training. Born in 1800, Henry followed the family tradition by being apprenticed to a seal and jewel engraver, but perhaps less deft with his fingers than his elder brothers, he was destined never to own his own business.

The system of apprenticeship was still predominently in use well into the 19th century, though during this period the need to be a Freeman of a guild in order to practice a particular trade in London slowly disappeared. At the same time legislation, either national or local, gradually was passed which took the place of the control which the Livery Companies had previously held over the conditions of employment, or in some respects the early trades unions or Friendly Societies served a similar purpose. Standards of workmanship were safe-guarded by becoming self-regulating as free trade developed, but also by various legal measures until today the whole subject has become highly complicated and includes not least the Trades Description Act. However, one of the great advantages of the apprenticeship system with its control of adolescents at a very vulnerable time of their lives, was recognised as highly beneficial to them and to society in general. It thus tended to continue to a large extent even when it ceased to be compulsory for a young artisan. During this term of training between the ages of fourteen and twenty-one, when a youngster goes through a period of growing-up, rebellious and character-forming, and also at a stage when his mind is at its most active and learning is relatively effortless, he was under full control of his Master. Often he lived in his Master's house, usually sleeping in the attic, eating with the family, and was under the jurisdiction of his Master's wife. Often there were other apprentices to keep him company, and from being the lowest form of life, the messenger boy and general factotem, he would gradually learn the trade from bottom to top, living in the atmosphere of the craft, talking, discussing, and putting it into practical effect every working hour of the day six days a week. On the seventh day he was usually free, and often this meant going home to his own family for a 'difference day' and a refreshing change of scene.

For all this supervision a fee was charged to the boy's father. Anything from £25 in this particular trade, was asked in some cases, increasing as the Master became more eminent. An apprentice, Joseph Beck, indentured to William Simms (1793) in 1846 was charged £200 which was very high and reflected William's standing. Sometimes, as with a son or a brother, naturally no fee was charged, or occasionally for the son of a close friend. Sometimes the fee took other forms in the records, as in the indenture for John Troughton to his uncle in 1756, when the 'consideration' was given as 'Love and affection'.

Apprenticeship not only taught the lad a trade, but also must have been a potent source of discipline and employment, as well as keeping youngsters off the streets and out of bad company. It kept them occupied. Of course every apprenticeship was not ideal, and Dickens has some examples of the less than successful, but Ramsden was a good instance of the system at its best, and one has every reason to believe that William Simms, father (1763) and son (1793), carried on this tradition.

One other word needs to be said on the subject. It was possible, especially as the 19th century progressed, to be apprenticed officially to a Master in order to assume the Freedom of his company later on, but to continue with another trade meanwhile. This happened in the case of William Simms (1793) who found he disliked working as a goldsmith and became an optician. It also appears largely to have happened with his brother, James (1792), who certainly learned the skills of jeweller and jewel case maker from Mr Barker, but ultimately followed his own father's trade of optical instrument maker, often using similar skills and deftness of hand with minute machine tools. A blatant and earlier example was William Simms senior (1763) who became a Freeman of the Butcher's Company, and only temporarily swerved from his chosen trade of optical instrument maker.

21st February 1815 not only saw young William (1793) become a Freeman of the Goldsmiths, but through this he also was granted the Freedom of the City of London. With about forty other young men he attended at the Guildhall to receive his certificate[4] of Freedom from the Lord Mayor of the time whose name was Birch. The occasion must have been momentous and exciting as being a big step in his life and the beginning of his independence.

William Simms (1793), now twenty-one and a Freeman of one of the most important Livery Companies in the City of London, was ready to set up on his own. With his contacts from his old tutor, and from the Ramsden-Bennett connection from which he must have had plenty of useful acquaintances, there was no difficulty in obtaining orders for his work for which he soon gained a name for careful workmanship. He doubtless inherited clients from Bennett who was getting old. The world situation too was still in his favour, with Europe recovering from the havoc of the Peninsular War, the retreat from Moscow, and the defeat of France at Leipzig in 1813. Napoleon was a captive in Elba, about to escape for the famous One Hundred Days, culminating in Waterloo, and across the Atlantic the unnecessary war with America from 1812 to 1815 also increased demand from both army and navy for scientific instruments. Moreover, wherever there was surveying proceeding in the world, William stood to gain orders for his levels and theodolites.

The previous year, perhaps with some idea of accommodating William (1793) in his own workshop once he was Free, William senior (1763) had bought the house and freehold of a property at No. 4, Broad Way in Blackfriars. He still owned the Doby Court house for which he was paying rates, but that was smaller and more importantly it was too far from the wharves along the Thames from where the ship's masters who were his potential customers, came. The new house had workshops at the rear of it, and was conveniently just south of Ludgate Hill from which it was reached via Pilgrim Street, or alternatively from St Paul's Churchyard by Creed Lane and Shoemakers Row. The 1799 map by Horwood shows it well. Blackfriars was a warren of tiny mediaeval streets which however had suffered badly in the Great Fire, after which it was largely rebuilt, but keeping the old street pattern. It had previously held the Dominican Priory of Blackfriars, founded in 1278, the nave of which lay immediately to the west of the pathway still known as Church Entry. The choir was on the east side of that pathway, which originated in the passage running north-south between nave and chancel normally found in a Friar's church and over which rose the steeple. After the Priory was dissolved in 1538 and partly destroyed, the site of the nave was used for burials right up to 1849. Round the corner, in Ireland Yard, south and east of the above, is the entrance to another burial ground where originally stood the Dominican Provincial's Hall, with the brother's dorter above. Here, after 1538, St Anne's Church was built to serve the precincts of the Priory of Blackfriars, but it was only destined to last a little over a hundred years, as it was destroyed in the Great Fire and never rebuilt. From then until 1849 that site too served as an

St Ann
Burial
Ground
(south of
Shoemaker
Row)

– unnamed

Broad Way

136 Fleet Street

London – Horwood 1799 – Fleet Street and Blackfriers. BY PERMISSION OF GUILDHALL LIBRARY, CORPORATION OF LONDON

35

alternative graveyard for the parish, and has since been paved over, partly using old tombstones, and edged with shrubs. In a corner on the right of the entrance still lie some stone remnants of the Priory.

These sites are described at length as they must have been well-known to William (1763) and Sarah, and even used as a playground by the younger children. After 1666, the Parish of St Anne's, Blackfriars had been joined with that of St Andrew-by-the-Wardrobe, which was a little to the south-east, and this is where the family must have worshipped. Sadly this Wren church was gutted in the Blitz of December 1940, so that its interior is now mainly modern. Part of its graveyard lying to the south was sliced through when Queen Victoria Street was being built in the 1860s, the graves and their stones being removed to other cemeteries.

Broad Way was, true to its name, wider than most of the other streets in Blackfriars, but was quite short and contained only 13 houses at William's (1763) time. From it the Simms boys could run down Water Lane to Earl Street which crosses it at the bottom and off which were the many wharves where they could watch the luggers unloading their cargoes of lime, timber, iron and other materials for the City. By walking a few yards up-river they could reach the Thames by Blackfriars Steps, just beside the bridge, then less than fifty years old. Waterloo and Southwark bridges were yet to be built – in 1816 and 1819 respectively – so there was still freedom for boats to pass up to the grand houses in the Strand, Westminster and Lambeth. Downstream, the other side of the broad stretch of tidal river, were the bustling wharves at Southwark with their fascinating selection of small craft and sails. The river was a busy place at this period, full of interest for boys, not least so Puddle Dock at the bottom of St Andrew's Hill. Another favourite visit for the younger ones was the Bridewell in Bridge Street because of the entrancing life-size wooden figures of a boy and a girl dressed in hospital uniform, which stood at the entrance and are now housed in St Bride's Church. These figures were widely to be found outside institutions and shops, and Dickens describes one belonging to old Solomon Gills in *Dombey and Son*.[5] He was known as the 'Wooden Midshipman', 'eternally employed outside the shop of nautical instrument makers in taking observations of the hackney coaches'. Dickens worked at Doctors Commons just south of St Paul's, as a journalist for two years from December 1828, so was well acquainted with such figures.

For young William Simms (1793) the future shone brightly, although at present he had no money to start on his own account in new premises. At first he retained the use of a bench in a section of his father's workshop at the rear of No. 4, Broad Way. He probably continued to live in his father's house there also, but he was a persistent and quietly forceful young man, and he also was producing some excellent work in these years, quite quickly increasing the number of his clients. His brother James at the same time was

36

continuing his father's tradition in the marine compass market, and business was good. Soon the working space became too cramped, and William needed the independence of his own menage, and room to employ his own assistants and apprentices. By about 1818, with marriage also looming on the horizon, he moved back up the hill to Bowman's Buildings, and lived there until that became too small for his requirements, but keeping his workshops there right up to 1826 when he joined up with Edward Troughton.

Marriages of William's (1763) children

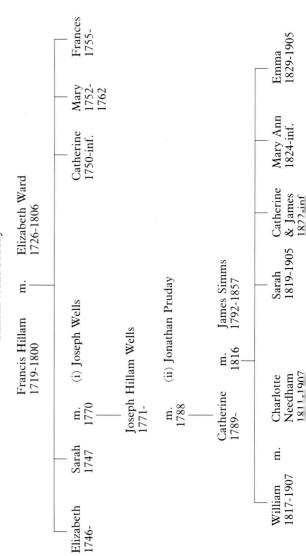

James 1792-1857	**William** 1793-1860	John 1798-1879	George 1799-1859	Henry 1800-1871	Frederick Walter 1803-1865
m. 1816	m. 1819	m. 1823	m. 1831	m. 1833	m. 1832
Catherine Pruday 1789-	Ann Nutting 1798-1839	Christian Sumner 1800-1850	Sophia Davy	Mary Ward -1857	Caroline Nutting 1804-1846

Hillam/Wells/Pruday

Francis Hillam 1719-1800 m. Elizabeth Ward 1726-1806

Elizabeth 1746-   Sarah 1747   (i) Joseph Wells   Catherine 1750-inf.   Mary 1752-1762   Frances 1755-

Joseph Hillam Wells 1771-

m. 1770

(ii) Jonathan Pruday

m. 1788

Catherine 1789- m. 1816 James Simms 1792-1857

William 1817-1907 m. Charlotte Needham 1811-1907   Sarah 1819-1905   Catherine & James 1822-inf   Mary Ann 1824-inf.   Emma 1829-1905

Nutting family

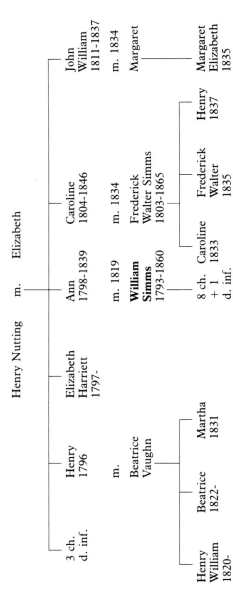
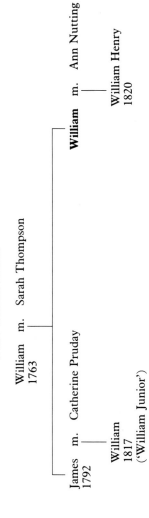

Henry Nutting m. Elizabeth

3 ch. d. inf.

Henry 1796 m. Beatrice Vaughn
- Henry William 1820-
- Beatrice 1822-
- Martha 1831

Elizabeth Harriett 1797-

Ann 1798-1839 m. 1819 **William Simms** 1793-1860
- 8 ch. +1 d. inf.
- Caroline 1833
- Frederick Walter 1835
- Henry 1837

Caroline 1804-1846 m. 1834 Frederick Walter Simms 1803-1865
- Margaret Elizabeth 1835

John William 1811-1837 m. 1834 Margaret

Four William Simms'

William m. Sarah Thompson 1763

James m. Catherine Pruday 1792
- William 1817 ('William Junior')

William m. Ann Nutting
- William Henry 1820

39

CHAPTER 4

1815-1824

THE YEAR WILLIAM SIMMS BECAME a Freeman of the Goldsmiths Company saw the great Battle of Waterloo. It exploded in June 1815, annihilating Napoleon's army, and became a landmark in the history of England, and therefore necessarily for everyone living then. At last there was peace almost for the first time since 1793. Up to then England had still largely remained a rural community, and outside the few big cities the market towns were quite small, pastoral and often very beautiful places. The people were fundamentally country folk, with the seasons of the different crops and the folk-tales of centuries ingrained in their thinking. Lady Day was still put aside for hiring labour and for paying rents. Harvest still had a festival spirit with genuine thankfulness. The fiddler still played in church and for the barn-dances. The agrarian revolution had advanced far, the fields were now mostly enclosed, and the majority of workers were tenant farmers or labourers. The large landowners controlled more and more acreage as they pushed out the boundaries of their estates. In the main everyone outside the industrial towns lived well, if simply, and the green pastures and orchards looked fresh and verdant, the arable land overflowing with abundant produce. Even in the towns it was still only a minority who lived in squalor, and the factory workers were in general better off than their first-generation parents or grandparents were when, unemployed and destitute, they left the land.

Waterloo brought to an end the long war with France and then with Napoleon, and thus to the previous very real fear of invasion from the Continent. Having conquered Napoleon at sea, and joined with Russia and Prussia to beat him on land, England found herself in a distinguished and much admired position to take a large share in the peace negotiations. She had won the war, not through superior numbers, but by discipline and training, and very largely by industrial pre-eminence and inventiveness. From now on the latter dominated her development and it was from this date that she truly evolved into an industrial nation. In 1815 most of the 13 million Britons worked on the land or in parallel trades. By 1831, half the population lived in towns. By 1871 the total population of the country had reached 26 million, mainly living in towns. In 1815 London had just about a million inhabitants. Only five years later this had increased by a quarter. A measure of industrial output that followed this expansion of population can be gauged by the fact that in 1815 the import of raw cotton from America amounted to 82 million pounds; by 1860 it had risen to 1,000 million pounds. The iron, coal and engineering trades, still relatively small except in towns like Birmingham where they formed the main employers, were rapidly working up to meet the years of railway mania between 1830 and 1850, and the huge explosion of manufacturing in the later three-quarters of the century.

To feed this enlarging population and preserve the price of corn, in 1815 came the first important Corn Law, which laid down that corn might not be imported until the price exceeded 80 shillings a quarter. This cost far outran what the increasing number of the poor could afford, and as they paid more for bread they had less and less to spend on other farm products such as eggs and meat and milk. The farmers therefore lost custom, and many of the tenant farmers had to forego their leases. Rents and tithes also increased with the price of corn, and by 1818 the peak of Poor Relief was reached at £8 million per annum.

Now began the intermittent riots of the destitute labourers in Bristol, Manchester, and in 1831 London and Dorset. The surge of emigration to Australia in search of better living conditions began. There was great social distress and unrest on the one hand, whilst on the other it was the beginning of the complex systems of social relief in hospitals, housing, orphanages and prisons, and not least in the lunatic asylums. It also saw the blossoming of great artistic and architectural enterprises during the Regency period; the great Nash terraces in London, and the classical houses and crescents in town and country. The refined furniture of the late 18th century was becoming heavier, more fanciful and gold-tipped, but still impressive. The influence of Egypt after the Battle of the Nile still showed in decoration and design right up to the rather deadening period of William IV. The Regency era, which commenced in 1811 with George III being permanently confined to care for his madness, was one of extravagance in manner, art and behaviour, extending into the 1830s before coming to earth with Queen Victoria's reign.

The most significant personal effect of the peace immediately after Waterloo was however, none of the above, but the noticeably enlarging number of unemployed and destitute on the streets. This was partly because industrial output previously concerned with the war effort, dropped dramatically, partly because of the flocks of returning soldiers, and partly the increasing plethora of farm labourers who could no longer find work on the land and came trudging into the towns. Beggars and itinerant pedlars and musicians were rife on the streets of London and at the annual

41

Bartholomew Fair, where the Simms children were only allowed to see the collections of wild animals but none of the other, less tasteful shows which made capital out of the misfortunes and degredations of war or birth on the dregs of human beings.

On the whole, middle-class families were very little affected by these events. Parson Woodforde in his diary commented briefly upon major news items such as the guillotining of Louis XVI or the Battle of the Nile, but immediately followed with a list of what he had had for dinner that day – boiled mutton, a 'soal', a couple of pheasants, damson tarts and cherries. The aftermath of war may have been bad for many trades, but for the Simms brothers engaged in scientific instrument production, there were always customers, governmental or private, to purchase their highly specialised goods. Even the jewellery trade which involved John and Henry, would barely feel the pinch, and their more practical offerings such as watch chains, seals, and compasses were still sought after.

James (1792), William Simms' elder brother, now working with their father at Broad Way, was making a good living from the manufacture of small instruments such as marine compasses, joint dials of all sorts, barometers, and probably simple telescopes, chronometers and sextants, or the earlier more favoured quadrants. In 1816 he married Catherine Pruday, at twenty-seven just three years older than himself, a country girl from Rutland. Catherine was the only daughter of Jonathan and Sarah Pruday of the remote little village of Wing, two or three miles over the fields and past an ancient maze, north-east of Uppingham. Sarah had been born in the next village of Ayston in 1747, the daughter of Francis and Elizabeth Hillam, whose family had farmed there for generations. She had first married a Joseph Wells of London about whom nothing is known, except that they had one son, Joseph Hillam Wells who was baptised at St Marylebone on 6th October 1771. Soon after this, his father died, and Sarah brought young Joseph back with her to live with her parents on the farm at Ayston. In August 1788 she married for the second time, Jonathan Pruday of Wing, retaining for herself the surname of Wells, which was a common enough practice then. Joseph remained with his grandparents at Ayston, and his step-sister, Catherine was born at Wing in October the following year. Eventually when old Francis Hillam died in May 1800 at the great age of eighty-one, leaving only daughters, Joseph inherited the farm, and his grandmother, Elizabeth lived with him until her death six years later when she was eighty. Contact between Sarah and the Wells connections in London must have been maintained, and through them Catherine became acquainted with the Simms'. In 1816 she and James Simms married, and their first son, William, was born in June 1817 at Bride Lane, a tiny street which runs from New Bridge Street, curling round to come up past the east end of St Bride's Church. Here he was baptised next month beneath its 'wedding cake' tower and within sight of Fleet Street. As a child this

42

William often went back to Ayston to stay at the farm with his Uncle Joseph, and when he learned to read, would amuse himself by wandering up the little path from the farm into the old churchyard to search out all the gravestones of former Hillams. These were clustered round the south door of the ancient parish church, and dated back to the 16th century. It was said that there had been Hillams at Ayston since the time of Norman William.[6] The beautiful bronzed ironstone of the cottages and the church on its little mound, surrounded by ancient trees, and with the old hall on the north side in its parkland, and the recently built Regency Hall, square, solid and elegant in its lovely garden complete with stone ornaments, heated conservatory against a south-facing wall, and imposing entrance gates, all this was a splendid place for a child to play.

By this time young William's (1817) Uncle William (1793) had brought his young bride home to Bowman's Buildings. Ann Nutting was only twenty when he married her, and he was nearly 26. The families had known each other for at least a generation. Her father, Henry Nutting, was a goldsmith, working at No. 38 Noble Street, just north of Cheapside in the City, an address which was to be used later by his son, another Henry, in his trade as a straw hat manufacturer. Ann was the eldest of the three Nutting children who are relevant to this story.[7] She was born at Noble Street, and baptised at the nearby church of St Anne & St Agnes (now a Lutheran church) in Gresham Street on 14th December 1798. Her sister Caroline was similarly baptised there on 12th August 1804, and lastly John William Nutting was born after the family followed the current trend of moving north to the newly-built terraces called after their creator, Pentonville. Here he was baptised on 19th May 1811 in the Parish Church of an area now mainly famous for its gaol. Owing to the fact that Ann was still a minor, her father and William Simms had to obtain a special licence, or allegation as it was known, from the Diocese of London before she could legally be married. This they applied for in person on the 4th August 1819 at Doctors Commons, and two days later William and Ann were united at the church of St James', Clerkenwell in the parish of which Henry Nutting and his wife Elizabeth and their children lived.

With no portraits to guide us, we may pause here to consider how William and his bride looked when they emerged from St James' that summer day. White had already become established for weddings, largely because all this century it had been popular for the diaphonous dresses made of materials such as muslin, tulle and taffeta then used. Ann was young, and came from a well-to-do family, though still within the social bounds of trade. Her tastes, tempered by her mother's opinion of what was fitting, veered naturally towards the latest styles now superseding the sweeping classical modes of the early century which favoured the high waist and the low neckline in spite of the northern temperatures. By 1820 waists were beginning to descend to their proper place, and necklines (at any rate

43

for day dresses) to rise. Skirts lost their trains and became fuller, with scallops and flounces, and shorter to just below the ankle. Sleeves were increasing in size from the miniscule puff of the Napoleonic era to longer and fuller shapes, and the 'leg-of-mutton' was appearing. Bonnets had been de rigeur for a decade, and being summer, Ann's was either of straw or of gauze to match her dress, and decorated with lace and flowers. Ringlets emerged from it either side of her face and possibly at the back also, or she may have drawn her back hair up over the top of her head to be held in place with a comb. No shawl was needed in August unless it was for modesty or decorative effect – in winter it would have been of wool or paisley, or she might have worn a cape or cloak of warmer material such as velvet. Her shoes were light heel-less pumps, as no lady could be expected to walk far, especially over the roads as they then were. She certainly wore white gloves, and may have carried a posy from the fields to the north. There is no hint as to Ann's height, but, as her new husband was tall, she had to stand on tiptoes on the church steps to receive his kiss on her forehead.

William's wedding attire is likely to have been conventional. The fancy styles of the 18th century had all but disappeared, and only the elderly like Troughton still wore a frock coat, breeches and hose, and wigs. Tricorne hats only appeared for ceremonials. Lace at the throat and wrists had been replaced by a white linen stock, often overworn by a black silk cravat, which just allowed the pointed tips of the collar to protrude up each cheek, and turned-up cuffs. His hair was cut short, worn with natural waves, shortly to become longer and bushier as fashion demanded. Top hats, still with curved sides, were now generally worn, and today William wore his best one of brown or buff to match his coat. This was single-breasted and cut horizontally around from the waist in front to form tails, probably rounded at their ends. Under it he wore a waistcoat of a light colour or slightly embroidered. His boots were of soft buckskin, worn under his nankeen pantaloons, which, starting broad at the top, narrowed below the knees and were strapped under his instep. Like Ann, he wore white gloves, and perhaps in honour of the occasion he sported a fob watch and a stick.

After the wedding the newly-weds returned to Bowman's Buildings, into which James and Catherine had now moved from Bride Lane, and where their second baby, Sarah (conveniently called after both her maternal and her paternal grandmothers) had been born that June. William and Ann's first baby was born just a year later and was baptised at St Botolph Without Aldersgate on 25th June 1820. He was called William Henry, and was thus the fourth living William in the family, a great confusion. First there was grandfather William born in 1763, now living at Broad Way. Then there was his son, William Simms, born in Birmingham in 1793, and as it turned out, far and away the most eminent of them all, now newly married to Ann Nutting. Next in age came William Simms' nephew,

44

William, born in 1817, son of James Simms and Catherine Pruday, and thus cousin to the new baby William Henry.

Four months after William and Ann were married the third of the Simms brothers, John, completed his apprenticeship. He was an enterprising spirit – a whizz kid we would call him today – and having heard that trade in small hardware was still booming in Birmingham in spite of generally adverse economic conditions, took himself off on the coach to that city. Doubtless he went to one of his Simms cousins who were still living there. Success followed him all the way. By 1823 he had returned to London as an agent for the Birmingham businesses, and found himself premises in which to carry out transactions in Belle Sauvage Yard, in rooms that had previously belonged to the Commercial Travellers Society, next to the famous old coaching inn off Ludgate Hill. The Belle Sauvage itself no doubt was the centre of many of his deals, positioned usefully as it was in the centre of the City and of an important stage for coaches which frequently departed from and arrived there from all the large provincial towns. Parson Woodforde often stayed at the Belle Sauvage during his trips to London or on his way to Bath, and delighted in its gourmet food and other comforts, only counter-balanced by the bed-bugs in its chambers which constantly attacked him.

John was plausible and persuasive, and made a successful business man, possibly engaging as a silversmith on the side. He remained in the St Brides parish over forty years, living first at No. 7 Shoe Lane, off Fleet Street, and then in a house in Peterborough Court which he rented from Edward Troughton, and later from his brother, William. In 1823 he married Christian Sumner of Warwickshire. Between 1824 and 1845 she faithfully gave birth to a constant flow of children, altogether no less than twelve in number including one pair of twins, Selina and Georgiana in 1832 who did not live. Amongst the others, probably all survived childhood, though not all married.

1820, the year that William Henry was born (and that, in which, almost imperceptably to the general public, poor George III slipped into eternity, and the Prince Regent became King), held other important family events. The baby's young uncle, Francis Octavius, the youngest of the Simms brothers, died in September in Broad Way at the age of twelve. Whether this was due to sudden overwhelming infection, still so common, or whether he had always had some potentially lethal disability is not clear. Perhaps it is significant that the only brother to call a child after him was the kind-hearted Henry. Neither William (1793) or John had a Francis amongst their numerous offspring, nor did James (1792) or Frederick Water, which indicates some distressing handicap which they did not want to recall. At any rate his death was possibly an influence on old William (1763) to think about retirement. He already had five of his seven surviving sons launched on their careers, Freemen of good Livery Companies, George having completed his apprenticeship that year. He announced that he would step down from his business on 30th June, and leave the whole thing, 'stock and implements and hackle then belonging to him'[8] to James (1792) and George jointly.

By 28th July the two new owners of the Broad Way enterprise had negotiated with a lawyer to draw up an indenture between them for a fourteen year partnership, to expire on 31st December 1834, or before that if one of them gave twelve months notice of quitting prematurely and paid a fine of £400. There were the usual safeguards of promises to consult and advise each other, keep books for mutual information, avoid debts, and share the profits equally. Their respective handwritings when they signed the huge document, were remarkably similar.[9]

James (1792) continued to live in Aldersgate, George may have remained at Broad Way for a time. Old William (1763) and Sarah certainly remained there, and to keep himself occupied, William (1763) acquired a tobacconist and snuff-making concern from a neighbour, Joseph Simms (probably no relation), who lived at No. 13. There is still a tobacconist round the corner in Carter Street, very unusual these days, and perhaps a great great great descendant of William's little shop which he ran in the downstairs-front of No. 4.

Next year his son, William (1793), took on the onus of Alfred Septimus as an apprentice at Bowman's Buildings. Since Francis' death the youngest of the brothers, Alfred, was very obviously a dullard, and was going into work a year later than most youths, to give him extra time to mature a little. He was to live with William (1793) and Ann, and to be given straightforward tasks in the workshop. Like most simple people he was probably quite happy with repetitive work, and therefore had his uses. He must have applied himself well, and caused no disruption, as he would hardly otherwise have been allowed amongst all the delicate instruments and glassware laying around on the benches. It was typical of his patient elder brother to tolerate this slow-minded boy at no pecuniary gain to himself, and to persevere to see him right through his seven years to acquire the Freedom of the Goldsmiths Company at the end of it.

1822 saw the arrival of three more newcomers to Bowman's Buildings as well as Alfred. In late January twins arrived for James (1792) and Catherine, a boy and a girl called after their parents and baptised at St Botolph on 3rd February. Both babies died in infancy. In May a baby girl, baptised Ann at St Botolph on 5th, was born to William (1793) and Ann, but also died. Such a sum of tragedy, even though so regularly occurring in the early 19th century, must have been hard to bear, and a shattering disappointment. As if this was not bad enough news for the grandparents in Broad Way, their worries were now concentrated on their sixth son, Frederick

46

Walter whom they had apprenticed (in March 1818) to a cabinet maker in Vine Court, Spital Fields, named Robert Wilmott, for the sum of £29. Robert Wilmott was a goldsmith, and his new recruit proved intelligent and nimble with his fingers, and showed an ability to draw accurate scaled plans for the furniture he would be making. However, Frederick was not happy. All his life he was to transfer from one interest to another, and now he was constantly complaining about his poor health which he attributed to his occupation. Neither was he able to become absorbed intellectually with his work. The boy was very bright, loved mathematical problems, and had high ambitions, but he had little perseverance. He had none of the calm unflurried persistance of his brother William (1793), though he had as good a brain. He wanted quick results, and felt he was being wasted sticking legs onto chairs, as indeed he was.

In December his chamber-master and his father agreed that his apprenticeship had not been a success, but in order to retain future Freedom, he should officially be 'turned over' to his father until his seven years were completed.

So Frederick left the furniture trade with relief, and returned to Broad Way where he was more at home amongst the optical instruments. But he was a restless soul, and instead of working all his hours at the benches there in order to make up for lost time, he went back to Mr Hayward, the naval instructor who had tutored him earlier, for more mathematics. Once he won his Freedom in April 1825, he found an assistantship with a surveyor, and at last for a time felt on safer ground.

★　　　★　　　★　　　★

Back in 1815, when William Simms (1793) first entered the world of business on his own account, he was largely dependent on his own resources to become known to potential customers. His fortune was to have a connection, via Bennett, with Jesse Ramsden, who remained the elder statesman of the mathematical instrument trade even after his death. This immediately set William up as a man of whom to take notice, even though it was a status which had to be maintained by accomplished workmanship. Like Ramsden he was fascinated by the problems of division of the circle which was so vital to the manufacture of accurate measuring facilities. He became known for the precision and dependability of his instruments, reputation he not only quickly achieved, but maintained. But he also needed to know the people who could advise and guide him, and also to bring him orders for his work. William (1793) grasped every opportunity to advance his career, not content merely to remain at his work-bench with his inventions, but to find recognition in appropriate circles. Very soon after he became a Freeman, such an opening presented itself – or, at least, he orchestrated an opening. He had constructed an original type of protractor using a principle of his own design which incorporated a long arm divided in tenths of inches, in addition to the usual brass semicircular limb, enabling the draughtsman to draw a radial line 'from a given centre to any extent and with any degree of inclination'. It provided an easy method of detecting 'any errors in its application and adjustments', and a facility in correcting them.[10] He carefully drew out a scaled plan of his protractor, wrote a description of its design and use, and composed a letter to the man he thought most able to advise him on how to bring it to the notice of influential men of science. This was Thomas Jones of Rupert Street, Haymarket, who early in his distinguished career had been apprenticed to Jesse Ramsden, and was therefore known to William's Master, Mr Bennett.

William could not have made a wiser move, as Jones soon replied with a letter full of approval and encouragement, recommending him to submit his drawings to the Society of Arts where many of the best known 'Artists in mechanical drawing are members thereof.'[11] William immediately followed this advice, and his invention quickly reaped its own recognition. It also brought him to the notice of Edward Troughton, an acknowledgement which was to influence his whole future. Indeed, he was destined in less than a decade later to become a partner with the great man, an event which to the young optician newly 'Free' of his apprenticeship in 1815, seemed totally unbelievable. William was a down-to-earth person, but even to him Edward Troughton was literally a star-lit figure, well-known throughout the optical world as one of the most important instrument makers then living. His name had been familiar to young William since early childhood when he had been taken down Ludgate Hill by his father to stare with awed fascination into the shop window of the Master at 136 Fleet Street, before passing on to the neighbouring toy shop to see the 'bell-ringers' from St Dunstan's Church, now resting from their labours. In 1816 William's design for his protractor and Jones' helpful response made the simple little device perhaps one of the most important instruments he ever made, as it became the first strand in the web of acquaintance between Edward Troughton and himself. From those early days at the Society of Arts, Troughton marked his potential, and thereafter his career with anticipation.

William had had the wisdom to attend lectures of the Society of Arts as soon as he became a chamber-master. He was from the first a frequent participant in its meetings[12] which then took place at various venues, one of which was the circulating library in Crane Court off Fleet Street, not far from his home. Its full title was 'The Society for the encouragement of Arts, Manufactures and Commerce', and it had been set up in 1754 at Rawthmells Coffee House in the quiet backwater of Henrietta Street, Covent Garden, by a group of men, mainly Fellows of the Royal Society, who realised that the great technical advances of the period in trade, commerce and the industrial arts, required an outlet. There was a need for a common ground both to promote discussion and to pool knowledge from which new inventions would be spawned. Young people starting in their careers, even children, required encouragement to develop their gifts and increase their involvement in technology. The Royal Society, which had been formed in 1662 was unchallenged in the world of pure science. The Society of Arts was formed to broaden the scope to technical advances. In 1770 it acquired its own headquarters at 380 and 381 Strand, and when the lease of that ran out, the Brothers Adam offered accommodation in the Adelphi where they built a house for the Society at a cost of £1,170 and an annual rent of £200 per annum. They had the vision to recognise its worth.

From its inception, the Society of Arts had offered prizes to youngsters for their productions of art and design. It also ran a busy series of lectures on a whole range of technical subjects, delivered by eminent men. William Simms attended these evenings with great regularity, not only for the content, but also for the acquaintance of fellow members, many of them with similar interests to himself. Very soon he became friendly with Bryan Donkin, one of its earliest members, who also became its vice-president and chairman of its committee on mechanics. Donkin was a civil engineer and an inventor, who had shown aptitude for both as a boy when he became proficient, and no doubt notorious, for making pea-shooters. As an adult he expanded his interests to a variety of projects including paper-making machines, printing rollers, and eventually astronomy. Here his interests overlapped with those of William Simms, who had been brought up in the atmosphere of optics and astronomical observation. It may be that the two men had similar personalities, though Donkin was much the older by 25 years.

William Simms also came to know Francis Baily who was a 'consummate man of business', and having earned himself a considerable fortune, was spending it on his fascination for astronomy. When William first met him, Francis Baily was absorbed by the forthcoming annular eclipse due to occur on 7th September 1820, which he himself would observe from Kentish Town. In 1818 Baily was to publish a paper on it.[13]

Both Bryan Donkin and Francis Baily had reputations for integrity and intelligence, and they were attracted to young William who was at the start of his career. They already were able to recommend his careful workmanship to their friends and amongst other members of the Society of Arts they introduced him to Colonel Colby. This was a vital link for William as Colonel Colby had, since 1809, been executive officer of the Trigonometrical Survey of England for which he had been working since 1802 under General Mudge. The latter had now become Lieutenant Governor of the Royal Military Academy at Woolwich, and Colby took his place in the Survey, which he ran with military precision from its headquarters in the Tower of London. He was fastidious about his instruments and his assistants, but again there appeared the 19th century respect for integrity and efficiency, and he gingerly ordered specimen levels and theodolites from William,[14] much to the latter's joy. Both fundamental instruments in land surveying, the role of the former was to ascertain the horizontal, the latter to measure horizontal and vertical angles, and thus levels, height and distance. These orders were really the commencement of William's success, and were probably the financial basis on which he asked Ann to marry him.

Early in 1820 General Mudge died, and Colby was promoted to be head of the Survey. He also became an FRS in April 1820, and the same year was appointed to a seat on the Board of Longitude. By this time he had proved William's excellence as an instrument maker and a man with whom it was congenial to work, and orders for surveying instruments, particularly theodolites, came thick and fast, enabling William not only to establish himself in the business, but to add his younger brother, Alfred, to his expenses.

It is at first sight surprising that William Simms was able to meet such eminent people on a friendly footing, and on their own ground. He had been brought up in a household which included astronomy in its parameters, although there is no evidence that his father was ever to give him much help in introducing him to the sort of people who could have assisted him to establish himself. Although old William was by no means so gifted or successful as this son, nor did he have a natural affiliation to men who were so distinguished, their names were well-known to him. Astronomy became very popular in the 18th and 19th centuries, and as more families reached a state of affluence during the rising prosperity of the middle classes, increasing numbers had the money and leisure to become amateur astronomers. The more wealthy of these even achieved a small observatory of their own. It was not uncommon for a man to own a telescope, even if only of low power, but as he rose in the social and financial stakes, the more powerful and accurate astronomical telescope became a desired object, until he reached the heights of a sophisticated equatorial capable of viewing objects not only on the meridian, but following their paths across the sky, and measuring their height and position.

William's father probably manufactured for the lesser end of the scale, for star-gazers who found the heavens interesting even if only from their top-floor windows. All his instruments had to be tested before they were sold in his shop, and as London became increasingly smokey, he had perforce to go to the edge of the City to find clean enough air to do this. As the early 19th century building spree developed, this became more difficult, and he needed to travel further afield to find an open space. To pinpoint a suitable hill above the grime, he had to drive the five miles to Greenwich, or a similar distance to Highgate, and even further to Sydenham. With this phase of work, he naturally learned a large amount of pure practical astronomy, and William, being a bright boy, accompanied his father on such outings. If the instrument to be tested was one for surveying, he was useful as an errand boy, moving object or instrument as required. He quite naturally picked up a helpful reservoir of information about relevant subjects, and when he started lessons with Mr Hayward this was augmented, and to it was added navigational skill which encompassed a familiarity with the heavens. His interest in astronomy thus received another fillip. Similarly when he went to work with Bennett, he first was employed as a general help with the instrument making, and as he became more qualified to do so, would be given the responsibility of examining the finished products completely before they could be sold. Thus his grasp of astronomy and surveying increased and his interest blossomed. Moreover, he could add to his knowledge from the various libraries which were opening at points throughout the capital, the more popular literature to be found at the circulating libraries, more technical at the various new institutes such as that in Finsbury Square. There were also lectures on the subject to which he was eligible to go, notably those of the Society of Arts. With such an astute brain, and a personal experience in making the instruments for the study of the stars, by the time he set up in his own business in 1815, he had gathered a pool of knowledge to exchange with men who now were his peers. No longer was he merely a technician, but well on the way to being an authority, and these older men soon spotted his potential. Moreover, his pleasant personality, which combined a certain amount of humility with a firm opinion based on rational foundations, endeared him immediately to other people, be they customers, friends or experts. His early introduction to the Royal Observatory due to acquaintanceship with Mr Pond's young assistants, increased his dedication until he was wholly involved.

The exact circumstances of the first encounter of Edward Troughton with the young man who subsequently became his successor, can only be conjectured, but it was impossible that their paths should not cross before long. Most trades in London were close-knit, and their families were known to each other, as exemplified by the intermarrying of the Simms family with other goldsmiths. Masters in a trade often apprenticed their children to their friends for which the fee was waived. It was inconceivable that Edward Troughton and William Simms should not know each other before the latter had been a chamber-master for long, meeting either quite accidentally at some neighbouring workshop, or at one of the gatherings of the Society of Arts, or a lecture elsewhere. The coffee shop was still a source of interchange of ideas, almost a club in its own right, and the one on Ludgate Hill may have been a favourite. Once William had received orders from Colonel Colby, their lines of communication narrowed, and later the Honourable East India Company was common ground.

Edward Troughton.

52

William Simms' (1793) future partner, born in 1753, was the doyen of optical instrument makers in London. When William transferred from his tutor to Mr Bennett's workshop, the name became even more familiar on a personal level. The distaste of Ramsden and Troughton for each other was common knowledge[15] since the latter's uncle John Troughton with several colleagues had instituted a petition to the Privy Council praying for the revocation of copyright of Dolland's patent of the achromatic lens in 1764. Somehow this feud had been fuelled on later occasions, and Ramsden was the only person in his life with whom Troughton maintained a quarrel. However, this old history was counteracted by the long list of Troughton's achievements, and by the time that William actually met him, Troughton had the highest of reputations for well-designed, beautifully executed, and minutely accurate instruments, for which William, still at the start of his career, had the greatest respect. Troughton's creations coincided with William's own field of interest, starting way back in the old man's early days when first his brother, John Troughton, perfected a new method of dividing a circle with minute accuracy, a proceeding which he completed with Edward's assistance in 1778. This was the foundation of precise measurement, and its successor made after William joined the firm in 1826 was even more refined, whilst William's own self-acting dividing engine invented by 1843, reached the zenith of perfect measurement then aspired to.

Troughton's other early specialities were in the refinement of the sextant, an instrument for measuring angles, and in particular used in navigation to ascertain the attitude of stars. He applied particular effort and care to this work knowing that the lives of seamen depended on his expertise and the pains with which he selected the lenses and mirrors concerned. He subsequently invented the British Reflecting Circle to counteract certain optical imperfections and patented the pillar sextant in 1788, nearly five hundred of which had been made by 1801. His other achievements were in the sphere of surveying, notably in the design of theodolites and levels, and even the more simple equipment needed in the field such as the lightweight level and staff. He was greatly involved in accomplishing accuracy in the common surveying chain, and later in the standard measures.[16]

The area where he became best known was that of astronomical instruments, starting in 1793 with the two-foot altazimuth circle for Count Bruhl, and in 1805 the Groombridge transit circle, with which he himself was dissatisfied to the extent of destroying the second one he made. The same year he completed the Westbury Circle for his friend, John Pond, who in 1811 was to become Astronomer Royal. By then, in 1810, Troughton's original six-foot mural circle was erected at the Royal Observatory at Greenwich, following which the rest of his life was engaged upon work not only for Greenwich, but for many other observatories throughout the world, completing the reputation which the 10-ft transit instrument at

Greenwich brought him on its completion in 1816. These were all highly sophisticated pieces of equipment incorporating telescopes for which he was only satisfied when they were in perfect working condition, regardless of cost to himself, either monatory or physical. He also carried out some experimental work with William Hyde Wollaston on the use of platinum and paladium on which to etch the all-important divisions on the circles of astronomical and navigational instruments. Silver was in use generally for this in the 1820s, and ultimately proved the most suitable material, but the initiative indicated the freshness of his mind.

Troughton himself was a 'character', and a totally different personality from William Simms; indeed one wonders how it was the two men were able to tolerate each other, let alone work together. William was a warm family man, philosophical about life and outwardly unruffled by adversity. He was kindly, and with a frank sense of quiet humour. In all the many hundreds of his letters still in existence, never once is there a malevolent or venomous remark about anyone. From his portrait photographs, he appears a bonviveur with a tendency to plumpness, and a smile never far from the surface. Troughton was quite the opposite, a thin, rather gaunt-looking bachelor who was abrupt and 'original' in his style of speech, and had a severity in his criticism,[17] which however was never unfair. His one known portrait, painted by Caroline Hassler whose father headed the United States coastal survey, betrays a middle-aged man with a thin aquiline face, unsmiling worried expression, and below the furrowed brow, distantly-focussed eyes. The two busts of him, both rather older, one by Chantry, the other by J. Devilee (1822) bring these traits into greater prominence; a thin ascetic countenance with deep unfathomable thoughts.

However, reports relate that behind Troughton's very firm opinions and eccentric manner, there was an extremely kind personality. It was this very positive characteristic which, with his total integrity, absorbtion in his work and particularly for its perfecting and suitability for its proposed use, that he shared with William Simms. He cannot have been easy to work with. He often failed to write down details of his projected labour, neglected to attend to accounts, either incoming or outgoing, and ran his business at a loss until William set things right.[18] His work occupied nearly all his time and energy, and he neglected himself, his appearance and his personal affairs. Untidy to the point of slovenliness, his tools and papers were in a similar muddle, although to himself they appeared in a logical arrangement. He was an eccentric, but because of his undoubted genius, his friends and acquaintances accepted his peculiarities as part of his personality because they respected his erudition.[19]

William Simms was not above forgetfulness or disorder himself. In February 1844 he had to write to the Astronomer Royal to ask if he had found a paper about a particular instrument that William had mislaid. 'I am in very great perplexity about the description – – – I went to the box where I usually kept it – – – I have looked in every place I can think of but without success – – –.'[20] Next day he wrote again to say he had found it and 'regret that I gave you any trouble about it'. On 4th June 1857, he had to send a workman to Greenwich ostensibly to deliver the precious eight-inch glass for the transit, but actually to look for his umbrella.[21]

However, the factors that brought the two men together were the honesty and single-mindedness for their work, their enormously high standards of knowledge and craftsmanship, highly developed inventiveness, and sheer hard labour. Moreover they respected each other and were tolerant of each other's faults, the ageing ascetic and the intelligent young family man, each with his sense of humility under the complicated matters with which they dealt, and undaunted by the heights to which they were asked to reach.

It is inconceivable that either man would decide to accede to partnership in a hurry without knowing very thoroughly the other's style of living and working. They had been familiar with each other personally for several years before 1825, probably since 1816 or even earlier, at the time when both were frequently attending meetings at the Society of Arts. This was the period when Troughton was heavily committed to making instruments for the United States coastal survey, having constructed the base-line measuring apparatus and an 82-inch standard scale for it in 1813. It was also soon to be the time of William's introduction to the Ordnance Survey, and it is more than likely that they discussed together the needs of Colonel Colby in his gradual absorbtion of the whole of England and Scotland into this gigantic map-making enterprise. Waterloo year brought heavy demands on Colby, but the following year he was again out in the field, triangulating Orkney and Shetland, then measuring the base-line near Aberdeen, and later in the decade surveying in the northern Scottish mainland. In 1821 he was busy verifying the observation difference between Greenwich and Paris, and by 1824 a survey of Ireland was being ordered and equipped.

Meanwhile India was again entering their sights, with its revenue survey re-commencing in 1822. Troughton had been making instruments for the Surveyor General's Office in Calcutta for some years, but William Simms also entered the arena at about this time. General Hodgson produced a paper describing the astronomical observations taken by the SGO between 1822 and 1828, and those of surveyors he had trained himself, in answer to the East India Company's request as to the best construction of theodolites for the revenue surveys in the North Western Provinces. He had 'consulted Mr Simms, and we agreed on the construction of the instrument described'.[22] The same theodolite is also referred to in Andrew Yeates' notebook in the early 1820s,[23] and it seems that William had a working relationship with Troughton for at least three years before the formal

55

partnership came into being at the end of 1825. In fact an altazimuth circle was jointly sent by them to India in that year and the next.[24] This conclusion as to their early collaboration is reinforced by the fact that in 1823 William repaired and re-divided the Westbury Circle which Troughton had made way back in 1800 for John Pond. It also confirms that William was well in touch with the Royal Observatory at Greenwich by now, and acquainted with the Astronomer Royal – still to be John Pond for the next twelve years – a contact which was to prove of mutual benefit over the rest of their lives.

The Astronomical Society[25] now added its voice to the general interest in astronomy, which once again had received additional publicity by the appearance in London of the annular eclipse of the sun in 1820. A great deal of highly specialised knowledge of the heavens had accumulated over the years, and astronomers felt the need to pool their resources by a central body which could equate the results of their observations, and disseminate them to other members. All the information should be gathered into a library covering every aspect of the subject, and comprise also a meeting place for participants. In 1821 a gathering of fourteen interested persons, which included Edward Troughton, Francis Baily, James South, and others later well known to William Simms, met together to discuss the formation of the new Society. Francis Baily became its first secretary, and was closely associated with the setting up of its constitution and methods of functioning. Troughton was voted onto its first Council,[26] and remained on it until 1832, becoming its vice-president 1830-31. William Simms was not elected to membership for ten years, and therefore was not allowed to attend its meetings even as a visitor. But his close connection with Troughton gave him access to its proceedings, even though second-hand, and so his name became familiar to a wider range of scientific men. Such communication with one of the most respected of the Learned Societies in England became a vital source of information and interest, and indeed of friends and clients for him.

In the summer of 1823, William made one of the most important friendships of his life, and with whom, particularly from 1835 he worked in close association. This was a brilliant young man, then only twenty-two years old, who was just down from Cambridge where he had graduated as senior wrangler and first Smith's prizeman. He was George Biddell Airy. Airy had already studied optics, chemistry and mechanics as a boy, in the library of his uncle, Arthur Biddell, at whose home at Playford, near Ipswich, he frequently spent his holidays. During that fruitful summer of 1823, George Airy went off to tour Scotland with his sister Elizabeth, but in the ensuing winter he was back in London staying with James South for whom Troughton had recently built a transit instrument for South's well equipped observatory in Blackman Street, and which, with his two equatorials were to be moved to his splendid new observatory built for him by Isambard Brunel in 1826 at Camden Hill, Kensington. At South's house

Airy met Sir Humphrey Davy and Sir John Herschal, and became deeply absorbed in astronomy, and it was in this inter-relationship of friends that William Simms also came to know these eminent men through his election in March 1823 to membership of the Society of Arts, proposed by his old mentor, Bryan Donkin.

In the following October Airy was elected a Fellow of Trinity College, Cambridge, and returned there as an assistant mathematical tutor, so that although he intermittently disappeared from William's orbit, the results of his endeavours in the form of various papers on physical astronomy and the undulating theory of light came to his notice. The friendship was a strange one, with their letters adopting the formal Victorian pattern, but frequently interjected with a personal remark. In the following thirty-seven years they came to know each other's every move, and indeed all their foibles, during their long association at Greenwich. The rather stiff references to the other's families hid an affectionate regard which was barely overt, and throughout their close relationship, they mainly tolerated each other's characteristics, though it is clear from their voluminous correspondence that William Simms had to exercise aeonian patience with the exacting demands of the frenetic Astronomer Royal.

However, this was, in 1823, well in the future. At home, William and Ann's next baby was born at Bowman's Buildings, and baptised at St Botolph's on 8th February 1824. This was Elizabeth Ann who was to become William's comfort through tribulation, and who even after her marriage was to remain living barely three miles away from him.

CHAPTER 5

1824-1830

THE LONDON OF 1824 WAS BECOMING more and more grimey, smokey and noisy. There was, in addition, a great amount of crime, much of it petty but none the less unpleasant, especially the frequent daylight robbery which occurred on the streets. The mail coaches clattered over the cobbles of Aldersgate with great commotion, adding to the clamour of the traffic and the street vendors. The lumbering hackney (or 'hired') carriages were even worse as there was a coach stand just near Bowman's Buildings where the pairs of tired old horses would wait for custom, until ultimately they rattled away on a mission with wheels rumbling, hooves ever beating and harness jingling. Bartholomew Fair, a joy to the children, especially the older of the two little Williams (1817 and 1820), was a rumbustious extravaganza of stalls, showmen, and ribaldry. It left litter and smells to add to the general din, and its wild animals brought to the Fair in waggons, held up the traffic and caused a jam amongst the carts and carriages. Pick-pockets were rife, assaults common. Frequently there were public executions before Newgate Prison, when there would be enormous gatherings of inquisitive gorping crowds of up to 10,000 people to witness the end of the miscreant. Even though the Simms children were kept indoors on these days, they must have been aware of what was going on, and of the tramp of people up and down Aldersgate making for the gallows outside the prison.

It was no wonder that because of all these disturbances, by 1824 William Simms (1793) decided that his little family would be better off out of London. That year, retaining his workshop in Aldersgate, and leaving James (1792) and Catherine to take over the whole house with their growing family, he and Ann moved out to Islington, away from the noisome smells and uproar and dust of the City. In doing so, they were only following current fashion.

Islington presented itself across the fields to the north of the City as a pleasant series of hamlets amongst pastures from where came the dairy products, the meat and the market garden produce for London. Since 1761 there had been a well-maintained turnpike to connect the south of Islington with Dog House Bar near the City, with two pretty little octagonal toll

58

houses built in 1808 at the southern end of Islington High Street. Until the very end of the 18th century the area had been open countryside, with clusters of dwellings at Highbury, Upper and Lower Holloway, Canonbury, Barnsbury and towards Newington Green. In an Anglo-Saxon charter it was recognised as Gislandune, meaning Gisla's Hill or Down. A little later, this became Iseldom, or 'Lower Town' or 'Fortress' in the Domesday Book, and in the 13th century 'pleasant Iseldon'. There were several estates within its boundaries, notably that of Ralph de Berners who gained a charter for land from the Prior of St Bartholomew in 1253, from which the name Bernersbury or Barnsbury derived. The original village centred around Islington Green, which was where the present Upper Street and Essex Road divide to run north. It was the last staging post for cattle and sheep drovers on their way to Smithfield Market, and therefore possessed an increasing number of inns where they could regail themselves or stay the night. By 1810 there were fifty-five of these hostelries in and around Islington. One of the most famous of these was the Angel, originally a hospice for pilgrims to the shrine of 'Our Ladye of the Oke at Iseldon' and for travellers to and from the heathland and towns to the north.

Islington Spa opened its doors opposite Sadlers Wells Music House in 1680, and by the early 18th century there were numerous pleasure gardens centred on inns or tea houses in the vicinity. The White Conduit Inn in Barnsbury Road which since 1641 had stood beside the waterway running south to supply the Charterhouse, was one of the most notable because in its grounds was created by Thomas Lord in 1782, the cricket club which later became the Marylebone Cricket Club. Here came the fashionable populace from London to enjoy itself, to take tea and to gossip, and to walk in the gardens and listen to the orchestra, even to take the waters.

In 1756 the whole district was opened up by the creation from an old country lane of the New Road which ran east-west to connect Paddington to Islington, and which later was renamed Marylebone, Euston and Pentonville Roads. The 15th century Parish Church was replaced by a new florid one designed by Launcelot Dowbiggin, under Act of Parliament for the prosperous community which had developed. From now on there were erected a series of delightful houses, squares such as Canonbury in 1790, and terraces, notably Highbury Place between 1774 and 1779 by Henry Penton, a voracious speculative builder. Here Charles Wesley frequently stayed at No. 25. In the Regency period came Cloudesley Square by Barry, Colebrook Terrace, and Duncan Terrace where Charles and Mary Lamb lived from 1823 to 1827. Later came Alwyne Villas and Alwyne Place, superior speculative houses with the pleasant New River Walk nearby. In 1820 the Regent Canal was formally opened, reducing the isolation of the area and at first enhancing its value by bringing in goods cheaply. Islington was now THE place for Londoners to live, their holiday area and the country-spa for its invalids. So popular did it become that its very convenience and attractiveness was the cause of its deterioration, and after 1841 an enormous burst of building took place in and around it of a rather meaner style of house which provided homes for the clerks and Pooters of the City offices who walked to work daily from their monotonous terraces. For the more affluent who could afford the sixpenny fare, there was Mr Shillibeer's two-horse omnibuses which commenced regular trade between the Bank and Paddington via the Angel in 1829. By 1831 the population of Islington had expanded to a mighty 37,000 souls.

William Simms (1793) had already in 1823 purchased a house in Camden Town. It was No. 14 Camden Cottages, called when he bought it 'Gothic Cottage' and was in King's Road. He held a ninety-seven year ground lease from Christmas 1823, expiring in 1920, at a ground rent of £7-10s-0d per annum. The landlords were the Marquis of Camden and the Prebend of Cantelowes in St Paul's Cathedral. It seems that William bought this little house, one of a row of nineteen similar, each in its own garden, and only recently built, as a speculation, or (as that was rather against his nature) merely for future use for one of the family. Situated in what until then had been open country, to the rear of them were fields. To the front were the outskirts of the new grid-planned Camden Town, with, just opposite, the pleasant curve of Brechnock Terrace. By 1833 the New Road to Tottenham (which later broadened to become the big Camden Road) cut through the middle of the cottages, which have themselves since been absorbed into a hardly detectable curve in the busy St Pancras Way. The Regent Canal, a recently opened attractive asset to the area, was only a short distance to the west, then a rural joy, now mainly overbuilt. To the south, after a small gap of fields was Somers Town, Euston, and the many new small streets round the Fever Hospital at Kings Cross, where thirty years later came the Great Northern Railway Station. William's little cottage in Camden was not inhabited until the end of the year of 1823, and its first Poor Rate paid next spring. The first tenant was George Millifont, who remained there for a number of years, to be followed by Isaac Webb Moore at a gross rental of £45. Late in the 1840s he was replaced by William's younger brother, Henry who lived there for nearly thirty years.

Barnsbury was but a step to the east of Camden, a rural step still, though soon to be devastated by the appearance of the railways steaming north from Euston Station, St Pancras, and Kings Cross. But for the time being the Regent Canal wended its pleasant way past the gardens of Barnsbury to the wharves of Camden Lock and then skirted the edge of Regent's Park, enhancing an area already picturesque and desirable. It was natural that William should choose No. 11 Barnsbury Row as his country retreat in 1824, from where he could with ease reach his Aldersgate premises daily. Upper Street, only a short distance away, was developing into a good shopping area where Ann could make all necessary purchases without the need to go into the City, and the family could benefit from the country air.

William and Ann had now been married five years, and he was a member of a respected trade, and known to have friends in high astronomical places. He had his country retreat at Islington, and fashion, which was aware of the increasing need for practical garments as the age of manufacturing rolled on, was providing increasingly suitable clothes. The embroidered thigh-length coat of the 18th century had left an atavistic remnant in the patterned waistcoat for evening wear, but otherwise coats were sober-coloured, 'tailed', and either single or double-breasted. They were worn over one or two plain waistcoats bordered with braid, and William would wear the latter on its own at work in order to keep his arms free, but always, of course, resuming his tailcoat to see a client. Trousers were developing from the tight-fitting pantaloons to become the drainpipes of later years, mainly in buffs, fawn, brown and bottle green. Boots (in memory of the army footwear of yesteryear) were still worn, often black 'Wellingtons' over his trousers, but increasingly the soft-topped 'Hessians' which could be worn underneath. In the evenings he changed into pumps, still sometimes buckskin, or just heel-less slippers. He wore his top hat continually, sometimes even at work, certainly when visiting. Its sides were becoming straight, but it was still fairly short. Gloves were a must; umbrellas had not yet appeared. On journeys by coach in winter, he wore his long voluminous 'Garrick' – a caped overcoat in checked tweed with big collar and cuffs, which covered him up well from the cold.

Ann's clothes now were also becoming more practical in that they were warmer than when she was a girl. Skirts were becoming fuller and reached to the ground, and her sleeves were 'leg-of-mutton' shape and increasing in size. She used shawls a great deal, indoors and out; in summer embroidered organdie, in winter wool or velvet, or she wore one of the new 'spencers' – small fitting waist-length jackets with turned-up collar and long, fitting sleeves, in dark velvet embroidered with braid. In winter she wore a redingote if she was journeying any distance, a sober cloak with shoulder capes in plain dark cloth, and she had a fur muff to go over her gloves. Her hair was now brushed smoothly back into a chignon, but still she left the ringlets before her ears, and usually a bonnet well back from her face and tied with broad ribbons. A respectable housewife, she wore her 'chatalaine' around her slim (almost certainly corsetted) waist – a chain from which to suspend her household keys and one or two useful domestic items such as scissors and thimble. Her shoes remained light pumps, although ladies boots, elastic sided and reaching just above the ankles, were to be seen occasionally.

★　　　★　　　★　　　★

During this same fateful year (1824) Edward Troughton made up his mind to approach William Simms (1793) regarding future partnership. He was feeling his age very acutely. His writing showed signs of a tremor, and this affected the minute manipulation of his fingers during his work. His eyesight was tolerable but by now he was severely deaf and had taken to using an ear trumpet. His brain was as active as ever though perhaps not so acute or flexible to new ideas, but he shied away from the routine labour of his business. He was, after all, over seventy, and whereas previously he could apply himself to his work nearly all his waking hours, now he soon wearied. The less interesting aspects of running a business such as sending out bills, tended to be pushed on one side.

However, to take someone else into the firm as a partner was a radical and disturbing move for him. He must now take cognisance of the other's opinion, and recognise that William would eventually take over the entire business, perhaps before his own death, so that he would have to move to the sideline and have no official voice in its running. He must have had enormous faith in this young man, who now at nearly thirty-two years old, had already made a name for himself. Moreover, he must also have liked him for himself. He would hardly have brought this outsider into what, after all, was his family firm in which he himself had worked his entire life since boyhood, some fifty-six years, if he had not felt he could come to terms with seeing him daily in his place. It says a great deal for William's sensibilites that the old bachelor wanted him to do just that.

For William Simms the offer was flattering. There was no one in London who approached Troughton's reputation. His clients would now be William's, and moreover his very large premises at 136 Fleet Street, which William would ultimately inherit, meant that he would have plenty of room there for workshops on the top floor which caught the maximum light, living space on the first and second floors, and kitchens in the basement. In addition there were the outhouses, and the other premises in Peterboro Court which were in part leased to John Simms and his rapidly expanding family, and also provided further workrooms for the business. The ground floor of No. 136 accommodated the shop which opened onto Fleet Street, into the window of which William had gazed as a boy, and more recently with informed interest when he visited the house. The room behind the shop was to remain Troughton's own parlour, a dark and gloomy affair, where he mulled over his problems, designed his instruments and sniffed his snuff. From his pipe which was never far from his lips, billowed curls of smoke that yellowed the ceiling and discoloured the many tomes lining the walls. These he constantly read and re-read, their contents on angling and optics, the two passions of his life, absorbing his mind, the former a relic of his Cumbrian childhood. For housekeeper he had his niece, Jane,[27] daughter of his sister Elizabeth Suddard, who remained with him until about the spring of 1832, which may have been the date of her death. At any rate she had died by 1835, as she is the only member of his family not mentioned in his Will of that year.

The address, 136 Fleet Street, which Edward Troughton and William Simms were about to share, had belonged to the former since 1782 when his elder brother John Troughton had bought the property from a well-known instrument maker, Benjamin Cole. Previously, Cole's father, another Benjamin, had had his business there, which he in turn had acquired from Thomas Wright in 1748, 'at the sign of the Orrery and Globe'. It should be explained at this point that an orrery is a device for portraying in three dimensions the relative size, positions and movements of the sun, moon and stars in their orbits. Whereas the planetarium is a room within which the heavenly bodies are viewed as from the ground to the sky above, the orrery would usually stand about three or four feet high in the library of a great house as a representation of the solar system, and by means of turning handles, the paths of the various cosmic objects be followed along fixed wires relative to one another. Smaller, simpler orreries were made for desk tops, such as Troughton's Small Orrery of 1800, which incorporated only the earth, the moon, mercury and venus. Larger examples were built on stands, such as those to be seen at the Science Museum at South Kensington. 'The sign of the Orrery and Globe' recalls the early days of shop fronts where the sign hanging over the door denoted and advertised the trade of the owner. There was no doubt from Thomas Wright's sign that his business was to do with surveying, astronomy and map-making. Wright was mathematical instrument maker to George II from 1747 until the King's death in 1760, and foremost amongst his many products for surveying and navigating, were the globes and orreries some of which are now in the national museums of Britain. Wright had inherited the business in 1715 from John Rowley who was 'Master of Mechanics to George I – great improver of maps, spheres and globes', and distinguished himself by making a telescope for Sir Isaac Newton when he became President of the Royal Society in 1703. He also made the original orrery in 1712 for Charles Boyle, Fourth Earl of Orrery. Previous to him the proprietor of this venerable firm was John Worgan, also an instrument maker, three of whose creations still exist: a circumferenter (c1670) and a Printed Compass Dial (1699) at the Museum of the History of Science at Oxford, and a Gunther's Quadrant at the Science Museum at South Kensington. The first, the circumferenter, is a magnetic compass with fixed sights for measuring horizontal angles, and therefore useful for surveying in flat country where there are few or no landmarks, and also (for the same reason) in mining surveys. The Gunther's Quadrant is a forerunner of the sextant, but because it comprises a quarter of a circle rather than a sixth, is more bulky. Like the sextant, with appropriate lenses it measures vertical angles, and as it is a hand instrument is useful in navigating, as well as on land surveys. Making such instruments, Worgan advertised his 'Shop under the Dial of St Dunstan's in Fleet Street', a print of which, dated 1737, shows quite clearly his shop which was little more than a booth. Thus there is an unbroken line of instrument makers in this firm working in Fleet Street which finally settled at No. 136 in 1718.

By 1825, when the Troughton and Simms partnership was coming into being, there were at least five other 'opticians', – the old name for optical instrument makers – in Fleet Street, and numerous others within easy walking distance, as well as any number of gold and silversmiths and jewellers. It was, indeed, a conclave for these very specialist trades.

The frontages of the tall houses which bordered the street were elegant and Georgianised. At the back of them was a maze of little courts and passages, a jigsaw puzzle of houses and small businesses, craftsmen's workshops, backyards and 'offices'. The area was full of small bookshops and printers, and the smell of ink and noise from the machines lay heavily over the yards and alleys. After the Great Fire of 1666, when unbelievably, no less than four-fifths of the City had been destroyed, the buildings were re-erected in brick, which was safer than the old half-timbered houses, but with very little re-arrangement of the streets, and the funds for achieving this were largely raised ironically by a tax on coal. By an Act for the re-building of the City of London, a partial standardization of the new houses was ordered, particularly in regard to fire resistance, and in the main streets, of which Fleet Street was one of only six, the houses were to be neither more nor less than four storeys high. The precise thickness of the walls at various levels was laid down, as were the size of timber scanlings and the ceiling heights of the several floors. The appearance of the exteriors was left to individual taste, but it was obligatory to have a 'penthouse' at the top of the grand floor to prevent drips from the eaves descending onto pedestrians below.

The sites of those houses were narrow fronted, and stretched back a distance at least double their width, with a tiny patch of courtyard or garden at the rear. From the main street, alleys, courts and gardens spread back, often in the position of a previous large mediaeval mansion, or on the site of its garden or connecting passage. These alleys were either lined with dwellings and workshops for the merchant who did not need a shop front in the main street (such as a lawyer or money-lender) or the man who had nothing to sell but the labour of his hands (such as a shoe-mender). The alleys were to be eight to ten-feet wide, or large enough for a coach where there was a big house at the inner end. Thus as many houses as possible were crammed onto the sites. All of them, except the poorest, had shallow basements (unless they were built on ancient foundations with crypts, such as Whitefriars Priory, or were old inns with deep wine-cellars) and an 'area' extending under the public footpath, in which were set the cast-iron covers of the individual coal-shoots. The back door opened immediately onto a court, be it ever so small, and then up two or three steps to the yard or garden, which remained at the original 'natural' level of the ground. In

Fleet Street, where space was at a premium, there were no steps from the front pavement down to the area, only some at the back of the houses.

Fire continued to be feared forty years after the 1666 disaster, and the 1707 Act ordained that there should be no more wooden eaves or cornices, and from then on roofs became hidden by a parapet. Two years later a further Building Act set windows back four inches from the facade in order to protect the wood of the frames from the spread of fire, and at the same time the idea of sash windows was imported from the Netherlands. Thus evolved the typical London terrace as exemplified in the facades of Fleet Street and many other London streets of slightly later date. When William arrived at his new business there had thus developed an harmonious uniformity of height and character in the houses, but with individualities of each shop detail. Later the penthouse projection proved unnecessary because of the introduction of compulsory rain-water pipes in the mid-18th century, and though some remained, others gave way to elaborate classical cornices above ground floor level as at No. 136.

The view from Fleet Street east to St Paul's was then unobscured by the later railway bridge built in 1864 at the bottom of Ludgate Hill, and the Fleet Market built in 1757 as a long arcaded erection, survived to 1829 when it was superseded by Covent Garden Market, and replaced by Farringdon Street. The Fleet Prison on the east side of the market remained until 1846, having been repaired after the Gordon Riots. The old Bridewell, rebuilt in 1668 in New Bridge Street, was still fulfilling its role as a prison for vagrants and women accused of immoral earnings. It had schools now for destitute children, and a new building was planned for the near future in its place. Blackfriars Bridge also remained as it had been built in 1769 until Sir William Cubitt rebuilt it a hundred years later.

Westerly in Fleet Street, Wren's Temple Bar marked the City boundary until 1878, and cut it off from later London in the Strand, slowing down traffic as it passed through its central arch. Nearby, between Fetter Lane and Chancery Lane was the old St Dunstan's Church with its cantilevered clock previously surmounted by giant figures which struck the hours on its bells, but which by this period according to Dickens had been removed to a neighbouring toy shop.[28] North of Fleet Street was Crane Court where the Royal Society met from 1710 until 1780. Johnson's Court was nearby, and the entrance to the Cheshire Cheese, famous even then as a favourite inn, and rebuilt in 1667, was at No. 145, only a few doors west of William's shop. Above the archway to the Inner Temple on the south side of the street was the timber-framed house at No. 17 which remains today. Hoare's Bank, founded by a goldsmith in 1690 and used by Dickens as the model for the bank in a *Tale of Two Cities*, was at No. 37. Tompion and Graham, the clockmakers, lived at the corner of Whitefriars Street, and above all towered the splendidly delicate masonry of St Bride's.

Fleet Street was noisy. It was busy from early morning until the night watchmen did their rounds in the evening with the clatter of traffic and the yelling of street vendors, or just with the people going about their daily business. The vibration from the passing coaches and carts was such that it seems the most implausible place for the delicate precision work such as that of an optician.[29] Troughton[30] overcame this difficulty by a method which determined the time or the declination, as the case may be, when an object vibrated equally on both sides of the diaphragm wire of an instrument, and jocularly insisted that such a condition was preferable to perfect steadiness. It certainly proved effective, though it provided one more hurdle to success.

No. 136 did not comprise a single house. Another dwelling, or messuage, to the north had recently been pulled down, giving more space to the courtyard, off which at least two other houses led. To the east, one was tenanted by James Fellowes 'or his undertenants', and partly backed onto Peterborough Court, that passage like a dog's hind leg which ran north from Fleet Street. To the west was the house tenanted by John Medhurst, a tailor, and abutting on the Globe Tavern. Another house to the north was tenanted by Thomas Curson Hansard. Belonging to Edward Troughton and William Simms (1793), besides the main four-storey house fronting onto Fleet Street, were the cellars, outhouses, and a tenement in Peterborough Court.[31] It is thus probable that some of their workmen were accommodated in the last house, and some of the dirtier jobs of the trade carried out in the outhouses where there was also a forge, though for major foundry work they went to Maudsley and Co. Instrument boxes and packing cases were certainly made on the premises, but the dust created had to be kept completely separate from the precision work on instruments. The whole establishment was at that time lit by candles, the old tallow ones or the later spermacetti candles introduced in the 18th century using the sperm of the whale which produced a clear steady light, and often protected in glass-sided lanterns so they were unaffected by draughts. The rooms, particularly those downstairs and in the close-knit outhouses in the yards, must indeed have been dark by modern standards. The agreement with the previous leaseholder, William Prevost of King's Road, Bedford Row in the County of Middlesex, ran from 31st December 1825 for eighteen years ('wanting one day') at £115-10s per quarter, and was to include all 'Cellars Sollars Rooms Yards lights easements ways urydraughts privies commodities advantages and appurtenances whatsoever'. There was to be no noisome trade, auctions, public sales etc etc.

Edward Troughton and William Simms jointly signed this document for the purchase of the premises, Troughton with a perceptible tremor, William firmly with a well-filled pen. From the wording it would appear that the latter was already installed at No. 136, in spite of the fact that, as usual, the London Trade Directory had yet to catch up on his movements. Perhaps he was running between the two businesses this year, and finally vacated

66

Bowman's Building the day of the signing, on 31st December 1825. His new apprentice, his young brother-in-law, John William Nutting, brother of his wife, Ann, was bound to him on 5th October at his old address in Aldersgate, but in fact may at first have been mainly employed in moving all William's belongings from there to Fleet Street.

At the time of the signing of the Troughton and Simms partnership, both men were engaged in work for the Survey of Ireland. Troughton also had fulfilled a number of orders for instruments to be used in India since the beginning of the century. When Colebrook was Surveyor General at Calcutta, his equipment included a 'circular instrument of 2 ft diameter[32] by Troughton' as well as a Ramsden quadrant. Colonel John Anthony Hodgson in his turn sent home from India to Troughton for a telescope and equatorial theodolite, sextant, spirit levels, measuring chains and a collection of books on surveying, all of which arrived in Calcutta on 14th November 1813. There was in the Surveyor General's Office a Circular Transit Instrument 'for taking horizontal angles', made by Troughton which was carried on its frame in a box 'in the manner of a Sedan chair'.[33] It took four coolies to lift it, but because of the hill climbing involved on expedition surveying, six of them were detailed for the job. It had been first used by Lambton in 1801, then by Warren in 1802-1805, and finally by Hodgson. Quadrants were falling out of favour for astronomical work by now, and most surveyors in India took their own sextant or preferably a reflecting circle, out with them from England in the early years of the century, the complete circle having more accuracy than an arc. Cheape used a sextant 'made by that incomparable artist, Mr Troughton', and possessed also an artificial horizon made by Troughton 'on a new construction'. The Indian surveyors also brought out their own theodolites; the one used by Jopp and Shortrede in the Deccan was from Troughton and Simms' workshop.

During 1824 and 1825 the Surveyor General at Calcutta was allowed to purchase an altazimuth circle for Rs 2,000, and a second one for Rs 3,000. The first of these was by Troughton & Simms.[34] It consisted of an altitude, an azimuth (hence 'altazimuth') and a transit circle of twelve inches diameter, was divided by Troughton, the vertical or altitude to single seconds, the horizontal (azimuth) to 5 seconds, with a micrometer with which to read it. This instrument thus provides evidence of William Simms' participation in work at No. 136 before the official start of the partnership in January 1826. Practically all the theodolites which Colonel Everest brought out for his Survey of India in 1830 were constructed by Troughton & Simms. They comprised one 3-ft and two 18-inch read by micrometers (or microscopes), four 12-inch, twelve 7-inch, and four 5-inch read by verniers,[35] a graduated sliding scale which subdivides the smallest divisions of the scale against which it slides. The 3-ft theodolite was the most impressive. Its horizontal circle (actually only 34 inches diameter) had been

67

hand-divided by Troughton and was read by five 'flying microscopes'. The vertical circle attached to the telescope was 18 inches diameter. The total weight of the instrument for packing was 20 maunds, 32 seers – nearly 16 cwt. No opportunity for testing it under Indian conditions occurred until measurement of the Dehra Dun baseline was in progress in January 1835, and then Colonel Everest declared it 'as perfect in performance as beautiful in appearance – quite a masterpiece'. This noteworthy instrument continued in use in India until 1873. Later it was renovated and presented to the Victoria Memorial Collection in Calcutta in 1916.[36]

Such a vast quantity of materials must have been under manufacture for a considerable time, in order to be completed by the time Colonel Everest departed for India in 1830, probably at least from 1827 when the original orders were submitted, perhaps earlier. Everest also advised James Bedford to ask for the East India Company pattern of small 7-inch theodolites made by Troughton & Simms for the revenue surveys in India 'making it an express condition that they be made by those makers alone'.[37] And then he reports that 'Mr Simms and I put our heads together to devise that form and – – – they are a splendid success. They cost too 20% less than Mr Gilbert's rattletraps'.[38] Thus Gilbert lost his expectation of half of Everest's order, and Troughton & Simms made the entire list. Not only that, but this close connection with work in India continued for the rest of William's life.

Meanwhile manufacturing progressed for the Survey of Ireland. From his first participation in the Fleet Street partnership, officially in January 1826 William was much absorbed with the intricacies of the huge and complicated geodesic theodolite ordered by Colonel Colby. Although primarily designed by Troughton, William Simms was responsible for the majority of the actual manufacture of this remarkable instrument (now adorning the Science Museum at South Kensington), Troughton finding himself too old and tired for concentrated labour at the work-bench, and thus some modifications initiated in the light of experience as the instrument grew, were introduced by Simms. Completed in 1827, it is inscribed with both men's names, as were all their products from the first day of their partnership. As an example of the intricate work they undertook, it is prime, its purpose ('geodesic') to measure a large portion of the earth's surface, allowing for the relevant curvature. It had in all eight microscopes, five of them on the 2-ft diameter horizontal circle, reading to 1-inch of arc, and the sixth at 180 degrees to the first. The two vertical circles of 12-inches arc are each read by a single microscope to 2-inches arc. The telescope is 27-inch focal length and 2.1 aperture.[39] This complicated piece of equipment was finally put together, tested, and packed in a number of specially constructed cases. It was then carefully transported to Ireland, where it was first set up on the southern side of Lough Foyle in October.[40] Colonel Colby had been working in Ireland since 1825, starting with a small party of sappers on the Divis mountain near Belfast, and with William's younger brother, Frederick Walter, then only twenty-two, to head his computing department. The whole operation was run as a military manoevre, with suitable precision, and no doubt fortitude by the participants.[41]

It is difficult for a layman to the world of surveying to appreciate to just what minute accuracy of measurement these 18th and 19th century investigators were set upon achieving, where a single inch fault in an eight-mile distance is not good enough for the Master of this craft. In 1784 the baseline at Hounslow Heath for the triangulation of England had been measured three times, first with glass tubes, then with seasoned deal rods, and thirdly with a coffered steel chain made by Ramsden. The length was found to be 27,404 feet, the discrepancy between the three measurements being three inches.

In Ireland, Colby demanded exact precision from his equipment, and he was dissatisfied with the apparatus he had for measuring the eight-mile baseline at Lough Foyle, and had instituted a series of experiments on the expansion and contraction of metal bars under variations of temperature, by which he devised the 'compensation bar', a combination of brass and iron, which was the basis of future measuring rods. Experiments similar to this are to be found described in William's later notebooks,[42] and interested him as a practical difficulty in achieving accurate measurement. Troughton had already contributed to the science of metrology by way of the Shuckburgh-Scale in 1796, and in 1813 he had made the baseline apparatus and the 8.2 inch standard scale for the United States Coastal Survey. Now he and Simms created the 10-ft Ordnance Standard between 1826 and 1827, and earlier using the calculations worked out by one of Colby's Royal Engineer Officers, Lieutenant Drummond, based at Furnival Inn in Holborn,[43] only five minutes away from their own workshop in Fleet Street, they constructed six sets of measuring bars for Ireland. It was from the baseline which Colby measured at Lough Foyle that the rest of the triangulation of Ireland followed, and the calculations of all the bases and distances between the trigonometrical points in the Triangulation of Great Britain and of Ireland were expressed in terms of Troughton & Simms' Standard. That their accuracy was extraordinarily high may be judged by the fact that when the Lough Foyle base was measured by tellurometer as recently as 1960, it was found to be only one inch different from that completed in 1827.[44]

Original records of the Survey of Ireland are much depleted for historical reasons. The fire at the Public Record Office in Dublin in 1920 destroyed some of the relevant documents, and after the Ordnance Survey transferred its files to Colby's new headquarters in Southampton in 1846, they just 'disappeared', perhaps finally destroyed in the Second World War blitz. There are however some remaining indexes from the early 19th century letters still at Phoenix Park, Dublin, though these consist in mere headings to indicate what the original letters contained, and in any case are not consecutive or complete. They were in a haphazard order when studied in the winter of 1989, and there were many gaps. Those of 1824 when the Survey was first ordered, are missing unfortunately, and the surviving ones run from March 1825 (entry No. 80) to November 1829 (2455), with a lone one in June 1839 (8608) and another in July 1854 (1310). Obviously there are many missing, but they do confirm that William Simms continued to be employed by Colonel Colby subsequent to supplying the earliest instruments for the Survey in 1824, and was engaged in repair and replacement of items well before he joined up with Troughton at the end of 1825. There are notes regarding the usual problems of breakages en route from London 'for want of care' (80), requests for further instruments (2455 in November 1829; 8608 in June 1839; and 1310 in July 1854). There is a request for a screw and nut for one of the 8-inch theodolites lately sent to Mountjoy without these articles (974 in September 1820). This is of particular interest as the screw in question was probably a micrometer screw of minute dimensions, unique in having been made on a screw-cutting lathe at Fleet Street, the lead screw of which was almost certainly manufactured at Bryan Donkin's works at Fort Place, Bermondsey. A number of the letters indicate the personal care which Colonel Colby took over studying the bills from 'Mr Simms' (and from late 1826, 'Simms & Troughton' – entry 1511), and haggling over which party should pay which item.

There is unfortunately no record that William actually visited the Survey or saw the geodesic theodolite and his other instruments at work in Ireland, although he may have travelled over to Belfast. But it was a tiresome journey involving a prolonged ride by coach in England to catch a steam packet across the Irish Sea from Holyhead, and would have taken him away from Fleet Street for well over two weeks at the very least. It is more likely that, if necessary, he usually sent a trusted and experienced workman to make any adjustments or to report on its performance, as he often did for Greenwich. He was himself fully occupied with the India orders, but also with repeated requests for further editions of Troughton's double-framed or 'pillar' sextants, copies of which continued to be made for the rest of his life. Troughton's Reflecting Circle also continued to find new purchasers, though at a decreasing rate. It used the same principle as the sextant, but since it comprised a full circle finely etched with divisions, was reckoned to be six times as accurate. With its attached telescope to read the angle, and therefore the distance, of the object to be measured from the fixed star or the moon, the vernier of the circle was viewed by a micrometer. The large transit instrument for Cracow, a telescope aligned in the north-south meridian, and thus with its clock able to measure in time and altitude the passing of stated stars, was mainly William's creation in 1828, though to Troughton's design and with his involvement. In addition to practical optics, No. 136 must have dealt with a large mail from the widely dispersed locations of Troughton's previous work, not only in England where calls constantly arrived for attention to instruments at Greenwich, Camden Hill and Blackheath, but also the Royal Observatory in Paris, the Observatory at the Cape, and from North America where the Coastal Survey continued, not to mention Ireland. Troughton continued to compose most of the descriptions of his instruments for the astronomical publications in which they figured, where his crystal clear prose with its complete omission of flowery sentiment, portrayed the item under discussion in unequivocal and detailed terms.[45]

William saw little of Airy at this time, as the latter was now Lucasian professor of mathematics at Cambridge, where he was promoting experimental physics with enthusiasm, particularly on the properties of light. He hoped to win the position of Astronomer Royal in Ireland, and even travelled to Dublin with this in mind in 1827, but returned empty-handed. It turned out to be a blessing in disguise as the following year he was appointed Plumian professor of astronomy at Cambridge, a Chair which had been created in 1706 with a legacy from Dr Thomas Plume of Christ's College two years previously. Recently funds had become available for an observatory in Cambridge, and in 1821 a splendid site was purchased from St John's College with a 360 degrees unobstructed view of the horizon, and away from the dusty atmosphere of the town. Moreover it was almost on the meridian which also ran through the tower of Granchester Church to the south, making a useful focus on which to set instruments. The architect for the new observatory was John Clement Mead, and during 1822 and 1823 he supervised the erection of his elegant two-storeyed Doric style building, designing also an east wing to accommodate the Director, and a west wing for the assistant. The first Director was appointed in 1824. This was Robert Woodhouse, whose duty it mainly was to set the observatory on its feet, and do what astronomical measurement was possible with only an equatorial and no assistant. In point of fact Woodhouse was a sick man, and was only able to keep things ticking over, finally retiring in 1827 to die. The Observatory Syndicate did not come into being until 18th March 1829, its first meeting being nearly a month later on 6th April,[46] almost a year after Airy found himself in the position of Director with only a transit instrument with which to work and still no assistant. He had, however, an increased income of £500 a year. On the strength of the latter, and a new assistant, Lieutenant Baldry, appointed in 1829, and with bright prospects, he persuaded Richenda Smith to marry him in 1830. He had been courting Richenda since he first met her six years previously whilst on a walking tour in Derbyshire where her father was Rector of Edensor, near Chatsworth. In 1828 he had started a system of frequent observations of the planets on a regular time-scale, reducing the results and publishing them without delay, his first small volume coming out in the spring of 1829. In all the work he

George Biddell Airy.
BY PERMISSION OF INSTITUTE OF ASTRONOMY, CAMBRIDGE

72

undertook at Cambridge, he was fortunate to be backed by a remarkable man named Richard Sheepshanks who was keen to promote the new observatory.

Sheepshanks, who was almost exactly the same age as William Simms, was the son of a wealthy cloth manufacturer in Leeds, from whom he inherited considerable riches. He followed a brilliant undergraduate career in mathematics by election to a fellowship at Trinity College, Cambridge in 1817. In 1825 he was called to the Bar, and now added theology to his repertoire, being ordained into the Church of England in 1828. Because of his inheritance, he was however in a position to eschew a professional appointment in either academic field, and instead followed his inclinations in science and particularly in astronomy. Already by 1820 he had a private observatory of his own for which Edward Troughton had provided the instruments. Having joined the Astronomical Society in 1825, he came to know Airy, and as well as his interest in the fortunes of the Cambridge Observatory, he co-operated with him in their investigations into the increase in gravity with depth below the earth's surface, which they unsuccessfully attempted in 1828 in the Dolcoath mine in Cornwall by measurement of pendulum movements. Thereafter the paths of these two men continued to cross, not least in their visits to 136 Fleet Street. Sheepshanks, being free of the ties of marriage and of the need for remunerative employment, was able to take an unbiased and objective view of astronomical affairs, and proved a valuable friend to William Simms in a liaison which continued all his life. They met frequently at 136, and after 1830 at the Astronomical Society, of which Sheepshanks became Secretary in 1829, editing its Monthly Notices for many years thereafter.

One other name deserves mention in connection with Troughton & Simms at this point. This was Andrew Yeates. Born in 1800, he was a member of a large family of opticians operating in and around Dublin, who at the age of twenty-one was sent to London by his father to learn more of the trade. The earliest optical instruments in Ireland were mostly made in England and shipped across the Irish Sea, and it was still usual for Irish makers to obtain their skills in the art of constructing instruments and preparing lenses from Masters in London. Some of these young men returned to Ireland to use and disseminate the knowledge they had gained. Others remained in England and set up business on their own account. Meanwhile astronomy in Ireland had been given a tremendous fillip in the last 50 years or so by the enthusiasm of wealthy amateurs, but these still acquired much of the equipment for their private observatories from English makers such as Edward Troughton and Thomas Jones. A prominent individual amongst these Anglo-Irish landowners was William Parsons, Third Earl of Rosse, who after a brilliant mathematical career at Trinity College, Cambridge, returned to his family seat at Birr Castle, Offaly, to experiment on methods of making large metal mirrors for telescopes. His fascination was in solving the problems of alloys of copper and tin in different proportions, in producing the castings himself, and in finding ways of polishing his great mirrors. From 1828 he used steam-power for this, and carried out all the processes in the manufacture of telescopes on the spot at Birr. His enthusiasm filtered across the educated classes in Ireland, who then wanted to own relevant instruments for themselves. A number of well-known Irish instrument makers thus appear in the 19th century to satisfy this demand, such as Thomas and Howard Grubb, and other reputable family firms of the 18th century such as Yeates, Mason and Lynch continued to thrive into the mid-19th century.

Andrew Yeates arrived in London in 1821, and by some means, perhaps directly, made himself known to Edward Troughton. From then until about 1833 he assisted in the workshops at 136. One of his notebooks[47] still exists, and indicates his interests. In the 1830s he did repair work for the Royal Observatory at Greenwich under Troughton's aegis, and finally after Troughton's death set up on his own at 12 Brighton Place, New Kent Road in London. Although he must have worked under William Simms (1793), his name never appears in William's letters, and it may be that it was Troughton who allowed the young man to remain under his wing though he himself was unable to give him practical help for the last years, only verbal advice from his armchair.

Yeates' notebook from those early years in London consists of a list of major instruments made by the firm, some long ago by Troughton alone, such as the Groombridge transit, sometimes with details of design, and sometimes with a drawing, as if he was ticking them off his list of study material. Occasionally he strays from the work-bench, with for instance, inserted in his table of scientific books the recently published *Loves of the Angels* by the Irish poet, Thomas Moore, preceded (rather surprisingly) on the previous page by a colour wash painting in blacks and greys of the God of the Underworld, Pluto, in Persian dress. He seems to have been a somewhat romantic young man, not untypical of his Dublin compatriots, and his flights of fancy perhaps indulged in working hours which would not have been approved by the industrious single-minded Troughton. His last entry in his notebook was on 17th April 1829.

CHAPTER 6

1820-1831

THE END OF THE 18TH CENTURY and the beginning of the 19th were remarkable for the small amount of scientific advance going on around the United Kingdom. Sir John Herschal even complained that mathematics was at its last gasp, and astronomy nearly so.[48] After the initial flare of interest in science at the restoration of the monarchy in 1660, and largely due to the restored King himself, the Royal Society was formed in 1662. It embraced the whole range of scientific thought, and it was not until the end of the following century when the Linnean Society was formed in 1788, that we find the first subdivision of scientific investigation into specialised departments. The Linnean Society received its Charter in 1802, by which time other distinct branches of knowledge were being recognised and provided with their own learned society. In 1799 the Royal Institution was formed, followed by the College of Surgeons in 1800, the Horticultural Society in 1804, and the London Institution for the Advancement of Literature and the Diffusion of Useful Knowledge in 1805. This last quickly received its Charter in 1807, the year the Geological Society of London was formed. Then came a plethora of provincial societies of which the Yorkshire Philosophical is one example of many. It was this last society which was largely responsible for the initiation of the British Association and its first meeting in York in 1831.

Since 1812 a Dr Pearson, cleric, schoolmaster and amateur astronomer, who had already produced a volume of astronomical tables, had had the ambition for the promotion of a society for like-minded men, which became a reality during a dinner party organised by Pearson in December 1819.[49] This was followed by a meeting of fourteen interested participants at the Freemason's Tavern, Great Queen Street, Lincoln's Inn Fields on 12th January 1820. The venue was not an unusual one, taverns being much used as clubs for the exchange of news and views then as had the coffee houses of the previous century. This gathering was the foundation of the Astronomical Society, at which a committee of eight men under the chairmanship of David Moore and with Francis Baily as secretary pro tem, was formed to consider ways and means, objects and rules. The first

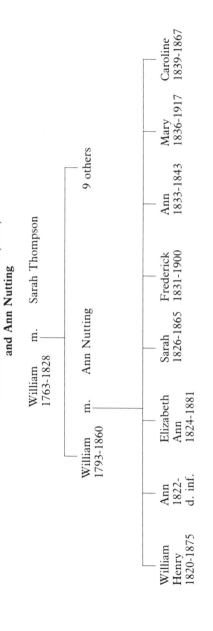

**Children of William Simms (1793)
and Ann Nutting**

William m. Sarah Thompson
1763-1828

William m. Ann Nutting
1793-1860

9 others

William Henry 1820-1875

Ann 1822- d. inf.

Elizabeth Ann 1824-1881

Sarah 1826-1865

Frederick 1831-1900

Ann 1833-1843

Mary 1836-1917

Caroline 1839-1867

meeting of the Society was held on Tuesday, 8th February at the home of the Geological Society in Bedford Street, Covent Garden 'at 7 o'clock in the evening precisely', at which any person recommended by present members could be considered a member without ballotting. Their 'address' or remit was for a society to form a complete catalogue of stars and other bodies upon a scale infinitely more extensive than any yet undertaken, a huge committment.

Unfortunately the 8th February meeting had to be curtailed out of respect for the death of the King, George III, which had occurred on 29th January. However, twenty-one members attended, and the total number of members was by then forty-seven. On 29th February, they met again, twenty-eight members attending. This time Edward Troughton was voted onto the first council, remaining on it almost for the rest of his life. Interest was particularly enhanced this year due to the expected solar eclipse on 7th September, a paper on which was read by Francis Baily at the December meeting, 1820. In January 1821 Troughton read his paper on the Repeating Circle and Altazimuth, and so the regular monthly meetings formed a pattern which was to continue. From November 1820 meetings took place in the Lincoln's Inn Fields rooms of the Medical and Chirurgical Society for the fee of 50 guineas per annum, and to pay for the use of the attics as a storehouse for their publications from 1828.[50]

The formation of the Astronomical Society in London had been preceded in Scotland by the formation of the Astronomical Institution of Edinburgh nine years earlier, and indeed the rumblings for an observatory in the Scottish capital had been heard since 1736 when the first proposals for its foundation had been put forward by the eminent mathematician, Colin McLaurin. A Trust Fund was set up, but because of the unsettled times, the project was not developed. Later in 1776 an optician named Thomas Short had leased land on Calton Hill, a precipitate little hill to the south-east of what was to become Prince's Street, on which he started to build an observatory designed by James Craig, the architect of the New Town in Edinburgh. Influenced by Robert Adam it took on a gothic appearance, but was never completed although Short lived with his family in one of the towers, using his own instruments for somewhat 'popular' astronomy. A small transit was ordered from Troughton[51] and a small subsidiary building erected in the grounds. In 1811 the cause of a scientific observatory was again taken up, and the Astronomical Institution of Edinburgh founded by a group of private citizens who inaugurated the 'New Observatory' designed in classical style by the President's nephew, William Playfair, in 1818. This elegant cruciform building on the apex of Calton Hill from where Colonel Colby had previously surveyed for his triangulation work, was not completed until 1824, and there were no further funds left to provide the expensive instruments envisaged. In 1822 George IV in a visit to the City, proclaimed it to be the 'Royal Observatory of George IV', an elevated title which seemed to put it on a par with Greenwich, but was at the time a hollow compliment to the empty establishment. However, the recognition by the King did stimulate the Government of 1826 to make a grant of £2,000 for equipment, and discussions had already been commenced with likely instrument makers. Troughton being too busy to undertake a transit instrument[52] for it, Frauenhofer of Munich was directed as early as November 1825[53] to proceed with one, which was estimated by Colby to cost £300, and by Professor Schumacher to 'not exceed £400'.[54] Next year Frauenhofer was fatally injured in a fire at Hamburg, and his associate, Repsold, took over the creation of the transit circle using Frauenhofer's 6-inch object glass. At the same time Troughton & Simms were requested to make a suitable mural circle and an altazimuth instrument. Troughton advised the Institution in February 1827 that the former should be 6-ft, 'as at Greenwich', costing 700 guineas, and the latter to have 'a vertical circle 3-ft diameter carrying a telescope of 4-ft, a lower circle of 2-ft or 2-ft and a few inches, and the axis to be downward' as 'the one he had previously made for Sir Thomas Brisbane, and to cost 400 guineas'. He and William ('my partner') considered that mid-summer of the year 1829[55] would see completion of both instruments and the altazimuth considerably sooner.[56] In February 1827 the committee accepted price and time schedule, and work began at Fleet Street.

During the 1820s everyone's thoughts were turning to the expansion of the manufacturing trades. One simply could not ignore the changes on every side, not to mention the rapidly increasing population. In the north there were cheap imports of cotton from America, and with it, continuing inventions for spinning, weaving and dyeing. In tandem with this there was a vast building programme of mills and factories, especially within range of the Pennines whose tumultuous streams provided power for the new machines. Midland towns also were entering into the revolution of industry, turning England into an urban society. Thomas Carlyle wrote in 1824 of the hurriedly contrived streets of Birmingham as being ill-built, ill-paved, always flimsy, often poor, sometimes miserable. He described the busy canals, the noise of machinery, the flare of furnaces, and in long evocative sentences, the sadnesses and poverty of the people. The steam-engine now was coming into its own, blowing the furnaces, pumping water, driving machinery, and beginning to be used wherever power was needed. In London the steamboats plying up and down the river became a more common sight by the middle of the decade, though young cousin William, son of James, being taken to Greenwich for a treat by his grandfather, old William, commented that they returned from the observatory by rowing boat, being unlikely to meet one of the new steamers with their treacherous wash.

The same year – 1823 – that the first of the Mechanics Institutes was opened in London to offer evening courses to young technicians as a supplement to their apprenticeships, the elder Brunel, the Hugenot Marc, began work on the first Thames tunnel at Rotherhithe. This caused considerable alarm at the very thought of burrowing beneath the river, and generated fierce debate and a good deal of sneering dissention, only fuelled on 2nd March 1825 when the opening ceremony was accompanied by a ceremonial feast when 200 of the hoypoloy sat down to a 'sumptuous collation'; and the first brick of the tunnel was laid by Marc Brunel, the second by his son Isambard. Thereafter Rotherhithe was visited by all London, eager to watch the sinking of the first shaft, and the cast-iron frames made by Henry Maudsley, the engineer whose foundry did so much work for Troughton & Simms.

Rumours of the first railways were also heard at this time. The Stockton & Darlington line opened for traffic on 27th September 1825, to the delight of the immense concourse of people assembled, and with 'Mr Stephenson' himself driving the engine, then the directors of the company and their friends in the following passenger coach, twenty-one open waggons fitted up with temporary seats for passengers, and lastly six waggon-loads of coal, making in all a train of thirty-eight vehicles, it was indeed an auspicious day. Between 1825 and 1835 no less than fifty-four Railway Acts were passed by Parliament to deal with the purchase of the land required. Meanwhile this was the heyday of the Turnpikes, well maintained roads between major centres of population, which eased the problems of travelling around England, provided one could put up with little sleep, and could afford the fares. Country taverns on the turnpikes became increasingly important as staging posts for the mail-coaches, and there was one located about every twenty miles, the distance a horse could canter without stopping. They offered rest and a meal to travellers as well as fresh horses for the next section of their journey. The three new Thames bridges in London, making five in all, increased greatly the access from the south, and now a railway bridge to Cannon Street was planned, though not completed for forty years.

In Fleet Street, William Simms settled quickly into his new position. There was no time to do otherwise. Like most young men with their way to make as a craftsman with an intellectually demanding skill, his working days were long and arduous, leaving little chance for other interests. This makes it only the more remarkable that, at a time when correspondence was written by the owners of such businesses themselves, as being usually too complicated or important for assistants to compose, the sentences were full, grammatical and well-conceived, occasionally with quotations from well-known writers such as Johnson, Pope,[57] or even the romantic poets. It is an interesting insight into the general educational standard of the period that even a man who had specialised as an apprentice at fourteen, had had drummed into him as a boy the production and appreciation of fluent English, and must assuredly have had access to the classics to be able to write so lucidly and with spirit and often humour, in a manner that few adults could emulate nowadays. This style of letter, respectful but sage, made ready friends of his clients as compared with the terse type-written communication of today.

William must seldom have been seen at Barnsbury Row in these busy months, other than at the weekend. His days were long and fully occupied, frequently extending into the evening, and he probably often stayed overnight at Fleet Street rather than call a hackney carriage for the journey home. In 1828 he added to his evening commitments by becoming an Associate of the Institution of Civil Engineers, of which Troughton was, with Telford, one of the original members and through many years was a constant attender at the meetings.[58] He heard with interest from Troughton details of the meetings of The Astronomical Society, and when time permitted, which was less and less, he attended lectures at the Society of Arts of which he had been elected a member in March 1823.[59] Saturdays, however, saw the shutters going up over the street windows of 136 in the early evening, and William made his way home to Ann and the family. There was now a new little baby girl in the household at Barnsbury Row, who was baptised Sarah after her Simms grandmother, on 15th October 1826 at St Mary's Church, Islington. Shortly before this event, and between it and Michaelmas, the family moved across the street, which was now called Cloudesley Road, to a similar but larger terraced house in Lower Islington Terrace. This was part of the Cloudesley estate, built on property of the Stonefield family, which provided a big square of elegant terraced houses, so typical of the previous century, with a large church in the centre of the square, and a road passing out on each side to form a cruciform pattern. Cloudesley Road was the first street to the west of the square, all of which was laid out shortly before 1824. The neogothic church, designed by Barry, was erected between 1826 and 1827 under Act of Parliament, but it did not however commence baptismal registers until 1829, so that Ann's next baby, born on 13th November 1828 was also baptised at St Mary's, on 10th December. He was named James after his uncle (1792), and indeed after his Simms great-grandfather (1710). This was the son who had a great deal in common with William Simms (1793), although perhaps a more solemn character. He was to prove a reliable, able and highly intelligent person, to whom William ultimately passed over his business. He also inherited the quiet but kindly sense of humour from his father. His first home at Lower Islington Terrace, although according to Sir John Summerson, built by one of five 'spec' builders working on the Cloudesley estate, and 'mere routine stuff', presents today a pleasing picture in its new incarnation as part of modern well-to-do Islington, as indeed it must have done when it was first erected.

Sundays were almost certainly retained as a family day. William Simms (1793) was in some ways a conventional being. He was certainly an affectionate father with the sort of quiet wry humour with which children feel comfortable. The 1820s were the beginning of what developed twenty years later into the Victorian era, with its hidebound approach to the 'English Sunday'. However, even before the young Victoria, who had been born the year of William and Ann's marriage, ascended the throne in 1837, and now still only a little girl, already had some influence on the middle class modus vivendi as the hope of the future. Her old 'Uncle King', George IV, was a highly painted, extravagant old roué, who had succeeded to the throne in 1820 after eleven years as Regent, and had refused to allow his wife to be crowned Queen. Having lost his only legitimate child, the Princess Charlotte, so sadly in childbirth of a stillborn infant, the pathetic old king became even more immersed in the social round and apparently oblivious of the needs of the country. His heir was now his sailor brother, whom the nation held in even lower esteem, but already the young Victoria had been seen in public, walking with her mother, the Duchess of Kent, in the gardens of Kensington Palace, where she led a quiet and disciplined life, far removed in every way from the Court. The disgust which people held for

Lower Islington Terrace.

81

the goings on of the King and his brother, was reacting into a gradually developing solidity of their own family life, and although church-going had more than an element of social requirement in it, there was also a need felt for propiety and ordered existence amongst the middle classes. Sunday would see family church attendance increasing, often twice a day, and with servants accompanying their master and mistress. Cold luncheon served at mid-day was followed by an afternoon devoted to reading, usually aloud where there were small children, and a country walk taken if possible. For William and Ann this may have been along the new Regent Canal to see the boats resting for the day at their moorings.

Sometimes they visited Uncle James Simms (1792) and Aunt Catherine Pruday and their three children at Bowman's Buildings. Particularly in 1826 when James (1792) was elected Constable for the Aldersgate Ward for the year, all the children including William Henry and Elizabeth Ann must have enjoyed looking at his Staff of Office, a rod about 6-ft long and one-and-a-half inches diameter, one half beautifully decorated with the Royal Insignia after the fashion of a Herald's tabard, and 'regarded by the mob' says his son William (1817) 'with great respect'. It was used on official occasions including his attendance at the Old Bailey Sessions, to one of which young William (1817) aged nine, was taken by him. James (1792) was also supposed to attend executions, the last public one of which in front of Newgate did not occur until 1868, although the last for fraud (that of Henry Fauntleroy, a banker) was on 30th November 1824, after a notorious trial at the Old Bailey, just opposite the prison. James did not relish this duty, so he would send one of his workmen, holding the Staff, to take his place. 'This was an evasion' says his son loftily, 'but it passed muster'. The constable's other duties were as a control on the night watchmen in the Ward. There was a growing criminal element in the City, and this was before the appearance of a trained police force. There were nine constables in the Aldersgate Ward, so James' turn came round every nineth night, and was not onerous as there was a great armchair in the Watch House where he could snatch a light doze at times throughout the night whilst his two superintendants, who were paid officials working under him, were expected to parade the Ward in turns, their aim being to see that the watchmen were doing their duty and not sleeping too long. James himself went round the Ward twice during the night with the superintendants to inspect the beats, and occasionally the Alderman, Sir Peter Laurie, made an inspection of the Watch House. Should there arise severe disorders, there was no alternative to calling out the troops, but as the soldiers could be callow and cruel in their handling of miscreants, they seldom were involved.

Other Sundays, family visits must also have taken place to the Simms grandparents at Broad Way. Old William (1763) and Sarah were now ageing, the former giving some cause for concern for his visible decline. His little business at No. 4 had added to it stationery as well as the sale of tobacco and snuff, but even this was too much for him. He became increasingly frail in the next year, and on 30th March 1828 he died at the age of sixty-five. He was buried in one of the churchyards of St Anne, Blackfriars, most likely in fact in that of the conjoined parish of St Andrew-by-the-Wardrobe, as the former were already full and due for closure. His grave was a double one with a stone laid over it. The date of his burial was two days prior to the bestowal of the Freedom of the Goldsmiths Company on his youngest surviving son, Alfred Septimus of 136 Fleet Street.

Within a year of old William's death – though it took longer, as usual, for the London trade directories to catch up with the fact – his sons, James (1792) and George had left Broad Way and gone their own ways. Details of their reasons can only be surmised, but as James' move was to 9 Greville Street, off Hatton Garden, it was certainly socially determined. Blackfriars was an unfashionable, pokey series of streets, dark because of their narrowness, and liable to crime. The space for workshops was limited, the address plebian. It was out of the area of the well-known jewellers and gold and silversmiths with whom James liked to hob-nob and Greville Street was altogether more elevated. At about this period also, George was keen to move westwards, also in search of social prefermant, which he soon claimed in the hand of Sophia Davy whom he married three years later, on 4th September 1831 at St Martin's-in-the-Fields.

For old Sarah the Simms brothers found accommodation within the Blackfriars' precinct, which she refused to leave and where she had friends. Unlike her husband and some of her sons, she was not a social climber. Her original home at the little village of Stone in Staffordshire had been humble – (although it must be said that her 'Uncle Thompson' was a friend of the celebrated Dr Abernethy) – and although her husband had big ideas, and acquired considerable wealth in early life, he is said to have lost it by unwise 'speculation', whatever that means. There was an undoubted streak of bravado in money matters in the Simms family, and a love of self-aggrandisement. It was apparent in his grandson, William (1817), whose diary indicates both conceit and a passion for name-dropping, but whose life was a series of moves without prolonged steady consistency. James (1792), father of this William, probably showed the same features, in that he failed to complete his fourteen years agreement with his brother, George, perhaps a similar character. Their brother, John, however, was a far more robust personality, persistent, enterprising but utterly purposeful as is shown by his continuation of his work and his existence in the same area once his apprenticeship and a few years in Birmingham were completed. One could argue that the steady members of the family were excruciatingly dull, but the facts are otherwise. Nobody could say that William Simms (1793), the most eminent brother, was dull when they consider his remarkable achievements, and John, who died a very rich man, must have been something of an entrepreneur in his agency to become so. Possibly he had a very persuasive manner. Henry, though less intelligent, was similarly utterly reliable. William Simms (1793) of Fleet Street had the best combination of all as he was highly intelligent, innovative, but consistent. Moreover it becomes very obvious in his letters that whilst he makes eminent friends without any effort, he retains his humility, thus becoming a most attractive personality. One supposes that in general he took after his mother, Sarah Thompson, in this, whilst inheriting his intellect from the Simms side of the family. At any rate Sarah refused to be chivied into leaving the area of Blackfriars she knew well, and lived on at Evangelist Court (just west of Broad Way) until 13th January 1834, when she died at the age of sixty-seven. She was buried with old William in the parish of St Anne's, Blackfriars.

There is a mysterious postscript to the story of Sarah and William (1763). In the 1860s the grand new Victoria Street was slashed through across Blackfriars from the bridge to the Mansion House, taking houses in the vicinity with it, as well as destroying part of the churchyards of St Mary Aldermary, and St Andrew-by-the-Wardrobe. Both churches now found themselves close to the busy new road, St Mary with its south-east corner only a yard or two from the crossroads with Cannon Street. St Andrew's fared slightly better as it retained sufficient space for an imposing flight of steps from Victoria Street up to its south door. The Simms grave, with many others, was removed with its stone as the new street advanced, as reported in 'young' William's (1817) diary in 1885. Where they were taken is yet a mystery, but they did not end up immediately at the then new City of London cemetery at Little Ilford, nor at the new private burial ground at Norwood, which saw later Simms burials. Further delving into parish vestry minutes may yet elucidate their whereabouts, but the Simms stone is most likely now being used as London paving, or even infilling beneath Victoria Street. The coffins were possibly removed in the 1860s to No. 13 Lambeth Hill or St Mary Somerset, both in the parish of St Andrew, and subsequently re-interred at Little Ilford in square 191 a century later in an unmarked communal grave when yet again building occurred on their resting place. If ever spirits became restless through lack of peace, surely those of Sarah and William must still be pacing the London streets searching for lasting repose.

Whilst all these family events were occurring in and around Broad Way, up in Fleet Street the seeds of another drama were being sown by the simple order for a telescope mounting, which prepared the ground for a prolonged saga causing endless unsought anxiety and aggravation to the participants. Mr James South was already well-known to Edward Troughton, who had earlier made a number of instruments for him, including a fine transit for his observatory at his Borough home in 1820, and more recently a number

84

of other important pieces of astronomical equipment for his new observatory at Camden Hill, beyond Kensington Gardens. Mr South had been one of the original fourteen men who had foregathered at the Freemasons Tavern in 1820 to inaugurate the Astronomical Society. He was not an easy man with whom to do business, as Isambard Brunel would find when he had severe altercations with him over the construction of the dome of the Camden Hill Observatory, a foretaste of what was to come to the peaceable partners at 136. South was a wealthy person, having married a rich heiress, and he liked to have his own way. It was during the autumn of 1829, on a visit to Paris,[60] perhaps in his capacity since May of last year as President of the Astronomical Society, that he purchased for the vast sum of £1,000, an object glass which was the largest in existence, of 11¾ inches aperture and 19-ft focal length. It had been made by the renowned French glass worker, Cauchoix, and had been in use at the Royal Observatory in Paris. Troughton & Simms received orders for its mounting immediately after South's return to London, and South and Edward Troughton had prolonged discussions as to its design. It was decided that two models of the proposed mounting should be made at Fleet Street, and that these should be immediately constructed and set up in secrecy in, of all places, Troughton's bedroom, in order that the design should not be 'pirated' by any rival amateur. Industrial espionage was even then rife. The object glass was then fetched by one of Troughton's trusted workmen to 136, a man called Norton, on 18th January 1830, and for the next seven months work continued on the instrument.

Meanwhile the polar axis was to be made (broadly, the stand upon which it was to lie), Troughton wishing to construct it of deal, Mr South a harder wood. William commented with his tongue in his cheek that 'South asked in the proper quarter (no doubt) for a supply of teak from one of the government stores'. South was surprised to find himself refused in spite of access to the 'proper quarter', and finally agreed to compromise with mahogany, whereupon he went, accompanied by Bryan Donkin to the timber yard of a Mr Aldridge of Aldersgate Street to choose the actual piece of wood. All was very carefully noted down in William's notebook, with names of witnesses, as he already recognised the slipperiness of his client. His own workman, Norton, the cabinet maker at Fleet Street, sent to the timber yard to give directions for the sawing of the block, and the polar axis was constructed by him on 2nd March 1830. Meanwhile the tube for the telescope was prepared in Mr Donkin's factory at Bermondsey, being too large to be produced in the small foundry at 136, and was transferred on 3rd December 1829 to Fleet Street on a temporary support which Mr South had had made for it. On 29th May William received from Mr Donkin a sphere 20 inches diameter for the centre of the declination axis, and by 11th January 1831, other parts from him, which were too large to be made in the factory at 136.[61]

85

By now the old reprobate king, George IV, had died, and his brother had succeeded to the throne as William IV. One of his first actions was to knight the President of the Astronomical Society, now Sir James South. Meanwhile the new knight was making a great nuisance of himself at 136, visiting almost daily, watching every step, often interfering with the workmen's progress, and generally driving them all mad, both employers and employed. Troughton intended the diameter of the declination circle should not exceed 10 or 12 inches.[62] He had altercations with Sir James who insisted it should be not less than 2-ft. Troughton gave way. Norton's workshop was similarly invaded by Sir James, where this interference continued, and then it was Mr Donkin's factory in the summer of 1831, where he complained that the axis was weak, more (William believed) from the shunting of the joints than from defective workmanship, 'but perhaps a little of both'[63] he admitted in his fair-minded way. The axis was consequently strengthened by sundry cast-iron pieces, and with trepidation, conveyed, well cushioned and packed, in a special cart to Camden Hill in September, where it was gently placed horizontally in the observatory under the eye of Sir James. He again insisted on having his own way instead of leaving the work to the specialists, and appointed a friend, Captain Robertson RN, to superintend the elevation of the instrument. During this delicate operation, almost unbelievably the tackle gave way, and just as it was being lifted, the huge instrument crashed down several feet, sustaining considerable damage to its lower end, and the frame throughout received a 'most violent shock'.[64]

Other tackle was procured, and at last the instrument was elevated, but the damage was done.

William's exasperation at the sheer wilfulness of Sir James is not overtly mentioned in so many words in his notes, but one can feel it exuding quietly but unmistakably from the pages. Troughton settled down with his pipe to give the whole project a great deal of thought, whilst William returned to the accumulation of other work waiting for his attention at 136.

1830 was a busy year in the workshops. The altazimuth circles for India, and all the other equipment ordered by Colonel Everest was completed and packed to travel with him on his departure in May. In early June Mr Henderson, then the Treasurer of the Astronomical Institution of Edinburgh, visited 136 Fleet Street to see how the instruments for the Royal Observatory of Edinburgh were proceeding. He found that now that Mr Simms had got the items for the Survey of India and the Observatory of Madras off his hands – – – he promised to commence immediately with finishing the Edinburgh altazimuth and to 'allow no other business to interfere with it'. It would be delivered before the end of July, and he himself would be the best person to superintend its erection on Calton Hill.[65] This was a telescope so mounted as to give measurements for the altitude of a celestial body, as well as its deviation horizontally from the meridian, having a graduated circle in either direction. This altazimuth was of course to be used in astronomy, but he also made instruments very similar adapted for surveying.

William fulfilled his promise, but work was heaping upon him and when it came to August he could not spare the time needed to travel to Edinburgh, stay a few nights and travel back, a total of nearly a fortnight. He therefore suggested that the Astronomical Institution send down a competent optician to stay in London, learn the details of the instrument and accompany it back by sea to Leith, and so to Calton Hill. In the event, John Adie,[66] son of Alexander Adie, a member of the Institution and an eminent optician, was chosen for the assignment, following which he would assist Mr Henderson to place it in the dome of the new observatory, his expenses to be considered as part of the cost of the instrument. He would also provide a barometer and two thermometers ('all of the best construction') and 'a portable time keeper for taking the time from the Astronomical Clocks to the Dome' – ('expense £6 or thereby').[67] Meanwhile Mr William Playfair was to examine the dome to make sure it was in good repair. The final cost of the project paid by the Barons of the Exchequer out of the Royal grant was

Altazimuth instrument at Calton Hill Observatory, Edinburgh.

87

to Messers Troughton & Simms for 'constructing the instrument £420, for pack cases, wharfage, carting, shipping etc £12-15s, and to Mr Adie for expenses, travelling, staying in London, and insurance on the instrument £22-13s-2d. Total = £458-8s-2d'.

The saga of the Edinburgh altazimuth has been followed in some detail as noted in the minutes of the Astronomical Institution, as they demonstrate the problems of distance in the early 19th century before the coming of the railways, and how difficult it was for an instrument maker to spare the considerable time needed for visiting the site to install his creations himself, as would be desirable. Whether Ireland, Brussels or India, the difficulty was there. The Edinburgh mural circle in 1830 was still in its early stages, and when completed in December 1833, a committee took on the problems of its transport and erection in the west wing of the observatory,[69] the details of which are less clear, although it appears from William's lecture to the Institute of Civil Engineers in 1834 that he did supervise its installation. Mr Rapsold however, did certainly travel from Hamburg to Edinburgh in October 1831 with the transit circle, which was placed in the east wing, offering 'to come at his own charge', but was paid £400 for the cost of the instrument, and £26-5s for his own expenses.[70]

Meanwhile mural circles for Madras and Cracow were shipped off from the Port of London, as well as an order from E. J. Cooper for a large transit instrument for his observatory at Markree Castle, County Sligo which would measure in time and altitude the progress of stars crossing the meridian there. Early in the year an important levelling instrument was finished for J. A. Lloyd to be used in his determination of the difference in level between the Thames at Sheerness and at London Bridge.[71] Moreover the firm received further recognition by virtue of three important personal events to honour Edward Troughton. From the King of Denmark he was presented with a medal following the creation of a zenith sector for use in the Holstein Survey by Professors Schumacher and Gauss.[72] At the Astronomical Society, now with its Charter and hence the prefix 'Royal', he became a vice-president for the year 1830-1831. Of lesser moment, but still a pleasant surprise was the dedication to Troughton of the second volume of Dr Pearson's book *Practical Astronomy*, published in 1829.

Meanwhile Frederick Walter Simms had become a useful contact at the Royal Observatory, Greenwich where the Astronomer Royal, John Pond, had increased the number of Assistant Astronomers from the single one of his predecessor to six, of which Frederick became one in 1829. He left the cold and damp of Ireland where at any rate he had learned the practicalities of surveying for which he was always grateful, to assume the equally poorly paid but more acceptable conditions at Greenwich. He had to eke out his slender income by giving lessons in navigation to merchant navy officers,[73] through which connection he became employed in surveying the new iron steamships, using methods taught him by Pond, to adjust their compasses to the altered magnetic field created by their ferrous hulls.

Meanwhile the face of London was beginning to change. In the shopping areas of the City the new methods of advertising businesses by innovative letters of their titles over the entrances was slowly spreading from the example of the more domestic establishments, and the new plate glass beginning to be inserted in their windows was first seen in one of the luxury drapery shops on Ludgate Hill to be quickly followed by other fashionable stores around St Paul's. Shopkeepers were learning the art of window dressing, though the more technical concerns such as instrument makers eschewed such frivolity and continued with but a token object in their flat Georgian windows, giving merely an indication of the nature of their trade. The gas lighting which began to appear more frequently after Waterloo increasingly illuminated the streets and now also the shop fronts, so that the City streets were becoming less gloomy and more exciting. Hoardings and sandwich-men were invented to advertise goods. Further west, Regent Street had been built in 1818, and even earlier the original Swan & Edgar store was opened by George Swan on the present Criterion Restaurant site in 1812, moving to the Quadrant six years later. Piccadilly already had its Fortnum & Mason since Queen Anne's day, and Oxford Street housed upholsterers, cabinet makers and carpet manufacturers by about 1830. The age of the bazaars was opening, the Pantheon for all sorts of goods in Oxford Street, and the Pantechnicon in Belgrave Square where one could buy everything in the travel line from dress carriages to light gigs. Baker Street had a horse bazaar, and Upper Street, Islington was becoming more and more competitive in its array of shops.

At Lower Islington Terrace another son was born to Ann Simms on 20th April 1831, to be called Frederick after his Greenwich uncle. He was one of the first babies to be baptised at Holy Trinity Church, Cloudesley Square, on 15th May. And from Greville Street, his cousin, young William (1817) was increasing his interest and knowledge of astronomy in his lessons with Mr Hayward at his house in Bartholomew Close, and visits to his Uncle Frederick at Greenwich, where he learned the names of all the staff in the observatory to flourish around amongst his school friends.

CHAPTER 7

1831

1831 WAS A YEAR WHICH ANTICIPATED great change in the ordering of the country. It was the year of the Reform Bill, which was going to effect not only the composition of Parliament, but as a result gave rise to a whole series of social developments. At the same period there were far-reaching events in William Simms' personal life, both at his work and in his social life, which in the New Year started to be closely associated with the Astronomical Society.

Ever since its formation in 1820, and even more so since his jointure with Edward Troughton in 1826, the Astronomical Society had been predominant in William's thinking, although as a non-member he was prohibited from attending its meetings, but eligible to send data and reports to its Council. So much a part of the astronomical establishment had he become by 1830 that in November of that year Troughton and Richard Sheepshanks put pen to paper to recommend him for admission for membership. They were backed in their application by five Fellows of the Society, F. Beaufort, Francis Baily, John Lee, W. H. Smythe and Timothy Bramah.[74] He was elected to the Society at its meeting on 14th January 1831, and formally admitted on 11th March. He was member No. 363. Thereafter for the rest of his life he was a constant attender at its meetings, and served on the Council on several occasions.

It so happened that his admission coincided with an extremely lively period in the Society's domestic history. At this same meeting on 14th January, Sir James South announced that he had attended a Levee on 15th December, when the King had signed the Society's autograph book as Patron, thus allowing the prefix 'Royal' to be added to its title. It was also decided at this same meeting that no president of the Society should hold office for more than two consecutive years. Thus by the time the Charter itself was signed by the King on 7th March, and a Special General Meeting called to accept it on 11th March, South, who had assumed he would be the first President of the Royal Astronomical Society, was prohibited from office by the fact of having just completed two years in it. In fury he absented himself from the next meeting on 6th April, when the new Council

No. 363

Mr William Simms, Astronomical Instrument Maker, of Fleet Street, being desirous of admission into the Astronomical Society of London; we, the undersigned, propose and recommend him as a proper person to become a member thereof.

Witness our hands this 12th day of November 1830

Edw. Troughton } From personal
Richard Shepherd } knowledge
F Beaufort Do
Francis Baily
John Lee
W. H. Smyth
Timothy Bramah

Proposed. Vol 12 1830
Elected Janry 14. 1831
Admitted Mar. 11. 1831

Troughton's recommendation, 1830.

was elected under Mr Bryan Donkin's chairmanship, and never again served on the Council.[75]

This rumpus occurred soon after South had published his pamphlet on 11th November 1830 against the President and Council of the Royal Society.[76] It also coincided with the row between Troughton & Simms and South over the mounting of the Camden Hill telescope, at a period when accrimonious letters were passing between the two parties, and in which the RAS was perforce involved through numerous of its members. The very fact that William Simms was backed to become a member by such eminent Fellows as Sheepshanks and Baily wholly vindicated their attitude towards William, and must equally have annoyed South in his campaign to blame Troughton & Simms for what he considered the mismanagement of the telescope mounting.

Troughton was feeling the need for more time for quiet thought and reflection on such problems. He was well over 75 years of age, and almost stone deaf. He had in William Simms a partner of five years standing in whom he had complete faith, and between them they had recently completed a number of capital instruments, with further orders in the pipeline. The altazimuth circles for the Indian Survey and for the observatory at Edinburgh had just been finished. Mural circles for Madras and Cracow were on their way to their destinations, and a small circle, two-feet in diameter, was now at work in the observatory at Paramatta in Australia (since 1826 in the possession of the British Government) with the exciting possibility of its results showing seminal differences from the Cape Observatory which, though on almost the same latitude, was at totally opposite longitude and weather conditions. At the RAS Troughton was a vice-president, and remained on its council another year, where he had been able to help the Society stand firm against the dissension which followed South's antics regarding the presidency. Moreover, the connection with Cambridge Observatory had been endorsed by an order under Airy's guidance for a mural circle there.

So it was that in 1831 Troughton handed over the business into William Simms' capable hands, together with the leasehold buildings and contents of 136 Fleet Street. The only conditions attached were merely that he, Troughton, should remain at 136 to live out his life in his gloomy back room, looked after by his niece and housekeeper, Jane Suddard, requirements very easily met with, as Ann and the five children were still happily ensconced at Islington. The business was to continue in its previous name – it would have been foolish of William to abolish such a world-famous title such as Troughton & Simms had become.

William may well have decided that in any case his young family were safer in the still rural surroundings of Islington, though how much longer it could remain distinct from London was a moot question. Building by

Penton, Leroux and Cubitt was proceeding apace, rapidly filling in the orchards and open fields between the City and the expanding villages and new towns to the north. However, there was increasing unrest in cities throughout the kingdom at the prospect of the Reform Bill which was shortly to come before Parliament. Up to now Britain had largely been divided between the rural areas under the aristocratic rule of local landowners, and the urban control of towns by industrial merchants. Before Waterloo the rural areas greatly outnumbered the urban, both in terms of square miles, and in the number of parliamentary seats, which far outweighed their relative populations. Now industrialisation was drawing more and more people into the towns, without correspondingly increased representation at Westminster. Moreover, even after 1815, Roman Catholics were still considered too dangerous to allow into the seats of power, and Dissenters nearly so. In 1828 there were two million Non-conformists in a total population of thirteen million, and by the repeal that year of the Test and Corporation Acts of Charles II which discriminated against non-Anglicans for religious reasons, their representation was righted. Moreover, the following year, 1829, the Duke of Wellington was responsible for the Roman Catholic Relief Act after which the latter could be admitted to Parliament. There were still oases of conservatism, notably the universities which remained exclusively Anglican until 1854 (Oxford) and 1856 (Cambridge) when for the first time Dissenters of all creeds could be admitted as undergraduates, though still not into the Divinity faculty, nor into teaching or administration, nor for Master of Arts degrees.

There was in addition, as well as the discarding of the boisterous and licentious way of living so prevalent in the previous century, an increase in genuine religious belief and practice. The majority of the clergy in the 18th century had been High Tories of dictatorial and often greedy life-styles. Many were younger sons of the aristocracy. In villages particularly, however, the clergy were not necessarily bad. In many they were a benevolent ruling force – such as Parson Kilvert – the only person in the vicinity who could read, the settler of problems, and adviser and mentor of all. However, when the Spiritual Peers voted against the Reform Bill in 1831, the mob immediately thought they were endorsing the prevailing inequality between rich and poor, and with enthusiasm rioted against the Bishops, stoning their coaches and even setting fire to some of the episcopal palaces – and with Trollope's wealthy Lord Bishop of Barchester and Mrs Proudie in mind, who could blame them? The rising Oxford Movement was insisting on the need to return to high spiritual values and Bible-orientated worship guided by sincere priests leading blameless lives, and ordinary people felt drawn to a moral awareness even if it was the middle class who initiated the return to church-going. From them the influence filtered through to the upper classes, and (often via their servants by example) down to working families. The Victorian burst of ecclesiastical building is one aspect of this, which though admittedly often a form of self-aggrandisement, did take note of the prevailing surge of religious interest, and although the Oxford Movement protested against the interference of the State in Church revenues, there was as yet no other authority to effect changes. The more forward-looking bishops were glad to co-operate with the reformed government to create the Bills of 1836 and later to reorder church finances and stipends to a rational and equitable level, which in turn made for a more sensitive clergy, supported by an active laity.

Meanwhile the labour force of the country was mobilising itself. In 1824, Trades Unions were given official legality. Up to then they had often assumed the disguise of Friendly Societies since the Combination Laws of 1800 made working-class organisation illegal during the French wars. Their growth and activity thereafter greatly increased over the next ten years. The labourer's wages, however, in the rural south remained low, and often consisted of bad corn and sour beer in lieu of cash, and moreover he could be turned out of his clay-built hovel at the whim of his employer. In the winter of 1830 starvation threatened the labourers who lived remote from the increased wealth of the industrial cities, and those from the area south of London gathered themselves into an undisciplined protest march to demand a wage of half-a-crown a day. There was terrible retribution on those who were caught, three of whom were hanged, and 450 transported to Australia as convicts. The national conscience was shaken. It was too near the centre of government to be ignored.

There were thus three areas of complaint; the mal-distribution of representation in Parliament, the problems of the Church-State issue, and the poor conditions still of rural workers. The Reform Bill aimed to right most of these wrongs by the re-distribution of parliamentary seats, the abolition of 'Rotten Boroughs' which now contained few or no constituents but retained a Member of Parliament, and the formation of new Boroughs in centres of increasing population. The franchise was now extended to the £10 householder, thus following the example of the American and French Revolutions by seeking to represent in Parliament the people and not their property. From now on, the owning of property was not the prime right to franchise, neither the lack of it a negation of that right.

It was only a beginning of reform, but a further sequence followed in the next forty years, and even into the 20th century. Back in 1831 its anticipation caused dissension, unrest, uniformed dismissal, and potential violence. There was a vastly increased interest in politics, and some meetings were attended by upwards of 200,000 people. The air was full of rumours, and the taverns buzzed with hear-say and discussion.

Unrest was particularly feared as it was recognised that a few firebrands could with ease influence a city mob to violence in which people and property who found themselves in the path of an excited rampaging rabble were liable to severe havoc. Even a crowd of fifty determined on destruction could not be deterred as there was nobody with the authority to tackle them. By the time things had reached such a stage, the army had to be called in and might take many hours to reach the scene. It was a frightening prospect for the ordinary citizen who had almost no protection from crime, and many of them remembered the domino effect of the Gordon Riots with horror.

The need was for a trained force of men who could manage to calm a crowd before such excesses had time to develop. There was an urgency also to detect and limit all types of crime in an orderly fashion, and to make the streets safe in which to walk about. The old system of watchmen at least had some deterrent effect, but depended on the honesty of the individuals concerned, and the discipline in which the local constable, an elected but unpaid post, held them. The Fielding brothers' creation of the Bow Street Runners decreased the crime of assault on messengers about the City, but this system was only operable over the area of central London, and was not officially controlled. The only wonder is that assault and rioting were not more prevalent, and says much for the honesty of the general public of all classes, and for the working of the Poor Law, however inefficient. Sir Robert Peel had been campaigning for a regular police force for nine years before he successfully saw his Bill through Parliament in 1829, allowing him to proceed. His body of 'Peelers' were formed in London immediately the Act was passed into Law, and caused an outcry at first with the indignant accusation that the Londoner's liberties were in danger and 'the wicked Tories were going to grind the populace like slaves and niggers'. When the new policemen appeared in their uniforms of blue belted jackets, top hats and truncheons, they were met with a burst of ridicule and contempt. However it was soon recognised from the experience of the Reform Bill agitations and of the starving Eastenders of London, that trouble was averted by the very presence of the police on the streets. The seething anger which had been gathering just below the surface in many parts of Britain ever since Waterloo due to the ensuing unemployment, the trade depression and agricultural enclosures, was in 1831 ready to break out into florrid anarchy. This it did with devastating effect in Bristol on 29th October for three days and nights, where great damage to property was reeked and the vivid scarlet of the sky reflected the raging fires below. London was spared from a similar fate, thanks to Peel's foresight, and other towns quickly formed their own police forces, so that by 1859 the whole country was served by regulated police control.

Coincidentally with the advent of the police, came permanent street lighting rather than that of the lantern-carrying watchman. The Gas Light and Coke Company had been formed in London in 1812 with the aim of piping coal gas to individual users, and by 1830 gas lighting was becoming general in the main streets of large towns. Gas was still expensive for heating, but as far as lighting was concerned a new form of burner was introduced during the 1820s which controlled the amount of air admitted to the gas current, and thus the whiteness and brightness of the illumination. Gradually, not only in streets, but also in homes and workshops candles were replaced by gas lights, and though the old ways which had satisfied instrument makers for generations were not easily discarded by the elderly, improved illumination was welcomed as a godsend by those with tasks of minute intricacy to perform. The gloomy little dens which constituted the workshop of the 18th century were a thing of the past by the time William Simms became sole master at 136.

From now on, London became a more orderly and safe place to live, influenced also by the general rise in moral tone which was apparent by the thirties and increased under Queen Victoria. The City of London continued to run its affairs in a democratic manner through its guilds and their constitution evolved over many centuries, with its own civic rules and regulations, but now its remit was more concerned with the general running of the City and its amenities, rather than organisation of its crafts and apprentices. Freedom of the City became an honour rather than a necessity for the trader. An increase in prosperity followed in the wake of the peace in the streets, and a long period of sobriety, thrift and well-being occurred after the Reform Bill was passed, with parallel reforms of the Poor Law quickly succeeding to the Statute Book, and a general awareness of social problems.

★　　★　　★　　★

Sir James South was abroad during the winter of 1831 until early the following year, and peace also reigned at Camden Hill, enabling Richard Sheepshanks to examine the contentious telescope and its mounting. It was a large instrument, with a 19-ft tube, and Troughton & Simms had never been happy about undertaking the work as it was not their normal line of business, being too large for their premises. They had from the start therefore refused to guarantee its performance, though they felt that as long as the mounting was accepted merely as a stand for the telescope, it would suffice. By means of a clock and micrometers, it could be used as an equatorial in order to fulfill South's wish to measure the positions and distances of the double stars.[77] Emphatically it was not intended to be an angular instrument, that is to say it was not suitable to be turned in different directions and elevations at will as would be a true equatorial telescope which is designed to do just this. However, an equatorial makes up for its increased mobility by consequent technical difficulties involved in overcoming the corrections needed in the measurement of refraction (the bending of light by a lens). Equatorials continued to be made for large observatories for some time – indeed, William Simms himself was to make the Great Equatorial for the Royal Observatory at Greenwich, completed in

1859. The transit instrument, fixed as it is in the meridian, does not possess this inherent problem. Nor does it demand such firm and expensive fixture, though its sightings are limited to the line of its position. The equatorial, on the other hand, can follow the moon through its orbit, and measure positions of stars throughout the sky. With a little ingenuity, South could have used this present instrument as an equatorial within limits.

However, it was true that, as Sheepshanks found, it produced a series of vibrations lasting 0.3 to 0.4 seconds when it was turned on its axis, and then let go.[78] Sheepshanks remedied this fault, which he diagnosed as due to a twist in the frame, by pinning the stays of the mounting by diagonal bracing, the result of which appeared completely to counteract the twist.[79] However, South refused to be placated, and resentful letters continued to pass to and fro between Camden Hill and Fleet Street through the summer of 1832. William's presence was constantly demanded at Camden Hill to set things right. On 4th May he spent the whole day there with a workman, to prepare the instrument for the following day when South intended measuring the planet Mercury as it passed over the sun, by which means he could test the accuracy of the equatorial. William and his man did not leave Camden Hill that night until nearly twelve, when they wearily took a hansom back to Fleet Street in time to have a rest before making their measurements of the diameter of Mercury from the 'little gazebo'.

The same day Frederick Walter was busy at Greenwich making his own measurements, from where he sent reports to the RAS of his results, comparing Mercury 'to a piece of coin pressed hard upon an elastic sphere'[80] as it sank below the sun's surface. On the 8th, one of the brothers, it is not clear which, sent reports of the Occultation of Saturn from Islington, presumably from William's house there, and again on the 9th came a report from Islington on 119 and 120 Tauri.[81]

South's experiments on 5th May were, as expected, a failure, not to mention a waste of the repeated visits which William had made to Camden Hill over the last year, owing to South's impatience and irritableness. He now forbade further work on the telescope, and Troughton & Simms had no alternative but to send him their bill for work done. It was not a great surprise to anyone who knew the circumstances and what had befallen at the RAS in the last three years, when South refused to pay. Letters continued to pass between him and the firm, and became more threatening and obstinate as time went on until finally the whole matter was turned over to their respective lawyers, as a great deal of time and expertise, as well as the actual manufacture of the mounting, had been expended, and the sum owed was considerable. Now, instead of between the participants, letters were exchanged between their legal advisers.

Whilst this personal turmoil was taking place, also in May 1832, at last the Reform Bill came up before Parliament again. There had been much parliamentary scurmishing, and fears that Wellington was preparing to prevent its passage by force, whilst 'King William, a perturbed and honest sailor, in such a gale as no State skipper had seen before',[82] brought back Lord Grey, and the Bill was passed. The country now settled down to elections for a reformed Parliament next year, and London quietened also.

It was a relief to William Simms to return to the relative calm of his family at Islington. He saw less of Frederick Walter, now the latter was working at Greenwich, and in any case Frederick was much occupied in attempting to increase his puny income from the Observatory by subsiduary jobs, as he was about to be married to Ann's younger sister, Caroline Nutting that summer. Their first baby, Caroline was born the following year. Meanwhile, old Edward Troughton was left on his own at 136 by the departure of Jane Suddard, and William was forced to give thought to the advisability now of moving Ann and the five children back to Fleet Street, where she could care for the old man, now increasingly frail, and seldom seen away from his dingy back room. Their eldest son, William Henry (1820), now twelve, was showing considerable promise as a mathematician, and William Simms saw that he needed further tuition in the subject from Mr Hayward as he had done himself, and as James' son, William (1817), had recently completed the previous year. That younger William was now apprenticed to his father who was a Freeman of the Clothworkers Company but carrying on his own trade in a dilatory fashion – he does not appear in the contemporary Trade Directories after 1830. At the same time, the need to have the family safely away from the troubles of London had disappeared now that the Reform Act had calmed the fears of agitation, and the only slightly worrying aspect was an outbreak of cholera, which had started on 10th February, and had claimed 5,000 victims by the autumn. Perhaps William was unaware of how much the epidemic had expanded, when he ended the lease at Lower Islington Terrace at Michaelmas 1832. On the contrary, one of the previous reasons for the original move to Islington – that of living in the country with fresh dairy products to hand, fruit from the orchards and vegetables from the little farms abounding to the north of the City, not to mention walks amongst the fields and lanes – had quickly disappeared as the countryside dissolved into speculative buildings, leaving very little greenery. By 1834 the population of Islington was a massive 37,000, and it was now merely a suburb of London.

The move back to Fleet Street meant that the two little girls, Elizabeth Ann and Sarah, could attend lessons in the vicinity, and James and Frederick could join them when they were old enough. For William Simms the move enabled him to contemplate a full days' work without the drain of a coach journey back to Islington at night. He was now visiting Cambridge frequently about the new mural, and probably also Edinburgh and even

Armagh (though this is not proven), and by basing his home on Fleet Street, he could leave the family with a clear mind knowing that John and Christian were just round the corner if needed. Even Ann's parents were now far from the City since they had moved out to Potter's Bar, chasing the receding countryside now that previously fashionable Pentonville was becoming so built up.

By the end of 1832 the move had been completed and the children were becoming used to their new surroundings and the strange old man whom they were adjured 'not to worry' in his dark parlour. Very likely he even slept in a corner of it where his bed had been curtained off as an alcove since the formidable stairs became too much for his strength. William and Ann lived on the first and second floors, and the top floor remained as optical testing rooms and observatory because of their superior light source. The kitchen, store-rooms and possibly the servants and apprentices bedrooms also were in the basement, and the coal-bunker was beneath the front pavement from where it was filled from the coalman's cart through a round grating. From here it had to be brought up all those flights of stairs by the serving maids for the living-room fires. There was a pump in the yard for them similarly to fetch water for the house.

However isolated Troughton wished to remain, it was essential for a good deal of passage from the 'offices' in the basement to the upper floors of the house, and however much the children were forbidden to disturb Mr Troughton, one cannot imagine that five children could have been constantly 'good'. On the other hand, Troughton was somewhat of a 'character', kindly in his own way, but an old bachelor unused to youngsters. The Simms children must have been much in awe of the recluse in his smokey den, his dirty wig on his bald head, his clothes stained with snuff and his ear trumpet at his side. They caught glimpses into his room as they passed through the hall or peeped through the bannisters as they crept up and down the stairs, but like all children they were very aware of the oddness of this individual, so unlike their father or even their Simms grandfather who used to live at Broad Way, and were either satisfyingly scared or hypnotically drawn to him. William Henry was an intelligent boy who in later life exhibited enterprise if not consistency, and it may be that Edward Troughton felt an interest in him, though conversation must always be restricted by his deafness and the need for William Henry to bellow into the ear trumpet to make himself understood. Elizabeth Ann and Sarah may have been sent into his room on errands, and the two little boys' perhaps occasionally wandered in out of curiosity. At any rate subsequent events showed Troughton's gratitude to the family when he specifically remembered Ann in his Will. This was tribute indeed to her care and his contentment in his last years, only broken by elements outside his control.

CHAPTER 8

1832

THE YEAR IN WHICH WILLIAM SIMMS found himself as sole proprietor in his firm was during a period of intensely hard work for him. He was now well known and respected as an efficient and accurate craftsman who was at the top of his trade, and could be relied on to produce a fine instrument. Moreover, he was a pleasant man to deal with, even under extreme provocation as when remarks from Airy, intended to be scathing, indeed proved as cutting as a new blade. 'I have now given you pretty good breathing time, and shall begin to work regularly upon you –'[83] writes Airy in November 1836, yet never once in William's own letters does a tone of more than mild irritation show itself.

Work on the Survey of Ireland was proceeding with military precision. The triangulation there could be carried across from the Scottish mainland even before the new baseline at Loch Foyle had been measured in 1827, and being full of widely-distributed mountains, Ireland was relatively easy to survey. Having emptied out Troughton & Simms' entire stock of theodolites – surveying instruments to measure distant land angles, levels and heights – as no other manufacturer had any completed examples, William continued to supply the survey both before and after the important geodesic theodolite of 1827. By 1829 Colby was in possession of 164 theodolites altogether, many of them from the Troughton & Simms' stable, and they also supplied most of the 576 sets of chains, each of 22 yards made up of 100 links, and the arrows for tethering them when measuring lengths. The primary network at Feaghmaan, County Kerry was completed in August 1832, and the first part of the Survey, that of Londonderry comprising fifty sheets, was published the next year.[84] Although mainly a military operation involving twenty officers and two hundred sappers and miners, the Survey employed up to two thousand local civilians such as schoolmasters who regularly checked the calculations, and when progress at first seemed disappointingly slow, Colby started to search for civilian draughtsmen to speed up the work.

Only a soldier of his experience and ability could have co-ordinated such an organisation. Even the smaller but equally complicated Survey for the

Bristol to London railway which Brunel was just beginning, did not involve so many people, though it cut straight through the countryside, including that of many different landowners. This at least, the Christian Socialist breathed with relief, was one piece of industrial development which did not use child labour. At long last children were prohibited from employment, for more than nine hours in one day or forty-eight hours in a week, by Lord Althorpe's Factory Act, which was primarily aimed at the textile mills. This advance almost coincided with the abolition of slavery throughout the British colonies, and was the beginning of a complex series of humane Acts of Parliament, of which the middle classes were at first barely aware.

In India Colonel Everest had resumed the Survey following his return from England in 1830, armed with large quantities of Troughton & Simms instruments including a large geodesic theodolite they had made between 1827 and 1830. They also supplied individual surveyors who were travelling to India with their own personal theodolites, as advised by John Anthony Hodgson, who himself had consulted 'Mr Simms' about suitable equipment for use by the Surveyor General's Office.[85] So also did Messers Jopp and Shortrede use a Troughton & Simms instrument for their Survey of the Deccan. Quadrants for astronomical work had passed out of favour, and sextants,[86] particularly Troughton's pillar sextant which combined strength with lightweight, or reflecting circles which proved even more superior, were made in large numbers by the firm, as were artificial horizons for surveying hilly ground,[87] which made use of the reflection of an object in quicksilver (mercury) to measure its height above the horizontal plane. After 1830 William Simms made a number of reverbatory lamps to Everest's order, which comprised an Argaud burner with glass chimney, fed from a reservoir of oil, and placed in the focus of a parabolic reflector. These proved to be very efficient except where there was a misty or smokey atmosphere.[88]

Conditions in the Indian Survey, as may be imagined, were often far from perfect. After the monsoon had subsided and the rains had drained down the sandy gullies, the heat became intense and the wind blew dust into every crevice. Before each developing monsoon the air was thick and heavy. Seldom was it condusive to the European to work, and results were long and often painful to obtain. Moreover the surveying parties were frequently far out in the wilds, many miles from towns and in contact only with remote mud villages. There was some chaffing at the ease with which their counterparts in the West obtained professional help when instruments went awry. It was no wonder that after travelling perhaps four hundred miles over stony roads in carts pulled by mules or oxen, the delicate equipment faired badly. 'If a screw gets loose at Greenwich, they bring up Mr Simms in a coach – here the instrument and its other instrument have to travel back to town and remain idle, and the Survey at a standstill until repaired and sent back by Dak.'[89] In 1833 this caused so many delays that Everest recruited artificers to man field workshops on the sites.

All over the civilised world it was becoming a status symbol to own an observatory, and these were often built and equipped with considerable lavishness but not always with the technical knowledge, proficiency or organisation to go with it. Even in Europe this occurred, in places such as Calton Hill in Edinburgh, run by the Astronomical Institution, and often in private observatories, although according to William Simms, the latter were more frequently business-like places where careful thought was taken over furnishing them. Examples of the former category were to be found in India where the reigning monarchs or Raj were often immensely rich, and anxious to display their wealth for its own sake. One such was the King of Oude, Nasar Uddin, who built the Lucknow Observatory in 1832, immediately ordering an altazimuth instrument from William. This reached Calcutta the same year, and an equatorial of more than 5-inch length made by William arrived in 1833, and was said to be far superior to apparatus already at Madras or Bombay which he had also made.[90]

Less successful were two astronomical circles ordered from William for the Survey in 1829, which did not arrive in Calcutta until 1832. These proved to be unsteady 'in spite of the firm using all their expertise to remedy the evil'. So much exasperation did they cause, that one of them came to be called 'Troughton' and the other 'Simms', but it was now recognised that this type of instrument was inherently top heavy, producing vibrations on movement.[91] However, the extreme accuracy of Simms' instruments was recognised, and rewarded by continued demand, frustrating though the time-lag of letters and goods must have been to all concerned. Ships leaving London and sailing, as they had to, round the Cape, would take anything up to three to four months to reach Calcutta. The recent 'Overland Route' to India, which involved a voyage to Alexandria, changing to a smaller vessel to travel up the Nile to Cairo, and then a carriage drawn by four 'wild' horses, across the desert to Suez, and there from another ship down the Red Sea and round to Ceylon and up to Calcutta, now reduced the time to about forty-six days. But the latter was hazardous to both people and goods. This however did not prevent the continuing connection of his firm with India.

William was by now much preoccupied with work at the Cambridge Observatory. It was to be another decade before he discovered amongst Edward Troughton's belongings what was probably the first known reference to the proposed observatory in a letter to Troughton from Thomas Catton FRS in 1817.[92] Built between 1821 and 1823 on land purchased from St John's College, making use of the slight rise of ground to the west of Cambridge on the Madingley Road, it was an imposing Georgian erection, perhaps too lavish for its aims. As Rev Richard Sheepshanks said in his article on 'Transit Instrument' for the Penny Cyclopaedia, 'It is not enough that a splendid building is filled with magnificent instruments directed by a consummate astronomer – – –'. He was complaining about the insufficient financial provision for an adequate staff to run programmes suitably elevated for such places, and for several years at Cambridge there was only a Dolland transit telescope and a single assistant to deal with the readings. Before George Airy was appointed to be Astronomer in 1828, with Lieutenant Baldry to come as assistant in 1829, and the promise of a second assistant later, virtually no planned work occurred in spite of the fact that the founders had ordained there should be regular meridonal observations with annual publication of results, but at first had not reckoned with the necessary manpower.

The original building of the Cambridge Observatory still exists very little changed from William's time, with an avenue of trees largely planted in Airy's day, running down the straight drive to Madingley Road. Ascending this drive provides an impressive view of the dignified Ionic portico in front of the main entrance lying straight ahead. Late Georgian in style, and although purpose-built, yet following the general neo-classical mores of its date, with symmetry, elegance, a triglyph frieze and pediment, it has a central dome to house the equatorial. This erection is mounted on independent circular walls within the centre of the building, thus divorcing the upper observatory room from vibrations and increased temperature in the rest of the observatory. The front aspect faces due south, and at a longitude of six degrees east, very near that of the meridian at Greenwich. The east wing constituted the astronomers house, and continues the Georgian elegance in its facade facing the Astronomer's Lawn, now surrounded by spectacular mature trees, many of great value. The assistant astronomer was housed in the west wing, the facade of which mirrored the east, but the internal fittings being somewhat plainer. Internally, the assistant's quarters were next to what became the transit room and central to that, the room in which William's mural circle was placed in 1832. The Astronomer's fine drawing-room at the SE corner of the building was complemented at the SW corner by another elegant reception room, although the fireplace now being removed from the former unfortunately, though cornice and central ceiling rose remain. Between the SE room and the ring-shaped hall with its central walled pedestal supporting the dome, is the splendid library still used as such, but with additional shelving carefully constructed to follow the design of the original ones. To the north of the hall is a small central wing designed to house the proposed zenith instrument, which in fact was never procured, and the space ultimately accommodated the boiler. A small secondary hall each end of the transverse corridor connecting the wings is charming in its shallow domed ceiling and its curved mahogany pannelled doors to the dining-rooms (now the astronomer's office to the east, and a common-room to the west). The front elevation also had one later projection of a single storey pedimented room connected with

103

Cambridge Observatory – eastern view showing entrance portico, dome, and Director's House.

the transit room, to house the collimator, used to set the transit instrument on the line of the meridian. Previously the tower of Granchester Church which is due south of the transit room had served for this adjustment. Behind the collimator room projection on the front facade are the vertical pilasters which originally contained the mechanism for opening the north-south shutters across the roof, with a break in the cornice at that point.

The original site of six-and-a-half acres on which the Observatory was built, was increased in 1890 and again in 1913 as requirements multiplied, and now reaches down to the Madingley Road, to house a number of later buildings belonging to the Institute of Astronomy, whilst to the north are the large new premises of the Royal Greenwich Observatory, transferred here from Herstmonceaux in April 1990. One other fact of practical interest was that the chimneys on the west wing, were dummies, smoke from the assistant's house chimneys being piped through ducts to the chimneys on the east wing, the prevailing westerly wind then carrying it away over Cambridge itself, whose own effluent also was carried easterly, and did not pollute the air above the precious instruments in the Observatory.

William Simms commenced his long and fruitful connection with the Cambridge Observatory soon after George Airy, whom he had already known for about five years, was appointed Plumian Professor and Astronomer at the University. His visits there were frequent, particularly during the planning and installation of the 8-ft mural circle which was ordered about 1829. The journey from London by coach was time-consuming and tiring, and consisted of about sixty miles of country toll roads. This would necessitate at least two changes of horses at stages along the way. He started out on his expedition warmly wrapped in his Chesterfield and cape, top hat and boots from one of several inns in the City – the Belle Sauvage on Ludgate Hill, the White Horse in Fetter Lane, or the Bull and Mouth in Aldersgate. The stages were at Ware, Puckeridge or Barley, where he could get down to stretch his legs and have a meal while the tired horses were exchanged for fresh ones. Once at Saffron Waldron he could see the pinnacles of Kings College arising above the trees to the north, and knew his uncomfortable journey with its variety of fellow passengers was nearly over. If Airy was not able to accommodate him at the Astronomer's House, there was The Olde Castle Inn or the White House Tavern in the town, and his workmen were put up in lodgings. The last few miles of his journey were normally taken in daylight as the Madingley Road was notorious for its criminal element and dubious taverns, and the shutters on the windows at the Observatory were not merely decorative, but a necessary defence, and were carefully closed once the daylight had gone. Cambridge itself may have looked beautiful, but even then was far from salubrious, and although since 1788 the main streets had been cobbled, lit, and occasionally cleansed, there were still few sewers – only two-and-a-half miles by 1849 and they did not in general take domestic waste. Only in 1853 was a public water supply commenced, and main drainage finally arrived in 1895. With the smoke from domestic fires, the fogs off the fens, and the odours of effluent of various kinds, Cambridge was still far from the pretty picture its colleges presented, and conditions up at the Observatory much preferable.

The 8-ft Cambridge mural circle was similar to the 6-ft one which Troughton had installed at the Royal Greenwich Observatory in 1812, and which had never been superseded. It was in effect a minutely graduated metal circle of enormous weight, whose function was to determine the declination or distance from the celestial equator of an object, solely on the meridian, by means of its telescope, and micrometers to read the circle scale. It was to be mounted on a heavy masonry pier in the line of the meridian, and to have special apparatus for supporting it when drawn out from the pier. William purchased the disc of flint glass from Sir James South for £25-0s-0d,[93] but in July 1830 still felt that it did not reach near enough to perfection to satisfy himself, having suffered by burnishing into the cell of its previous apparatus.[94] By early 1832 the main work on the mural was completed, and it was carefully packed and transported by waggon 'with all its various parts' in the care of one of his workmen to Cambridge, where it was set up on the prepared pier. William then proceeded to graduate it, a task he always seems to have undertaken himself with his most important assignments at this period. It was a procedure that could spell success or disaster for the instrument's future.

At last, on Christmas Eve 1832, he directed his account for the circle to the Vice-Chancellor and Observatory Syndicate for a total of £1,168-1s-6d, including time and travelling expenses for himself and his workmen, and carriage of the instrument to Cambridge, a sum of £42-0s-6d.[95] Characteristically he admitted one item (that of applying platina bands to the micrometer heads) could be 'left perfectly open, to be allowed or disallowed', as they 'were made under the conviction of their being an improvement, we believe without any direct authority'. Perhaps a workman had taken undue initiative, which William was in agreement with but had to cover. The total bill was up on Troughton's original estimate of £1,050, as the divisions had taken longer than expected, 'requiring considerable outlay'.[96] This was one of a number of occasions recorded in various archives when poor William's calculations were underestimated, and he had apologetically to explain to his client the reason. It is easy to understand how in the construction of such complicated instruments it was difficult to assess accurately the time factor in the costs. The materials could be exactly judged, but should there be any delay due to a snag in workmanship or design, or even by accident, the extended time still had to be paid for, and obviously each occasion caused him embarassment, and as we would express it now, a problem with his cash flow. To the Vice-Chancellor he requests payment as soon after the finishing of the work as the 'necessary forms will allow'.

Airy received the mural circle for his under-equipped observatory with relief. From its position in the room to the left of the central hall it could be used to measure declinations of stars to the south without being blocked by the young avenue of trees, and he was now able to increase his routine observations. For this he also acquired this year an equatorial by Troughton's old friend, Thomas Jones, which was erected in the dome of the Observatory and to his great satisfaction, and doubtless after a good deal of complaining, was sent a junior astronomer, James Glaisher the following year, to work under Lieutenant Baldry.

Whilst the Cambridge work was proceeding, other orders were taking shape, including the extensive variety of lesser items to be found in his shop and in his catalogue. The other important capital instrument to be completed in 1832 was a large transit for the private observatory at Castle Markree in north-west Ireland. This belonged to the Cooper family, a fine castelated house which had been rebuilt several times, the last in 1802. Edward Joshua Cooper, an astronomer of considerable ability, was born in Dublin in 1798 and inherited the running of the estate from a father also interested in the stars. Edward travelled widely before returning to Markree in 1830, where he proceeded to erect a private observatory for himself, which he 'furnished most richly',[97] commencing with the 5-ft transit mentioned which had a lens by Tulley, and succeeded this with a refractor mounted by Thomas Grubb in 1834, and a mural circle and a comet seeker both by Ertel in 1834 and 1842 respectively. Here Cooper with an assistant produced systematic meridian and meteorological observations from which

Markree Castle and Observatory, about 1832.

the government published in four volumes a catalogue of the stars, and later 'Cometic Orbits' and other notes. There is no firm evidence that William visited Markree himself, and it may be that the distances and time involved were a deterrent in this pre-railway era, forcing him to rely on despatching a trusted workman to set up the transit. It may even be that although he and Troughton had submitted a design for a mural for Markree, it was Ertel of Munich who won the order because William had not personally supervised the installation. Competition between the instrument makers was even then exceedingly keen, but William Simms was very busy elsewhere, and was pressed for time.

CHAPTER 9

1833-1834

ONE REASON FOR WILLIAM TO URGE Cambridge University to settle his account without delay was that Sir James South had refused to pay his large bill which was owed to Troughton & Simms for the equatorial. Moreover not only that, but William had spent a vast amount of extra time on the instrument during 1832 in trying to right the vibration that had so infuriated Sir James. He was therefore well out of pocket, and needed the cash to pay for materials for the work now in hand at Fleet Street which included a mural circle for the observatory at Edinburgh and another nearing completion for Cracow. There was also now the exciting prospect of building a large new telescope for Cambridge Observatory due to the recent gift by the Duke of Northumberland to the University of a splendid 12-inch lens made by the French glass worker, Cauchoix, which would involve William in many journeys to Cambridge to confer with Airy on the design of the mounting, and then wooden models to be constructed, and ultimately materials for the equatorial itself.

Sir James continued to withhold payment, and after a great deal more time had been wasted in writing letters to him without result, William had put the matter in the hands of a lawyer. All through 1833 the latter exchanged missives with his opposite number acting for Sir James, until finally in December court proceedings were instituted against South for non-payment. It was a complicated business, and professional witnesses spent many hours at the Camden Hill observatory, often with a considerable amount of intentional hampering and irritation by South's servants there in spite of John Nutting paving the way with the footman to let them in.

It was a highly distinguished group of scientists who were involved in examining the polar axis of the instrument, including Messers Pond, Baily, Riddle, Dolland, Donkin, Penn, Bramah, Jones and Henderson, and Captains Beaufort and Smith,[98] all names very well known in the world of astronomy. Professor Airy came down from Cambridge to have a look at it with Richard Sheepshanks. No effort was spared to give an authoritative and fair opinion of the position, whilst William's young brother-in-law, John Nutting, who was now Free of his apprenticeship with William but

Parents of surviving Simms children, including cousins

James	**William**	John	George	Henry	Frederick
1792-1857	1793-1860	1798-1879	1799-1859	1800-1871	Walter
m.	m.	m.	m.	m.	1803-1865
Catherine	i) Ann	Christian	Sophia	Mary	m. Caroline
Pruday	Nutting	Sumner	Davy	Ward	Nutting
1789-	1798-1839	1789-1850		?-1857	1804-1846
	ii) Emma				
	Hennell				
	1811-1888				

Surviving children born in 1820s and before

William	William		
1817	Henry		
	1820		
Sarah	Elizabeth	Martha	
1819	Ann	Christian	
	1824	1824	
Emma	Sarah	Sarah	
1829	1826	Elizabeth	
		1827	
	James	John James	
	1828	1828	

Surviving children born in 1830s

Frederick	Adelaide		
1831	1830		
Ann	George	Charles	Caroline
1833	1833	1834	1833
Mary	Charles	Jane	Frederick
1836	1836	Ellen	Walter
		1836	1835
Caroline	Frederick		Henry
1839	Walter		1837
	1838		

Surviving children born in 1840s and 1850s

Walter	Georgina	Arthur
Hennell	Frost	George
1847	1840	1840
Lorina	Julia	Edwin
Maria	1843	Henry
1849		1844
Arthur	Maria	Edward
Hennell	Sophia	George
1853	1845	1845

still worked with him, attended these sessions and afterwards wrote notes of the proceedings. William Cubitt, at present involved with building the south-east railway, was expected to attend, but asked to be excused at the last moment, probably as he was himself in trouble with Sir James at the time. The latter briefly appeared at the earlier of these night-time sessions at Camden Hill, but departed, leaving his servants to act as sentinals. Another night Nutting notes 'Lyall and the butler had us in charge'.[99]

Mr William Henry Maule had been appointed arbitrator between the parties, a highly amusing man of the greater erudition, well known as the wit of the English bench. Counsel for Troughton & Simms was Mr Starkie, and for South, Mr Drinkwater Bethune, both men of esteemed repute.[100] Proceedings seemed likely to be awe-inspiringly sharp as steel, and after commencing at the end of 1833, took up the whole of the following year, the first six months being devoted at Mr Maule's direction to William to complete the original project.

Coinciding with all these problems, William's home life was disrupted by the arrival of another baby girl, who was baptised on 18th October at St Brides, only a step away from his home in Fleet Street. This baby was called Ann, which signifies the deep affection which William had for his wife. They already had a daughter named Elizabeth Ann (the Elizabeth being after her Nutting grandmother), and before her a baby who had been baptised Ann before she died in infancy. Ann Nutting has left few hints as to her personality, but this repetitive insistence on her name must be one interesting indication of the regard in which William held her. Another pointer is the undoubted esteem which Edward Troughton had for her in the way she cared for him. A third, which we shall come to later is her friendship with Professor Challis' wife at Cambridge, where she stayed at their home at the Observatory, wrote letters to her asking for advice about her children, and sent presents via the packages which were put on the coaches for Cambridge. The Challis family were very evidently fond of her.

Baby Ann had been forerun in May by a little cousin, a first daughter born to her Aunt Caroline Simms and Frederick Walter in Greenwich. That baby was christened Caroline at St Alphege, the neo-classical Hawksmoor church near the Royal Observatory. The Simms family was yearly expanding its size. Henry, who was by now married to Mary Ward and was living south of the Thames in Kennington, was producing his eight children over this decade. James (1792) and Catherine Pruday had by now completed their family, with only three surviving children, their eldest, William (1817) now apprenticed to his father, a Freeman of the Clothworkers Company, and two girls, Sarah and Emma. George had married Sophia Davy, a widow, at St Martin-in-the-Fields in September 1831, and took her back to join James and Catherine at 9 Greville Street. The fourth of the brothers, John and his wife, Christian Sumner, of whom they were all so fond, were rapidly increasing their brood, and went on doing so until 1845. 1832, however, was a bad year for them, when their twin daughters, Georgiana and Selina, both died in infancy, and 1833 saw no new babies at their home at Peterborough Court.

How Edward Troughton coped with the problems of the enlarging Simms tribe is not recorded. It seems probable that Ann had the children well disciplined, and kept them away from the old man's room. His last years were overshadowed by the South lawsuit, though at home he seems to have been content. His name appears nowhere in William's notebook on the case, nor in the account of it in the Royal Astronomical Society History. By 1831 his handwriting was particularly irregular, and it seems likely that he was unable to take any practical part in the manufacture of instruments for the last three or four years of the partnership with William, and after retirement was too aged to make a useful contribution to the South case, although in private he must have mulled it over continually, and often discussed it with William. In none of the archives consulted has any reference been found to him personally during these years except the fact that he seldom left his room, and in addition in September 1834 there is the thoughtful evidence of his Will. His 25-ft zenith telescope erected by John Pond at Greenwich Observatory, and the subject of a recent paper by Pond was no doubt avidly discussed with William, and another matter at Greenwich which would interest him was the new Time Ball. This commenced its daily one o'clock drop from the southern turret of Wren's original building in 1833, an event of great significance, being the first official visual time signal of high accuracy given to mariners, from which they could set their chronometers, and therefore the first attempt at uniform time across the world.

1834 started badly for William. In the first week of January his mother, Sarah Thompson, died at the home she had made for herself at Evangelist Court, Blackfriars, after old William's death. She had been born sixty-seven years before in Stone, a small pottery town north of Stafford in 1867, and been married to William for forty-three years. Early on in their married life together she had suffered the disruption of coming with him and their two elder babies to the big City, so different even then from Birmingham at that pre-industrial period. They had first lived with his parents, James (1710) and Hannah Ann Collins at White Cross Street, then at Doby Court, and after their death, at Bowman's Buildings and subsequently at No. 4 Broad Way. After Sarah moved to her last home, James and George had transferred to 9 Greville Street, Hatton Garden, and the Broad Way premises, which old William had bought freehold, and the income of which he had left in trust to Sarah, was rented to W. Arrowsmith & Co, merchants. Finally in 1835 the house, yard and workshops at the back were sold 'for the most money and best price that can be reasonably had or gotten' to the

112

Time Ball, Royal Observatory, Greenwich.
BY PERMISSION OF NATIONAL MARITIME MUSEUM, LONDON

113

'Penny Story Teller' offices, a concern which also published a useful periodical entitled *The Doctor*. The proceeds of the sale had been bequeathed jointly to James (1792) and William (1793), the two eldest of old William's eight sons. No mention is made in the Will of the other five surviving sons, a strange omission, as only John was well established already. Possibly this was in respect of the fact that Alfred Septimus was being cared for by William Simms since 1821. The Will is undated, so it cannot exactly be judged what the circumstances were of the family when it was written, but it was probably made at the time in 1820 when he handed over his business to James (1792) and George. Henry and Frederick Walter were then still apprentices, although Henry was due for his Freedom the following year.

Any spare time which William Simms may have had in the early months of 1834 were taken up with the preparation of his case for the South lawsuit. On Thursday, 29th May the Court of King's Bench began its deliberations. Owing to the complexity of the case there was an enormous jury of forty-eight men appointed to consider it. Almost all were merchants, mainly in the City of London. There were three bankers and one esquire.[101] In June William was obliged to write to the court complaining that he had suspicions that Sir James was attempting to prejudice Mr David Pollack who was due to become a referee in the case.[102] On 21st July he went up to Camden Hill with Richard Sheepshanks and George Airy, and on 24th the large number of eminent assessors examined the polar axis of the equatorial, an exercise which was repeated several times.[103] The summer of 1834 was prolonged and hot, and people were swimming in the New River at Islington as well as the Thames, and London must have been sweltering in conditions unconducive to study.

Day-to-day work could not cease. Adjustments to the mural circle at Cambridge were necessary, and later probably a visit to Edinburgh Observatory[104] which had just acquired its first Professor of Astronomy and Observer in the able person of Thomas Henderson. Here William set up the completed mural circle about which he lectured shortly afterwards to the Institute of Civil Engineers at the request of the President, Mr Telford. He also lectured to the Institute on the subject of 'Graduating Astronomical Instruments', taking material from Troughton's paper of 1809 for the purpose.[105] An equatorial was also completed for Brussels, and sent off possibly in the care of a trusted workman – there is no evidence one way or the other as to whether William went over himself, but an order was also put in hand for a mural circle for the same observatory.

In a short description such as this of the life of one man, few details of the manufacture of each of his instruments can be included. They are, moreover, of more specialised scientific interest rather than of general historical regard. But a word is needed here to indicate the extent of the care with which William's products were tested and retested, the results tabulated, compared with others of the same type, and finally re-assessed in their final position. The story can only be gleaned from the workbooks which remain, but they indicate the meticulous attention he paid to obtaining the precision for which he became famous. For instance, in 1830 one reads that Mr Hussey's micrometer scale was divided into $\frac{1}{50}$th of an inch, each of which was equivalent to five-and-a-half revolutions on the micrometer screw, and $\frac{1}{100}$th of this on the vernier.[106] This brought the fraction down to $\frac{1}{27,500}$th of an inch, a figure not unusual in this work, comparable sums being used when he was testing micrometers for the standard scales with Francis Baily in January 1835[107] (when $\frac{1}{20,400}$th of an inch is recorded). Instruments destined for locations with extremes of temperature, such as the 6-ft mural for 'Khrakow' which was tested in the workshop on 8th, 10th, 11th October and Saturday, 29th 1831 for variations at different degrees Fahrenheit, and the tabulations of results take up six pages of closely written figures.[108] The Edinburgh mural circle took up nine pages of figures at the beginning of January 1834 and three days in which they were 'cleared off and prepared for examination'. No wonder William sometimes got his accounting estimates wrong. Certain notes, foreign to today's technician are jotted down, such as at an examination of the Edinburgh altitude circle in 1828 the observer had his 'face towards the window in all trials', and on the dividing of the declination circle of the Shuckburgh equatorial in the autumn of 1828, two sets of figures are given in the six pages of results, one by lamplight the second by daylight[109] – the latter being noticeably the better. Perhaps the most remarkable thoroughness is recorded in 1838 when testing the mural circle for Lucknow, which 'began in summer and proceeded into October', a span of three to four months, and producing no less than eleven pages of tabulations.

Whilst carrying on with his own work, William was keeping a weather eye on Brunel's survey for the Great Western Railway which was now well under way. It was a remarkable feat of organisation and tenacity, and once the route was decided and the land purchase agreed, the actual work of measuring and projecting onto maps and plans involved a vast undertaking. The most difficult terrain was that between Bristol and Bath, a civil engineer's nightmare of crags, ravines, torrents and tunnels, not to mention the River Avon which repeatedly crossed the proposed path of the track. To follow Brunel's progress provided an absorbing study for William, and precisely the kind of use for which he had made his theodolites and levels for Colonel Colby. Brunel's difficulties, including those of the appalling weather conditions were familiar to him from the reports from the Survey of Ireland, not only the official run-down, but more graphically the descriptions by word of mouth from Frederick Walter. Comparing the two sets of problems provided him with plenty of detailed mathematics and thought which he could discuss with his brother, who, with fellow feeling for Brunel, took a deep interest in the work.

Frederick Walter had discovered that assistantship at the Royal Observatory did not combine well with marriage, and notwithstanding the demonstrable hazards of practical fieldwork in the adverse weather conditions of northern Europe, he was drawn to returning to his old stamping ground on the railways. He had completed five hard years at Greenwich, working at all sorts of hours to comply with the routine observations required from the assistants, and continuing to give lessons on navigation in his spare time in order to supplement his poor income. The survey for the railway to Dover was being planned, and at a word with Henry Robinson Palmer, a Vice-President of the Institute of Civil Engineers,[110] Frederick Walter decided to leave the Royal Observatory for the more inviting and lucrative pastures of the South-East Railway. He and Caroline continued to live at Greenwich, where their second baby, Frederick, was born in 1835, and from Greenwich it was easy for him to travel through Kent to sites on the proposed track. When he later went for a spell to Paris to study the handling of asphalt, Caroline may have remained at Greenwich, which was a good deal more salubrious than the City where her brothers and sisters lived.

Frederick Walter had for some time felt that there was a lack of clear textbooks for students of navigating such as his own pupils, and also students of surveying or indeed of astronomy. There were plenty of treatises on the subjects, erudite, often verbose, and always far above the head of the newcomer to these disciplines. Now that the City colleges were in full swing, and even for men attending private tutorials, there was a need for a basic guide from which to learn the principles of the subjects, with clear descriptions and diagrams of the instruments available, and of the paths which light rays passed through them to give answers to the problems to be measured. In his spare time after he left Greenwich Observatory, Frederick Walter composed just such a book,[111] badgering his many scientific acquaintances for technical information to include in it. William no doubt provided much of this. It embraced details of the construction and methods of adjustment of each item, and indications for their use. At the end was an appendix which included methods of surveying for ordinary roads, the better quality toll roads, and for railways, and this was followed by various tables for the student's use, and lastly a detailed catalogue of instruments made by Troughton & Simms, who also published the book. Scanned today, Frederick's first edition of this classic reads with continued clarity, so undated is its English and its practical approach to the subject. Not a scrap of flowery language is to be found in it, each sentence being planned and shaped for easy interpretation, one leading to the next in logical succession, and yet complete in itself. The engravings and diagrams similarly show succinct intelligibility, with a directness of style and lucidity

116

of prose which indicates a strong uncompromising personality. The student who admits to having read the book will be allowed no excuse for ignorance, and must have welcomed its advent.

Whilst Frederick Walter was composing his book, England was continuing to seeth from the twin miseries of unemployment and high prices, particularly in the large cities, and very markedly so in London. It seemed as if at any moment the bubble would burst, to spread anger, riots and civil disorder in uncontrollable abandon. Although the police force was now in position in London – indeed there was a large police station only down the road from Troughton & Simms at No. 119 Fleet Street – and it was able to hold petty crime at bay, there was a constant fear of insurrection. London was a very crowded place by now, containing not only the wealthy, the busy craftsmen and the merchants, but intolerable numbers of beggars and prostitutes. The noise in the streets was multiplied by the vagrants shouting for alms, playing their flutes and penny whistles in an attempt to earn a few coppers for their sustinance. Drunkards rolled along from the gin-shops where they had been drowning their sorrows, and the usual din of carriages and waggons, hand bells and barking dogs continued unabated. Over all, frequently hovered a pall of thick fog, partly smoke from the many chimneys, partly mist from the river and its marshes. For a poor man, even one in work, where the pay was often insufficient for the barest living, life was hard and threatening.

The social fabric of England was, however, beginning to be upholstered and renovated, and the blessings of improvement were in sight. The year before had seen the first effective Factory Act which attacked the plague which employed children from the age of five for intolerable hours in the textile mills, so that they had to be dragged to work in the mornings by their equally exhausted mothers, half asleep. Lord Althorpe's Act was to be followed by further legislation effecting both women and children, and gradually all factory operatives. At the same time the Poor Law was amended in 1834, following the report of a Commission supported by Edwin Chadwick, the reformer and disciple of Bentham, on the appalling conditions in impoverished areas of both town and country. The Act of 1834 distinguished between the able-bodied destitutes who were now to be treated uniformly over the whole country, and the old and frail who needed different provision, and orphan children who required special care. It was after this that the Bridewell Hospital, newly re-built in 1829, and so familiar to the Simms family in its location in Bridge Street round the corner from Fleet Street, became less a House of Correction and subsequently a home for destitute children. Moreover the responsibility for all these facilities was transferred from the parish vestries, who were only too keen to refuse entry to their own territory to anyone who might be a charge upon the rates, to newly elected boards of Guardians. From now on the appalling sight of a dying vagrant or a heavily pregnant destitute being bundled over the border to the next parish became a thing of the past. At the same time the state of the prisons were being brought to the notice of the public, often by such people as Elizabeth Fry and Charles Dickens in their different ways. Dickens' descriptions of Debtors' Prisons which he had known during his father's sojourn in the Marshalsea, and his own visits later to the Fleet which he described vividly in *Hard Times*, caused an uproar. The workhouses also stimulated his pen to force the public to become aware of the inhuman conditions there and in the slums, as in *Oliver Twist*. The poor farm labourers of Dorset produced their own notoriety at Tolpuddle, from which the men were sentenced to be transported for seven years, and the sight of the hulks on the Thames waiting to take convicts to Australia gradually rose to the conscience of ordinary people, and were vividly pictured in *Great Expectations*.

It is hard to imagine kind-hearted men and women such as William and Ann Simms, tolerating so many excesses of cruelty. The blight on the streets of London, the conditions of their own Fleet Street, crowded, smelly, beset with intolerable poverty, and with the Fleet Prison round one corner and the Bridewell round the other, today would cause immediate concern. Then, it was normal, and had been so all their lives. Born during the French wars, they had been brought up in this mèlée. With our own experience of incomparably better social conditions, it is difficult to accept that it was permitted. But the winds of change were steering parliamentarians such as Wilberforce, Shaftesbury, and Elizabeth Fry's brother-in-law, Fowell Buxton, towards the task of reforming the law, and creating provision for the masses. It was a hundred years and two world wars until the Welfare State was truly in position. But first Parliament was to receive its own domestic blow that October.

William must have climbed to his little 'gazebo' in the roof at Fleet Street, taking the bigger children with him when he realised the walls of his workshop were glowing orange in the autumn light. The western sky was unnaturally reflected with a huge firey glare. An enormous conflagration was blazing in Westminster. Less than two centuries after the Great Fire, Londoners were still very sensitive about fires, and rumour about this one soon travelled as far as Fleet Street. The fire-engines from the City, mere waggons supplied with hoses and a tank of water each, with bars the length of the vehicle for pumping, were soon being rushed by their crews along Fleet Street and through Temple Bar westwards. The House of Commons was ablaze.

This was an event which was to effect William in a personal manner as the standards of length which were held at the House were consumed, and required replacement. The Royal Astronomical Society was now involved. It had had the foresight early in its existence to realise that as a professional body it should own its own standards. In March 1830 it therefore requested

Francis Baily to undertake this very arduous task. He was a wealthy man, highly intelligent and innovative, and passed his time in scientific investigations and invention. Once given this assignment, he instituted a large number of experiments to compare different metals in a range of temperatures, using a novel form of testing in which were three thermometers let into three brass tubes held within each other. The results were compared with the Imperial Standard Yard, later destroyed in the fire.

Meanwhile at 136 Fleet Street, two events occurred, the old complementing the new. In September Edward Troughton, now aged and ill, and reaching the end of his days, composed his last Will and Testament, disposing of all his worldly goods which he had not already handed on to his partner. John Nutting happened to be in the workshop when Troughton was ready to sign, and was sent for to the stuffy dark back room to witness his signature. A second witness was found in the person of Edward Lovelock, the son of William Simms' aunt, Sarah Simms, who lived in Chapman Street, Islington, and may have been merely visiting, or more likely have worked for William. As if to right the balance of the imminent departure of his old partner, in November William signed an indenture with his eldest son, William Henry, now fourteen years old, as apprentice for, as he thought then, a seven year period. A bright boy, tutored in mathematics by the ubiquitous Mr Hayward, William was proud to have his son working with him in his firm, with the prospect that in due course the lad would be able to take over the reins.

Across the road at the King's Bench, Mr Justice Maule worked on at his papers on the South case, and the QCs concerned settled down to a watching brief. All became quiet, and there is no further record of its progress for another three years.

Simms family mid-1830s

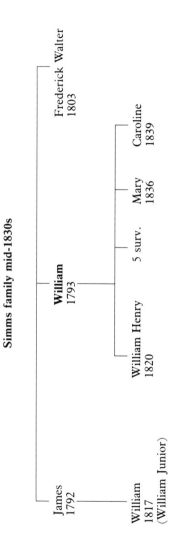

CHAPTER 10

1835-1836

1835 WAS REMEMBERED IN ENGLAND as the year of the Golden Harvest. The fields around the murky towns glowed with their ripening crops in the hot sun, as if the word 'hunger' would never again occur. The population rate was steadily rising with a visible acceleration, and this year reached fourteen million. The Municipal Reform Act which served as an addendum to the Reform Act of 1832, came into use, and from then on, the newly instituted borough councils were elected by those rate-payers who had occupied their property for at least three years. Thus were included not only wealthy industrialist Whigs, but also lesser merchants, supplanting thereby the previous Tory influence, and changing ever further the balance of power. Paid officials were now appointed to carry out the bye-laws, and by this Act the local councils gained jurisdiction over the police, and over property owned by the municipality.

The middle classes were becoming yearly more serious-minded, particularly in their religious practices, with the proliferation of every sort of relief society to alleviate the cruelties of impoverishment. It was now firmly in the mind of thinking people that the appalling spectacle of ragged, shoeless beggars of all ages which they could witness in their own streets even if they never dared to go into the notorious slums of the East End, represented genuine suffering. More and more literature was produced to bring the plight of the poor to the notice of the populace. Dickens was only one of the authors engaged in this, in his case often pouring ridicule on the law or even on the charity workers where they presented hypocracy. Mrs Jellaby in *Bleak House* with her obsession with Africa whilst at the same time neglecting her own children attracted his scorn, as did the grand ladies dishing out alms in order to couple their names with well-known nobility, such as occurred with Mr Boffin in *Our Mutual Friend*. Where Dickens had not himself experienced the conditions of extreme poverty as he did in the Marshalsea, or in his boyhood job at the blacking factory on Hungerford stairs, he made a point of visiting them, complementing his tour with a stinging description in his novels in such classic manner that they demonstrated their authenticity.

Somerset House, venue of the Royal Astronomical Society from February 1835 until 1874.   BY PERMISSION OF PETER MENNIM

By no means all the charitable work undertaken at this period was carried out for selfish reasons, and orphanages, almshouses, dispensaries and even hospitals sprang up under voluntary control and gifts, and were run by committees of thoughtful lay members who gave a great deal of time and conscience to their work. Smaller projects included societies to provide all sorts of necessities for the poor, be it coal, blankets, shoes or even soup and bread. The giving was becoming more and more genuinely inspired, and one can hardly blame local big-wigs for enjoying the kudos that was bestowed on them by having their names emblazoned on a Hospital or Church Honours Board. It was a huge step forward from the attitudes of the previous century which largely ignored want or pronounced it comfortably an Act of God. Prisons too received their share of publicity, and this year saw the appointment of inspectors who had to report back on the conditions in Britain's jails. The rate of change was slow, but it was at least a beginning. Mistakes were made, as when Outside Relief was brought to an end, so that only those within the dreaded workhouses received benefits, and subsequently only when need became dire, and possibly even death was pending, would a poor soul knock on the workhouse door, so much hated was its regime. Only the gin shop in the slums thrived, the sole way other than death to obtain relief from misery. Its results were little counteracted by the campaign against inebriation which sought to prevent the evil of drink without attacking the hunger and wretchedness which caused it.

Changes in communications were developing all through the 1830s with the coming of telegraphy and the construction of the railways, yet it was the next decade which saw the enormous boom in the creation of railway companies and the ever widening network of lines to a quite astonishing effect. Euston, opened in 1838, the first of the great London stations, was being planned, and even then gobbled up some of the new town of Camden, later to be devastated with its neighbour, Agar Town by the building of King's Cross at Battle Bridge nearby. Even so, the area just north of the Regent Canal was still being developed into respectable new streets and terraces, the most delightful of which was Barnsbury Square by Thomas Cubitt, which has survived the ravages, or more accurately arisen from the ravages, of time, to the present day.

Great as were the effects ultimately on William's personal life by these social upheavals, nearer home were two important events. The first was the increasing frailty of Edward Troughton, who now was over eighty, a great age at that time, and failing visibly. His life gradually slipped away that spring, and he died on 12th June, 1835. The house was hushed as the great man left the place which had been his home for fifty-three years since his brother John, to whom he was then apprenticed, had bought it from Benjamin Cole in 1782. With all his oddities, he had been affectionately regarded by his adopted family of Simms. His death was recognised as the end of an era by the many distinguished men whose society and friendship in life he esteemed the most valuable part of his reward.[112] All the Learned Societies with whom he had connections wrote glowing and appreciative obituary notices about their old and respected colleague, that of the Royal Astronomical Society covering his life in detail, including an extensive bibliography and a personal recognition of his qualities of intellect, integrity in his work as well as in his dealings with other people, and a heart-warming note of his kindness to colleagues and juniors.[113]

Troughton's Will is interesting as being of his time in that he remembered all his nieces and nephews individually, but also two specific social projects, one the Charity School run by his church, St 'Bridget's' in Fleet Street; the other the new-fangled London Vaccine Institute. Inclusion of the latter is particularly remarkable in such an old man as being so avant-garde. It was not quite forty years since Edward Jenner of Gloucester introduced the process of innoculating human beings with cowpox to protect them from the feared and very prevalent smallpox, an action thought by many' to be unnatural, unethical or at the very least dubious. The first Vaccination Order was published in 1829, only five years before Troughton made his Will.

His executors were Rev Richard Sheepshanks (now at Trinity College, Cambridge), William Simms, and Troughton's nephew-in-law, James Fayrer of White Lion Street, Pentonville who was married to Nancy Suddard, daughter of his sister, Elizabeth. Fayrer was an optical instrument maker in his own right, and on occasion undertook work for Troughton & Simms. All three executors received £100 each for their trouble. The business had of course been disposed of to William when in 1831 Troughton had retired, so the Will merely dealt with the personal residue in a series of legacies. The famous codicil leaving £100 to 'Mrs Simms the wife of my late partner' was only added on 23rd February that year, and had been witnessed by John Nutting and by another of William's juniors, Robert Lawrence. Typical of Troughton's carelessness with money – so diametrically the opposite of his care with his instruments – was his omission to pay James Fayrer various sums owing for work done, and finally the following July the executors were able, with counsel's agreement to pay him £573 of debts, increased to £613-5s-0d by interest payable, before the estate was finally wound up in January 1839. The executors' account shows a surgeon's bill of £5, the nurse £1-2s, the funeral £4-15s-8d, and the undertaker a huge £92-5s-8½d. For an unostentacious man this last item was a remarkable total but included a burial at fashionable Kensal Green Cemetery (only opened in the countryside beyond Marylebone two years before) which many famous names in the astronomical world attended. A bust by Chantry was placed with the Royal Observatory at Greenwich, and a lesser one completed by J. Devilee in 1822 is now in the Vickers Instrument Archives in York.

Six days after Troughton's death, George Airy took up the reins as Astronomer Royal in succession to John Pond. He found matters at Greenwich in a great state of disorder, and wrote that the whole place needed turning out.[114] It was not entirely Ponds fault that the records had been left in such a muddle. He had been vastly overworked, and even though he left Greenwich with six assistants where there had been only one when he arrived there in 1811, the routine work for the Admiralty with chronometers, and with observations resulting in quarterly publications took up much of his time, and his greatest achievement was in 1833 when he produced a catalogue of 1,113 stars, which proved to be of the highest accuracy. He updated the equipment in the Observatory including the addition of Troughton's 6-ft mural circle in 1812, and his transit instrument in 1816, and generally improved the standard of astronomy into the modern era. He was a sick man when he left the Observatory in the summer of 1835, and it was only a year until he died at his home in Blackheath.

Airy must have burst into Greenwich like an explosion. With his enormous energy, he set about modernising its methods, and gradually its instruments. A man of great orderliness of mind, from that moment he never seems to have thrown away any document however trivial. Moreover he was an obsessional filer, which makes him a gift to the historian as all his letters, bills, results, and even the most lowly tradesmen's accounts are preserved, and carefully indexed by him in old age. From an invoice for new knobs on the nursery door in the Astronomer Royal's house to highly technical descriptions of his astronomical methods, it is all there in the RGO archives at Cambridge, duly dated and in order, and even bound in some cases, no matter how scrappy the bit of paper concerned. His own letters were copied onto the thinnest of tracing paper, anathema to archivists as it creases and easily tears, and is often very difficult to read. William's letters in the same archives, however short and hurriedly written are, without exception, beautifully presented, easy to decipher, usually dated and addressed, and often with a personal touch in the last sentence. Frequently showing signs of haste, they nevertheless almost exclusively are finished off correctly – 'I am, dear sir, Your respectful and obedient servant, W. Simms'.

Airy was an inimitable disciplinarian, and could be harsh, with reprimands that wilted his colleagues, but every now and then from his notes slips a small phrase that gives the lie to this characteristic, and his letter to William after his little son, Walter, died in 1853 is typical. With William he seems to have got on well, probably due to their complementary personalities, and the fact that William soon learned not to allow his blustering to flurry him. Airy was dictatorial and ambitious, did not suffer fools gladly, worked phenomenally hard, and expected everyone else to be as single-minded as he was himself. The large portrait of him at the Royal Society, now housed at Carlton House Terrace overlooking The Mall, shows a highly intelligent face, a youthfully questioning expression, and a slim athletic figure. William, equally hard-working, was a much more pliant character, lacking the complete self-confidence that Airy possessed, but in a quiet manner, usually unobtrusively got his own way. William hated a row. Airy could blast forth if circumstances directed. William was a very experienced instrument maker who produced highly accurate goods, and was as reliable as was possible with such a complicated trade. Airy knew his man, having worked with him for seven years at Cambridge, and experienced his expertise. Had he not had complete confidence in William's abilities and reliance on his opinion, not to mention an underlying respect for the man, he would never have continued the happy liaison that had developed in spite of Airy's hasty manner, to the end of William's life.

One of the first of Airy's actions at Greenwich was to insist on the appointment as his chief assistant of a brilliant Cambridge mathematician, Robert Main. Now only twenty-seven, Main had the previous year graduated as sixth wrangler from Queen's College, and was then elected a Fellow, whereupon he took Orders. He produced a stream of erudite papers on astronomy over the years, and remained at Greenwich until the very month of William's death in 1860. His letters to William are always extremely proper, with none of the fireyness of Airy's communications, and his advent ensured that the work which Airy had initiated at Cambridge, culminating in a catalogue of 726 stars published for 1828-1835, continued in an orderly fashion at Greenwich. Main was a Fellow of the Royal Astronomical Society, and William was now meeting him socially at the Society's gatherings, since February 1835 held in their own rooms which until recently had been used by the Exchequer, at Somerset House. There is no evidence of a particularly warm relationship between Simms and Main, and it remained correct and formal.

Airy's translation to Greenwich opened a new era for William Simms as although he had been familiar with its observatory from childhood when his father had taken him to see Troughton's big instruments, and he had on various occasions since attended there professionally, not least when Frederick Walter was one of Pond's assistants, he now found himself at Airy's beck and call. An unsolicited note would be delivered at 136 by a coachman whose orders were to bring him back to Greenwich to see to an instrument which was faulty. One gains the impression that, easy-going as William undoubtedly was, and anxious to please, before this had been continuing for very long, he quickly learned to cope with the importunate Astronomer Royal who had to be taught that he was not the only client on William's list. There was, for instance, a mural circle reaching completion for Brussels, and any number of items for the Indian Survey.

William was corresponding at this period with Sir John Herschel on the application of the collimating principle to the examination of the mural circle, and on the collimator error of astronomical instruments in general.[115] The Land Revenue Survey in India was demanding further equipment, and put in a huge indenture in January 1835 for every conceivable instrument, including nine theodolites to be sent as soon as possible.[116] Contact on a much smaller scale was maintained with Edinburgh by the delivery in September by mail-coach of an annular micrometer, price £6-65s, and 'wires to the Transit Instrument'[117] (? from the clock). In addition, throughout these years work was proceeding with Francis Baily on the Standard scales, to which, sometimes indirectly, there is repeated reference in the archives. Scales were in constant demand for surveys the world over, in order to compare all measurements with the official lengths, the latest being the 6-ft tubular scale for the Euphrates Expedition in December 1834.[118] In January 1835 William divided a 5-ft scale for Baily which they then compared with three others: the RAS scale, that made for Professor Schumacher, and another for Professor Struve for Russia, and all four were studied at varying temperatures. Results showed no change with temperature, but a minute discrepancy between the four was found, leading Mr Baily to direct that his own scale be shortened by the equivalent of 7.40 divisions of the RAS micrometer, which was equal to nine divisions on William's own micrometer.[119] Bryan Donkin's gun barrel scale now entered the equation in March 1835, which equalled the Parliamentary scale at 62°F,[120] and myriads of figures follow in the notes. In April the tubular standard scale is compared with the others. The mathematics continues, the columns of figures lengthen, pages of notes in which Mr Baily's name repeatedly appears are laboriously written out in William's own technical notebook.[121] The concentration on measurement is intense throughout the year.

Airy was combining his new work at Greenwich with continuing direction at Cambridge of the construction of the Northumberland telescope, where the new dome to hold it was already being built opposite the south-west corner of the main block, and was now at the plastering stage.[122] A note from William in August addressed to Airy at Cambridge discusses the wooden model of the tube, and approves Airy's proposed method of packing the braces, but a week later William indicates he must have the model back at Fleet Street for alterations rather than attempt them at Cambridge. He had also, in his position of executor with Sheepshanks of Troughton's Will, sent some of the portraits belonging to Troughton up to the Observatory 'that had for so many years adorned my late excellent friends sitting-room'.[123] In December he received a request from Airy accompanied by designs and description for an estimate to make magnetic apparatus, followed by further technical correspondence between them. This is the initial glimpse in his letters to William of what was Airy's first major development at Greenwich, that of regular observations of the Earth's magnetic field there, which eventually began in 1838.

The correspondence between Airy and William Simms in 1836 serves as a good example of Airy's impatience, and William's efforts to appease him. The problem was probably that Airy was running between Cambridge and Greenwich, whilst William had other things on his mind. In addition, Airy's successor at Cambridge, Professor Challis, was already installed there, and William found himself writing to Challis about the Northumberland telescope on some occasions, and to Airy at others. Before the year was a week old, Airy sent directions for the micrometers for his magnetic apparatus,[124] and received a technical reply from William the same day.[125] A cry went up from Greenwich on 25th January for alterations to the mural circle, and William undertook to be there next day, bringing a Gunters Scale with him.[126] On 22nd February, Airy was complaining the zenith tube was lacking '2 or 3 eye-pieces – can you give me any information please?' and adding 'I do not at all like the plan of the micrometer generally'.[127] William replied next day that the zenith micrometer had been returned with all its screws but he would 'come to the Observatory on Thursday afternoon, if convenient to you, and look at it'[128] and at the same time would like to discuss the Northumberland telescope, which he was now planning to put as many of his men to work on as he could without them getting in each other's way. He also planned to go to Cambridge himself to check on the dome. In May a storm blew up over Airy's allegation that two dark glasses for the eye-pieces of the equatorial had not been returned from the workshop. Main urged their rapid restoration to Greenwich, and the very next day Airy wrote impatiently for them – 'as soon as you receive this, to rout up all the sun glasses' from the sextants, spy glasses and telescopes of all kinds – – – 'and to fit them somehow'.[129] On the 10th May, Main sent the two eye-pieces down to Fleet Street by carrier – William had called Airy's bluff and cannot fit them whilst they are at Greenwich. However he does find time to fit up and send an antique telescope for Airy's young son George, a gesture of his fondness for children, and, one suspects, to bring Airy down to earth.

Nevertheless, in June there was a peremptory demand from the Observatory for thermometers. William immediately sent nine – his entire stock. He also sent the model of the lower end of the zenith micrometer,[130] followed next morning by a note. In August a furious letter came from Airy:

'WANTED. A common micrometer.
WANTED. A common micrometer.'[131]

But he had met his match, and William calmly informed him the micrometers were as yet unfinished, and he was going away for a few days – no doubt to see his family holidaying at the seaside.

In October peace seems to have been declared, or at least an understanding had been reached between the two men. William requested Airy to come into the workshop to discuss the zenith micrometer[132] that has caused all the fuss, since planning the work would be so much easier by having the breech end in town. Next month he completed the thread which had taken longer than expected,[133] and later in November Airy was again irate because work on the Northumberland telescope was held up due to a strike of the men at the iron foundry of Maudesleys, an example of the newly developing power which the workers had discovered they had over their employers. Airy as usual was exasperated over what he considered a triviality, and in November wrote for information about the equatorial, whose craftsman, Field, was 'beyond my power'.[134]

One way and another William had his hands full. Another baby girl, Mary, had been born to Ann in the spring, and more worrying was the suspicion that William Henry (1820) was not settling in as he should at the business. Already he was showing signs of dissatisfaction, and talking of going to Cambridge University when he was old enough. For this he would need further tuition in mathematics and classics, and William had to face the fact that this son was not destined to remain with him in the firm, and indeed was spending more and more time at his studies and elsewhere, and less at the practical work at the workbench. In fact he was following the widespread trend of increasing wealth to dictate a better education, including that leading to a university degree, without which he was likely to remain in the despised class of tradesman. William Henry may have been merely trying to better his social class, or he may genuinely have disliked the hard manual work of an instrument maker. He undoubtedly was a bright boy, and could have yearned for an academic life such as his father's many friends had, or he may just have been kicking against the traces of apprenticeship, and wanted more fun. There may indeed have been a combination of reasons. His cousin 'William junior' (1817) (as he came to be called after 1836), son of his Uncle James (1792), who was only three years older than he was, also had high-flown ideas, but also seemed content to tinker about occasionally at the workbench. Technically he was apprenticed to his father, but found the huge range of orders at Fleet Street more to his liking, especially the names of well-known personalities and observatores that were on everyone's lips there.

William junior had been born in June 1817 to James and Catherine Simms at their first house in Bride Lane, and spent most of his childhood in and around Bowman's Buildings in Aldersgate, that is, when he was not holidaying at his mother's old house at Ayston. From an early age one imagines him to be one of those irritatingly inquisitive children who are constantly fiddling and poking at objects that do not belong to them. In his case, his quick brain and natural inclinations towards mathematical instruments drew him to his father's workbench at Broad Way, and when occasion arose and he could dodge Edward Troughton of whom he doubtless was in awe, to the workshops at 136 Fleet Street. As a small child his grandfather, old William (1763), who now that he had passed his business over to his sons, had plenty of time to spare, would take the boy to Greenwich on the horse-bus, and sometimes back by the river on the off-chance that they would see one of the new steam-boats which were just beginning to appear.

At fourteen these jaunts had to stop as then he was officially apprenticed to his father in order that later he would be able to obtain the Freedom of the Clothworkers Company, one of the major Livery Companies in the City of London. Now he had to settle down to consistent work, but occasionally his uncle Frederick Walter would take him to visit Greenwich Observatory where he was one of the assistant astronomers. Frederick Walter must have noticed the boy's attitude and intelligent grasp of elementary optics, and wished to encourage him in the art of practical astronomy. It certainly seems to have enthralled young William (1817), so much so that afterwards he well remembered the then Astronomer Royal, Mr Pond, his chief assistant, Mr Henry, and the other assistants by name. But then, William (1817) enjoyed name-dropping. His greatest thrill, however, was his first observation of a star's transit, which he made at the Observatory with Troughton's Transit Instrument, then considered the best in existence, but which was later dismantled and its object glass fitted to the Reflex Zenith Instrument.

In 1836 young William's (1817) apprenticeship was interrupted by illness, one of the frequent fevers that continually attacked Londoners in their unhygienic surroundings. Cholera was rife and although not named as such he was evidently very ill. Instead of returning to the foggy atmosphere of the Broad Way workshop, he was sent away to convalesce at Dover, where his uncle Frederick Walter was surveying for the South-East Railway on the exciting projects for the harbour and the line tunnelling through the chalky cliffs from Folkestone. Young William was an arrogant youth, and thought the railway was where he himself could make his fortune. In retrospect, he may have been right, but at the time his parents, James and Catherine, thought otherwise, perhaps sensing his indiscipline, and sceptical of a career in what was then so untried and speculative. Although Brunel was now busy with building the Great Western Railway, the scale of future development was quite unseen by most people, and was rightly thought to be too risky to commit a youngster's future. On 1st November, William junior (1817), therefore, being quite recovered from his illness, started work on an official basis with his Uncle William (1793) in Fleet Street. He was nineteen and still had two years of his apprenticeship to run. Somewhat blasély he claimed that his uncle needed him as a confidant now his own eldest son was going to university, and he, William junior, was kindly giving up his independence in order to go into business with him. But in fact it may be that Uncle William (1793) recognised his arrogant young nephew's shortcomings as well as his talents, and that this employment would save him from drifting from job to job, and ensure that for the next twenty years at least, he fulfilled his intellectual potential.

Thus it was that he commenced his career at Fleet Street having already dabbled in the workshop there for about the last three years. His nose was now, however, kept firmly to the grindstone in the daytime, and in the evenings he attended the London Mechanics Institute in Southampton Buildings off Chancery Lane, for classes on relevant subjects. Later he wondered to himself how on earth he had managed to work so hard at that period of his life, and envied his contemporaries who were earning huge sums and making their names with such apparent facility in the railway mania then all the rage. Irritated by what he thought might have been, he turned to music as a consolation – what he called in his diary, 'a musical fit', though he did not enlarge on what instrument he favoured, and tried not to think of the opportunities such as his gifted Uncle Frederick Walter was enjoying in the laying out of the South-East Railway under Sir William Cubitt's aegis.

William junior (1817) can thus be seen as a Walter Mitty character, resourceful but self-opinionated, so much so that one soon becomes used to taking his remarks at less than face value. He was the nephew who later, in 1885, wrote the informative and ungrammatical diary, from which one gathers the impression that he was of a much less steady character than his younger cousin, James (1828), or indeed than his Uncle William (1793), who was employing him. He seemed to dance from one enthusiasm to another in an age when the work ethic in the middle classes was a necessary adjunct to reliable income and reputation. However, his diary picks up some interesting historical facts about the contemporary conditions in London which are illuminating to read about firsthand, and it is a pity he did not continue his descriptive writing, improving his clarity from the undisciplined out-pouring which has to be unravelled to be understood.

★   ★   ★   ★

The year in which William junior (1817) joined Troughton & Simms, he must often have walked across Blackfriars Bridge to the south side of the river and then to a little way east of Southwark, where there were great goings-on, better viewed from the top of St Paul's than from the new London Bridge, but best of all from Nunhead Hill behind Peckham where one could still enjoy a panorama of London, from the docks to Battersea. Gradually from the north of the Borough rose a line of graceful arches like a Roman aquaduct stretching three miles away to the south-east towards Greenwich. The end near London Bridge was in a poor slummy area, where instead of the old timber-framed coaching inns around Guys Hospital were a clutter of dark dirty streets. But once Bermondsey was left behind, the rest of the way was green and pleasant. This was the first local railway to be opened in London, running out to the country even before the stations at London Bridge and Greenwich were completed, and was an offering to town-dwelling Londoners of a day out in the rural surroundings of Kent. The 'Greenwich Railway' was opened with pomp and splendour at a great banquet on 14th December 1836, at which the Lord Mayor of London was present, after which he and some of his more illustrious guests made a special ceremonial trip down the line to Deptford. At first only intended for pleasure, this railway rapidly became used for commercial reasons because of its proximity to the City. Eventually a new access station in the same grand manner as the later King's Cross (also designed by Lewis Cubitt) was built in the Old Kent Road at the Bricklayers Arms, but proved unpopular with passengers because of its greater distance from the City. Nor was the station which was built in 1843 in Bermondsey any more used. The railway, however, spawned its own extensive house-building in the south-east of London, and so became more and more busy. It is probable that William Simms (1793) did not patronise the railway for his journeys to Greenwich, at any rate in the first years of its life, as a coach could take him door-to-door without the trouble of changing conveyance or having to walk each end of

131

the route. Coaches are still mentioned in his letters until the mid-40s, and even later. But it is more than likely that, with other Londoners, one of the main Saturday afternoon treats which he gave his family was to take Ann and the children on a railway excursion to Greenwich and back, perhaps returning in the good old-fashioned method by boat, and probably taking tea with Caroline and Frederick Walter and their children whilst there.

Note: page 126

Collimation is the process of adjusting the line of sight, which in a linear instrument and by means of a second telescope, is thereby brought to the centre of the object glass, and should intersect at right angles with the wires placed at the focus. This must be done to ascertain any deviation there from before observations can be obtained correctly. By the nature of a mural circle, the principle must be adapted, as was exercising William Simms' mind just now.

Note: page 127

Gunther's Scale – called after an English mathematician, Edmund Gunther (1581-1626), it is a large plane scale which is engraved with various lines of numbers from where the answers to practical geometric and arithmetic problems can be deduced, using compasses as an aid.

CHAPTER 11

1837-1838

ONCE AGAIN A RECURRING SITUATION arose. William sent his bill of costs for work done on the zenith instrument to Airy, who, as so often, objected to its being larger than the estimate for the job – quite an amount larger this time – in fact £23-10s-0d as opposed to £12-14s-0d.[135] The reason proffered by William was the usual one that the time taken on it exceeded that anticipated, but also an extra micrometer had been added at Airy's request, and Airy had also induced him to alter the mode of suspension of the plumb line, to make an extra support for the slider, and to move it by a new rack and pinion, instead of by simple sliding. It seems that Airy was in the habit of ordering little extras and modifications as the jobs went along, and then expecting the bill to be unchanged.

Poor William had a severe bout of influenza this month, and 'such a headache as I never before felt'.[136] There was a germ going round the workshop, and nearly a third of his men were away ill, including the one he had sent to the Observatory about the clamps for the mural circle.[137] Airy too, had been struck down with sickness, and was taking some time to recover. The weather was dreadful, and William kept putting off a visit to Greenwich in case by going out, his own convalescence was prolonged. Between January and late March 1837 he had recurrent infection, and had to send one of his best workmen up to Greenwich in his place to overhaul the Bradley Zenith Sector. Going to Cambridge to make required adjustments to the mural circle was out of the question, although even there a workman had been able to do most of the work.

Construction continued at Fleet Street all this year on the Northumberland telescope, and at last in November it was ready to load onto a waggon with especially strong horses, at Deighton's yard at the White Horse, Cripplegate, and set off under the care of a workman named Potter. It was due to arrive at Cambridge next day at noon, and William arranged to travel there with Airy shortly afterwards. 'In a few days I trust we shall see the Collosus upon its legs' he breathed with a sigh of relief.[138] Airy and William were to be put up at Professor Challis', but meanwhile Airy worried himself about the wisdom of sending Potter in charge. William, however, knew his

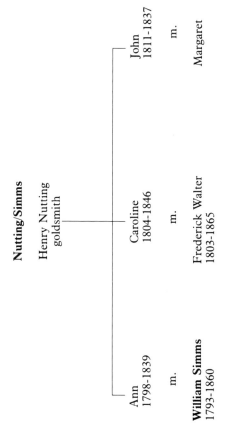

Nutting/Simms

Henry Nutting
goldsmith

Ann
1798-1839

m.

William Simms
1793-1860

Caroline
1804-1846

m.

Frederick Walter
1803-1865

John
1811-1837

m.

Margaret

men better, and was well aware of the pride they had in their work.[139] After many months of concentrated and meticulous labour in charge of the project, Potter was the most unlikely person to allow any harm to come to the equatorial, such was the pride in their work which these craftsmen had. A sophisticated instrument like this became their own particular baby, and a source of great satisfaction to them.

Alas, it seems likely that William had to postpone his visit. His brother-in-law, John Nutting, who was only twenty-seven, had been ill for months. Married only a short time and with a baby daughter of two-and-a-half called Margaret Elizabeth after her mother and paternal grandmother, he died of consumption at his home, 72 Hatton Gardens on the morning of 25th November. This is the first time this dread word is mentioned in the family's history, but then, John's death took place in the very first six months of compulsory registration of deaths in England. Trained by William in his workshop since 1825, his loss was severe, since he had an orderly mind and a quick brain. While he had been ill, with its inevitable result, William had fortunately been able to bring in his brother, Henry Simms to take John Nutting's place as a clerk, which as the business flourished, was needed as a separate entity quite apart from another instrument maker. Henry was reliable and hard-working, and made a niche for himself in the firm with which he remained the rest of his working days, probably until the move to Charlton in 1866.

June 1837 was the date of another death, this time of national importance as it was also the end of an era and the start of a bright new one. William IV, who had been known to be failing for some time, managed to stay alive in order to celebrate from his bed one more anniversary of Waterloo on 18th June. He died early in the morning of the 20th. A rather mediocre king, he was at least more popular than his elder brother George IV, whose extravagances and debts brought the monarchy into severe disrepute. When he died in 1830 everyone was either unmoved, or blatantly pleased to see the end of him. William IV made many mistakes of judgement, but he was more humane and approachable, and the country ended up by holding him in some affection. Although he never married his mistress, Mrs Jordan, because of her total unsuitability for the position of Royal Consort, due to her birth, her amorous past and her career as an actress, the country did rather admire his devoted family life with her at Bushey Park, where she bore him no less than ten children, the Fitzclarence tribe. In spite of having other affairs, he remained faithful to her in heart until it was born in on him that he must marry legitimately in order to produce a male heir. It was a remarkable fact that from the huge family of thirteen children which George III and Queen Charlotte produced, only one grandchild, a girl born in 1819, was eligible to ascend the throne. Princess Victoria's father, the Duke of Kent, had died when she was a baby, and she had been dictated to by her mother throughout her childhood, and now that the throne approached, her mother insisted on taking her for a tour of the country each year to show her off to her future subjects. This embarrassed Victoria, whilst it utterly enraged her Uncle William, who in any case loathed the Duchess, not without reason. She was rude, sneering and slighting to him; moreover she prevented him having any contact with his little niece, a great sadness as he and his Queen Adelaide, whom he married in 1818, had no child of their own. Brought up in the navy, bluff and often foul-mouthed, he was known to Nelson, but not really a shining star in the opinion of the Admiralty, William IV nevertheless had a friendly and jovial, if unpredictable exterior. In addition he had had the sense to back Lord Gray in his successful efforts to see the Reform Bill through Parliament. His short reign paved the way from the careless excesses of George IV and the Regency, to the thinking and disciplined years of Queen Victoria, during which the country gained self-respect and social awareness, and the changes for good foreshadowed the Welfare State of the 20th century.

Just as Britain was celebrating (albeit with some reservations) the advent of their new queen, so there was joyful anticipation at 9 Greville Street on the birth of a baby girl at long last to Sophia, wife of William's brother, George. They had been married for six years without producing a live baby, and so great was their happiness at the arrival of this one, that they patriotically named her Emma Victoria. She was baptised at St Brides on 7th August. Alas, their joy was short-lived, as like so many of her contemporaries, the little mite was dead in a few days, and poor Sophia had to come to terms with the fact that she would never have a family of her own. She must make do with her many nephews and nieces-in-law.

★　　★　　★　　★

The New Year of 1838 was only a few days old when Airy was already restlessly putting pen to paper to write to William about Thomas Jones. Jones had for many years been a close friend of Edward Troughton's, having started his working life as an apprentice to Ramsden in 1789, when Troughton was already in partnership with his brother John Troughton. They had both been closely involved in the formation of the Astronomical Society in 1820, and now after having made a name for himself in his craft during fifty years, sadly he was becoming blatantly inaccurate in his results. A good and faithful friend, his colleagues were loathe to hurt him by derogatory remarks, and hence Airy's letter to William Simms asking him to call in to check his methods of construction on the clock for one of the instruments for Greenwich – 'I should be glad if from time to time you could just look at him and correct his notions'.[140] Both men were fond of the old boy and William had reason to be grateful to him for his encouragement over his protractor design way back in 1816. Other examples of this kindly dissembling occur in the archives, and demonstrate William's capacity for tactful handling of a difficult situation without hurting the other participant.

William was busy at the time on a copy of Troughton's rain-gauge for Cambridge, which he had shown Challis on his recent visit to Fleet Street. Both this and an anenometer (an instrument for measuring the course, force and velocity of the wind) with its lock were put on a waggon for the Observatory at the end of January, from the White Horse, Cripplegate.[141] The mural circle for the Observatory at Lucknow was nearing completion, but its small telescope was temporarily sent up to Cambridge whilst the one there was being adjusted. The equatorial completed for Liverpool the previous year in time for the British Association meeting, needed his attention, necessitating a journey to Lancashire about now – a time-consuming business which he could not shirk. His workshop was buzzing with orders for India, even more than previously, as he had now officially replaced William Gilbert as supplier to the East India Company for their many and various surveying needs.[142] In Scotland, Colby was resuming work on the Survey, whilst the Irish Survey continued with the appointment of William Yolland, a brilliant young army officer in the Royal Engineers as superintendent for the Board of Ordnance of the publication of astronomical observations. Yolland worked in the headquarters at the Tower of London, in Dublin and in the field, surveying.

William Simms had, since his introduction to the Royal Astronomical Society in 1831, proved an assiduous member. He enjoyed the monthly meetings at which he met all the names famous in astronomy at the time, many of whom he knew intimately, and could call his friends. Early in 1838 he was elected to its council for the first time, and now was committed to an extra meeting each month. His old friend, Francis Baily, was President that year, and took the chair, and William found himself amongst colleagues including George Airy, Lieutenant Roger, Sir John Wrottesley, Professor Challis, Reverend Robert Main, and others. There were fourteen members on the Council altogether, and they discussed all matters pertaining to the Society, from the most trivial domestic, to astronomical of the utmost complexity. His first Council meeting occurred on Friday, 9th March at Somerset House, when the appointment of a new Assistant Secretary was discussed, an innovation designed to take some of the everyday work off the shoulders of the two Secretaries, George Bishop and Augustus de Morgan. The duties of the new employee were examined in detail and listed, down to such mundane issues as seeing that the Society's apartments were kept clean and that incoming mail was noted down in a special book for the purpose. The salary was fixed at £80 per annum. Papers submitted to the Society were also carefully sifted, and decisions made as to which should be published in the Monthly Notices and which read to the Society at their gatherings. Council meetings had recently been moved from their previous evening hours to afternoon at four o'clock, enabling members to return home in comfort, if not always in daylight, at their conclusion.[143] William proved not to be amongst the most vocal members of the Council, but when he did have his say, his colleagues learned that his few words were worth paying attention to, as thoughtful results of experience, without superficial comment.

Meanwhile at home the Simms family shared the nation's excitement over the extraordinary race to New York by the first steamships to cross the Atlantic, the *Sirius* and Brunel's *Great Western*. Both had been launched the previous year, but the little *Sirius* which belonged to the St George's Steamship Packet Company of Cork, and was intended for home waters, was chartered to deputise for the *British Queen* which would not be ready before its rival, *The Great Western*. After some modification, *Sirius* left for New York on 28th March, calling in at Cork for coal, and arriving at Sandy Hook on the 22nd April with only fifteen tons of coal left in her bunkers. *The Great Western* only left her moorings in the Thames at 6.08 am on the 31st March. There followed, less than two hours later, the disastrous fire around her boiler flue and its lagging which badly injured the vessel's creator Isambard Brunel. The great ship returned briefly to Bristol for repairs (leaving Brunel on Canvey Island to recuperate), and finally left for New York the following Saturday, 8th April with only seven hardy passengers aboard. It arrived off Sandy Hook fifteen days five hours later, triumphantly on St George's Day, and returned to England in a mere fifteen days, to the pride of its builder, still very ill, and to the nation. Later that year, on 24th July, *The Royal William* arrived in New York, having crossed the Atlantic in eighteen days twenty-three hours, the first steamship to do so from Liverpool. After this victory, to cross to New York became commonplace, and in fact only four years later, Dickens did so on a lecture tour.

Many of William's friends at this time were men of means, whose inherited wealth enabled them to spend their time in the study of whatever was their pet subject, in most cases astronomy. Mention has already been made of Sheepshanks, Baily, and Sir James South who all were wealthy men. The wonder is that the appetite for knowledge and exploration itself provided a goal for much patient and sophisticated investigation, with no thought of monetary gain to the participant. This is a feature of Victorian England which in the 20th century had been lost through the rigours of death duties and taxes, and with it the independence to study for its own sake. In this context it must be regretted, as it provided an atmosphere of enthusiastic academia unbesmurched by the mundane influence of monetary considerations. These highly intelligent men studied and experimented only because they enjoyed it. Very occasionally women too followed lofty scientific or literary paths, though for them there were many hurdles unassociated with finance. As early as 1835, Caroline Herschel and Mary Somerville were elected Honorary Members of the Royal Astronomical

Society,[144] even though women were not eligible for ordinary membership until the end of the century. Men, however, who had contributed to astronomy were admitted as Fellows regardless as to their official appointments. There was a network of friendship amongst the Fellows whereby any interested acquaintance of theirs who showed erudition in the subject, would willingly be accorded access to the place of work of other Fellows, often a very well-equipped observatory. Instances of this appear continually in the archives. In May 1838 a 'Mr Eyston, a friend of mine, and a lover of Science'[145] was introduced by William to Professor Challis with a request that the latter should show him the instruments at the Observatory. William himself had to remain in London to attend on the annual Visitation at Greenwich, which, introduced in 1831 in Pond's time, had provided a rigorous scrutiny of the accounts, the instruments and the general conduct of the Observatory.

At the beginning of June he dispatched the clock for the equatorial to Cambridge in the charge of the workman who had made it, together with some other parts. He and William Henry travelled there on the coach which left Fetter Lane at 10 o'clock on 10th June, in order to enter the latter at Pembroke College on the 11th.[146] They stayed at the Challis', and remained for several days so that William Henry could explore Cambridge, whilst his father worked on the equatorial. The polar axis was causing William concern, and his workman was instructed to do some preparatory work on it before he himself arrived.[147]

Back in London the next excitement was the Coronation on 28th June, and bunting was going up in all the streets, and scaffolding in Whitehall and around the Abbey. Crowds poured into London from the country and everyone's relatives whom they had heard nothing of for years, suddenly expressed a desire to come and visit them. People were sleeping in the streets and the park, and the buskers and peddlars were doing a roaring trade. Gypsies and barrow boys filled the pavements with their wares. Shouting, singing, waving, and even dancing filled the streets. At midnight the church bells rang in the new day, and at four o'clock the guns in the park answered with volley after volley, oblivious of the early morning drizzle. Surely William steered his family and all their hangers-on, through Temple Bar and down the Strand to Whitehall to see the people and the processions and the bands marching along from Buckingham Palace, and at last the little Queen in her fairy-like carriage drawn by cream-coloured ponies brought especially across for the event from Hanover. By now the sun was shining brightly as if to do its best to greet the new reign, and when it set late that summer night, its glow was taken up by a magnificent show of fireworks set off in the park.

Next week the weather turned, but in spite of the rain, Ann and the children and a vast array of luggage were dispatched by coach to Dover for their usual two months summer holiday at the seaside. William accompanied them to their lodgings, saw them settled in safely, and then returned to Fleet Street to cope with the work which always accumulated when he was away. At home he had Sarah Newall to look after his wants and housekeep for him, his servant from Shropshire who had already been with him many years. She was now a widow of fifty-four, and an integral part of the Simms household. Once home again he dispatched a workman to Cambridge with orders to replace the object end of the equatorial which he carried with him on the coach, together with a book of poems by a Mr Dales, 'with Mrs Simms' respects to Mrs Challis, to whom and to the children please remember me'[148] – probably a thank-you present for her hospitality on a previous occasion.

Next month William took a few days off and went down to Dover to see his family. But Airy was not to be put off, and on 4th August, after he had 'ever and anon jogged Simms respecting the Northumberland work',[149] he called a cab and went down to Fleet Street to hurry things along. He was politely received by Henry who, as general factotum, was now well familiar with the work of the firm. He showed Airy the latest letter on the subject of the telescope from Professor Challis, and ushered him out with the promise that he would draw his brother's attention to remarks about the declination rods.

Poor William arrived back a few days later feeling as if the amount of work that had heaped itself up at Fleet Street in his absence, had made the trip hardly worthwhile. He wrote to Airy proposing they went together to Cambridge next week, probably on the Star on Thursday if he himself could dispose of his backlog of work by then, otherwise one of the early coaches on Friday morning.[150] That weekend he was able to arrange with Challis for a tutor who could give William Henry (1820) special cramming in Greek, notably 'the first on Thycydides',[151] which he required for matriculation. All the likely Greek scholars he knew in London seemed to be out of town for the summer. In the event, William Henry travelled with him to Cambridge, and seems to have stayed with the Challis' as he was able to report back to his father later that month on the bothersome polar axis.[152] Mrs Challis, meanwhile, had sent down to Ann full instructions as to what William Henry would need to furnish his rooms at Pembroke, clothes, food, and so on,[153] and by the time William fetched her and the younger children home from Dover in mid-September,[154] there was only a fortnight in which to gather all his requirements together and have them sent on a waggon to Cambridge. William Henry followed the last week in September and duly matriculated that Michaelmas.

It is interesting to speculate on the two Williams' (1793 and 1820) choice of Pembroke College for the younger one. Presumably they favoured it at the advice of Professor Challis, but another draw may have been the unconventional one that it had a planetarium in one of its courts. This had been erected by a previous Master of Pembroke Hall, Roger Long in 1765 when occupant of the Lowndean Chair of Astronomy and Geometry. A well-known astronomer who published an important work on the subject in 1742 and 1764, Long's planetarium was a revolving sphere 18 feet in diameter, to accommodate thirty people, and demonstrate the movements of the stars around them. Such originality must have appealed to the successors of the creators of the early orreries.

It must have been shortly after the family returned home from Dover that William (1793) had some sort of severe illness for which he was kept indoors under the charge of a surgeon. He managed his business from his room, and directed a workman to travel to Cambridge to deliver the completed brass rods (? for the Northumberland telescope), hoping to follow himself on 20th October.[155] He was able to bring his accounts up-to-date whilst he was convalescent, including bills for work completed at Cambridge and Liverpool. Henry who had taken over the accounting since John Nutting became fatally ill, no doubt paved the way for William in this respect, although his billing did need to be checked for its occasional flaw. Another job which may have filled William's time in bed was to read Frederick Walter's latest publications on which he had advised during their creation. The most famous, which ultimately ran to a sixth edition in 1875, was that on levelling, produced in 1837. Now came the results of Frederick's sojourn in Paris, *Practical Observations on the Asphaltic Mastic*, and *The Public Works of Great Britain*, a large tome which he had edited. In preparation was his Treatise on Mathematical Drawing Instruments, to come out the following year, and to run to an eighth edition in 1860.

At last in December, light shone through the winter fogs and months of illness, with the publication of Mr Justice Maule's deliberations on the South lawsuit. Troughton & Simms had won. William was enabled thereby to recover from Sir James the sum of £1,570. Costs were to be divided between William Simms and Sir James, and the parties respectively were to pay their own expenses for the case. These for William amounted to £100 for his Attorney and £29-12s-11d for his expenses incurred during the arbitration, including the cost of making moulds for models, his workmen's time at Camden Hill, coach and cab hire, and refreshments for his workmen and his witnesses.

Thus came to an end one of the most celebrated industrial tribunals, a cause of anxiety and a great deal of extra labour to William, and a nagging sadness which darkened the last days of Edward Troughton, who never heard the successful outcome which vindicated his firm. Sir James does not disappear from the archives subsequently, continuing his erratic way through life until he surfaced again to public gaze in 1842, with his famous auction.

Sir James South.

Throughout the hearing in 1835 and in his final judgement in 1838, Maule exhibited shrewdness and studiousness, but his handling of the case gave plenty of scope for his usual mockery and lack of tactful flattery. There was no trace of real sympathy in the way he dealt with either party – he was interested only in the legal niceties of the case rather than necessarily a fair result, and his sarcasm could be devastating. In the end, William did well to obtain what he received from the verdict from so unpredictable a judge, and albeit he himself brought the case against South and had witnesses of high repute to vouch for the integrity of the equatorial, he still had to pay for his own expenses, not least in the continual aggravation of Sir James' oddities and barbs, and Mr Maule's heavy irony. However, with his friends' help, he emerged with the most important ingredient, that of an unblemished character, both for himself, and for his skills as an instrument maker. His life had been overshadowed for nearly a decade by the wretched telescope, and Christmas 1838 must have been lightened by the shedding of this burden, though others were gathering.

142

CHAPTER 12

1839

WILLIAM HENRY (1820) CONTINUED TO CAUSE his parents concern. After a term at Pembroke College, where, judging by his account for beer with the college butler, he led an abstemius life, there is no indication as to whether he was unwell, or simply did not fit in with college life, but something was not as it should be. The Challises offered help, and he went to stay with them at the Observatory in the New Year.[156] By 11th February he was home again in Fleet Street, and his father wrote to Professor Challis that 'his case appears a most alarming one'.[157] Six weeks later, at the end of March, William was again pen in hand writing to Challis to say that the young man would be back in Cambridge in another fortnight, and he would himself also be there about then. The equatorial was almost finished, and he enclosed some oil stone dust for the lower pivot 'for grinding, which will do no harm if it does no good'[158] – typical Simms optimism.

There was, as usual, a great deal going on in the workshop, but William made time to examine the Fuller theodolite for the Royal Astronomical Society, and at the Council meeting on Friday, 8th March he reported his results and conclusions on this creation of Thomas Jones, made for the reassessment of some of the stations upon the Trigonometrical Survey of England.[159] The same week he was able to supervise the packing of the mural circle for the observatory at Lucknow, and see it onto a ship for India, together with a sheet of instructions for its use. A 2⅓-ft transit instrument completed for the Mayor of Louth also received its written instructions, which were sent to the Rev Mr Jeans for his information in its use.[160] In April he heard that his 5-ft achromatic telescope with a lens by Tulley mounted equatorially had been presented by Richard Sheepshanks to the Royal Observatory at Edinburgh.[161]

On 10th April he felt able to leave home for a few days and accompanied William Henry back to Cambridge, longing to get away from London 'to recruit my health, having been a close prisoner for some time'.[162] Ann was very unwell. A week later he returned home after an unsuccessful visit in so far as viewing anything through the Northumberland telescope was concerned, because of the consistently cloudy nights, but was satisfied with

Available help at Ann's demise 1839

William

Elizabeth
Ann
15 yrs

James &
Catherine

John &
Christian

George &
Sophia

Frederick Walter
& Caroline

William's children 1839

William
Henry
19 yrs

Elizabeth
Ann
15 yrs

Sarah
13 yrs

James
11 yrs

Frederick
8 yrs

Ann
6 yrs

Mary
3 yrs

Caroline
4 mths

144

the instrument itself, and very pleased with its dome, which not only functioned well,[163] but was an attractive addition to the grounds of the main observatory, having been designed in much the same style. He quickly dealt with the part of the telescope which he had brought home with him in order to effect some modification, and packed it off on the coach to Cambridge, enclosing a parcel for William Henry at Pembroke 'when you send to the town'.[164]

The previous autumn, Ann had found she was again pregnant. Her last baby, Mary, had been born in April 1836, a healthy child who was now trotting about the house in Fleet Street, 'helping' the servants, and, holding her father's hand, could walk down the road to the Fleet Bridge and back, eyeing with excitement all the passers-by, the traffic, and the horses. This present pregnancy did not run smoothly, but some time in April 1839 Ann gave birth to another little girl, to be called Caroline after Frederick Walter's wife. When the baby was baptised on May Day at St Brides, Ann was already gradually going downhill, and probably did not go to the church. The new baby was healthy, and thrived, although she probably needed the services of a wet nurse, whilst the faithful Sarah Newall looked after the sick mother.

May passed with William Henry remaining at Pembroke until late in the month, when term ended and he set off to Ireland with a friend for the long vacation. His father struggled on, finding it difficult to fulfil all his obligations including the regular meeting of the RAS Council at Somerset House, but had to decline the usual invitation to dine with the Visitation party at Greenwich at the end of the month. As well as routine work he was writing a paper which he was to read to the assembled RAS on 14th June on his deliberations resulting from his patient investigation into the quality of optical glass made at the direction of the late Dr William Ritchie by Messers Chance & Co of Birmingham. Ritchie had died unexpectedly from fever in September 1837 during his experiments on the manufacture of this glass, hoping to produce lenses to surpass those made on the continent, from where at present 'English opticians were dependent when a large object glass is to be worked'.[165] William Simms bought up most of Ritchie's stock of flint glass in order to compare it with discs made by Guinand (then at Neufchatel), by the Stangate Glassworks near Lambeth, and by the Falcon Glass House, Whitefriars. Although 'there were several pieces of very excellent crown',[166] only three of the twenty-nine discs of flint glass were reasonably free of striae and veins, and after much mathematical reduction of these, he was forced to the conclusion that Ritchie's glass was no different from other discs made in England. Ultimately a government commission refused to provide funds for further experimental work on the methods used, taking into account Simms' report, and that of Dr Samuel King on a telescope constructed by Dolland with an object glass made by Ritchie's method.

As always William's exposition was clear and humane, and when he sat down having completed his report to the Society, he was followed on the dais by a colleague, Edward Dent FRAS, the maker of fine clocks and chronometers, who was to compare results on the transit clocks of the observatories of Greenwich, Edinburgh and Makerston.

Later in June, William slipped out again for the RAS Council, perhaps glad of an excuse to forget his troubles at home, and to meet his friends, and also in July, but that month he felt unable to stay a night away from home, with Ann so ill, and sent his nephew, William, to Cambridge to fix the chronometer on the telescope and attend to all the wishes of Professor Challis.[167] William Henry, he supposed 'was by now in Ireland, making a tour for a few weeks',[168] no doubt calling in at Armagh, Birr Castle and Markree on his way.

As anxieties for this son and for Ann heaped upon William's head, yet he was able to appreciate the deep sorrow of the Airys who had just lost their little boy, Charles. They took the child's body back to Playford, near Ipswich, to be buried adjacent to the house where they had had so much happiness, and whilst they were there, Richard Sheepshanks paid one of his frequent visits to William's workshop. This time, however, he brought the devastating news that the Airy's elder son, George, had succumbed to the same infection as his brother, and died whilst at Playford for Charles' funeral.[169] This double tragedy left William deeply affected. He knew these two boys, and as always with children, was fond of them.

Armagh Observatory.

Alas, now it was his own turn to mourn in this year of continual trouble and upset. His life was shattered as his beloved Ann increasingly became more and more jaundiced and weak and sickly, until on 23rd August she died, leaving William to care for their eight children. The eldest, William Henry, was nineteen, and very uncertain of himself or his future; the youngest, Caroline, was only four months. In between these two came Elizabeth Ann, aged fifteen, Sarah aged thirteen, James eleven, Frederick eight, Ann six and Mary three. Even in these days of high maternal mortality, but after seven previous successful births, it was an unforeseen calamity.

Ann's death was one of the earliest to be recorded officially since compulsory national registration commenced in England only two years previously. It was a new-fangled arrangement with which the servants had to deal, rather than the nearest and dearest of the departed. Examining the blotted and badly-written certificate of Ann's death, one feels that the registrar, Septimus Wray, had not yet got into the way of things, whilst Sarah Newall, who had been present at the death, was unable to sign her name and had to make her mark as an X.

The cause of death is interesting. It was registered as 'diseased liver'. Since she had given birth only four months previously, one is drawn to the conclusion that the two events were connected. She had certainly been ill enough in late pregnancy to keep William at home, and may have had severe toxaemia, or even eclamptic fits, which could have left her liver badly damaged. Chloroform was just beginning to be recognised, and although Queen Victoria was the first Royal personage to have it administered at the birth of Prince Leopold in 1853, it was first officially used in childbirth in 1847 before its potential dangers were known, and it is possible that even earlier it was sometimes a part of a medical man's armamentarium. A delayed effect of high dosage could be liver necrosis. Another fascinating possibility, in view of the fact that her granddaughter-to-be, her son James' daughter, Eleanor, died at thirty-five from cancer of the pylorus (confirmed by last minute ameliorative surgery in 1899) is that this also was cancer, either of the pylorus, pancreas or the liver itself. A less likely cause was malaria, which still lurked in the marshes of the lower Thames, but more common would be an infectious hepatitis culled from the unhygienic drains and water supply, or even due to Weil's disease from the rats living in the Fleet ditch, now covered since 1766, but still draining the area including the Fleet Prison on its east bank.

Whatever the cause of Ann's death at so relatively early an age as forty-one, it altered the family's life. As William had no sisters to call upon in this emergency (the only two, the twins born in 1795 had died in infancy), much of the housekeeping must have devolved on young Elizabeth Ann. William's brother, John, who lived only round the corner in Peterborough

147

Court and Christian (when she was not busy with her own growing family), would have been a valuable source of practical advice. George and Sophia, being childless now their only baby, Emma Victoria, had died, had no experience upon which to draw. James and Catherine, who lived with George and Sophia at Greville Street, were likely to provide more support since their two eldest children William and Sarah (1819) were grown-up, and only Emma (aged ten) a child. Henry was in any case working at 136 but a bit of a bumbler; and his poor wife, Mary, was too fully tied up with her own ailing children to be much use. Possibly Ann's sister, Caroline Nutting came to take over the reins temporarily but she had her own family concerns at home, now 2 West Square, between Lambeth and Newington. Somehow therefore Elizabeth Ann had quickly to learn how to manage to deal with the servants needed to run this large household, and undoubtedly Sarah Newall, the old retainer from Shropshire, was her best ally.

Ann's death was registered in St Brides parish, where her funeral service was held. St Bride's graveyard was however nearly full, as can be seen by the present height of the paving above the level of the neighbouring pathway. Burials there actually ceased in 1853, after which the City of London Cemetery at Little Ilford came into use in 1856. There were in addition private concerns who owned burial grounds. One of these with a high reputation was the South Metropolitan Cemetery Company which purchased a large area of land in 1837 at Norwood, about eight miles south of the City, way out in the country near Sydenham and Dulwich. It was a beautiful area on a gently sloping north-facing hill, and with trees and grass and a carefully planned pattern of curving coachways and paths leading up from the impressive and massive wrought-iron entrance gates in Norwood Road. It became the resting place for eminent mid-Victorians, who were commemorated by equally imposing, even majestic, memorials, mini-temples and lofty mausoleums. There is an account of Mr and Mrs Charles Dickens attending the funeral here in 1857 of Douglas Jerrold, the actor and playwright, a grand affair of which Dickens spoke very strongly of the extravagant way it had been conducted. 'Mourners had worn bands of black crepe round their arms with the initial DJ, and the car for the coffin was like that provided for the Duke of Wellington.' After the ceremony Hans Anderson who was Dickens' guest, was driven by Mrs Dickens to the Crystal Palace for the first of the Handel festivals when *The Messiah* was given before an audience of 12,000 persons.

Ann Simms' funeral was less ostentacious. William chose a beautiful site for her grave at Norwood, at the top of the hill near to where a chapel was later built. It was far away from the gate, and peacefully reposed facing the distant view of the City she knew so well. Next to it was a broad drive which was, much later, dug up and used for further burials. He bought a plot 6 ft 6 ins × 2 ft 6 ins at the cost of three guineas in 'Square 64' of consecrated ground, the depth of the grave being 20 feet, which would in time be able to accommodate eight adult burials. The following year he purchased a further strip of one foot, so that the total area of the vault was 7 ft 6 ins × 3 ft 6 ins, at a cost of £4. The reason for this extra space was most likely so that it could accommodate a table slab commemorative stone. Sadly this has now (1989) completely disappeared, but in its stead have grown up many forest trees, whilst beneath them there is a riot of blackberry bushes and wild shrubs. Ann's grave is clear of overgrowth and difficult to locate except in relation to other named graves on the official plan. (A new, inscribed headstone was placed on the grave in February 1992.) It is opposite another huge stone slab the other side of what was once the central drive, and which is inscribed to Thomas England. It appears likely that this Simms vault is to be next in line for further modern interments. However, in spite of this intrusion, the place remains a quiet resting place, unaffected by present-day traffic and bustle, as it was the day she was laid there.

★　　★　　★　　★

After Ann's death there is a gap in the archives until Airy, who most certainly did not mix business with personal affairs, had on 3rd October written to William to complain about his billing for the Northumberland telescope. 'You really must learn to frame estimates letters – – – the great excess above the estimate is exceedingly vexatious',[170] he complained. The annual accounts at the Observatory meant that Airy had to keep within his budget. William seemed to throw up the slipper, and announced in reply that it would have to wait a few days while he went down to Margate[171] to see his children whose usual summer holiday had perforce had to be postponed this year. However, in spite of his inclination to answer Airy in kind, his usual good humour reasserted itself, and when he had calmed down he returned to his desk before catching the coach, to try to explain to the unsympathetic Airy that his workmen's time was hard to judge in advance, and that preparation of the workshop for a job of this size and complexity took up more than a third of the cost of the project. He conceded that thereby his premises were improved, and he was therefore 'not anxious to press the item at all, or any part of it'.[172]

It seems that as usual Airy got his way, or at any rate a compromise was reached, whereby William did not charge for the carpenters work.[173] One suspects that he got the worst of the deal, due to his dislike of anything approaching a row. Poor William. His affairs seem to have been in a muddle in spite of Henry, who probably was not a forceful character. They both appear to have inherited the placid outlook of their country forebears at Ayston, but things could not just be left to look after themselves. In mid-December he had to admit to Airy that he had lost the estimate for a double image eyepiece and position circle.[174] Airy supplied the answer without doubt from his filing system, but one can sense his sigh of irritation. It was a trifling contretemps compared with the unhappy events in both their lives this year, and perhaps both men were edgy and ready for the short break at Christmas.

149

CHAPTER 13

1840-1841

AFTER ALL THE ANXIETIES OF 1839, the New Year started on an optimistic note by the reception at the Cambridge Observatory of a communication from Alnwick Castle written on the last day of the old year. His Grace the Duke of Northumberland wished his appreciation to be conveyed to the Vice-Chancellor at St John's College and to the Syndicate of the Observatory, for the completion of the telescope and building, 'which I presented to the University'.[175] Praise indeed from their noble benefactor.

This cheerful mood was reflected in the popular attitude to the forthcoming marriage of the Queen to Prince Albert of Saxe-Coburg, her cousin through her mother's family. Less fervent than the preparations for the Coronation twenty months previously, yet there was acute interest from a personal point of view as if to one of the family, in the wedding of their young sovereign. Victoria was petite, vivacious and not quite twenty-one. Her bridegroom was good-looking, upright, and if an unknown quantity, at least preferred to the Duchess, his future mother-in-law. Besides which, the English were a romantic nation, and revelled in this young love, particularly the Londoners who could watch her driving from Buckingham Palace to the Chapel Royal at St James', clothed in her white wedding dress trimmed with lace, happily bowing to the onlookers despite the February rain. Later, after a reception at the Palace, the young couple emerged in their carriage, she now in a white travelling dress and bonnet edged with swansdown, and surrounded by well-wishers on horseback or in gigs, en route for Windsor. A group of Simms children must inevitably have been amongst the cheering crowds to watch them pass by. At last the gloom of the previous year was lifted, and the six months mourning being at an end, the Fleet Street family returned to a routine life.

The last year had been so busy that it was a relief to William when in January 1840 the latest biennial elections to the Council of the Royal Astronomical Society did not include him. Now he was both mother and father to his children in so many ways, he really could not afford the extra time required to attend the council meetings, which swallowed several hours of precious daylight each time they occurred. The following six years' relief from office was welcome, although he remained a faithful member of the Society, and was religiously present at virtually all their ordinary gatherings at Somerset House. At these meetings he was amongst friends as well as clients, one of whom was Sir John Herschel Bart, son of the renowned astronomer, Sir William Herschel, who had discovered Uranus in 1781. It is typical of events that William now found himself in January advising Sir John on the best instrument for his investigations into the Law of Refraction. The 36-inch theodolite suggested by Sir John is too small, but the 3-ft meridian circle has an azimuth of 2-ft, which would best answer his requirements. William's letter is short and to the point, and dispatched by post on the 27th to Herschel's home at Slough.[176] As important to astronomy as his father, Sir John pioneered the study of the physical constitution of the stellar universe, and although working in a separate field from Airy, served as one of the Visitors to the Royal Greenwich Observatory.[177]

Shortly after this correspondence, Francis Baily arranged with William to use part of his premises for his experiments on the Neopolitan Standard Scale.[178] This he was comparing with the Standard belonging to the RAS, to which he had originally contributed. Measurement had long been an interest of William's, following in the footsteps of Troughton who had made the five-feet Standard Scale for Sir George Shuckburgh in 1796, which became the foundation of all subsequent scales owing to its extreme accuracy. Indeed it was barely five years since the extensive investigation of Baily's own scale, made for him by William (see Chapter 10). Troughton & Simms' technical design book has several instances of work on the subject of survey measurement and computing scales, ordnance chains and measuring calipers, and bars for measuring baselines,[179] particularly around 1850, when William's son, James, acquired a life-long interest in metrology. It was also in 1840 that William Gravitt came to Fleet Street to discuss his new 'Dumpy' Level,[180] the forerunner of which was Troughton's Improved Level, introduced about 1812.[181] The function of the surveying level is to find the horizontal. Troughton had already improved on earlier models by introducing the long spirit bubble into the tube of the telescope, and mounting a compass firmly on four legs over the tube. He erected the whole instrument rigidly on its supports. Gravitt's new level advanced further by using a short telescope tube of only 12 inches with a large aperture object glass and short focal length, so that it had the light and power of a larger instrument without the inconvenience of its greater length. Its short squat shape soon gave it the nickname of the Dumpy Level, which it affectionately retained to this day. William Simms now co-operated with Gravitt to make his new instrument which eventually superseded all previous levels because of its light weight and ease of use in the field.

Like all parents of large families, William never seemed to be entirely free of anxieties over his brood. No sooner had one trouble subsided than another raises its head. William Henry was back at Pembroke this term as usual, with his health 'quite re-established',[182] but he was fidgety and unsettled, although the Challises kept an eye on him, and reported back to William. He returned again to Pembroke for the summer term, but then left it for good at the end of May 1840, though there is no suggestion that he was rusticated or sent down. He was plainly a great worry to his long-suffering father because of his erratic ways, and it seems very likely now that his troubles had all been largely of a psychological nature, and not primarily due to physical illness.

William Henry's little sister, Ann, who was six years old had on the other hand for some time been causing a different kind of concern. The child was not robust, and the death of her mother cannot but have affected her. Ever since her baby sister's birth the household had been upset, first with illness, then death, and then with all the traumas of a normal family life. William had written to Mrs Challis in the autumn of 1839 to ask her advice about his little Ann, and from her motherly being received sensible words of wisdom which evidently helped, as Ann came through that winter quite well – 'much more comfortably than I had reason to expect'.[183] She was delicate, and the London fogs must have exaccerbated her bad chest. She needed the extra care such a child was given in those early Victorian days; many layers of woolly clothing, hot compresses, and the good old kaolin inhalations, camphorated oil rubbed on her chest, and extra rest. To the fore in the family doctors' prescriptions now came his advice for some sea air, and in August, William took four of his children to Hastings for a fortnight; probably Mary and Ann, and the two younger boys, James and Frederick. Hastings was now coming into its own as a resort, and family holidays were de rigeur. Although garments for the occasion remained formal, and hats and boots were worn on the beach, there began to appear the bathing machines that the Regency period had made popular at Brighton, and which subsequently became commonplace at all watering places. The atmosphere was relaxed and happy. Lodgings were taken within easy reach of the beach, and the fresh air and the southern sun positively enabled William to revive and enjoy his children. He had left his nephew William (1817) to look after things at Fleet Street, under the eagle eye of his Uncle Henry, who was rather apt to put a spoke in William junior's enormous wheel of self-confidence, but knew that William senior (1793) could be quickly brought back home by means of a note sent by hand on the coach. Alternatively he could try out the new, official, postal service.

The passage of letters had by this spring been reorganised by Sir Rowland Hill, and the systems passed into law on 10th January. The new Penny Post commenced on 6th May, by which a uniform rate of 1d per ounce, pre-paid by a stamped envelope or stamped paper at a recognised post office, ensured its delivery in the town of the addressee. Up to now there had been a multiplicity of out-of-date postal laws and methods of sending mail, often haphazard and unreliable, depending largely on which area one lived. The most common method was by the mail-coach, the earliest of which had commenced the run from Bristol to London in 1784, carrying only four inside passengers, and an armed guard on top. This was a daily service, and travelled both ways, taking about sixteen hours each journey. The arrangement was so eminently superior to sending letters by the ordinary crowded stage-coach, that it was rapidly introduced on an increasing number of routes. As late as 1800 one would see the postman, wearing his official hat and jacket, ringing his bell in all the main City streets, and offering for a penny to take mail to the General Post Office then in Lombard Street. London Penny Post was particularly slack, and had many receiving houses for mail, often merely a sack left in a local inn which was handy for the coaching station. There were five principle offices, the chief at Throckmorton Street off Bartholomew Lane, and also at Westminster, Soho, Queen Street near the Tower, St Saviour's Church, Borough, and Temple Office in Clare Market just off The Strand.

William's early letters often show the brown triangular 'paid' mark, but later ones merely say 'Post Paid'. More often he used personal messengers including his own workmen, which was more convenient, quicker and reliable, but Clare Market was his nearest official office, and a boy could quickly be sent down through Temple Bar, turning right up through Clement's Inn, to post a letter there. Envelopes were only just appearing in 1840 and were not by any means universally used.

In Hastings William was allowed to put work to the back of his mind. It was a lovely place for a family holiday, with plenty to watch around the fishing harbour, and above it the old Norman Castle to climb and explore, whilst out to sea there were larger vessels, either sail or steam, or a combination of both, passing by on their way to the Solent. His thoughts even so may have wandered to Cambridge to where he had recently introduced Professor Bartlett from West Point Academy, so that he could discuss with Professor Challis the erection and equipping of an observatory in the United States.[184] Where, William wondered, would this be? His connections with North America had continued since Troughton's work for the US Coastal Survey between 1812 and 1815,[185] and it seems likely he kept in contact continually with transatlantic progress in optical work.

William returned home on 15th August, leaving the children in the care of one of their Simms' aunts, probably Aunt Caroline Nutting, to enjoy the rest of the summer at Hastings. The last months of the year become remarkably devoid of recorded activities until one realises that the time was filled with planning for a move from No. 136 in the near future. The lease of these premises would come to an end at Christmas 1843, and it had become all too clear that both house and workshops were inadequate for his large household, the servants that were now required for its upkeep, and the

153

continually increasing amount of trade he was attracting. The workshops consisted of a multiplicity of small rooms and outbuildings in the big yard at the back, scattered in a higglety-pigglety fashion, without foreplanning. It was also noisy, being next to Peterborough Court (later incorporated into the *Daily Telegraph* building), and the conditions must have left much to be desired.

About this time, a larger house, with an extensive yard, became free two doors to the west. These premises had belonged to Mr Bundy, a travelling-trunk manufacturer, and William hurried to buy. His nephew, William (1817), reported him in his diary as having built a new house and factory on the site, but there is no evidence of this, and a print of the street facades shows that the whole row of houses maintain the pleasant and sturdy uniformity of Georgian design, still to be seen in a photograph of 1923, although by now there are alterations. All these neighbouring buildings were of equal depth from front to back, and it seems more likely that he revamped the house for his own requirements, retaining all that he could of the older house, thereby saving himself expense. The land at the back was used to enlarge his workshop floor space and improve the layout and conditions generally.

No. 136 was a two-bay house; No. 138 was three-bay. Both houses had four good-sized floors not counting the basements, and No. 138 was double-fronted on the ground floor, although oddly, the front door was not quite central. Both houses had steps at the back up from the basement to the yard, but no front 'area' steps. He even built a new 'little gazebo' on the roof – but London was becoming so filthy now the steam-engines were belching forth their grime to add pollution to the smokey air, that it may have been necessary in any case to take his instruments elsewhere for examination. At any rate, now that he was free from the Sir James South debâcle and had received his payment through the Court, he was able to finance his new building with ease.

Early in 1841, William moved the family temporarily into lodgings, and took on new subtenants at No. 136 Fleet Street, whilst the dust and dirt of the building at No. 138 was in progress. About the same time, John and Christian Simms purchased No. 141, and moved round with their present quota of seven children and one little live-in maid of seventeen, leaving the noisy house which Troughton had first leased them in Peterborough Court, thankfully behind. Their new house was over the entrance to Wine Office Court, much of which John and his son George subsequently bought up for their agency business, using the old wine warehouses for storage. Along the passage from their house was the famous Cheshire Cheese Inn, built over part of the remains of the old priory of the White Friars and with the aroma of its famous saddles of lamb and barrows of beef daily roasting.

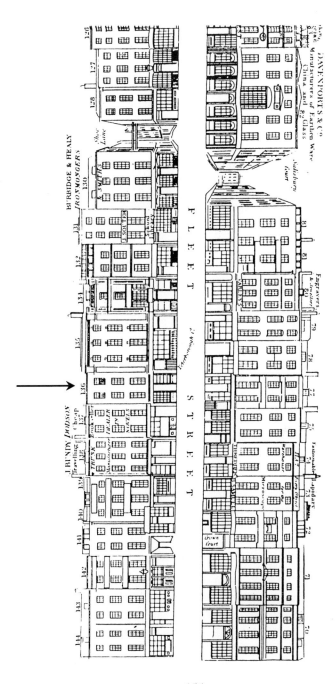

Fleet Street – Tallis's Street Views, 1838-40.

155

William's ground-lease for No. 138 Fleet Street ran from Christmas Day 1841 for eighty years, and in the event the house was occupied by the firm precisely until Christmas 1921. The ground rent, due each Midsummer Day, was fixed at £150 per annum, payable to the landlord, the Parish of St Bride. The tenant was to insure the premises, the Parish to include the cost of the insurance with their other property at the 'Hand-in-Hand' office, and to add the amount to the rent each year. The vestry clerk was to retain the policy.

This move of William's serves to demonstrate the rapidly increasing wealth of the country as a whole at the beginning of the Victorian era, leading eventually to enormous prosperity for the remaining decades of the century. Britain was becoming the workshop of the world, and William's blossoming affluence only mirrors that of employers as a whole. The world wanted goods from this country because of the expertise it knew was here, and British manufacturers worked hard to provide for their clients. Labour and raw materials were cheap. Enterprise and ability did the rest. Nevertheless the years between 1839 and 1843 were known as the Hungry Forties, the harvests were poor, and there was much agitation for the repeal of the Corn Laws to bring down the price of bread. This did not occur for another six years after William's move to No. 138, and by then he had plenty of reasons to move out of London altogether. He had now the foresight to extend his ability to provide all the instruments he could for the opening up of the world of the British Empire, and the exploration and road-building that followed. In addition there was now the entrance of the railways into the equation, whilst the huge increase in ship-building and navigation developed in conjunction with world trade, provided a never-ending demand for his products. His new factory was his answer to this demand, and he had the vision to meet the challenge. It is difficult to judge just how many men he now employed at Fleet Street. Certainly he still had to parcel out work to other firms and colleagues such as clockmakers and dial-makers, and nor did he have more than a small foundry, or space for large items. The census of 1851 does not help, and one can only make a guess based on the manner in which he was able, almost without fail, to send a workman at a moment's notice to Greenwich or Cambridge or any one of his private clients when circumstances demanded. When the larger factory was later built at Charlton by his son, James, it employed a hundred men, so it seems reasonable to suppose that the Fleet Street factory accommodated at least fifty men and boys, a far cry from the few apprentices and journeymen employed by Troughton before 1826. The hunger for accurate mathematical instruments throughout the world was insatiable.

The various archives reveal little to indicate the difficulties encountered in running the business during this year when presumably the old workshops were still in use, and then gradually work moved over to the new factory. The only indication of such complications is in the dearth of correspondence remaining from that year of 1841. Part of the house at 136 was sublet to a young couple, John and Sarah Heptalwight, and their thirteen year old daughter, Diana. He was a painter, perhaps working for William at this period. 138 was not included in the national census which had its initial run that year, for obvious reasons. The bricklayers were busy there. Probably a number of William's own men were transferred to building work, and certainly his joiners would take on the carpentry for the new constructions. The rest of them carried on with the orders constantly arriving on William's desk, and were required to keep the normal flow of work under control. Henry seems to have retained his place in the front shop, but the only letter from him this year which has survived is one to the Astronomer Royal, tactfully headed 'Fleet Street', without a qualifying number. It was merely to inform him that 'Mr Simms' was out of town, but had given instructions to Messers Maudesleys (the iron founders) 'to prepare the bar or bars for the Magnets'.[186]

In July William had another visitor from the United States, a Mr Cranch of Cambridge, Massachussetts. Mr Cranch was one of those wealthy and intelligent men who were independent enough to use their money to further their interests in astronomy, and travelled where they willed. He was probably referred to William by Mr Hassler, the director of the US Coastal Survey, and well worth William's while to cultivate as owning or planning to build an observatory of his own, would be very likely to order equipment from him. As so often, William was able to advise, and then set him off on the coach to Cambridge, bearing an explanatory note to Professor Challis[187] requesting him to show the American round the Observatory.

Practical optics must have been vested with problems for the workmen this year, with dust a worse than usual hazard. The everyday orders had to be fulfilled so that the firm's income was maintained. Much of the bread-and-butter work was for repairs to instruments previously constructed by the firm, or sometimes by other instrument makers; at other times there were modifications required in the light of the owners' experience, or for some particular occasion such as for the solar eclipse expected in July next year. Greenwich was perpetually named in the order book, this October for work on the micrometer of the zenith instrument.[188] About the same time a transit instrument by Ramsden belonging to Mr Froude required repair.[189] William Froude was an engineer at present working for Brunel on the Bristol and Exeter railway, and a friend of Frederick Walter, and it can be assumed that the faulty part was detached from the main frame by one of the workmen, who brought it back to Fleet Street for the work to be done, after which it was carefully packed and returned by the same man, who refitted it and tested it in situ. Another of the men was engaged in making a new 7-inch sextant for Professor Schumacher's observatory this autumn.[190] William found that workmanship was of a much higher standard if the same man followed a job through from beginning to end, fulfilling a pride in its efficiency. Very often the man's name is included in the notes in the workbook or correspondence – this time it was Hawkins.[191] This induced a personal interest in each instrument (as well as the reference for problems), and generally a family atmosphere in the factory at large. There was no question of a production line in this very specialised business. Every product was carefully given the full attention of its individual maker, and very often with the full co-operation of the client who frequently had drawn his own design, and knew exactly what he wanted by way of construction or repair. Airy was a prime example of a customer who had a precise notion of his requirements. Occasionally William had to point out difficulties or inadequacies obtaining to its execution, and advise some modification, but usually he fell in with what Airy ordered.

Just now William was working on methods of illuminating the lines in a dark field,[192] and notes of his thoughts were copied down into the workbook so that the senior designer could check his methods. Into this fascinating compendium went notes on all sorts of work in hand, the exact size of a diaphragm sent for repair by Captain Boileau of the Bengal Engineers, now working on the Survey of India; the design of a pediometer for one of the Surveys, probably that of Ireland, using a scale of three chains to an inch; instructions for refilling one of Troughton's mountain barometers, written out in careful longhand – 'If there is any reason to suspect that moisture is lurking in the quicksilver, expel it by a heat of about 220 etc. etc.'[193] – instructions sent to Major Sabine in Ireland for his magnetic theodolite, or for the Ordnance Survey Signal Station telescopes; diagrams of the protractor for the Royal Marines at Portsmouth, or for a Dipping Needle (to show the inclination of the magnetic needle to the horizon at any given place) sent to Mr Heron at Glasgow. Troughton's rain gauge, a pendulum by Thomas Jones (for repair?), an artificial horizon (see Chapter 8) for Mr Sheepshanks, now living at Reading with yet another observatory attached to his house, and a level for the Royal Military Academy at Woolwich. Such was the range of orders coming in, and when at the beginning of 1842 the last of the work-benches were transferred through to the new factory behind No. 138, it must have been with a sigh of relief that William and his men watched the departure of the builders, and settled down into the craft for which they had been trained, now in much improved conditions of space and arrangement.

CHAPTER 14

1842-1843

LONDON WAS STILL SUBJECT TO agitations and mob violence in spite of improved control of disturbances by Peel's policemen. Ever since 1839, there had been bad harvests and rising cost of bread. The Corn Laws still prevailed, ostensibly to 'maintain the price of food', so that the labourers in farms or factory suffered increasing deprivation and hunger, and moreover foreign trade was being hampered by the rising cost-of-living at home, which in turn affected the industrial well-being in the towns. The axiom of free trade was being purveyed across the country and at Westminster, and every now and then burst out into angry scuffles.

Intertwined with the Anti Corn Law reformers were the Chartists who demanded democratic government. They aimed to extend the franchise to every man regardless of status, to have secret ballots, and gain freedom from the property qualifications for parliamentary candidates. They also insisted on wages for Members, and argued for equality of numbers in each electoral districts so that the remaining Rotten Boroughs/Districts should go. Poverty was once again being tackled, but for the government to increase its activity in this field, it needed more income.

Up to now a large number of commodities had been taxed to provide funds, including glass which most affected William, but also leather, paper and timber, all used in his business. Various foods attracted import duty, and the whole system was complicated. Since 1815, at a time when the cost of the army and navy had decreased, and the old Property and Income tax levied in 1803 to prepare for the threatened invasion by Napoleon, had been withdrawn, there had been no specific tax on wealth. Now in 1842 Peel reimposed an income tax of 7d in the £, but at the same time removed excise duty on no fewer than 750 articles. Many raw materials as a result now came into the country free of duty, and manufactured goods had a common rate of 10% tax, thus greatly simplifying the system. Only the Corn Laws doggedly remained for the present, but at a reduced level; soon, however, even they were overtaken by events. Peel paid the price for his reforms, and was voted out of office, but because of his foresight, exports which had been static in amount and range since Waterloo, began to expand in a constant and

159

ultimately vast degree, and with agriculture also improving, the coming prosperity of the 1850s and 1860s was set in motion.

William Simms was far too gentle to be a political animal, though as a City manufacturer he probably had Whig sympathies. The present laws of duty and tax affected him directly in his business as well as personally, and he approved of the abolition of tariffs even if he did not exactly welcome the tax on his income. Unfortunately for him the excise duty on glass was one of the few items not rescinded this year, and he had to continue to pay high prices for it until 1846. Nevertheless this January 1842 saw him at his most genial. Having consulted the order books, he composed two accounts for work completed at the Cambridge Observatory, and sent them to Challis 'with respects to Mrs Challis, and my regards to the young people – – – Wishing you many happy New Years'.[194] Four days later he was able to pack the finished wire plate of the transit instrument in a piece of tubing for safety, and send it on the coach, aptly named The Telegraph, to Cambridge.[195] By the end of the month, a clamp for the Northumberland telescope followed on the same coach, together with instructions for using the 'finger and thumb method' for its handling.[196]

Normally William seems to have sent small goods by one of the ordinary stage-coaches, but if speed was of the essence, then he resorted to the mail-coach. This stopped every 7-10 miles for fresh horses along the way, thereby increasing its overall average rate to 8 or 9 mph. It carried usually only four passengers, and if they were overlong in stretching their legs at one of the staging posts, the coach was liable to leave without them, as punctuality was paramount, and remarkably often adhered to. The velocity with which they travelled could, however, be uncomfortable, even dangerous, and it was not unknown for a mail-coach to topple over, particularly at corners. But that was in some passengers' eyes compensated for by the speedy arrival at their destination and the security of having a guard armed with a couple of blunderbusses. For some of the more delicate pieces of apparatus which William wished to send to the various observatories, damage was less likely to occur on the stage-coaches, and long-distance passengers also preferred the stage-coach, which trotted along at about 12 mph, and from which he would be provided with meals en route and a comfortable bed at a staging inn for the night. On the mail you sometimes received a quick meal, but more often you took a picnic to eat while travelling. In the 1840s about twenty-seven of these mail-coaches left the new GPO buildings in St Martin-le-Grand every evening at eight o'clock, having loaded up with passengers and luggage from the neighbouring inns. The booking office was in nearby Little Britain off Aldersgate. The coaching inns mentioned by William Simms included the White Horse in Fetter Lane which was only a short walk from his home, the Bull and Mouth in St Martin-le-Grand, the Cross Keys in Wood Street (rather further off, near Cheapside), and the famous Belle Sauvage on Ludgate Hill, in a room off the tiered courtyard of which John Simms ran his agency business. There was also the Bolt in Turn in Fleet Street. The statistics of some of these coaching firms was remarkable. William Chaplin, who owned the White Horse, and in 1825 also bought the renowned Swan with two Necks in Lad Lane, the Spread Eagle in Gracechurch Street, and the Cross Keys in Wood Street, had an underground stable for 200 horses, and in 1830 employed 2,000 people, 1,800 horses, and had part ownership of no less than 68 coaches. Another owner patronised by William Simms, Edward Sharman at the Bull and Mouth, sent his coaches on long-distance hauls to the north of the country, including Holyhead, Manchester, Liverpool, and the Scottish cities, and it will have been on one of these coaches that Simms or his workmen, and certainly his brother, Frederick Walter, travelled to Ireland during the Survey. The Manchester Telegraph left London at 5.00 am, and reached its destination that evening at 11.00 pm, having covered 186 miles at an AVERAGE speed of 10 mph, a quite astonishing achievement. The early Victorian travellers must have been extremely resilient to withstand this sort of treatment, and required the ability to cat nap between the many stages to remain in good condition on arrival. That they continually were making such journeys says much for their enthusiasm for adventures.

Tough the travellers may have been, but in March 1842 William Simms was so unwell as to be unable to go even up to Greenwich to check a micrometer, and had to send his nephew, William, in his place.[197] He was at the time engaged in making an equatorial for his old acquaintance, John Wrottesley[198] for whom he had previously provided certain instruments for his new observatory at Blackheath ten years ago. Wrottesley was a lawyer who was one of those who assisted in the founding of the Astronomical Society, and was its secretary from 1831 to 1841, when he became its president for the usual two-year stint. 1841 was a busy year for him as he also succeeded to his father's title as Third Baron Wrottesley in March, became a Fellow of the Royal Society in April, and thereafter removed his observatory to the family estates at Wrottesley Hall in Staffordshire. His astronomical work, though as an amateur, enabled him to catalogue certain fixed stars, for which he had received the Gold Medal of the Royal Astronomical Society in 1839. His new equatorial was of 129-inch focal length by 7½-inch aperture, and when completed at Fleet Street, was loaded onto Reeves' cart, and transferred in the care of a workman to Stafford, where doubtless William was pleased to visit its owner.

By June William was well again, and hoped to complete another clamp for the Northumberland telescope by the end of the month.[199] He was having difficulty in dividing the vernier for the hour circle of the equatorial as his engine was not large enough for the purpose, and he asked if he could borrow 'the other vernier' from Professor Challis from which to copy the divisions. But Mrs Challis who kept a motherly eye on William, thought he needed a holiday, and invited him up to stay with them at Cambridge.

161

However, much as he would have enjoyed a visit there where he felt so much at home, his younger children were down at Brighton for the summer, and he wanted to spend every moment of spare time with them,[200] thoughtful as ever of their lack of a mother. Airy was at the Superga near Turin this month in order to observe the total solar eclipse on 8th July, so there was peace from that quarter just now, and William was able to work without interruption. He sent off the completed clamp to Cambridge by the 'Telegraph' on 8th July, enclosing also a book of Bessel's which he had borrowed,[201] and was then free to travel down to see the children, always a joy for him.

He was back in Fleet Street by the 28th July, sending off on the mail to Cambridge 'a steel spring with brass centre and screw'[202] requested by Challis. A small telescope recently completed for Mr Francis Beaumont was sent to Greenwich for checking.[203] Beaumont was mainly working on hydrography, but also in the determination of longitude, was a contributor to the Society for Diffusion of Useful Knowledge and a Fellow of the Royal Astronomical Society. In September he and his new telescope went off to the Continent for a tour, after which the instrument was to be returned to William for further review.[204]

In December came the final incident in the South equatorial saga, fully reported with undisguised glee by *The Times* three days before Christmas. William himself mentioned it quizzically in a letter to Airy on 15th December; indeed it was impossible to avoid the huge posters plastered everywhere in the Kensington area and some other parts of London as well as in the daily papers. At South's direction these advertised the public auction of the scrap that had been once his great equatorial at Camden Hill. Having crudely hacked to pieces the whole of the mounting, South organised its sale at his observatory, to be held on Wednesday, 21st December between 11 and 12 noon. The language of the advertisement was intemperate, to say the least, with quite extraordinary statements of a highly libelous character against Troughton & Simms, Airy, Sheepshanks and everyone to do with the 'botching up' of the instrument, and indicated the unbalanced personality of its perpetrator. It says much for his friends at the Royal Astronomical Society that they took it in good humour, and mounted no action against South. The sale went through, the heaps of metal being carefully weighed on a balance set up in the garden for the purpose, and a trail of scrap-metal dealers carted it away. The tube and circle had been wilfully damaged by his order, to prevent them being bought by an instrument maker and reused in their present form, but the brass with which they were made remained unsold even at 8d a pound.

To a man of William's temperament such wanton destruction of many hours patient craftsmanship, cannot but have been severely hurtful, yet his philosophical outlook enabled him to put the whole calamity behind him, and nowhere is there any evidence of vindictiveness as a result, only a kindly humour that any man could behave so ridiculously.

Sir James South remained a member of the RAS, and no doubt their paths met on occasion, but like most of his contemporaries, William did not take him seriously. After all, South had by his own actions lost £8,000 over the transaction, and this from a highly intelligent man. His later work included observation of various comets, and he showed some genuine approbation for instrument makers as a class after all in his letter to *The Times* of 16th April 1845 after examining the 6-ft reflector at the Earl of Rosse' seat at Birr Castle, in central Ireland.

A far greater tragedy than the psychotic ravings of a colleague was now darkening William Simms' life. His little girl, Ann, was visibly losing her battle against tuberculosis. Only ten years old, the illness was perhaps superimposed upon congenital defects of lungs or heart, as mention is several times made earlier of her chest complaints. John Nutting was the first of the household to die of phthisis, such an appallingly prevalent disease at this period, the cause of which was not yet recognised. Possibly Ann's mother had harboured the germ, but the scourge it was until the middle of the 20th century, is only too well demonstrated over precisely the same years in the Bronte family of Haworth, where the mother and two elder sisters died in 1821 and 1825 respectively, and then in quick succession Branwell and Emily died in 1848, Anne in 1849, and Charlotte in 1855. Its very name, 'consumption', was picturesquely correct, as the wasting and gradual decay of the victim's body took many months to occur, unless a sudden haemorrhage brought an abrupt end to his or her life. Sometimes there was partial healing, and an intermission of the hacking cough, and further episodes delayed. A child who was affected, usually went downhill fast, and in Ann's case, Christmas 1842 must have been entirely given over to her care, with the growing realisation that the wracking symptoms must soon cease of their own accord.

Ann Simms died on the last day of January 1843, nursed as always by Sarah Newall, who also visited the registrar's office next day to present the death certificate and sign the details with her mark. The little girl was buried on 6th February in her mother's grave on top of the hill at Norwood cemetery, and William went back to work with a sad heart. This was the third Ann who had died during his married life. His letters written in January never betray his personal feelings, with one exception; two days after the funeral, he wrote on black edged notepaper to Challis, a business letter to describe the method whereby the iron founders poured metal into moulds, ending 'I have lost my dear child who has been a sufferer from pulmonary disease. She died on Tuesday in the last week'.[205] A more emotional comment would have had less impact on the sympathetic family at the Cambridge Observatory. William was not an extrovert who easily showed his feelings.

Earlier letters that year never indicate the upset at home. It is tempting to feel some smugness on William's behalf when he writes on 7th January to the Astronomer Royal to mention the fact that Troughton & Simms' account with the Observatory for the quarter ending 30th September 1842 had not yet been paid.[206] The perfect Airy had been found wanting – a rare occurrence, and a pretty answer to the innumerable times he complained about William's slowness in delivery. It was comforting to know that Airy too was actually human.

At the time William was preparing a paper for the Royal Astronomical Society on a new arrangement for the altitude and azimuth instrument. This he read to the Society on 13th January 1843, concealing completely the deep grief in his soul now his little girl was fading away. It was a short exposition, accompanied by a model of the instrument and a large clear diagram. With these before his erudite audience he explained how he had perforated the vertical axis to fit the speculum 'with an achromatic object glass having a diaphragm in its focus, so as to serve in conjunction with the spirit-level upon the instrument as a vertical collimator'. Thus he could adjust the line of sight passing through the object glass.[207]

The paper was totally to the point and devoid of frills or emotion, and when it was published in the Society's Memoirs in 1846, the same flat restraint was evident.

The American government had by now decided on a site at Washington for their new observatory, and had appointed as director Lieutenant Gillies of the US Navy. He was to visit Oxford and Cambridge to study their observatories,[208] and called on Fleet Street in early January prior to travelling north, where William was able to show him the nearly completed transit instrument for Oxford. Now that Hassler had died during this year, the new connection with the United States was welcome to William as it initiated a series of orders, commencing immediately with a 5-ft mural circle for Washington, and another for West Point.[209] Maudesleys were to cast the metal parts in one piece in the near future.[210]

Meanwhile a correspondence was carried on between William Simms and William Bond of 'W.C. Bond & Sons' of Congress Street, Boston, Massachussetts who was in charge of the Harvard College Observatory instruments, and later became its director and then a professor at the College. At the London end, Joseph Cranch acted as go-between, and he and William Simms had discussed suitable instruments for Harvard in late May 1843 when the latter had proposed a transit circle of at least 3-ft, which, with four reading microscopes 'of the most perfect kind' prepared for fixing to stone piers, would cost £350. A zenith sector of 8-12-ft like that which Bradley, the 18th century Astronomer Royal, used at Greenwich, though with refinements, would cost not more than £400, 'perhaps less'. William recommended the shorter length for the zenith telescope as it would the more easily be reversed in direction, and would have an arc of vision of about 20 degrees at the 'zenith' of the sky, unlike the present one at Greenwich which had an exceedingly limited range of arc.[211] Further letters between Bond and William Simms do not appear that year in the Harvard Archives, and we find the next exchange in January 1845 when Bond placed a firm order for the transit circle and an equatorial telescope with William, the former to be similar to the one Troughton had made for Stephen Groombridge in 1806, but sturdier.[212]

Repair work for the East India Company filtered in – a theodolite for their steamship *Memnon* needed adjustment in both altitude and azimuth,[213] and a tell-tale to be made to show the position of the helm. This last was 'objectionable' as it did not work without banging the hand in its movements.[214] Three Standard Chains for the Admiralty required re-measuring under defined conditions of temperature, and adjusting. The temperature of the workshop was noted as being 53°F,[215] the month being January. The men at Fleet Street were certainly not pampered. There was also a connection with the Inspector of Artillery at Woolwich, Lt Colonel Dundas, who sent a list of the guns now in use, with the diameter of the bore of each, and of the shot in every case, and also an order for measuring calipers to check them.[216]

On 5th April William and his second son, James, went together up Ludgate Hill and round St Paul's to the new Goldsmith's Hall in Foster Lane, which had only just been rebuilt on its old site to replace the previous one erected after the Great Fire. This latest erection was sumptuous, with a beautiful livery hall and court room and a string of elegant reception rooms. How much of this splendour James would be able to see on this visit is uncertain, but he only had to look up from the street, especially at night, to see one of the great sparkling chandeliers and a fine stuccoed ceiling. Here James was officially bound Apprentice to his father 'to learn his art of an Optician for seven years from this day'. They then followed on to the Chamberlain's Office in Guildhall just round the corner, where they joined a small crowd of other fathers and fourteen year old sons, and waited their turn to enroll James' indenture. The terms of this contract were very similar to those which his father had sworn before him, and his uncles and his grandfather, and which James duly signed in the presence of Robert Michum for John Lane, Clerk to the Company of Goldsmiths in the City of London. This was the beginning of a life-long affinity between father and son, and for James the start of over seventy years connection with the firm of Troughton & Simms. Of the three sons of William and Ann Simms, he seems to have been the most able. Certainly he had the greatest application and single-mindedness. A serious and conscientious young man, he also had a quirky sense of humour rather like his father but quieter, but which like

165

him was always kindly directed, and never ever vicious. In later life James became much loved by his workmen and their wives, and by his own grandchildren, as much for his generosity of thought as in material matters. The biography of his grandson, James Simms Wilson,[217] who was so like him in character and looks, cites endless instances of his gentle manners which could provide amusement for himself as well as for others by quietly pointing to the absurdities of life.

★   ★   ★   ★

Airy was just now engaged in checking the major instruments at Greenwich, and recently had examined the divisions upon the declination circle of the Jones equatorial at Cambridge.[218] The readings being difficult to see, he told William to make a double microscope to ease matters, and this was duly sent up to Challis. Now Airy found the same problem with Troughton's zenith sector at Greenwich, and ordered an exact copy of the micrometer for this instrument as well.[219] William wrote to Challis on 16th March asking him to send the first micrometer down to him by the earliest available coach so that measurements could be taken for a replica, and the second micrometer was quickly made. The Cambridge one was given back to Challis when he called later in the summer, leaving an eyepiece with William as a further guide for cutting a screw.[220] Challis was a very much easier man to deal with than the Astronomer Royal whose peremptory demands could be most wearing. Like any good tradesman, William jumped to attention to carry out his wishes. With Challis the demands seem to have been wrapped up in warmth of approach, perhaps less business-like, but altogether more human. The First Assistant at Greenwich, Robert Main, was a combination of the two astronomers. He was entirely correct and clear in his official orders, and there was no excess verbiage in his letters, which are always precisely to the point, impersonal, and systematic.

'Gentlemen', his letter to William on 23rd November commenced. 'The Astronomer Royal directs me to request that you will have the goodness to send a person to the Observatory tomorrow the 24th inst. to do the following work:', which he then carefully enumerated 1, 2, 3. He ended by permitting himself the only flourish of the communication: 'I am, Gentlemen, Your obedient servant, Robert Main'.[221] Airy's letters by contrast are far more discursive, informal, and his thoughts immediately transferred to paper, though he usually ends in a formal manner, in the shortest possible way. He has to rush on to the next activity seething in his busy brain.

Division of the circle was a matter particularly on William's mind this year. For months, indeed years, he had been experimenting with methods of improving this most laborious task, which not only took up a great deal of

166

time, but had to be done with exact accuracy to achieve maximum results by the instrument in question. To the layman the problem appears at first sight to be simple to solve. If you want a circle to be divided into four you draw two lines across it at right angles to each other to form a cross; if in eight you bisect the right angles already formed; if sixteen you bisect the half-right angles – the 45 degree angles – and so on. But how do you divide a circle accurately into 360 degrees as you need to be able to do in any measurement of the world and its sky. Further, how do you then divide each degree into 60 minutes, and still be able to read the result with ease and precision, confident that you have the correct result, and that every minute has been given the same interval as every other minute, with no space left over. The complexity of this conundrum had been exercising the ingenuity of instrument makers for centuries, but notably for the last eighty years. Troughton's dividing engine completed in 1793 had been an improvement on Ramsden's eighteen years earlier, but still used enormous resources, mental and physical, of the operator. William Simms' dividing engine was essentially the same as Troughton's in broad design, though with further improvements, but its great advance was in the fact that it was self-activating, and could carry out the whole process without the personal exhaustion generated by previous models. Power was provided by a counter-pivoted weight, which as it fell, transferred energy to the machine. For many months he experimented with his ideas, finding that the power needed required so large a drop that he had to make use of the courtyard outside one of the upper windows of his house, whereby the weight could fall over several storeys to the ground. Where such height was not available, he accepted that a boy (James?) turning a winch could do as well, or of course steam power which was used in most modern factories, would negate the need for boy or weight.[222]

On 9th June 1843 William presented his Paper of his Self-Acting Circular Dividing Engine to a gathering of the Royal Astronomical Society. His exposition was clear, concise, and as usual, without a trace of self-aggrandisement. To read the script now, one of the startling features is its elegant prose in which the sentences are beautifully rounded, the vocabulary broad yet unequivocal, and the meaning entirely straight-forward. There is no doubt that, short as his school days were, he was well tutored in the English language, and must have read widely in the English classics to acquire such facility of literary style. His everyday letters also exhibit this same ease of expression, and every now and then include indications of a cultured repertoire. Unfortunately all his books other than scientific, passed after his death to Elizabeth Ann, and have been lost, but like all gentlemen of the time, he certainly owned a well-stocked library, which in his case was not only for show. If we may judge by some of his descendents, books on travel would particularly have commended themselves to him, and as very many of these were published in the mid-

Victorian period, he probably possessed a great number, with special reference to the places where his instruments were sent. His brother, Frederick Walter, had this same flare for perspicacous elegance of language, as can be seen in his scientific treatises which are clarity personified, but also in his book describing his journey to India.[223]

In June William was ready for a holiday, and took his family down to the Isle of Wight for the summer. Who exactly this included this year is problematic, but Elizabeth Ann (now nineteen) probably acted as mother of the party which consisted also of Frederick, Mary and Caroline. Sarah likely went as well. William as usual saw them settled into their boarding house, stayed a couple of weeks, and then returned home. The island was joining the popularity of other south coast resorts for family holidays, easily reached from London by the Portsmouth coach, and a rowing boat to Ryde. No one yet knew that Queen Victoria and Prince Albert were considering a home of their own, and at Peel's advice were about to buy Osborne House on the north-east coast of the island, with its marvellous views across the Solent to the ships sailing from Portsmouth, directly north of what became their main reception rooms. The lovely beaches and country walks appealed to the Queen just as much as they did to her more humble subjects, and the trip from Portsmouth was a thrilling adventure for town children. Thomas Cubitt, the builder of the new wings at Osborne was already well-known to William Simms as the man who had bought up six acres of the Barnsbury Estate some thirty years ago to build the terraces and squares where William had lived in Islington in the 20s. He will have watched the rise of the strange towers at Osborne in the following years with much interest.

Next month, on 19th July, the Prince Consort travelled from the new Paddington station by special train driven by Gooch and Brunel to Bristol, where with great ceremony and rejoicing, he launched the steamship, *Great Britain*. This huge vessel, made for the Liverpool to New York passenger trade, was merely one further indication of the country's growing domination of world commerce and manufacturing, and the Great Western Railway on which the Prince journeyed, one of the leading innovations of the new age of rail travel. It was however early days, though potential passengers were excitedly poised to use a number of lines being built, and which would open shortly. Moreover they were increasingly keen to buy up shares in the growing array of railway companies. In October William went to Paris to see Monsieur Guinand, the eminent manufacturer of glass. The journey was still fraught with hazard, as the line to Folkestone was only open to goods traffic and both that and the one to Dover from London Bridge did not have through trains until the following year. Even then Dover passengers had to make their own way from the town station to the quay, as the Admiralty Pier was not yet erected. From Dover they boarded one of the Admiralty mail packets which sailed daily to the continent, to find that the French railway had not yet come through to Calais. It would not do so for another five years and even then would follow a round-about route to Paris. Easier would be the Folkestone voyage to Bologne, though again there were difficulties at the embarkation port due to the steep ramp down to the boats which was not open to passenger trains until 1850. The new Folkestone harbour and hotel were in progress of being built, as William well knew, Frederick Walter being one of Cubitt's engineers on the project. The main line railway from Lille to Paris was already open, but neither Calais or Bologne were linked to it until 1848. This autumn of 1843 therefore, William would have to travel part of the French portion of the journey by coach, and probably took the Bologne crossing as involving the shorter distance to Paris. He had doubtless been to Folkestone many times in the course of its construction to see his brother's work, particularly the tunnelling which especially interested both men, and now the enormous earthworks being created for the harbour defences at Folkestone a source of absorbing fascination. His big burly form uncurled itself from the South-Eastern carriage which was little different from the horse coaches to which he was accustomed, and quite as uncomfortable, and slowly ambled round the vast dykes, his quizzical smile and his top hat giving little cause for comment to the navvies who were used to visitors.

Once in Paris he went to inspect M. Guinand's furnace where he produced optical flint and crown glass. William made full notes of all he had seen,[224] and had long discussions on the different methods of manufacture, polishing and the differing types of instrument for which the glass was suitable. How long he stayed in Paris is doubtful, but the whole journey from London, with a night on one or other side of the Channel had taken at least two days, so he is likely to have remained several nights. Whether he left any order with Guinand there is no reference. It may have been a preliminary canter, for it was another month before he received a note from Airy on 27th November asking him to come to see him 'either to my ½ past 3 dinner or in the evening, to talk over my Altitude and Azimuth Instrument',[225] William already knew of Airy's plans to acquire this instrument for Greenwich, but designs were at an early stage. He replied on 28th that he would be at the Observatory the following day 'at 5 o'clock or soon after'.[226] Unlike Airy he could not waste precious winter daylight with impunity. Plans went ahead, and William undertook to make a wooden model of the proposed instrument, and sent a firm order to Guinand for the object glass. A fortnight later, Airy went down to his uncle, Mr Biddall, at Playford, near Ipswich for the Christmas period, requesting any com-munications to be sent to him there.[227]

This was the first year that the Christmas card made its appearance. Designed by J. C. Horsley for his friend, Sir Henry Cole, Patron of the Arts, an edition of 1,000 copies were on sale in London that December. The words printed inside each card were much as they are today – 'A Merry Christmas and a Happy New Year to You' – the picture on the front one of family festivities. Decorations to celebrate Christmas had always been present in England, but the Christmas Tree, German and mediaeval in origin, and introduced into this country in the early 19th century, was much popularised by Prince Albert who saw to it that there was always one at Windsor. The Victorians decorated their Christmas trees with candles, candies and fancy cakes hung from the branches by ribbon and paper chains. These trees remained the centre of Yuletide rejoicings, becoming synonomous with the Family.

A year of mixed fortunes, 1843 was on the whole a memorable one, and anyhow there were still two small children in the Simms household as well as the older members of the family to enjoy the excitements of Christmas, so it was probably celebrated as usual even though small Ann was not there this year to join in. Numbers instead were augmented by the many young cousins who lived nearby – the children of James and Catherine, of John and Christian, of Henry and Mary, and of Frederick Walter and Caroline. For Elizabeth Ann in her position as 'Miss Simms', and proxy mother to the family, there were weeks of culinary preparations to be completed for such a large and festive gathering.

CHAPTER 15

1844-1845

AT THE BEGINNING OF JANUARY William wrote to Airy to let him know that the model of the altazimuth would shortly be ready for his inspection. Meanwhile much harrying of Guinand, the glass maker, produced no reply, and once again William wrote to him urgently that he needed suitable discs to work for the optical parts of the Greenwich altazimuth.[228] At the same time various pieces of modification for the Northumberland telescope were proceeding, including that on the rods, and he had also decided that the telescope circle arch was too large for his dividing engine, so that he was forced to construct an outrigger, 'the radius of which shall be suitable for the work'.[229] He was obliged to request extra days' grace in which to complete this 'having a good many plaguesome things heaping upon me just now'.[230] The normally placcid William seems to be experiencing irritating problems with his customers, and work was evidently going through a bad patch. Guinand however at last responded by sending the requested glass,[231] but now William's blacksmith had declined to take on the metalwork of the altazimuth as he had neither the space nor power to grapple with anything so large.[232] In all this hassle, William himself had managed to lose Airy's written description of the instrument, and after searching everywhere for it including in the box containing a small preparatory model, he at last discovered it in his workshop where it should have been all the time, much to his chagrin, and no doubt to Airy's impatience at such lack of order. The main model, however was ready and packed up by the end of February, and was forthwith dispatched by steamship, *The Orwell*, to Ipswich where Airy was staying at his recently purchased cottage at nearby Playford.[233] The same month William received a firm order for a transit circle for Harvard – 'to have 8 micrometers, 4 for each face – particulars to follow'.[234]

A month later, there comes the first ever mention of William travelling by train to see a client, when he left London on the 8.30 am for Ipswich to have discussions with Airy on the plans for the altazimuth, and no doubt many other items of mutual interest. His London station of departure was then at Shoreditch, opened in 1840, and later to become Bishopsgate Goods

Wells/Simms/Needham

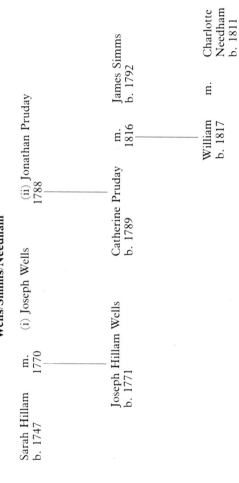

Sarah Hillam
b. 1747

m.
1770

(i) Joseph Wells

(ii) Jonathan Pruday
1788

Joseph Hillam Wells
b. 1771

Catherine Pruday
b. 1789

m.
1816

James Simms
b. 1792

William
b. 1817

m.

Charlotte
Needham
b. 1811

Station. The line between Colchester and Ipswich was the most easterly part of the Eastern Counties 'railroad' from London, and had opened only the year before. It was not yet suitable for delicate goods such as optical instruments however carefully packed, and they had a lengthier but safer journey by sea, or if for an inland destination, by coach. The railway, however, cut down the travelling time by more than half as these early trains operated at about 25 mph as opposed to 10-12 mph on the coach, and moreover the stops at the various stations were brief, and not to be compared with the staging posts at inns along the toll roads, which now rapidly began to go out of business and often disappear altogether. It was still necessary to go to Cambridge by coach although there was a train as far as Bishop Stortford by May 1842, and another from Bishop Stortford to Newport (16 miles short of Cambridge) the following year. The schemes for new railways and the enthusiasm (not to say gambling) of shareholders was by 1844 becoming cyclonic, so that in the three years 1844, 1845 and 1846 alone, Parliament passed no less than 438 Bills authorising 8,470 miles of track costing over £180 million. In Leeds it was not uncommon for 100,000 shares to change hands in a single day – to and from all grades of society ranging from titled aristocrats and country parsons to mill operatives. Some people over-stretched themselves with gullibility or greed. In the latter category was the entrepreneureal George Hudson of York who ultimately fell from being 'The Railway King', to disgrace and bankruptcy.

Frederick Walter Simms was deeply involved professionally in the railway boom by his connection with the South-East Railway, and in 1844 published his classic book, *Practical Tunnelling*, which had a wide circulation particularly amongst railway surveyors and engineers, and indeed is most readable even today. It was the usual Simms monument to unambiguous clarity of exposition and elegance of language on all aspects of the organising and planning, as well as the practical problems of railway construction. Mr Cubitt (later Sir William) appointed three resident engineers under himself, who were each responsible for a different section of the line between London and Dover, that nearest London being allotted to Frederick Walter. This stretch involved several tunnels, the most notable at Bletchingly and Saltwood. Bletchingly is 1,324 yards long, and is situated just east of Red Hill (as it then was) where the Dover line diverged from the south-bound Brighton line, turning due east in a bee-line for Tonbridge. Saltwood is near Merstham just north of Red Hill, and measures 954 yards. As both were on straight sections, he was able to use a transit instrument of his brother's to ensure alignment, building temporary wooden observatories each end of the tunnels. He possessed a considerable fund of geological knowledge, but even so was badly hampered by quicksands at Saltwood, which required fifteen horses working long hours to pump the excavations dry. He employed fifty-six miners and fifty-eight labourers, and noted with appropriate coldness that conditions for these men were appalling as they

173

were consistently wet through, and at the early stages often bent double, so that they needed a four-shift day. Many of them became ill, so he commented in his matter-of-fact way.

The trial shafts for Frederick's section of the line were sunk in February 1840, the wider working shafts in August, from which driving the headings of the tunnel was finished by Christmas. Excavations 'pushed on with the utmost vigour night and day' until 1st November 1841, when the last junction at Bletchingly was keyed in. Extensions, entrances and brickwork were completed by May 1842, and that tunnel was opened to the public on 26th May, within the contract parameters. The Saltwood tunnel was finished a year later in June 1843, shortly before the whole line from London Bridge to Folkestone was ready for use, whilst the blasting of the chalk 'Round Down' between Folkestone and Dover on 26th January 1843 opened the way for the last part of the project to be built along the cliffs between them.

It was at about this period that William's oldest son, William Henry, was appointed to the position of Surveyor General in Ceylon. It is uncertain what led to this post. Born in 1820, he was twenty when he left Cambridge and started to tour Ireland in search of his soul. He seems to have been a restless young man, and his movements are difficult to follow. The Survey of Ireland was on its final stages, but he may have sought work under Colonel Colby, who had previously recruited his uncle Frederick Walter. Later, William Henry very likely assisted that same uncle on the South-East Railway. However it came about, he gained sufficient knowledge and reputation to branch out on his own with the work in Ceylon where roads were being built under a developing colonial system. Expropriation of land to form large plantations in which to grow tropical products for export, required facilities to transport the goods to the ports, mainly Colombo. William Henry remained in Ceylon from about 1843 or 1844 until about 1856.

His cousin, William Simms junior (1817), working at Fleet Street on the creation of the Standard Yard, was turning his thoughts to other, more delightful matters. He was frequently to be found during his holidays at the home of his mother's step-brother, Joseph, in Northamptonshire. This was the son of Sarah Hillam and Joseph Wells, who had been born in St Marylebone parish of London in 1771, and had returned with his mother to Ayston when his father died, subsequently inheriting the Hillam farm in 1800. Latterly however, he lived at Weldon, Northamptonshire, to where William Simms junior (1817) henceforth directed his visits, and here he was rewarded for his faithfulness in 1843 by meeting Charlotte Needham of Wymondham, Leicestershire. She is said to have been a distant cousin of William's through his mother's family. Certainly the Wymondham parish registers were full of Needhams, as is the churchyard in all its rustic seclusion replete with Needham graves. Here in the beautiful early English parish church of St Peter's, William and Charlotte were married by the bride's brother, the Reverend Charles Needham, vicar of the neighbouring villages of Sproxton and Saltby, on 29th June 1844. After the wedding they returned to their home at 9 Granville Square, Pentonville (at that time newly built in classical style, and in 1990 still impressive), and whilst William concentrated on dividing instruments for the Ordnance Surveys' Triangulation of London, Charlotte tried to accustom herself to living in town, so different from the remoteness of Wymondham. When he announced in 1848 with some aplomb that he was the one who placed the theodolite in the 92-ft wooden structure on the Cross of St Paul's, her pride was only paralleled by his own, further enhanced when the Standard Lengths were ready to be installed at Westminster under the careful guidance of Rev Richard Sheepshanks in 1855.

The official Standards of Length with which Troughton & Simms became involved, are in fact the criteria from which all other linear measurements can be verified, essential to obtain a consistency of results, and to which can be referred all other scales for determining length. Length is only one of many Standards which control the characteristics of objects, agreed over many years of public useage, and derived from simple though rough and ready traditional methods available from time immemorial to the peasant as well as his master. The length of a man's stride or the distance from his outstretched fingertip to his nose sufficed in the early days of barter to assess the length of his plough or of his cloth. Length was one of the most basic measurements, as was size in terms of weight or volume, and throughout history wherever there has been an exchange of goods, there has been a need in the market place for a uniform check on quantity and quality in order to uphold fair trading. One of the first functions of town elders, councils or mayors was this control of commerce and to provide their own tangible standards for comparison of goods. Many town hall museums have such measures in their keeping.

Originally local in origin, as towns became less isolated with the appearance of durable roads, and trade developed into a countrywide activity, so was the need perceived for national Standards for reference throughout the country, to be kept in the capital and available to all. Finally, International Standards were evolved in the different trades, at any rate in principle though because of traditional differences they did not always coincide. Nor do they today. In addition, the production of reliable Standards became complicated when it was accepted that their actual readings varied with the conditions under which they were used, particularly in the case of Length, where temperature affected some materials more than others. The aim was to produce a compound substance whose overall properties were as stable and inert as possible, and for those

175

deviations which were inevitable there must be reliable tables to calculate results.

The story of the development of Standard Lengths is a long one to which reference has already been made in earlier chapters. The need came seriously to the notice of army surveyors when accurate maps were required after the 1745 rebellion in Scotland, and it was recognised that a proper network of roads was required in order to control the Highlands and open up hiding places of the clansmen. The flagrant errors in old maps now encouraged the use of carefully controlled Standard Lengths from which measuring rods and chains in the official Yard (or ell in Scotland) could be graduated, and from which General Roy ultimately achieved his triangulation of southern Britain in 1783. By the 19th century the Ordnance Survey was taking the need for standardisation very seriously, and Colonel Colby was engaged in triangulation of the whole of Great Britain. By Act of Parliament in George IV's reign the Imperial Standard of Length was defined and produced, and made available at the House of Commons, only to be re-created after its destruction in the fire of 1834.

The gestation of the National Standards of Length had been long and hard, not least because of the mix of different men, all with strong personalities, which had been involved. There had been clashes of temperament all along the line. There had also been problems in connection with the composition of the measures, some favouring one metal, some an alloy to overcome the effects of temperature. There was the question of how the lengths should be supported without affecting their freedom to expand or retract, and lastly how they should be illuminated in order to obtain an accurate reading. A comparable number of problems arose regarding the instruments for their verification.

From time to time experiments appear in William Simms' workbooks, which were associated with this research. Others were done by Francis Baily (as an adjunct to his work on the pendulum prior to 1838) even before the Government Commission on the Standards appointed him to his official position. From 1843 Baily launched into the work, only to have it unexpectedly curtailed next year by his death. The final version of the Standards and their accompanying instruments were at last arrived at by Richard Sheepshanks after fourteen years of patient experimentation involving thousands of readings of length and temperature, all of which he carried out in the basement of Somerset House. From these results Troughton & Simms prepared the finished products and their authorised copies which were legalised and delivered in 1855 to the new House of Commons and various other sites including Greenwich.

★　　★　　★　　★

In April 1844 Airy's fertile brain was ever creating new endeavours and developments at the Royal Observatory, but he seems not to have had any finite drawings of its lay-out from which to plan extensions. He asked William senior to request his brother Frederick Walter, who was more relaxed now the South-East Railway was in working order, what he would charge to draw up scaled working drawings of the whole complex.[235] For plans and sections such as Airy would require, Frederick reckoned this would cost £70.[236] Airy quickly withdrew when told the sum – 'I must pull in my horns a little' and, restricting his price to £20, requested that Frederick should come to his house at the Observatory, and work on plans up to that amount.[237] This was clearly an unsatisfactory arrangement from FW's point-of-view, and one is driven to the suspicion (as probably was Frederick) that Airy was attempting surreptitiously to drag professional work from his quarry at a lower than professional price. Here were two strong-minded men facing each other over a costing, and the outcome can only be guessed, as the archives do not tell us whether these particular drawings were eventually executed for the amount Airy imposed. Frederick was hardly likely to lower his price since he was not a regular 'tradesman' as was his brother. Moreover, this year his work had been recognised officially by his election to the Royal Astronomical Society, which greatly increased his standing.

★　　★　　★　　★

Railway mania continued and increased, and London was subjected to its share of smoke and smog from the funnels of the trains. However, there was some compensation to be found in 1845 when Gladstone, then President of the Board of Trade, brought in a measure whereby every railway company must provide at least one train a day on each line, incorporating covered third class carriages at a cost to the passengers of a penny a mile. Thus railway travel of reasonable comfort and protection from the elements was provided for the lower classes, who quickly started to make use of it for Sunday outings and trips to the country.

More and more railway companies were completing their proposals for new lines, and on 29th July the track between Shoreditch, Cambridge and Ely was formally opened amid great pomp and circumstance, the railway to Norwich having opened just previously. In Cambridge a huge marquee was erected, and 600 people were entertained to lunch by the Eastern Counties Railway Company, to the music of the band of the Coldstream Guards who had travelled from the Tower of London on the special train to mark the occasion. Public transport from Shoreditch to Cambridge, Ely and Norwich commenced next day, though no trains were allowed to stop at Cambridge on a Sunday for fear of crowding the town and colleges with riff-raff from London. Sadly the very commonlands that many townsfolk were aiming to visit for their picnics were now out-of-bounds by their enclosure, which was increasing in speed and extent by the General Enclosure Act

177

passed this year. It was ironical that it was not so much villagers who were objecting to this loss of public access, as the urban population who depended on these open spaces for their leisure enjoyment. Eventually the Commons Preservation Society was formed nearly twenty years later, and the process was stopped, leaving areas such as Epping Forest and Berkhamstead Common as open public places of delight in perpetuity.

Railway mania was not confined to England, or even to Europe. In India, entrepreneurs were jostling for position in the great rush to build lines. It was quickly perceived by the Honourable East India Company that they had much to learn from the experience of 'unseemly struggles' which had taken place in England over acquisition of land and bribery of owners to sell when it was not seen to be in their interests to do so. The enormous volcanic effect of the railways in their slicing up of land, heaping up of unsightly embankments, bridges and cuttings, may have caused excitement and glamour for some, but in so many places they completely raped the local countryside, not to mention the suburbs of towns where huge areas of housing were subjected to the view of viaducts and bridges from their parlour windows, their gardens and washing lines to smuts and smoke from steam-engines, and their peace to the roar of locomotives. It was a competition between those who foresaw the financial benefits of rail travel and transport of goods, and the existing features of the country, with its peaceful village landscapes.

The East India Company saw the need for a railway network in India if it was to reach commercially into the 19th century, and decided to call in a competent engineer to give some order to the overall plans. Nor did they wish for the panic for railway shares to reach the level it was approaching in England, with the threatened collapse of so much capital which did in fact occur when the bubble burst in 1847, causing dire results for many innocent shareholders.

On Saturday morning, 17th May 1845, Frederick Walter received out of the blue a letter from Major General (later Sir Charles) Pasley, requesting him to call at the Board of Trade in Whitehall. Wondering what was afoot, Frederick called on him that same morning, when Pasley asked him if he would consider going to India in an appointment created by the Honourable the Court of Directors of the East India Company. Frederick went home to consider the proposal with Caroline.

In many ways this offer came at an opportune moment for them both. Frederick Walter was forty-two, and now had a wide experience of civil engineering, surveying and geology. He had largely completed his current assignment on the South-East Railway and was looking around for pastures new, filling in his time with writing a stream of practical papers on his accumulated knowledge. Domestically he and Caroline were at a low ebb. Two of their three children, Caroline born at Greenwich in May 1833 and

Henry born there November 1837, had died. Only the middle child, Frederick, born in January 1835, had survived, and he being ten was considered old enough for them to leave in England in safe hands, wrench though this involved, particularly as it was not known at that time how long they would be away. It was, however, perfectly normal for colonial servants such as Frederick Walter, to leave their children in the healthy climate of Britain rather than subjecting them to the very well known risks of fever unprotected by today's immunisation procedures. In the event, young Frederick was placed in the care of a clergyman in Margate, who would treat him as a pupil, and oversee his general welfare. Perhaps he even visited his uncle Alfred Septimus at Mrs Fish's establishment on his free days. (See page 192.)

On 3rd June Frederick Walter was introduced to Sir Henry Willcock, Chairman of the Honourable East India Company, taking with him testimonials from Sir William Cubitt and Mr Bryan Donkin, to be told that he was required to leave England within six weeks in order to arrive in Bengal during the rainy season so that he might inspect the scale of the normal annual floods. He was to take Mr John Fraser as his assistant, and to depart from England on 20th July. Quite a breath-taking timetable.

Frederick and Caroline took their leave of all their relations on 19th July, having probably taken their son to Margate previously so that they could see him safely settled in. They left Nine Elms Station in South London that evening by the 5.00 pm train for Southampton, arriving at 8.30 pm. Next morning, Sunday, was enlivened for them in a highly poignant manner by the chimes of church bells, forcing them to realise something of the extent to which they were about to miss their home country. They sailed at 11.00 am aboard the P & O ship *The Great Liverpool* down into the Solent where they waited for a pilot. Their cabin had pride of place, as befitted such important passengers – on the upper deck at the stern, opposite that of the Captain, an RN officer named McLoed. Their last act before leaving home waters was to write to young Frederick, with who knows what feelings, handing it to be posted by the pilot who guided them round the west end of the Isle of Wight for their last sight of England.

Seventeen years later, as an elderly, lonely and ailing recluse, Frederick Walter wrote a fascinating book about his and Caroline's journey to India, and their early days in Calcutta, which he presented to his son and his wife, Caroline Frances. Their whole voyage, including the overland route via Cairo and Suez occupied forty-six days, a considerable reduction from the three to four months taken by the sea route round the Cape. The Suez Canal was not opened until 1869.

The spring of 1845 seems to have been blighted in London by illness. Airy was laid low in March,[238] but struggled up in May for the eclipse of the moon, quite invisible through the smog of central London. William junior

179

also was suffering from some infection and off work for a time. Mundane orders arrived at 138, such as for 'best ether' for Greenwich,[239] and the same for Colonel Sabine who was continuing his experiments on magnetism as well as superintending observatories across the world as a whole unit. A sketch arrived at Fleet Street from Airy of his proposals for the polar axis of the new equatorial for Liverpool Observatory which William was to make, and a maximum-minimum thermometer used for measuring the temperature of the Thames came in for repair.[240] Occasional letters from Ceylon gave indication that William Henry was involving himself in astronomical observation in his spare time, mainly regarding the Great Comet which he had seen from Colombo on 31st December 1844 and in early January, describing in a memorandum to his father written on 15th January 1845 its characteristics, which were duly passed on by him to the Royal Astronomical Society.[241]

At home John and Christian produced the last of their huge family, now numbering twelve, when Maria Sophia was born on 11th June. James (1792) and Catherine had their three surviving children headed by William junior (1817), and George and Sophia remained childless. Henry and Mary Ann were struggling with their eight children, with repeated journeys up the hill to Highgate Cemetery to bring the four that did not survive. News in England was mainly of Brunel's *Great Britain* which sailed to New York from Liverpool on 26th August arriving in fourteen days, twenty-one hours, and returning in fifteen-and-a-half days to a tumultuous welcome. Then reports started to trickle in from across the Irish Sea of the destruction of almost the entire potato crop by blight following a continually wet summer. Already the Earl of Rosse had left his work on his huge 6-ft reflector at Birr Castle – 'The Leviathan of Parsonstown' which had just been completed – so appalled was he by the calamity besetting the peasants on and around his estates in Offaly. Instead he turned his attention to attempting to relieve their sufferings, and his great telescope with its two 72-inch mirrors each weighing four tons, remained neglected for three years until 1848. The fearful stories of famine began to arrive by degrees in London, at first hardly credible, or at least immediately put down to the Irish improvidence and forgotten, and only later when starvation was a blatant fact, believed with horror.

The condition of the labourers in Ireland had for years been intolerable, and the likelihood of early death from disease compounded by under-nourishment was rife. The poverty was indescribable. There was virtually no work and no wages except the most meagre. There were no industries, and few towns. There were no shops, for no one had any money to spend. Even the farms were seldom large enough to employ labour, and the peasants had to exist on their own tiny patches of land. Years ago, during the last quarter of the 18th century, they had discovered that the potato was easier to grow than wheat or oats, and all that was required was to dig a 'lazy bed' which needed only a quarter of the acreage of wheat, plant the seed potatoes, and wait for six weeks or so for them to grow and multiply. The potatoes could be stored in the ground, and used for the pigs and chickens as well as for humans. The only tool required was a rough spade. Soon the Irish peasants existed on this single crop, and in spite of occasional warnings of the danger of this system when the crops failed, as they did every few years, they soon lost the knowledge, the seed and the tools to grow alternative food. Somehow this diet enabled them to remain alive, and even to reproduce themselves to a far greater extent, so that between 1779 and 1841 the population increased 172% owing to a combination of early marriage and their Roman Catholic religion. By 1845 the total population of Ireland was eight million, almost all illiterate and in rags.

The 1840s saw a succession of poor harvests, and now in 1845 the continual rain soaked the tiny patches, until suddenly in the autumn the potato blight devastated the main crop potatoes, leaving a slimy mess in the fields upon which the peasants depended for their basic food. Ghastly scenes of starvation followed, and those men and women who had means or strength left, deserted the stricken land for Glasgow, New York, Liverpool – anywhere where there was hope. From these cities the Irish spread out, putting down roots and making new lives for themselves in many of the big towns, including London. Many of the men worked as navvies on the new railways, and over half a million were on relief work on the roads in Ireland. A terrible battle with death was joined.

Hennell – Goldsmiths*/Morpeth/Simms

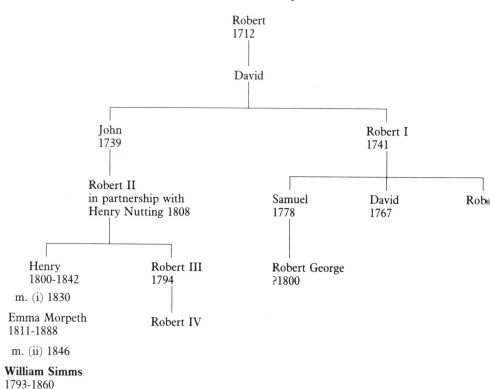

Robert
1712

David

John
1739

Robert I
1741

Robert II
in partnership with
Henry Nutting 1808

Samuel
1778

David
1767

Rob»

Henry
1800-1842

m. (i) 1830

Emma Morpeth
1811-1888

m. (ii) 1846

William Simms
1793-1860

Robert III
1794

Robert George
?1800

Robert IV

* Partly extracted from *London Goldsmiths* by A. G. Grimwade.

Simms' children June 1846

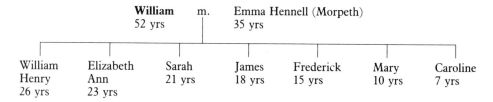

| **William** | m. | Emma Hennell (Morpeth) |
| 52 yrs | | 35 yrs |

| William Henry | Elizabeth Ann | Sarah | James | Frederick | Mary | Caroline |
| 26 yrs | 23 yrs | 21 yrs | 18 yrs | 15 yrs | 10 yrs | 7 yrs |

182

CHAPTER 16

1846

HARVESTS IN BRITAIN HAD BEEN poor in 1845, and because of the restrictions on prices of imported corn, labouring families found it hard to make ends meet. At length, to resounding acclaim, in 1846 came the repeal of the Corn Laws. Passed in 1815 with the aim of restoring agricultural prosperity at the expense of the consumer, it was fiercely resented in the towns, setting urban and rural life apart. After the repeal there was an increased rate in the urbanisation of the country, increased wealth and population of the towns, until already by the 1851 census, half the island's inhabitants were urban.

One result of this surge to the towns was the opposite effect produced by those who could afford to move away from the increasingly dense crowds in streets and tenements, out to the peace of the countryside, constantly withdrawing further and further away from the heart of the cities. William Simms was one of these. However, he had another reason for a change of home. Whilst the problems of the Irish were gathering pace and the Industrial Revolution expanded, his own work progressing well, William made a decision to remarry. Things at home cannot have been easy since Ann's death in 1839. The new baby, Caroline, had to be reared, her elder sister Ann to be cared for until she died in 1843, and young Mary brought up in a large, busy household. Their brother James had already been apprenticed to his father in 1843, to the mutual satisfaction of both, and continued to live at home. Elizabeth Ann and Sarah between them ran the household at 138, which may still have included their young uncle, Alfred Septimus. In May 1846, William Simms took on another apprentice, Joseph Beck, the son of a City wine merchant, at the huge premium of £200, which incidentally tells us something of William's standing at the time. Joseph may also have lived within the Simms' household, so there were thus at least six, maybe seven, adults living there, not counting servants, and two young children. William's third son, Frederick, born in 1831, also started work this summer, though there is no record of formal apprenticeship. In the 1851 census he is still noted as living at 138, with the faithful old Sarah Newall remaining there to look after him.

Once more William married into the world of goldsmiths, although this time his choice fell on Emma Hennell, the daughter-in-law of one. Emma had been born a Morpeth, her father, Thomas, having died before her first marriage, but noted in the Parish Register as a 'gentleman'. He may well also have been a working goldsmith or jeweller, the bonds of these crafts, especially of Liverymen, being so strong and intertwined. Emma had first married Henry Hennell of the well-known family of London goldsmiths. Henry was a son of Robert Hennell, himself the son and grandson of a goldsmith, and from 1808 in partnership at 38 Noble Street in the City with Henry Nutting. There were also Hennell cousins, Samuel and David, and their father, another Robert, working as goldsmiths at 5 Snowhill, just off Newgate, so the whole atmosphere was one of craftsmanship. Henry Nutting was the father of Ann, William Simms' first wife, and of Caroline (married to Frederick Walter Simms) and John (who was apprenticed to William Simms until his death in 1837), and it is therefore perhaps not too fanciful to suggest that Henry Hennell was actually named after his father's business partner. Emma must therefore have come to know the Simms family very well long before she married into it, including the old folk at Broad Way. The distances between all their homes was only a short step at the time of her first marriage.

Henry Hennell was born in 1800, and instead of following in the family craft, he was apprenticed at fourteen to an apothecary, John Hunter, a Freeman of the Worshipful Society of Apothecaries, and resident in London. The 'consideration' for his apprenticeship contract was nil,[242] which indicates family ties between John Hunter and the Hennells, or long-standing friendship. After serving seven years, Henry was duly admitted to the Freedom of the Society of Apothecaries on 1st May 1821,[243] and took the usual oath. He thereupon became an employee of the firm authorised to manufacture drugs within the premises of Apothecaries Hall, a large complex of buildings in Blackfriars just south of Broad Way and west of the ruins of St Anne's Church. Burnt down during the Great Fire like St Anne's, it had been rebuilt in Carolingian style, and exists to this day on the eastern slope overlooking New Bridge Street and the site of the Fleet ditch. Henry soon rose to become Chemical Operator in charge of the factory hands, and was evidently held in high regard by the Court of Proprietors at Apothecaries Hall. He lived in one of the houses (in Blackfriars) belonging to the Society, and it was from this house that he was married to Emma, and where they resided for their short and evidently childless marriage.

Emma was only eighteen[244] at the time of her first marriage, which, as she was a minor was by licence with the consent of her mother, Marie Morpeth, recently widowed. One is drawn to the conclusion that either Emma was a wilful girl who insisted on marrying at an unusually early age, or else her mother saw a good match which would absolve her from looking after her daughter and her expenses any longer. Marie had at least ten children, only one of whom, Edward, was older than Emma, and the youngest, twins Henry and Mary, were only three years old, so their exhausted mother must have breathed a sigh of relief when Henry Hennell and her Emma were married at their mutual Parish Church of St Andrew-by-the-Wardrobe for St Anne's, Blackfriars on 21st July 1830. The official witnesses were Edward Morpeth, Emma's elder brother, two Hennell relatives, and a friend, Lorina Clarke, whose Christian name Emma admired so much that she stored it away in her memory for future use.

Twelve years later, on the morning of Saturday, 4th June 1842, there was a terrible explosion at the drug factory.[245] Emma probably heard it from her home only a few hundred yards away. She knew that Henry was to spend that day manufacturing medicinal compounds from fulminating ('explosive') mercury, and that it was a very hazardous process, so much so that Henry would not allow his factory hands to carry it out because of the risk. It was an unstable material only requiring a smart blow to set it off, and is used to this day in the initiation of the firing chain of most artillery weapons throughout the world.[246] In spite of experience and care an explosion occurred, killing Henry outright, though there is no mention of other casualties.

The shocked Committee of the Court of Proprietors met later that same morning to express their regret at the great loss to the Society and to the widow (conveyed to her by their chairman, H. Robinson, Master, at an opportune moment). Moreover they resolved that funeral expenses should be met out of their own funds.[247] A fortnight later they elected Henry's successor at a salary of £200 pa. In mid-July they received a well-constructed letter from Emma, perhaps dictated by her mother or her father-in-law, begging for an annuity 'as out of his pay of £220 pa Henry had saved nothing' for her subsistence. She was immediately presented by the Society with £50 for her present support, and the promise that they would further discuss her plight at their next meeting in December. This was not soon enough for Emma's needs as she had meanwhile been told she must leave her 'tied' house in Blackfriars before the end of September, and required to know her 'expectations'. Thus the Special Court of Proprietors resolved to grant her at once an annuity of £50, to commence at Michaelmas 1842. In December they received a grateful acknowledgement from the widow, written from her new residence at Clapton,[248] then a small village to the north-east of the City. Later she moved to the better quality four-storeyed house in Upper Stamford Street, a few contemporary remnants of which still exist just south of the present-day Waterloo Bridge.

Owing to the close liaison between the Hennells and the Nuttings, it is safe to assume that William Simms was deeply affected by this tragedy, and from the first gave comfort and hospitality to the young widow who was only nine years older than his eldest son. From this paternal interest in her, friendship blossomed into close affection, and four years later, he married her, still in her early 30s. He was eighteen years older than his new bride. They were united at the austere neo-classical church of St John's, Waterloo Road on 10th July 1846, just round the corner from her house at Upper Stamford Street. St John's was an auspicious beginning to their happy years together. It was one of the four 'Waterloo' churches built by order of the Commissioners between 1822 and 1824 in the enormous parish of Lambeth as a thanksgiving for the great victory against the French in 1815. The architect, Francis Bedford, was a local man who had travelled in Greece, thus echoing the classical in the portico at St John's, and in its tower. The view which met Emma and William when they emerged from the ceremony onto the broad steps of the church, was to change radically soon afterwards when, two years later the pretentious neo-classical entrance to Waterloo Station arose at the terminus of the Nine Elms line.

Everything one reads of Emma indicates that she was clearly conscious of current fashion trends, and is likely to have followed as nearly as her small income from the Society of Apothecaries allowed to the example set by Queen Victoria in her choice of wedding dress six years previously, back in 1840. This had been of a very simple design in white satin woven by the impoverished Huguenots of Spitalfields, and trimmed with Honiton lace. The skirt was gathered at the back and pleated at the front around the front-dipping waistline, and the sleeves were elbow length prolonged by drapes of lace. Full-skirted as dresses were by the mid-1840s, the crinoline had not yet reached this country as it did with an explosion in April 1855 when the Empress Eugenie accompanied Napoleon III on a visit to England wearing the first example here. However, the increasing number of underskirts and petticoats worn by women in the 1840s paved the way for it, and the length of skirts (now sweeping the ground) agreed with the decorous fashion of the time. Except for evening wear the normal clothing for the middle-class woman had more than a hint of primness, and though the huge skirts had several rounds of flounces and lace, the necks were high, the patterns simple and the sleeves extended down to the knuckles. Bonnets, although decorated with ribbons and flowers, lacked the flamboyancy of later hats, evolving from coal-scuttle shape to the poke bonnet with a large brim which half-obscured the face. By the time of Emma's wedding in 1846, the bonnet had become smaller and closer fitting, and was worn over a white linen cap, the frill of which framed the face. The Queen had broken with tradition at her wedding by wearing a spray of orange blossom given her by Prince Albert, over her head instead of a bonnet, and as this immediately became popular, it may be that Emma followed suit, though as a widow she may have felt a bonnet more in keeping. Her gloves were again white and her shoes had small, shaped heels. Her reticule (unnecessary now that she could hide her possessions in her large skirt), was replaced by a dainty parasol.

William's attire for this second marriage was more sombre than for his first, not because he and Emma were both widowed, but because fashion so dictated. His plain dark trousers were cut in a fuller style and had no instep strap. They were probably of the same material as his coat which is likely to have been a single-breasted cutaway with rounded tails finished with braid – a forerunner of the modern morning coat and worn over a lighter but plain waistcoat. Alternatively, as this was a formal occasion and he was middle-aged, he perhaps wore a new dark frockcoat with matching trousers and waistcoat, which was beginning to be much used as City wear. His boots, now laced, were obscured by his trousers, and his hat was a black silk topper, considerably taller than his earlier hats though not yet quite a 'stovepipe'. His cravat was smaller than previously, almost a tie. His collar was starched and still pointed upwards, but less obtrusively now. His hair (which was naturally balding) was parted on the left, shorter, mildly side-whiskered, and brushed forward. He certainly wore white gloves, and possibly held a stick, and as a mark of his growing eminence a gold watch with its chain suspended across his waistcoat.

William and Emma's marriage was witnessed by his eldest daughter, Elizabeth Ann, who seems to have seen him through every crisis of his later life, and for whom he had great affection. She was only thirteen years younger than her new step-mother. Their other witnesses were, once again, Edward Morpeth, Emma's elder brother, and Edward Hennell, her brother-in-law. Again William was married by licence, this time to avoid the attention created by the proclamation of banns, but more importantly that it was the custom of the middle classes to do so.

It was natural that neither William nor Emma would want their new home together to be where he had already lived, with its associations with his first marriage. In any case, No. 138, although a large house, was now increasingly needed for workrooms, and the family was finding its quarters swamped by machines and such-like paraphanalia. He and Emma would have more children, who needed space and fresh air, neither to be found in Fleet Street. They also wanted to escape from the crowds and the fogs of London as their peers were doing, and from the recurrent infections contracted from an overloaded water and drainage system, and the disgusting smell of the Thames. A relative of Edward Troughton already lived at Carshalton in Surrey, where he and his father before him, ran a tailoring business. It was natural that William and Emma's thoughts should now turn to this area, which although distant from the City, was rapidly becoming more accessible as the railways were busily pushing through new lines. The track from Brighton to London Bridge was already completed, and its station at East Croydon had been opened in 1838. The West Croydon to London Bridge line waś even more convenient, and was opened in 1839. Moreover, William knew that Carshalton Station (renamed Wallington in 1868) on the line from West Croydon to Epsom was due to open in 1847, and

187

until then it was easy to drive in his own coach the three miles to West Croydon to pick up the train to London Bridge, which was within walking distance of Fleet Street. Like many other professional people then and since, he welcomed the opportunity which the new railways gave him to leave his work and worries behind him each evening, and to make for the country.

Carshalton was indeed then deeply in the country at the foot of the Surrey hills and at the head of the little river, Wandle. An attractive and ancient village, which retained many of its mediaeval buildings, it had a network of underground springs which ensured that it was a fertile farming area, virtually untouched until the 20th century. Its principle edifice, besides the old church, was Carshalton House, built in 1696 by a wealthy tobacco merchant, Edward Carleton, later used by Thomas Scawen, and then by Sir John Fellowes, a financier. There was also Carshalton Place[249] on the site of the manor house of Thomas Scawen, and a splendid Queen Anne rectory. The present church has Norman origins and a Saxon predecessor although it underwent enlargement in the 19th century after William knew it. Even today the two village ponds have survived, as also have several of its ancient houses, but the plastic era has dug deeply into its High Street, although it is possible with the aid of early photographs to visualise it as it was in its Victorian guise.

On 25th March 1846, with his marriage in view, William Simms signed the ground lease of the house and gardens of the beautiful miniature estate of Bramble Haw at Carshalton for a period of sixteen years and twelve days, at a ground rent of £100 per annum. He also leased the adjacent meadow of Westcroft for nineteen years less twelve days from the same date at a rent of £19 per annum. There was a sitting tenant on a part of the land used as an orchard, whose name was Jessie Richardson, a carpenter, for a rent of £1 a year, and whose lease was to end at the same time as that of the house. William, true to form, insured his new property for £1,000.

Bramble Haw had been open waste land until 1780, when it was sold jointly by Earl Bathurst and trustees for James Scawen, son of Sir William Scawen, to John Allfrey, a carpenter of Carshalton. Between that date and 1786 the exquisite little classical house was built, and immediately sold to Edward Benyon of Slynes Oaks, Chelsham, near Croydon, who the following year leased the land to Thomas Potts, gentleman, of New Broad Street, London, for a term of thirty-one years. It was next leased to Robert Burra in 1820, and finally sold leasehold to William Simms in 1846, Robert Burra remaining the agent for the ground landlord, Edmund Benyon.[309]

The house was typical late 18th century classical style, built of mellow stone, and when William lived there, a perfect three-bayed cube, with a refined and delicate moulding at the top of the base course and in the cornice and frieze. The frieze was fluted, and at intervals was set with sunray

188

Bramble Haw. (Peatling Papers).
BY PERMISSION OF LONDON BOROUGH OF SUTTON HERITAGE DEPARTMENT

paterae of grey terracotta matching the colour of the stone. Above the low parapet was an attic storey with a Mansard roof, dormer windows and an unostentacious central chimney stack. Below this was the main bedroom floor, and then the piano nobile with windows only in its outer bays. Lowest came the semi-basement. On the east was a classical porch with two sentinal columns and matching pilasters, and five steps down to the drive. The front door had a fanlight above it, and led into the delightful hall with its steep but elegant stairway and balasters, all with well detailed mouldings. The hall fireplace also had good woodwork, and, typical of English design of the period, was set in a corner. The panelled doors to the living rooms were high quality, as were the open bookshelves in the library at the front of the house, and the cupboards beneath them. The other front room was the little dining-room, said to be exquisite, and at first designated as the 'Common Parlour'. The mantlepiece was noteworthy as being of Portland stone slabs. The drawing-room faced west over the garden and was the largest room, a dignified space with two columns at the door end, and possibly at the other end also. These echoed those at the front porch, being neo-classical, with attic bases on a low square plinth, and capitals which appear from photographs to be simply carved with fluting and a ring of other decoration,

189

possibly egg-and-dart, with a square abacus above. There was a splendid cornice and skirting, and large wall panels to which much later were added swags and drops which detracted from its original Georgian simplicity. The wooden mantlepiece was a fine 'Adam' one described as with 'composition ornaments'.[250]

To enjoy such a house as William undoubtedly did, indicates his taste for architectural delights, and the fact that he added none of the excressences and the out-of-character oak panelling and plaster frippery that came later underlines this sensitivity. The grounds also speak highly of his feeling for simplicity and quality. Near to the house was a degree of formality in the walls and the small pond and fountain. Otherwise there appear to have been large stretches of grass and many large forest trees. The site was a peculiar triangular shape due to the confluence of Acre Lane and Westcroft Road to the west of the house. Flowing through this end of the grounds near the apex of the triangle was the little stream, the Wandle, which having supplied the water for the lakes and conduits at the great Carshalton House, ran through William's land and subsequently down to Marchant's Mill where it turned the waterwheel for grinding the corn. The deeds for Bramble Haw include the right of James Scawen's trustees to make up the river's banks and to keep it clear, as well as to enter William's grounds and inspect the water at any reasonable time.

Along Westcroft Road still stands William's coach-house, a gabled early Victorian brick building, E-shaped, with steep roof, and probably once with barge-boards. Of recent years it has been converted into a dwelling. A few yards east of it are the remains of the stable, 18th century but partially rebuilt by the Carshalton Society in the 1980s. Its wooden gables form the pigeon cote, and the barn now serves as an impressive gateway to a back lane running to garages and gardens of the many semi-detached houses built over the entire site in the 1930s. South of the little stable yard is a small 18th century house which was probably used by the coachman in William's day. It is simple, dignified and rendered in white, and it is still occupied. The imposing carved stone gateposts at the main entrance to the estate have disappeared from the corner of Acre Lane, although a hump in the ground indicates the position of the south-easterly one. There was another entrance half-way along Acre Lane running directly north to the house, which could conveniently be used for travelling in the Croydon direction. It has now been built over. There is also a single plain stone gatepost still standing far down Westcroft Road, which is carved with the date 1792, but which probably belonged to the next property. Westcroft Farm on the other side of the road, built in the 16th century, still stands, but has additions and alterations, and its farm buildings are now converted to dwellings. The friendly little Wandle has disappeared from view, but some of William's trees, notably along what was his front drive, still survive high and magnificent, as does the monkey puzzle tree in his front garden. A raised area in the present back lane where it converges down into a narrow passage veering westwards, indicates the footings of his house.

During the early summer of 1846 the Simms family took possession of their new home at Carshalton, and all the happy – and the sad – memories of the Fleet Street homes were carefully parcelled away in their memories. It was as if the remaining members had launched out anew to a fresh start in a very different life. The clean Surrey air was not only a boon to their health, but to the star-gazers amongst them a great advance on the murky skies of London. To have space for the children to run and play was a wonderful experience, the little village shops more leisurely, the small mediaeval church on its knoll by the ponds so different from the formal classicism of the Wren churches they were used to. Everywhere was more spacious, even the coachman's quarters. The London vendors crying their wares in the street, often ringing handbells to attract customers, were replaced by tradesmen calling directly at the house with horse and cart, the latter piled high with fresh vegetables, meat, dairy products, or coal. The kitchens at Bramble Haw were roomy, and by 1851 there were three female servants living in the main house, with gardener and coachman down by the stables.

Although retaining one or two living rooms at Fleet Street for use when working late, as so often occurred, either by himself or by his apprentices, William now turned his face in his free time to being a country gentleman. Modest and quiet as always, with his new young wife he soon attracted friendship. At first viewed as 'trade', when they realised his sympathetic qualities and total integrity, his clients became his friends, and this probably extended to the great houses in and around Carshalton. There is no indication that he spent much time socialising for its own sake. Indeed, his attendance at the various learned societies to which he belonged left him few evenings for such exchanges, not to mention the huge amount of time he spent with clients, experimenting on the instruments he was preparing for them.

His second son, James, continued to live at home after his apprenticeship ended in 1849 and indeed for another ten years. Elizabeth Ann was still with him, and Sarah also was unmarried, and so remained at home. Also the children, Mary aged ten and Caroline aged seven. It was perhaps Alfred Septimus whose life was most changed by William's remarriage and move to Carshalton. It seems likely that he remained living with his elder brother after his apprenticeship was completed in 1828 until some time between Ann's death in 1839 and the marriage in 1846. The granting of Alfred's Freedom of the Goldsmith's Company came only a week after his father's death in 1828, and it may be that Alfred went to live with his widowed mother, Sarah Simms, at her new abode at Evangelist Court for a while. Possibly after her death in 1834, or maybe at an even later date he developed further symptoms such as fits or a deterioration of his mental condition which decided William that he required care of a full-time nurse. Margate was well-known for its bracing air, splendid beaches, and the Royal Sea Bathing Infirmary which had been started by old James Simms' friend Dr Lettsom, the Quaker physician. Certainly by 1846 Alfred had been taken down to Margate to a Mrs Fish, who cared for him at William's expense until Alfred died in November 1875. (See page 179.)

★ ★ ★ ★

No word of William's intended marriage comes through the extant letters that spring of 1846. Instead we find that by the end of January the carrier had searched out a boat to Ipswich sailing from Nicholson's Wharfe on the Thames, which could accommodate all the rotating parts of the Greenwich altazimuth instrument, leaving at Fleet Street only the circles to be divided,[251] a process which could quickly be achieved now William had his self-acting engine.

In February he wrote to Challis that William junior (1817) had been taken ill again, and was not at work, but even so the rods for the Cambridge equatorial had been completed and would be sent with a workman who would carry out the dividing and engraving, expected to take four days to complete.[252] A week later he wrote again to introduce a friend, Mr Irsse,[253] 'who desires to see the Observatory'. After a further week we find William's workman leaving London by the eight o'clock train, to arrive in Cambridge soon after 11. As always with his men's welfare in mind, he asked for someone at the Observatory to direct the man, a stranger in Cambridge, to 'some decent house where he may get a lodging'.[254] But he did not pamper his employees; in fact a note to the man in question was sent 'by way of putting in the spur',[255] when he proved to be taking overlong in completing the job. Time, even then, was seen as money. Labourers, even craftsmen, were relatively cheap, but must be employed economically.

The most heartening item of news in the scientific instrument world that spring, was the repeal of the excise duty on glass in February. Optical glass was expensive, and had to be brought in from abroad to maintain quality and costs. Up till then all further experiments following on from William's own work on Ritchie's glass had provided no way of improved manufacture at a reasonable financial outlay, and William found himself unable to purchase suitable flint glass for the Liverpool equatorial now being made at Fleet Street.[256] In April, therefore, he arranged to go to Munich to inspect a telescope which the prominent instrument maker, Merz, was making for the United States, and look into the question of supplies of flint glass for his own use and also an object glass for the proposed transit circle for Harvard and for a transit instrument nearly completed for them.[257] He asked Airy if there were any tasks he could accomplish for him whilst he was there.[258] Airy, always awake to any opportunity which presented itself, replied

192

immediately listing five items, all to be carried out with the utmost discretion, not to say stealth, as Merz was not to learn anything in return, or even to realise the implications of William's actions. First William was to look for the methods for constructing a 2-inch telescope which could be incorporated in the construction of the Liverpool telescope (about which Merz was to remain ignorant), and if possible to 'get a trial of it, at any rate get its size and length'. Secondly, he was to see if he could 'learn, examine or try anything about the 1-inch equatorial which Merz (was) making at Sir John Herschal's order'. Thirdly, he asked William to buy on private account two large prisms, which he described. Fourth, 'If you can find something like surprising of his different instruments, I should like to have them', and fifth, 'Pray do not fail to bring a form copies of his period catalogue'.[259]

A remarkable list of orders, the old fox. Here was blatant commercial espionage by a master, who was already planning his new range of instruments for Greenwich, its transit circle, its reflex zenith tube, and a chronograph, all to be completed within a few years, but to produce first every reason why the Board of Visitors should sanction the expenditure. He was beginning to mount his battle order.

There is no record of William's reply, hardly surprising in the circumstance, as it was doubtless verbal or otherwise private. That this kind of secrecy had to be maintained there are other examples, a notable one being when Edward Troughton had the model of the South equatorial kept in his own bedroom at 136, safe from prying eyes. Airy's requests, however, not only shed light on this aspect of optical manoeuvre, but also on the time element with which William was likely to allot to this visit to Munich, not counting further excursions into Austria and Bavaria which he may have made. It was a huge journey of about 800 miles the other side of the Channel, which even though now possible by train, would still take two full days and nights even if he did not stop off anywhere on the way, such as Paris or Strasburg. At the least he must have been absent from London for two or three weeks.

Before he left home, William was able to complete drawings and instructions for a transit instrument for Professor Bache, director in Hassler's place of the Coastal Survey of the United States of America.[260] This was one of a family of new instruments for the Survey, some capital ones for which plans were already in the pipeline. In fact the American market continued to send to England for optical goods, and William had a good relationship with Harvard College at Boston, Massachussetts,[261] for whom he was just now planning the 4-ft transit circle and by June had completed a mural circle.[262] The India Survey[263] also was ticking along, and a further theodolite was in the making for that area, with the likelihood of many more as Frederick Walter continued his surveys.

193

In January 1846 William Simms had been re-elected to the Council of the Royal Astronomical Society, now under the chairmanship of Captain Smythe RM. Simms was absent from the first meeting of the new Council in February, perhaps due to the terrible winter weather combined with domestic matters. Next month on 13th March he was present, also submitting a communication (No. 619) from his son, William Henry (now in Ceylon) on his observations of the Great Comet of 1845. In April he missed another Council meeting as he was by then on his way to Munich, as also in May. June saw preparations for his marriage together with general settling down at Carshalton, rendering his attendance at Somerset House impossible, and from then until November there were no summer meetings. However, in spite of another severe winter, he attended meetings in December, and again in January when he was re-elected for another year, and in February and March 1847. It was during this session that the timing of the Council meetings were reconsidered, owing to the difficulty that members were having in contending with the stormy winter nights, as well as combining their visits to Somerset House with other social appointments including the Society's own functions: From about now the meetings were held in the afternoons to suit all.[264] In April 1847 William presented another communication from William Henry regarding sextant observations of Wilmot's comet, an erudite offering deep in mathematics. Next month he absented himself from the Council meeting as it coincided with the birth of Walter Hennell, the eldest of his and Emma's three children, but the next three meetings he was present. In January 1848 he failed to be re-elected, perhaps at his own wish, as his time was already fully occupied including with his new domestic responsibilities. He is noted as being a quiet member of the Council's deliberations, but that when he did hold forth, it was with knowledge, conciseness, and of proved value. He did not embellish for the sake of speaking. What he said was to the point, and he did not talk just to be noticed.[265] It was an honour to be a member of this elite gathering, of which he was very sensible, but his professional and private lives already demanded much of him, and his health seems more and more to have limited his activities.

In Calcutta, things were going less smoothly. Already Frederick Walter was experiencing the antagonism of railway enthusiasts who had their own ideas as to where the new lines should run, and who objected to the authority of Frederick's new broom sweeping away their preconceived notions. Ignoring their opinions, he set off to survey the feasible routes for the railway. But his concentration was shattered almost without warning in April by the sudden prostration of his wife, Caroline, who within a few days succumbed to that great dread of all 19th century travellers from which they had little defence, fever. She sank rapidly beneath the flood of infection, and died of cholera on 18th April, only seven months after arriving in Bengal. India had once again exerted its merciless power, always a hazard taken by itinerant Europeans as a worthwhile risk, indeed a duty to Empire building. The weather in Calcutta was torrid, with hot damp temperatures, and little wind to relieve the heat. The monsoons were expected soon. Caroline was buried next day at the New Burial Ground, Circular Road, Fort William by the English chaplain, Archdeacon J. Daltry. She was only forty-two. Frederick Walter, stunned, erected a gravestone on which was a text from 2nd Corinthians chapter 5, v.8 – 'absent from the body to be present with the Lord'. Then he had no option but to return to his work as Superintendent of the Committee of Railroads, though the heat, the arguments and the loneliness began to take their toll.

The news of Caroline's death must have arrived in England about seven weeks later, at the end of May. The Simms family was devastated, young Frederick with his tutor at Margate, unbelieving, an eleven-year-old trying hard to be a man and to hold back his tears. It was to be another four-and-a-half years before his father came back to him.

★　　★　　★　　★

Only one more entry appears in the main RGO archives for that year. On 4th December William wrote to Airy, who had completed his examination of the altazimuth at Playford and sent it back to Fleet Street for its final stages, to say that the dividing of the instrument could be proceeded with without further delay. Soon it would be ready to transfer to its permanent home at the Royal Observatory, Greenwich.[266]

In Airy's own archives, in the section headed 'Correspondence with tradesmen', another letter from William, written from Fleet Street on Boxing Day, answers the former's question about the price of transit circles, which is not without interest. A 2-ft transit similar to one he had made for Mr Beaumont, now in the possession of Mr Dawes, would cost £220. A 3-ft one like that recently constructed for a Mr Peters of Buckingham would be £350, and a larger one of 4-ft just like the one he was engaged on at present for America, would come to £500.[267] Even taking into account his overheads and his workmen's wages, William was now in the top league with a very good income, well in line with his lovely home at Carshalton. Victorian England was becoming evermore prosperous, and there was a great pride in achievements, not only personal but in Britain itself and the growing British Empire.

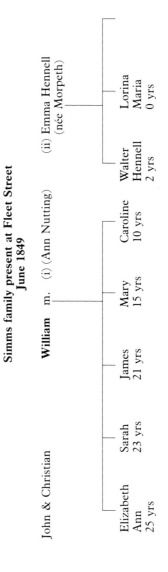

**Simms family present at Fleet Street
June 1849**

John & Christian

William m. (i) (Ann Nutting)

(ii) Emma Hennell
(née Morpeth)

Elizabeth
Ann
25 yrs

Sarah
23 yrs

James
21 yrs

Mary
15 yrs

Caroline
10 yrs

Walter
Hennell
2 yrs

Lorina
Maria
0 yrs

CHAPTER 17

1847-1849

1847 WAS A YEAR IN WHICH ALMOST the whole of the continent of Europe was rumbling with discontent. Made up largely of a great number of small states, the united Germany that later became a nation under Prussia, was at this time yearning for Republicanism. Bavaria, Schleswig, Holstein, Gotha, and several others were seething like a cauldron with revolutionary ideas which were only waiting for the lid to be raised for the whole conglomerate to boil over. In Italy it was a similar story. A number of small states under the Austrian Empire, struggling for self-determination and unity. France had passed through eighteen years of peaceful but dull monarchy, headed by the now elderly Louis Philippe, cautious and uninventive, but determined to keep France out of war, against Russia to support Poland, against Holland from whom Belgium cheerfully seceded under its new King Leopold of Saxe-Coberg in 1830, or against Austria over Italian nationalism. It was over thirty years since Waterloo, and many Frenchmen who were then children had grown up in the unexciting atmosphere of 'Le Roi', and yearned for the glow of success and magic of Bonaparte, forgetting the bloodshed and misery which his excesses engendered. France, like nearly all of Western Europe was becoming restless. Only England under Queen Victoria, and little Belgium under Victoria's Uncle Leopold, remained calm and flourishing, whilst mighty Russia in the east was firmly controlled by the Tsars who were awaiting their next chance of Imperialism.

Even in England there were grumblings from the industrial centres, particularly the mill towns of the north, where the Chartists had continued their struggles for factory improvements ever since Lord Althorp's Factory Act in 1833. The repeal of the Corn Laws in 1846 fanned the fire of revolt, gradually spreading discontent across the country amongst the working classes. From their midst sprang an employer, Fielden, who was one of Lancashire's largest cotton spinners. Fielden knew the factory floor intimately both as operative and as boss. It was this man who had the driving ability to carry the new Ten Hour Bill through Parliament in 1847, whereby no women or youths were allowed to work more than a ten-hour day, thereby effectively reducing also the male working day to the same amount, since the men were unable to complete the mill processing without them. This measure was of enormous importance as it opened the sluice-gates to a whole range of factory law and inspection which could never have been contrived in the piecemeal cottage industry of the past. Moreover, once again the middle and upper classes were jerked into recognising the appalling conditions that men and women in the factories were enduring, turning attention now also to the mines, and to the whole range of industrial plant and workshops. Inevitably attention was also drawn to the plight of children in general, and in particular to the working practices for children. The Victorians were developing into great family people, and although previously they had taken the conditions of the slums dweller for granted as an act of God, or even hardly believed that such squalor actually existed for some, now by various paths the truth was brought home to them through the activities of reformers within Parliament and without, supplemented by literature of the period, much of it written primarily for children themselves. 'Water babies' ranks high on the list, but there are other fairy stories, not all English, which revealed the same cruelties as those besetting the chimney boys. The flow of novels and articles continued from the able pen of Charles Dickens, bringing the horrors of the London poor into the drawing rooms of the upper classes, to increase his readers' sympathetic understanding of children.

The famine in Ireland continued throughout this year with all its ferocity of 1846. By January half a million Irishmen were employed on relief work on the roads of the province, and more than two million were receiving food handouts. All were destitute, and to multiply the problems, there was now a policy amongst the big landowners to change the land from tillage to pasture since the repeal of the Corn Laws brought down the price of wheat. To keep the peasants away from their estates, their poor hovels of mud and stone were bulldozed to leave their inhabitants with nowhere to go but the workhouses, not all of which would accept them. Too weak to work or even to walk, many of the poor souls collapsed on the roadside to die. Others managed to cross to England, and still others went on board the 'coffin' ships bound for the New World. But the conditions for these would-be emigrants was said to be worse than in the slave ships, and of the 89,738 en route for Canada in 1847, no less than 15,330 died before they arrived. In Ireland itself nearly a million died of starvation, or its attendant diseases. The harvest again completely failed in 1847, and by 1849 the population of eight million had been reduced by famine and emigration to 6½ million, of which almost a million were maintained by the workhouses.

The astonishing fact is that such shocking events hardly obtain a mention in English history books of the 20th century, so little effect did they have on the course of happenings here. Most indexes have no reference to them, and one can only surmise that the Irish potato famine had very little impact outside Parliament where the cost of maintaining the population was the principal source of anxiety. Only in the large cities was the influx of the Irish noticeable, or in small pockets of the lesser towns, and when the crops the next year were successful, and the famine was over, the whole disaster was wiped from the memories of most people, who like William and Emma were shielded from any excesses by their comfortable home circumstances – and only on their visits to the City was the increase in the numbers of Irish beggars and Irish labourers all too apparent. Away in the peaceful countryside at Bramble Haw this spring of 1847 they instead greeted their first baby, a boy who was baptised at Carshalton Parish Church on 20th May, the first of a number of family events to take place at that beautiful church. He was named Walter after his uncle in India, and (somewhat oddly) Hennell after the family of Emma's first marriage, who were, after all, friends and partners of the Nuttings.

William had the gratifying achievement this year also of completing a major instrument for the Greenwich Observatory, his highly successful altazimuth telescope. On 29th January he was able to announce that the dividing of the altitude circle had just been completed.[268] In April, after a little contretemps over William junior (1817) who had taken it upon himself to depart from a visit to Greenwich without first making sure that Mr Main had no further tasks for him that day, William (1793) was able to assure Airy that whatever remained to be done to complete the altazimuth, would be carried out immediately.[269] The very same day he found himself apologising once more to Airy, this time on behalf of brother Henry who had got himself in a muddle over his accounting, and had overcharged × 10 for an item. 'I was startled when I saw what had been charged – – –'[270] expostulated poor William. Henry was faithful and honest, but none too bright. He had mixed up the decimal point.

However, all was forgiven, if not forgotten, in the drama of conveying the altazimuth to Greenwich. Reeves was required to provide two of his strongest horses for this load, and one at least of William's most competent men who had been involved in the creation of the instrument accompanied it to make sure no chances were taken with this precious convoy. Thus it arrived at Greenwich, its function to provide observations which did not coincide with the meridian, notably movements of the moon. With this beautiful piece of equipment Airy was now able to correct lunar tables to a high degree of accuracy, as also the relation of the heavenly bodies to each other and to the moon, which was his prime task as Astronomer Royal, and from which other measurements, particularly time, were extended.

The new altazimuth required unobstructed views of the whole sky, and a three-storey building had already been constructed on the old walls of Flamstead's Observatory in the south-east corner of the Upper Garden at Greenwich, opposite the Octogon Room, using the original north-south orientation of two of the walls. Over this was built a special dome to house

199

The Royal Observatory at Greenwich. Flamstead House is at the lower right, the Meridian building just above it, and the dome (altered in 1894) for the Great Equatorial further left. The small dome amongst the trees just above this is the 'new' altazimuth pavilion (1898), and top left is the New Physical Observatory (1899), now a planetarium, which has 'Simms' carved over a window on the south of the west wing. The transit circle is in the centre of the Meridian building behind the gable opening.

BY PERMISSION OF NATIONAL MARITIME MUSEUM, LONDON

the new telescope, and there it remained fulfilling its task until superseded by a further instrument designed in 1898 by Sir William Christie and made by William's son James, for which a new little building of classical proportions was erected to the south-east of the Meridian Building.

That winter was long and cold, and Airy occupied much of it at Playford by drawing out his designs for his new transit circle, discussing it stage by stage with William, both at the cottage and in London. It would combine the functions of the transit or meridian telescope, which determined Right Ascensions of heavenly bodies, and the mural circle which with a clock attached, measured the declination of stars, thus recording simultaneous results by a single observer rather than the two men required (in separate rooms to avoid noise distraction) for observations on the separate instruments. It was a complicated piece of equipment, first designed in England in the late 18th century by the Reverend Francis Wollaston, but more well known by the one made by Edward Troughton for Stephen Groombridge at his Blackheath observatory in 1806. Its proved accuracy in the latter instance probably encouraged Airy to go ahead with his own transit circle for Greenwich, which subsequently became the archetype for a whole family of later instruments of a similar design.

In March 1848 Airy visited Bramble Haw to examine the model of his proposed transit circle, and the problem of adequate lighting was talked over, but no decision reached. William's own solution was to add prisms to the telescope, a method which Airy later claimed as his own, though with some doubt.[271] Some polite argument over whose invention the arrangement actually was took place later when in 1851 William was drawing up the written description of the transit circle, but although he humbly bowed to Airy's assertion that it was his, one is left with grave doubts as to the truth of the matter. Perhaps some 'industrial espionage' was again being used to serve Airy's purposes.

★   ★   ★   ★

Early the next year – 1848 – hopes of peace in Europe were disrupted unequivocally on 23rd February when the barricades went up in the poorer sections of Paris, followed by severe rioting. By 27th the French royal family began to arrive as fugitives in England carrying few possessions but those in which they stood up. Louis Philippe himself crept into Buckingham Palace from Newhaven on 3rd March, thankful to be away from the mob fury, and Louis Bonaparte, Dutch nephew of the Emperor, after a brief flirtation with the French government, withdrew also to Britain to bide his time with cries of 'Vive La Republique' echoing in his ears. In Berlin rioting broke out in March which was bloody and widespread, and in Italy fighting subdued Austria's claim to sovereignty.

In England the Chartists threatened to march on London, and Queen Victoria, who had only just given birth to Princess Louise on 18th March, travelled to the safety of Osborne on 8th April with her six children, whilst Albert tried to find accommodation and clothes for the French royals. Poor Victoria immediately felt isolated from the centre of activity[272] and longed to be back in London where the shopkeepers kept up their shutters and boarded up their doors, whilst the aristocracy brought in estate workers from their country houses to defend their London mansions. In the event, the gathering of demonstrators on Kennington Green only numbered some 23,000, rather than the anticipated million, and the threatened march turned into a damp squib of a cab drive to hand in a petition at Westminster. William's relief must have been considerable as he surveyed his precious altazimuth awaiting its last finishing touches before being transported to Greenwich. Moreover he had also at Fleet Street a large number of other vulnerable instruments nearly or completely ready for disposal to their buyers, amounting to a considerable total value. These included a 7-inch theodolite which Airy was to examine for an unspecified client, and which was sent up to Greenwich on 5th April. There was a series of equipment for Professor Bache of the US Coastal Survey including a transit instrument,[273] and a zenith and equal altitude telescope;[274] a telescope and equatorial stand for Mr Bonditch of Cambridge, Massachussetts; also a further equatorial for Boston, Mass[275] (? for Harvard College), just completed. Work was also proceeding on the Liverpool equatorial using glass from Munich, and an equatorial clock with centrifugal pendulum to work in conjunction with it.[276]

William continued to have problems with obtaining good glass, and in January this year wrote to Airy[277] of his expectation of receiving from Paris in the near future two discs of flint and two of crown glass. Alas when the parcel eventually arrived at the beginning of March, both the 8-inch discs of flint glass which it contained were so imperfect that he had to return them.[278] The object glass he had brought from Munich for the proposed transit circle for Greenwich, and had since been working, had cost him the huge sum of £300,[279] which amount included no profit to himself. Even so Airy managed to beat him down without apparently too much difficulty to £275, 'if on further examination you are quite satisfied'.[280]

William was weary. He had had a number of worries besides the problem of the glass, and London was an unhealthy place to be this summer, suffering a sudden severe epidemic of cholera, the first since 1832. There is evidence that his youngest daughter, Caroline, had not settled down with her new step-mother, and the latest baby, Walter was not as robust as his half-brothers and sisters. Perhaps there was some jealousy on Caroline's part, both of her step-mother and her step-brother, not wholly unnaturally. On 6th April William retired from the threats of the Chartists, his clients and his suppliers, to travel down to Brighton 'to recruit my health which has declined lately',[281] leaving Henry and William junior (1817) in charge of the business. A walk along the front would blow away the London cobwebs, and his evenings could be entertained by reading Frederick Walter's 'report on the Diamond Harbour Dock and Railway Company' which had recently arrived from Calcutta. Perhaps for light relief he took along a copy of Dickens' latest offering, *Dombey and Son*, which embraced all the parts of Islington, Camden Town, Mrs Pipchin's establishment at Brighton, and Dr Blimber's school nearby, which he knew, as well as the evocative descriptions of Soloman Gill's instrument shop in the City, so like his own father's.

This holiday cannot, however, have done the trick, as in June he was again confined at home, unwell.[282] Was this the start of the nephritic illness from which twelve years later he died?

Before this, however, back in Fleet Street in early May, he was offering to lend Airy two telescopes for some project or other, now that he was certain that it was Mr Dawes who was going to be operating them. He had considerable respect for William Dawes with whom he had had numerous liaisons, including that over his methods for illuminating telescopes, a subject exercising his mind at present with regard to the larger instruments now passing through his hands. Dawes had his own observatory at his home at Camden Lodge, near Cranbrook in Kent,[283] where his 2-ft transit circle had been made by William, originally for Mr Beaumont and with which an equatorial by Merz and Mahler he discovered fifteen Double Stars between 1840 and 1859.

On 30th January 1849 the entry in the firm's workbook notes the completion of four object glasses, each of 8-inch aperture. One was for Mr Peters, another for Mr Airy for his new transit circle at Greenwich, a third was sent to Alabama, and a fourth was now in Mr Airy's hands for examination, destination obscure.[284] A copy of Airy's report is written into the workbook, but is followed in mid-February by a letter from the Royal Observatory to complain that too much colour in the lens is obscuring the view of the stars, notably Venus.[285]

There are now repeated allusions in William's letters to the increasingly detrimental atmosphere of London. A good example appears in February this year when he writes to Airy that adjustments needed to the altazimuth instrument would be better done at Greenwich if possible, under Airy's directions, as William was at the moment 'staying in town and have an atmosphere filled with the smoke of surrounding steam engines'.[286] Waterloo Station had recently been opened at the termination of the Nine Elms line across the river, accommodating an expanding volume of traffic. In addition to problems of dust and fog, William also had lacerated his thumb, which made it difficult for him personally to carry out the work necessary because of the pain and 'inconvenience'.[287] Fine optical work was becoming more and more fraught in the centre of London, and the indications are that often when possible he worked at home where he could set up the instruments in the garden at Bramble Haw without fear of pollution. This year however was not one of those periods, and in April he was in London attending a meeting at Somerset House when he was able to assure the Fellows that he had solved the problem of glass production in England.[288] He had been liaising with the great firm of Chance & Co in Birmingham, with the able assistance of Monsieur Bontemps of Choisy-le-Roi, who was a refugee from the fighting in France last March. Bontemps was an old friend of William's, having been one of his acquaintances in Paris, and was immediately to contact him on arrival in England as an emigré. To Bontemps had been communicated by Guinand's son the method that had made Guinand Pére, Fraunhofer, and Merz and Mahler famous for their glass making, and since Europe was for the time being cut off from England for commercial intercourse, so it was expedient for Bontemps to pass this valuable information, previously a close secret, on to his English friend.

William lost no time in acquainting Messers Chance with the details which, no doubt, they were overjoyed to obtain. They entailed careful 'stirring of the melted glass till it could be stirred no longer, and then chilling the pot somewhat quickly, by which the melted mass split itself into blocks, each sensibly homogeneous'.[289] From this product, optical lenses devoid of veins and cracks could be made, and from now on it seems likely that William used exclusively English glass. By March 1849 he was able to write to William Bond, the director of the Observatory at Harvard that he now had all the facilities for making clear flint glass, and had a good supply of it for which in July he received Bond's congratulations on his achievement.[290]

William Simms continued to carry on a lively correspondence with William Bond over these years, some regarding the new instrument for Harvard, some communications (very politely) indicating need for reimbursement from the College Treasurer for his trip to Munich the previous year. In June 1847, he received via Messrs Baring Bros in London 30 guineas, only £20 of which went into his own pocket, the other £10 being divided between two of his workmen for 'their extra labour during my absence'.[291] Once again he expressed his own confidence in the object glasses he had then acquired. He also indicated in a gentlemanly manner that it was usual for him to receive part of the cost of expensive instruments such as the transit circle ('now in a very forward state') in advance – he suggested £200 to be going on with – 'but I by no means press it' – 'lack of it will not slow the work, nor receipt of it accelerate it'. In this same letter (April 1846) we hear the first indication that he would be prepared to come to 'US of America' on Bond's invitation.[292]

Other letters follow, (one from Bond to order a micrometer for 'our great telescope') though some are evidently missing from the Harvard Archives. With triumph he writes on 30th March 1848 that he has completed graduation of the (transit) circle, and now has only the fitting up and adjustment of the micrometers to achieve, which will take him a fortnight. He aims to send it by ship out of London to avoid the risk of the train journey to Liverpool, still somewhat erratic. By 22nd June it has been carefully packed and shipped, together with 'a telescope for Mr Bonditch' on board the *Swan* from London to Boston, thus concluding all Bond's present orders – 'but I hope not to be long without one' he hints.[293] Alas, in September he had to write to the Treasurer at Harvard to remind him that Messrs Baring had had authority only to pay him up to £200 sterling, and that the balance of £120-14s-8d is still due – 'not that I am in any hurry about it',[294] he disarmingly concludes. More urgent is his warning in the same letter that the reversion (turning over to face the opposite direction) of the transit circle is a hazardous business, and most liable to damage, and he will send Bond some of Airy's papers to describe the risks involved. In November William acknowledges two letters from Bond in which he reports that the mounting for the transit circle is nearly completed – 'Mr Airy will use collimators on his new transit circle rather than reverse it' he hints. Incidentally, he has nearly finished Mr Bonditch's micrometer.[295] Nevertheless in December Bond writes to say he has satisfactorily completed the arrangement for reversing his instrument, and now has a further problem with condensation between the two faces of the flint and crown glass in the lens. To remedy this he (Bond) was extracting the glass when necessary from the tube to wipe the surfaces clear of moisture. Horrified, William replied, ignoring the ill-advised reversing of his precious instrument, but strongly deprecating the separation of the lens from its bed – 'on some unlucky day one of the glasses will be broken', he warns. He suggested instead that Bond should wrap waterproof cloth around the edge of the lens, and use Canada Balsom and 'Master Varnish' to exclude the air.[296] He also thanked for Bond's detailed description of the Harvard Dome, but says his own will be much smaller.

One of the instrument maker's greatest problems, however, now recurred. This was the successful carriage of the completed item to its new home without damage. Even within England mention of the carelessness of the carrier is frequently complained about, and the larger instruments were often accompanied by a workman, preferably the one who had made it, who on arrival would unpack and position it, and even carry out preliminary adjustments. Overseas this was, of course, out of the question, and however carefully these delicate pieces of equipment were packed and labelled, the sailors or the agents who dealt with them were less conscious of their fragility and value, and damage, often severe, was sustained en route by careless handling, even dropping, or by rolling in rough seas when they were poorly roped to the deck. This was a constant and expensive threat, which was realised in the case of the Harvard Transit Circle. Bond professed no knowledge of such poor handling in his observatory, and complained bitterly about the resulting discrepancies in the division caused by a strain or blow on one of the arms of the circle. A long involved letter to William Simms resulted, rejecting any fault on his side of the Atlantic. But how to remedy the damage, particularly as the instrument could still be used as a transit telescope, and was indeed already involved in the on-going Government Survey. Further correspondence between the two men ensued, William warning Bond that if he takes the screws out in order to take the axis to pieces 'it will be good for nothing'. 'Still holding myself at your command in this matter.'[297] Finally it seems to have been decided that it should be returned to London the following spring, though no word of this is to be found in William's workbook, and it is possible that he himself visited Boston that autumn of 1849 'to show(n) you some of the nebulae through our great telescope' – the surviving records are inconclusive.[298] However, he was back in London by 25th October when he disclosed in a letter to Bond the excellent results of sliding scales in computing, and also acknowledged an order for a new transit instrument for Boston,[299] the transit circle presumably now being used for its original purpose. One wonders whether Bond's propensity for reversing the latter had in fact been the cause of the damage he attributed to careless transportation.

William remained resident at Fleet Street for several weeks after the significant April meeting of the RAS regarding the production of glass, the reason for this prolonged stay being not entirely clear, but possibly a combination of pressure of work, the painful condition of his hand made worse by the rumbling journey to and from Carshalton each day, and perhaps the need for surgical attention which could only be found in London. At any rate, his and Emma's next baby, a girl, was born in Fleet Street, where the attentions of Sarah Newall, and perhaps of John's wife Christian, were welcome and calming. The baby was baptised at St Brides as had been three of her elder step-sisters, on 15th June 1849. Her names give cause for comment, as they were unusual, and this follows a pattern which Emma tended to take. She was given the somewhat theatrical name of Lorina after Emma's friend, the only Lorina that has come to light in the International Geneological Index for London. Her second name was Maria, again unusual but this time after Emma's mother and sister, though her step-sister was a Mary which was a very common name. It is noticeable that all the children of William Simms and Ann Nutting had 'normal' down-to-earth names, each commemorating an older relative, whilst all three of Emma's children have some unusual facet in their names which are none of them – except Walter – from the Simms side of the family, and even Walter had been given popularity by *Dombey and Son*. The assumption must be that William's first wife was conventional, but his second wife was avant-garde, and liked to follow the latest fashion.

After this baptism, William and Emma retreated to Carshalton as rumours of further cholera in London were rife; in fact that year produced one of the most severe epidemics on record with 14,000 registered deaths in the capital alone, a re-run of the visitation on the previous year. By September it was thought safe for the children to go down to Brighton for their annual trip to the seaside, taking servants and linen and vast quantities of clothes on the train with them, and leaving the older members of the family behind. As usual William accompanied them to see that they were comfortably settled in before returning to London, and fetched them home again a month later.[300]

Airy had by the autumn developed his plans for the new Reflex Zenith Telescope with which to replace Troughton's zenith sector at Greenwich. This is an instrument precisely mounted on a vertical axis to observe the passage of stars crossing the zenith meridian, and transferring the result to an attached clock. The vertical alignment minimises the effects of atmospheric refraction, and the telescope can be used to gauge the distance of the star concerned from the observer. It was an addition to the armoury for the precise determination of time. William was to construct the new instrument using the object glass from Troughton's old transit telescope installed in 1816, and now to be dismantled, though considered in its time to be in a class on its own. Airy had to give thought also to the housing of his projected new instruments, and whether the transit circle could be accommodated under the present meridianal roof-opening built in 1748 for Bradley's transit instrument from which Britain's first Ordnance Survey maps were based, or whether some alteration to the building was needed. It was at first unthinkable that the meridian itself could be altered, though in the event that is what happened. Airy could be most radical if occasion demanded.

The general public, as usual, had no inkling of all this. Emigration was one of the main topics of conversation just now, not only of the Irish to New York where they developed a thriving colony imbued with gross anti-British antagonism in some quarters. The poorer classes of England and Scotland who were finding it impossible to make a living were also joining the bandwaggon to Canada, and now to Australia, the influx to the latter reaching a peak in 1853-54 with a large number of artisans unconnected with the booming Gold Rush obtaining passages for the lengthy voyage. Three hundred thousand men, women and children left ports in Britain in 1849, and the flow continued until the 1880s by which time 2½ million people had voluntarily sailed for these new countries.

Even so there was a shortage of dwellings for the new urban population in England. Jerry-building of potential slums increased in the industrial towns all this decade, with often no attempt to repair the older terraces, so that the number of houses of appalling standards of material and condition multiplied alarmingly. Still there was insufficient accommodation, however primitive, and crowding of those there were increased to a horrifying extent. The one-room family was common in the east end of London, where cellars were rented out to those who could not afford room-space above ground. Houses were sub-let, until there was anything from a dozen families living in one four-floored tenement. Even quite respectable people endured these sort of conditions. The 1841 census for No. 136 Fleet Street showed the following relatively modest list of tenants: John Heptalwight, a painter, and his wife Sarah and daughter, Diana aged thirteen; Richard Wood, a publisher, Elizabeth Lea, servant (presumably to Richard Wood), William Calvert, compositor aged sixteen, Ann Marshall aged sixteen, servant; Edward Frieburg, aged fifteen (occupation undisclosed), Edgar Parks (thirty-one), ironmonger, and Mary Powell (thirty-eight), servant, with Leonard (eight), her son. These seem to fit into three groups and therefore probably had a floor each, which gave them ample space, until one remembers that their water came from a single source, and their effluent ran out through a single drain. Even so they were relatively well off. Most dwellers further east were without drains, or, even worse, with drains in poor repair which released their contents onto surrounding ground. No wonder that cholera made in-roads into the slum population of towns, less often in the country villages which had natural drainage from small communities. Parliament was so shocked by what it discovered after the 1848 bout of cholera that before the year was out it had passed the very first Public Health Act which whilst having no powers of compulsion, did at least point to the need for action to end the chaotically insanitary results of industrial 'progress' which housed its victims in utter squalor. In fact one of the pressing reasons for Ordnance Survey study of London was precisely to judge the number and state of its drains.

CHAPTER 18

1850-1852

NOT WITHSTANDING ITS SLUMS AND its social problems, Britain was now a prosperous country. One only had to glance at the shops in Ludgate Street for confirmation of this fact. At numbers 9 and 10 Mr Everington was purveying rich Indian shawls. At the bottom of Ludgate Hill was another business selling damasks, muslins and shawls. In St Paul's churchyard were the retail and wholesale emporia of George Hitchcock and Sons, silk-mercers, linen drapers, haberdashers and carpet manufacturers. There were silks from Spitalfields and Lyons, velvets from Genoa, shawls from China, France and Paisley, ribbon from Paris and Coventry, delicate laces from Valencienne, Honiton and Buckingham, and carpets from Kidder-minster, Brussels and Axminster.[301] In Tottenham Court Road Maples' furniture store, opened in 1842, and Fanny Heal's feather-bed and mattress manufactury, were both thriving. New Oxford Street had recently been laid out through the dubious rookery of St Giles to cater for more shoppers. The beggars continued to thrive.

The artisan now wore much the same clothes as his master – a dark morning coat or jacket with matching trousers of straight cut, and a waistcoat of similar or slightly contrasting colour. The ubiquitous top hat of polished beaver or (for grand occasions) black silk, completed the picture, both within his family and in his job whilst his children now had a chance of education at the National Schools. The uniform wretchedness of the lower classes in the thirties was becoming polarised to the very bottom of the social pile, and with rising wages and cheaper food, there was time for most people to have some leisure pursuits at home, and Saturday afternoon outings to the Regent's Park zoo or the panorama. The level of literacy was spreading out over the various classes and a third of labouring families owned one or more books. The free library was widely used and the new railway excursion tickets gave thousands of people the joy of a day at the sea or in the country.

Into this atmosphere of growing confidence crystallized the idea conceived by the Prince Consort for a 'Great Exhibition of the Work of Industry of all Nations'. It was to be a 'pageant of peace, morality and industry'. The Prince was President of the Society of Arts which was the main organiser of the Exhibition, and he chaired most of the preparatory meetings, guiding the plans into a scale that was grand yet catered for all kinds of people in its optimistic pride in all things British. Although the whole country gradually had its appetite whetted for the project, the English optical industry remained quietly working away at its own pursuits throughout 1850 and early 1851, and very little notice was taken of it by the organisers. Plans for Paxton's huge house of glass, though personifying recent recognition of the value of light and air to the individual, failed to reach as far as optical uses of glass in the English market, by some remarkable oversight which had managed to entice various continental manufacturers to exhibit. Only religion had come to terms with the astronomers, claiming that 'the heavens declare the glory of God, and the better the telescope, the greater the glory'.[302]

William had plenty to occupy his mind this year without bothering with exhibitions. In early February he was in Oxford to see the heliometer,[303] a micrometer for measuring the apparent diameter of celestial objects and their distance from one another. Whilst he was there, instructions arrived at Fleet Street from Airy about 'sliding rules', accompanied by designs for them, and when William returned he had to apologise for not attending to these requirements immediately. A new measuring tape was made for Airy, but turned out to be sadly inaccurate. The usual workman to construct these items had left Troughton & Simms, and his successor was a 'bungler', according to William.[304] Reeves, the carrier, was also in trouble again for his carelessness in breaking a repaired thermometer[305] by failing to pack the goods securely into his cart. Once more the good name of the firm was in the hands of incompetent underlings, causing poor William a good deal of irritation. His workbook for 1850 names a series of 'gentlemen' as well as professional astronomers and scientists for whom he supplied instruments. A compound microscope for the Reverend Samuel King, Rector of Saxlingham Nethergate in Norfolk, a keen geologist, entomologist and traveller, in May,[306] and another for Mr Ewbanks, a brass-founder with a wide range of scientific interests, now living in USA, in August, were detailed. An equatorial for Sir William Keith Murray was finished in September, accompanied by minute instructions for fixing it, starting with a description of 'the fixing of the iron plug in the southern pier' and including small diagrams in the margin.[307] This was an example of the client installing his own instrument without the assistance of a Simms workman, who could hardly be spared from the workshop, so great was the pressure of the firm's output in these years.

Now that the London air was so murky, and the successor to Troughton's little observatory which William now had constructed over No. 138, and which contained a clock, a transit instrument and an ordinary equatorial of the zodiacal form,[308] was itself requiring a replacement, William determined to build his own observatory away from the City. He

210

had been considering its construction for some time, and had already (see Chapter 17) asked William Bond at Harvard for advice on the dome. Moreover, Bramble Haw was eminently suitable for an observatory, being well in the country and on land gently rising to the Downs. In his book *The Achromatic Telescope*, published in 1852, he admits it is possible to leave the stand of a transit instrument or an equatorial in the open air, and to carry out the instrument itself when required, but by the time its adjustments are completed, 'in nine cases out of ten, the evening which promised to be fine, turns out cloudy and unfavourable, and nothing in such a case remain for the astronomer, after all the labour of carrying out and adjusting his instruments but to remove them from their stands and replace them in their boxes. A few such disappointments with the fruitless exposure to the night air, and perhaps some unpleasant inroad upon the health, have a wonderful effect in chilling the ardour, even of one who commences with good preparation and with no common degree of zeal'. Here speaks the voice of experience.

William believed that the observatory was merely a rain-proof cover for the instruments, and therefore the simplest arrangement would suffice for

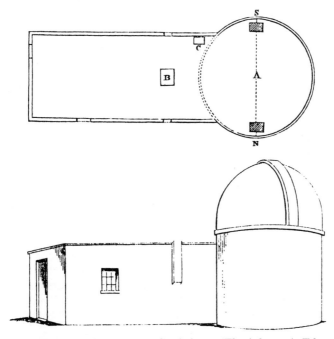

Plans for William's observatory at Carshalton – (The Achromatic Telescope).

211

good astronomical results, the instruments being the important element, together with the observer himself. His own observatory planned in the spring of 1850, could not have bourne out this precept more clearly as it was utilitarian in the extreme, and was made by a local builder called Mr Walker. To be constructed mainly of corrugated iron, a new material recently introduced, it was to be 14-feet long by 7-feet wide, and 7-feet high. Half of the length was to be permanently covered, but on a slight slope in order to carry off the rain, and the other half removable, running on collars along two bars of iron. There was to be a window in the covered end, and a door on one of the long sides. According to Robert Main's article in John Weales 'London and Vicinity exhibited in 1852' the finished article was in fact 16-feet long and nearly 8-feet wide, the sides merely a framework of deal covered with sheets of asphalt felt. The equipment consisted of the three pieces transferred from the 138 observatory, and in addition, outside the new observatory itself, was an achromatic telescope on a stand, particularly noted as having an English object glass. In the covered area of the little building was a table and chair where the computing could be carried out. According to the Peatling Papers,[309] it later had a dome, although no actual evidence for this has been found in spite of William's known preference for one. In his view the best type was of conical construction recently employed by the Reverend Samuel King at Saxlingham Nethergate, or alternatively the more complex cylinder and dome erection sometimes used. As in the case of most private owners, William's little observatory probably died with him. At any rate it was not mentioned in the final catalogue of the demolition survey of Bramble Haw in the 1920s.

In the last few years since the increasing fogs bedevilled him, it may be that William was forced to test most equipment elsewhere than at 138, possibly at Greenwich or on one of the hills within easy reach of Fleet Street. Sydenham was a likely neighbourhood, and after 1854 could be reached by rail from London Bridge Station. It is not clear where the smaller items were tested. Certainly there must have been a location other than the City for the most delicate, and there is little indication where this work was generally carried out. The science of astronomy was yearly increasing in popularity amongst all classes down to the artisan and clerk, and numerous publications were appearing to assist the amateur astronomer by charting the 'celestial bodies', some scientific, others somewhat plebian. The Society for Diffusing Useful Knowledge was the first organisation to produce a large star chart for this new clientele, and this was followed in the middle of the 19th century by smaller pocket-sized compendiums, notably that by Richard Procter of Brighton whose helpful little book published in 1871 as a companion to the earlier 'Webb's celestial objects for common telescopes' ran to seventeen editions. It was intended for public libraries and schools. The Penny Cyclopaedia was an earlier offering for the top end of the market, and employed eminent writers such as Richard Sheepshanks, whose articles were suited to a range of intelligence, lucid and comprehensive as they were.

William's shop catalogue reflects this wide range of interest by the less wealthy parts of society in its large number of smaller pieces of equipment, and it may be assumed that the more lowly of these were made by individual craftsmen working in their own little businesses around the Fleet Street area to supply William with what he could sell in his shop. His brothers, James (1792) and George in Greville Street may very likely have provided some of these items. By the 1851 census, they were named as brassworkers, rather than compass or joint dial makers as previously, and possibly they were subcontracted by William. His larger or more expensive items, especially those ordered by specific customers, always received his personal care, as is clearly apparent in his letters, no matter how busy he was.

During this year of 1850, William and Professor Challis engaged in a lengthy correspondence regarding the latter's pet instrument which he had recently invented and was some sort of calculating machine[310] of which he was inordinately proud. The first extant letter about it is dated 16th March from Fleet Street, and requests that although the work on it is almost finished, William needs further explanation on the construction of the lamp.[311] There was then trouble over the special table for the machine, with which William's cabinet maker let him down badly as 'it is already bent most awfully'.[312] He therefore decided to use brass rather than wood for the table as it was essential to obtain complete stability, but in April he found a firm of mahogany workers whom he thought reliable, and he finally abandoned the idea of metal. His son, James, who this year completed his apprenticeship, brought the machine with him at the end of March by train, hoping to pick up a porter or a fly at Cambridge Station[313] to carry it up to the observatory. Some new apparatus connected with the Cambridge transit was still awaiting division,[314] and somehow the 'machine' was still not sent by early May because of a fault in the dividing,[315] which turned out to be a discrepancy between decimal parts of an inch and the twelfths and twentyfourths that Challis required. A whole letter hurriedly pencilled all over with calculations of fractions follows from William,[316] and finally on 11th May he beseeched Challis to put off the Observatory Visitation to 20th as at the same time as he was struggling to finish Challis' work for Cambridge, he was being heckled by Airy to go to Ipswich with his nephew, William (1817), to make preparations for dividing the transit circle for Greenwich.[317] On the 14th he wrote to Airy that he was off to Ipswich that day to put some points upon the circle for the purpose of cutting the divisions upon the engine, and would send to Greenwich on Thursday for the 8-inch object glass for cleaning and return. A few days later he reported that the stains on the valuable object glass could not be removed without re-working it, but he did not think they would injure its performance.[318]

'It is some time since I mounted one of my object glasses of 8-inch aperture for America' he reflected thoughtfully. 'With clock motion, micrometers and all needful things in the best style,' he was to be paid £800 for it, but if he was to repeat the order, he thought it could be done for £100 less.[319]

In early August William turned his attention to comparing a scale he had made for a customer in Canada with the tubular scale which he borrowed for the purpose from the Royal Astronomical Society,[320] but by the 13th he was at the end of his tether due to all the calls upon him that he decided to go off for a fortnight's recuperation – 'with the hope of servicing my health which has suffered lately'.[321] Brighton may have been his destination once again as it was so easy to reach now he lived near Croydon on the main line from London, but there is no evidence of his whereabouts which could just as well have been Ireland or France. Airy was away from Greenwich just now, and the August sun was anything but conducive to work in Fleet Street, so it was a good time for William to be absent, as were many Londoners now the family summer holiday habit had established itself.

By the end of the month William was back in Fleet Street completing work on the object glass for the Greenwich transit circle. He sent it up to the Observatory in the care of a workman on 12th September.[322] A week later he was there himself, arriving before 10 o'clock in the morning to inspect the instrument and discuss with Airy further work[323] on both the transit circle and the zenith instrument, both now approaching completion.

★ ★ ★ ★

As autumn wore on news arrived from India that Frederick Walter would soon be back in England for good. The irritations and frustrations of the work there had continued without remit. He missed Caroline badly as she had provided commonsense and a calm home where his other associations gave very little satisfaction because of a constant battle with entrenched ideas and positions. Finally his advice for the route of the proposed Calcutta railway was rejected in spite of his careful reasoning and logical exposition of his survey results, and the last straw was the weather which wore him out physically. Once Lord Hardinge, the Governor General, had retired soon after Frederick and Caroline arrived in Calcutta, the trouble had begun with the Indian officers concerned with the survey, and the East Indian Railway was ultimately built near to the Ganges, far away from the coal-fields, and by a circuitous route, completely contrary to Frederick's recommendations. By 1850 he was thoroughly disheartened and was not at all well. He was only too glad to give up the post and to come back to the recognised but lesser hazards of England. His young son, Frederick, needed him as no one seemed to do in India. The boy was now fifteen, and was studying for an entrance to Kings College Hospital medical school. It was high time he had a parent's advice and interest.

Frederick Walter arrived in England as the autumn fogs presaged winter, to find William, his brother, busy but harrassed. Business was good, but his main clients were demanding. Far worse was the nagging anxiety over William's little son, Walter, who had not been well for some time, perhaps since birth. There was no acute illness, and the family doctor could find no label for whatever ailed the child. Possibly a congenital disorder of then unknown cause, possibly the dreaded tuberculosis attacking in secretive but merciless style, the child was seriously ill, failing to thrive, to play, and finally to eat. William's mind must yet again have returned to *Dombey & Son*, but in his optimistic way, he continued to hope. His last letter to Challis that year was black-edged, a forerunner of what was to come. This time it was only a narrow black edge. The contents were to request the moon's place (position) on 1st June 1850 for the purpose of reckoning an occultation observed by William Henry (1820) in Ceylon. A brief concluding sentence thanked Challis for his kindness[324] – it was for some sympathetic action connected with the death of John Simms' wife, Christian Sumner, which had recently occurred on 27th November at 141 Fleet Street after a distressing battle with cancer of the breast. She had always been a favourite sister-in-law, and the fact of William's mourning notepaper was a just tribute to this lady, who almost certainly had seen his family through the difficult years after Ann's death. Her demise can have done nothing to cheer her other brother-in-law, Frederick Walter, and that Christmas was blighted by dark foreboding, which was realised soon afterwards on 17th January 1851, when the little boy, Walter Hennell, quietly died at Bramble Haw. Non-plussed, the doctor signed the certificate, naming 'decline' as the cause of death, and the coachman, James Lovell, was sent the same day to register it. Three days later the little coffin was transported to the top of the hill at Norwood Cemetery, to be buried with his half-sister, Ann, and her mother.

Common though child death was, William and Emma were inconsolable. This was their firstborn, and now Lorina Maria was their only baby, about eighteen months old at the time. The older family of Ann's children, except for William Henry, were all at home to give comfort, but still the sadness remained. Airy wrote to William the day the child died, though somehow he dated it 27th January, an unusual slip – 'I am much grieved at your domestic calamity'[325] he said, and sent it to Fleet Street by hand. William's reply was immediate – 'I am much obliged by your kind note of this morning'. Then he continues on official matters – 'With respect to the Transit Circle work, I am not in want of the money at present and can therefore wait without inconvenience'.[326] Airy was evidently behind with his financing from the Visitors.

215

1851 was one of the most eventful years of William's life, leaving little time for mourning. England was blossoming out into its most affluent period during which trade doubled its volume in the twelve years up to the early 1860s. The news of gold discoveries at Ballerat and elsewhere in Australia increased the scramble for emigration, not all of which by any means was due to tales of rich finds, or indeed to poverty at home. Often it was for the sheer excitement of travel and exploring new fields of endeavour. Much of it was assisted from official sources, but also there were a great many families who emigrated on their own initiative or by dint of personal contacts in the place of their hoped-for destination. The fact of the lengthy journey to Australia seems to have had very little deterrent effect for those with the youth and the will to go. Emigration to Canada and America also continued, particularly from Scotland and Ireland, shortly to be followed by pilgrims to South Africa after gold was discovered there. The emigrants formed one of Britain's main exports, so that British expertise and customs were carried to all parts of the world, increasing trade thereby with the Home Country to these far off places, and thus creating further wealth in Britain itself.

The Prince Consort's Great Exhibition was not merely a British product, but an attempt to bring together into his huge Crystal Palace the art, culture and industry of the world to the glory of peace for all time. It was the inauguration of the golden age of Victorianism, and Queen Victoria herself took great personal interest in the preparations. She visited its site at Hyde Park at the end of January, and then again with her children a month later. Finally in early April she came once more when it was in the throes of last minute chaos, touring the whole palace, and after the Grand Opening on 1st May she visited it numerous times, systematically viewing each stand and department, upon which she commented at length in her diary, especially on those that particularly attracted her.

William Simms was inundated with work this year, when two of his most famous instruments, his transit circle and his reflex zenith telescope, were reaching completion and came into use at Greenwich. So also were many other important products, some noted in his workbook for the year, which give an insight into the enormous activity proceeding in the factory behind 138 Fleet Street. The Civil Engineers Department at Lahore received an unspecified number of standard levelling instruments and twenty Y levels.[327] There were telescopes of 1¾-inch aperture to be sent also to Lahore, and in November a Universal equatorial for India.[328] 'Philosophical apparatus' was made for Senior Don S. Montago.[329] A number of capital instruments were at the design stage for different private observatories, completed during the next year, and he was in frequent touch with Colonel Sabine who was now at Woolwich[330] experimenting with magnetism.

During the early months of 1851 it was realised that though several well-known foreign instrument makers were exhibiting at Hyde Park, England was very poorly represented in spite of William Simms being the leading British maker and a world name in the trade. Dolland had several exhibits, but this was insufficient to represent British achievement in this special sphere. The organisers therefore 'urged and requested him' late as it was, to contribute to the optical stands in order to maintain Britain's high reputation.[331] Rather at the last minute, therefore, William put on his thinking cap and entered as an exhibit the transit circle with the interior illumination which he had made for Mr Pritchard's small observatory at Clapham, and over which he had had the argument with Airy about the inclusion of a prism.[332] Troughton's altazimuth – the Westbury Circle – made for John Pond at the beginning of the century was also included, as was Challis' calculating machine and a number of other new instruments.[333] The resulting section of the exhibits was still rather patchy, but better than before. Since William's nephew, William Simms junior (since February an FRAS), was one of the officials in charge of the optical arrangements, all was set out to as much advantage as possible, particularly as the latter had himself divided the later instruments on the new Dividing Engine, as he was so fond of telling visitors. Even so there was a shocking last minute scramble to sort out the exhibits, and on 16th April William wrote to Airy that Ertel's one exhibit, a portable altazimuth with axis view, was still not yet unpacked.[334] William himself had been to Hyde Park twice the previous week, but the confusion was so great that the commissioners both for the Zollarium and for America advised him against removing his instruments from their boxes, for fear of damage. It was not until 6th May, five days after the official opening of the exhibition that William Simms junior was able to set up Ertel's instrument,[335] its maker having given up in despair and gone home.

However, once open, the Great Exhibition was an enormous success, and anyone who could possibly travel to London to see it, did so. Whole families made a day out of it, and often repeatedly came back. Excursion trains ran from all parts of the country, and although Kings Cross Station was not quite completed, the Great Northern line, only opened in 1850, put down its passengers at Maiden Lane a little further north, from where they were taken by horse omnibus to Hyde Park. The final closing date for the Exhibition was extended until 15th October by which time over six million people had visited it, and a profit of £186,000 was made from which to plan for the South Kensington museums.

During the Exhibition juries appointed for each section discussed and reported on all exhibits, recommending the best for Council medals, and the runners-up for Prize medals. The Zollarium jury strongly recommended William for a Council medal and were put out when the Council of Chairmen refused to acknowledge this, and awarded only a prize medal to

217

him. Ertel also received a prize medal for his one exhibit, but Merz who only entered an equatorial, was awarded the Council medal. In the Navigating and Surveying sections also William received a prize medal for a sextant and a reflecting circle, which was a little unexpected as the designs were old ones of Troughton's although the actual instruments were new,[336] a contradiction which caused comment, though not from him.

Back at Fleet Street the reflex zenith tube was in the finishing stages, and a week after the opening of the Great Exhibition Airy came along to 138 to view the instrument and join William for dinner – 'a mutton chop shall be ready at ½ past 2'[337] cooked by the faithful Sarah Newall. At the end of May the telescope was carefully packed[338] and transferred gingerly to its home at Greenwich where it occupied Bradley's Transit Room, replacing Troughton's 10-ft transit instrument which had occupied it since 1816. Next door to the east was the room which Pond had built in 1809 for Troughton's 6-ft mural circle, but which was now converted to receive the new transit circle. This change involved a removal to the east by nineteen feet of the Greenwich Meridian, the equivalent of .02 seconds of time, an amount which at that period was insignificant for practical purposes. From now on this famous instrument procured the basis of Greenwich time, combining the work of the transit instrument and the mural circle, and continued to do so until 1954, although in the meantime was replaced in 1936 by a new transit circle made by William's great grandson, James Simms Wilson.[339] It was indeed a seminal instrument, copies of which continued to be made for other observatories across the world including that for the Cape of Good Hope next year. It still occupies its original position as an exhibit at Greenwich, and is used now for teaching and demonstration purposes.

Time – even the new Railway Time soon to be introduced at Greenwich – does not stand still, and no sooner were these two great instruments installed that summer of 1851, than Airy's thoughts were centred on Christianstadt in Sweden, where a solar eclipse was expected to be seen in good conditions on 28th July. A number of Fellows of the RAS were planning to travel to Sweden, and to accommodate his own party, Airy hired numerous telescopes and stands from William for the occasion.[340] How much prior notice the latter had is doubtful, but as usual he managed to produce the required selection as if out of a hat, very much in the same way as he had come up with large numbers of surveying instruments in earlier years for Colby in Ireland and Everest in India. There is no evidence that William accompanied Airy to Sweden, but it remains an open question, although he certainly took a personal interest in the event.

Frederick Walter was now recovering from the exigencies of working in India. He had had a series of illnesses due to inflammation of the liver since his return the previous autumn, presumably an infectious hepatitis contracted from the hopelessly inadequate water supply and sewage

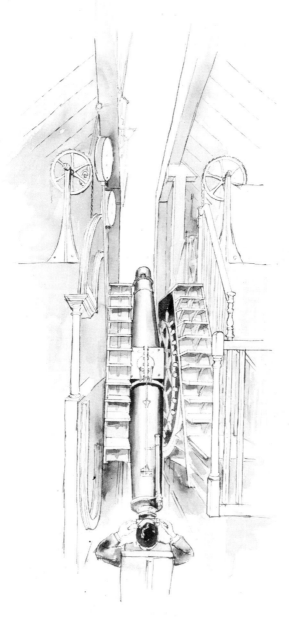

Airy's transit circle.

219

facilities of Calcutta, upon which ironically he had reported whilst there, but it also seems likely that he underwent some sort of nervous breakdown.[341] During 1851 he was sufficiently improved to be appointed to the position of consulting engineer to the Mid-Kent Railway Line, working on the section between Rochester and Canterbury. This was a return to his old stamping ground where the local farmers had been so opposed to giving up their land to the railway in the 1840s. Frederick Walter was involved in the building of the tunnel at Sevenoaks, but never to the extent of his earlier work, and illness seemed to dog him so that he was even unable to give evidence before a Committee of the House of Commons regarding the route of the line, later known as the London, Chatham and Dover. He had a much less easy-going temperament than William, nor, because of circumstances, did he have the same family backing. He was becoming both hypochondriacal and desperately lonely, with a grudge against the great disappointments of India. He soon gave up any professional involvement, and spent his time reading and in scientific experimentation of an unexacting kind. A sadly disappointed man, with all his hopes centred on his only child, Frederick.

One more important family event occurred this year – the marriage of William's eldest daughter, Elizabeth Ann on 4th September to Henry Lee at Carshalton Parish Church. The official witness this time was Sarah Simms, sister of the bride. The bridegroom was a furrier whom Elizabeth Ann had known for at least five years, and for whom William had respect. The son of a furrier, James Lee, of Lambeth, he was probably not in the position to marry her earlier in spite of this being the heyday for such luxuries as furs. Perhaps he was still apprenticed to his father, but certainly money was a problem as later in the decade, William lent Henry £800, a very large sum. After the wedding Elizabeth Ann and Henry went to live at the Waldrons at Croydon, so William still had this much-loved daughter near at hand. Their house, part of a crescent, still exists a short distance south of the High Street, and near to the old Brighton Road.

A delightful incident occurred as the year was drawing to a close, which reveals more of the character of the two participants in such kindly scullduggery than all the reports and letters in the world. In November Airy wrote to William asking him to collude in some secretive work with the aim of saving the reputation of the elderly Thomas Jones. Jones had been a contemporary and good friend of Edward Troughton, and had a life-time of highly admired optical work to his name, for which he was much respected amongst astronomers. His had been the first equatorial at the young Cambridge Observatory, and he had supplemented Troughton's mural circle at Greenwich by a second one. Earlier he had been one of those who formed the Astronomical Society in 1820 and later made a transit instrument and a mural circle for Armagh Observatory. Born in 1775, he was now failing to understand new methods and ideas, and in particular was unable to grasp Airy's instructions in connection with a double eyepiece.

Frederick Walter Simms.

'The old man does not understand the theory a bit – – – it is the most spirit-breaking work that I have ever tried' complained the exasperated Airy. Unwilling to dismiss Jones from the project, yet equally unable to penetrate the cloud of his incomprehension, he asked William Simms if he would agree to make the eyepiece secretly to Airy's design, and engrave it with the maker's name, Thomas Jones, 4 Rupert Street, Haymarket, so that Jones would be none the wiser, assume it was his own,[342] and receive the credit. William had good reason to grasp the chance to repay Jones for his earlier kindness to him, as it had been he who had first encouraged William to go ahead with his new design for a protractor in 1816, which was the start of William's recognition by the optical world. He thus immediately replied that he would be glad to co-operate, to make the instrument and to sign it with Jones' name,[343] a piece of unselfish deceit which can only have been rewarded by later seeing the pride in the old man's eyes. Behind Airy's stiff exterior and William's kindly smile there was a mutual feeling of sympathy for the ageing optician. Thomas Jones in fact died the following 29th July, so this was probably 'his' last instrument.

CHAPTER 19

1852-1854

AFTER THE FLURRY OF 1851 with all its eventful activity, 1852 was miraculously subdued, with only two major exceptions of a personal nature and one of national significance. Work at Troughton & Simms was progressing in its usual vein, exacting but unspectacular, which increased all the more the impact of all these events. Whilst life in William's workshop could rarely be humdrum, the early months of 1852 contained a typical mix of orders with few of any prominence. Correspondence during this year both with Cambridge and Greenwich is almost non-existent, and no major astronomical instruments seem to have been completed for national observatories, although this apparent absence of communication may be illusionary, and due to poor preservation or disposal of letters for one cause or another. Equally it may be due to more personal contact rather than written discussion, or it may have been caused by illness, or by failure to keep proper notes. Archival material, after all, depends largely on careful filing at the time.

The Great Exhibition had given a boost to the optical trade as to many others, and because the microscope provided the largest contribution to the mathematical instrument section, it received the greatest attention. In 1852 the effect washed back to the manufacturers, and in William's workbook, details and diagrams appear, notably for Smith Eldon's compound microscope,[344] whilst his 1852 catalogue denotes a range of microscopes costing from one guinea to the considerable sum of £24-0s-0d. Besides this product, several private clients received their orders, including further 'philosophical apparatus' for Senior Don Montago who was experimenting with pulleys and weights.[345] More relevant to William's own interests was Mr Collingwood's[346] wish to equip his private observatory, following William's advice that an equatorial and a transit circle would well suffice for his needs. The latter, William wrote, would be suitable if given a 5-ft focal length and 4-inch aperture, 'with a declination micrometer in the eyepiece to facilitate the taking of direct and reflected observations'. The circle was to be 36 inches diameter, with four micrometers to read to single seconds of arc. The illumination also is described in his letter, as are the collimators. The cost was to be £450 exclusive of packing and shipment.[347]

At Bramble Haw 1853

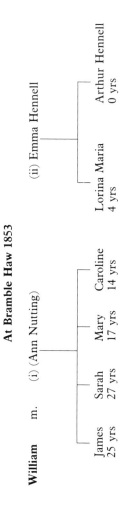

William   m.   (i) (Ann Nutting)   (ii) Emma Hennell

James — Sarah — Mary — Caroline   Lorina Maria — Arthur Hennell
25 yrs — 27 yrs — 17 yrs — 14 yrs   4 yrs — 0 yrs

The most acceptable personal order that year was from Mr Carrington.[348] Richard Carrington had been born in 1826, and so was still a young man. Whilst at Trinity College, Cambridge, like many other undergraduates he had attended Professor Challis' lectures on astronomy, becoming so inspired by them that he determined on a career in that subject. In March 1852 Carrington resigned his first appointment as observer at Durham because of the poorly equipped state of the observatory there, and started to build his own observatory at Red Hill, near Reigate, for which he conferred with William, regarding the type of equipment suitable for his very highly developed needs. William designed for him a transit circle of 5½-ft focus, taking his Greenwich instrument as its model though with reduced scale. He also designed an equatorial for him of 4½-inch aperture, and both instruments were installed by the middle of June, mainly by William Simms junior working under the instructions of Lord Rosse of Birr Castle. From this nucleus Carrington produced advanced observations of the circumpolar stars, which work finally earned him the Gold Medal of the Royal Astronomical Society in 1859.

Unlike his nephew, William senior's character was to work away quietly and efficiently, caring little for publicity. He felt assured that the excellence of his products would bring their own acclamation. To such a man, who although a leading manufacturer in highly sensitive wares was so reticent about his skill, it must have come almost as a shock when in 1852 he unexpectedly received an auspicious-looking communication by hand from the Royal Society, then still at Somerset House. On opening out the thick notepaper, he was astounded to learn that his name had been put forward for election to a Fellowship of the Society. To become a Fellow of this august circle was surely the peak of any man of science' career, and for William, who was so humble regarding his own achievements, an event truly overwhelming. It was the recognition of many years of painstaking application of complicated optical and mathematical principles. It recognised the successful completion of some of the world's most accurate tools for measurement, underlying all the erudition to be found in the map-making of the Ordnance Survey. It was also a reward for long hours of intricate and specialised work to produce the apparatus for others to achieve great advances in astronomy, navigation and surveying. A compliment, an accolade, and best of all a sign of the regard in which his fellow scientists held him. It was with considerable pride that he realised that he was now distinguished by the official style of William Simms FRS, FRAS. Coming so soon after the glowing tributes to his virtuosity by the jurors at the Great Exhibition the previous year, it went some way towards making up for the slur of the Council of Chairmen who had negated his Council medal for a prize medal.

William's sponsors for the FRS numbered twenty, all very well known names in astronomy and surveying, including of course George Airy. The list reads like a catalogue of mid-19th century achievement. It included John Couch Adams, the Cambridge mathematician and discoverer with Le Verrier of the planet Uranus; George Rennie, builder with his father of the London bridges; James Glaisher, the director of magnetic and meteorological services at Greenwich, and reporter on the Great Exhibition; William Cubitt, builder of the South East Railway and countless other projects; Lord Wrottesley, for whom William Simms had made an equatorial in 1841 and who was to become President of the Royal Society in 1854; William Gravett of Level fame; Isambard Kingdom Brunel, now embarking on his 'Great Eastern' project;[349] and old friends such as Richard Sheepshanks and Bryan Donkin. It is significant that William's oldest client from his earliest days before he joined up with Troughton, Colonel Colby, was not on the list. His surveying days were now at an end, and in October that year, he died at his home at New Brighton, thirty-two years after he himself had been elected an FRS.

The second outstanding event which marked out 1852 as the zenith of William's career occurred at about the time of the bestowal of his FRS. It was the appearance of his most well-known publication which he simply entitled *The Achromatic Telescope*, a masterly account of the technicalities of the instrument and its various mountings, especially the equatorial, in his usual lucid and slightly humorous style. It was this book which included a treatise on private observatories including his own in Fleet Street and Carshalton, from which one gathers a range of information about the social mores of the times, and of the character of the man himself. The book was printed by Taylor & Francis at Red Lion Court, Fleet Street, and published by Troughton & Simms. A copy was naturally presented to the Royal Astronomical Society, on whose shelves it can still be found today, as indeed it can in many reference libraries, public and specialist. It was well received at the time, and contained a good deal of sound common sense combined with rather more erudite descriptions and diagrams. A heart-warming example of the former is contained in the advice to use a soft silk handkerchief or carefully chosen chamois leather for wiping a lens – 'better to avoid meddling with the object glass'. It became a seminal book on its subject, and is as clear in its facts as it was the day it was written.

It was probably during this year, perhaps in honour of his election to Fellowship of the Royal Society that the first of the two known extant photographs of William were taken.[350] The collodian wet-plate process had been perfected recently, and was patented in 1851 by Frederick Scott Archer. Much speedier to produce than the calotype, and quicker to expose than the daguerrotype, it rapidly became popular even with amateur photographers, and photographic 'rooms' were set up where professionals developed their wares. The carte de visite was yet to come two years later, when thousands of portrait photographs began to be made, and all families who could afford them had their own family albums. In 1852 personal

226

portraiture, however, was by no means uncommon, much of it of high quality, and such a mark of William's eminence would appeal to Emma's sense of propriety.

William's portrait photograph is incredibly realistic. It shows an attractively open character, only confirming what is conveyed in his writings. His kindly intelligent face betrays amusement at the whole procedure, a smile hovering around the corners of his mouth and eyes, the only permanent reminder in his otherwise line-free face of his attitude to life. Clean-shaven, with regular features, he impresses by his unambiguously frank appearance. He is neither rotund nor lean, though the beginnings of a double chin are perceptable over his neck-cloth and stand-up collar, and there is the suspicion of balding – a family feature – as his hair is brushed forward in the manner of the time over his receding forehead. Taken at the very height of his career, this handsome man inspires confidence and calm. A most interesting study of personality before ill-health compromised his life.

On 18th November of this eventful year, Fleet Street was witness to the most extraordinary and moving event, when the Simms family had a grandstand view of a remarkable procession accompanying the funeral cortege of the Duke of Wellington, who had died three weeks previously at Walmer Castle. Since 10th November the body had been lying in state in the great hall at Chelsea Hospital. On 11th the Queen and the Royal family had visited the hospital to pay their respects, and on 12th the nobility and gentry who had tickets filed past the bier. Thereafter a vast mass of pushing, shoving, emotional humanity fought and struggled for admission, quite overwhelming the police, who had to have reinforcements from the army to keep order. Up to 65,000 persons passed through the hall each day, of which certainly the Simms adults formed some, and probably the older children too, in a wave of patriotism generated the year before at the Great Exhibition. The following Wednesday a squadron of cavalry guarded the coffin on its way to the Horse Guards, from where it was accompanied by a huge military parade representing every unit in the British army and some that were not, to St Paul's Cathedral. The Prince Consort determined that this was to be the 'most wondrous of military pageants', and had designed the enormous funeral car, twenty-seven feet long, of bronze partly taken from the guns used at Waterloo, and covered with allegorical subjects proposed by the Prince. It now rests in the crypt of the Cathedral. The streets were heavily decked in black, and a million-and-a-half souls who lined the route in spite of the heavy rain were so overawed by the display that not a sound came from them as the great carriage rumbled by. Only the tramp of marching feet and the strains of the Dead March in 'Saul' and other lugubrious melodies chosen by the Prince, could be heard to the accompaniment of jingling of harness and the minute-guns in the Park. As evocative was the sight of the Duke's horse led by his groom in the procession, with his master's empty boots, reversed, hanging from each stirrup.

The windows, balconies and roofs along the way were crowded with silent spectators. At No. 138 Fleet Street Emma, surrounded by her family who had come up from Carshalton for the event, was so moved that the name of Arthur Wellesley was filed away in her romantic memory for future use.

$$\bigstar \qquad \bigstar \qquad \bigstar \qquad \bigstar$$

One possible reason for the paucity of correspondence in 1852 is that William was again in Munich, though the date is uncertain. Specifically he was examining glass for the transit circle ordered by Harvard College, USA,[351] and incidentally doubtless visiting the workshops of Ertel and Merz. An off-shoot to Switzerland to see the glass manufactury of Daguet probably followed. He thought the Munich instrument far too expensive at 42,000 florins (about £3,554-14s-0d English money), as including merely the instrument, whilst the cost of packing, transport to the coast, and shipment to America were extra. His own prices were much less formidable, and his advice to Challis for a transit he thought suitable for his use was a mere £450 for one like that which he had made for Mr Collingwood, or £550 for a larger one. An equatorial to go with it could cost anything from £150 to £650 according to the size of the object glass. If this discussion was for a transit circle for Cambridge Observatory, Challis was to be disappointed as it was another twenty years before William's son, James (1828), made a great instrument for his successor with money given by Miss Sheepshanks in her brother's memory, a highly successful instrument which was still in working order in the 1940s, though not used regularly after about 1919.[352]

William commenced the New Year of 1853 at Carshalton with 'sickness', and letter-writing was delayed.[353] He had had to say goodbye to his youngest son, Frederick, now twenty-two, who set sail to Sydney, Australia, at the beginning of January, as so many young men were doing. Frederick was a civil engineer, though details of his life are scant. Up to now he had been living at 138 in Sarah Newall's care, from where he was probably apprenticed to one of the many firms at work in the construction of railways, roads and bridges. A likely employer was William Cubitt on the South East Railway or on the later Great Northern, or indeed recently on the erection of the Crystal Palace for which he had been knighted by the Queen at Windsor in December 1851. Frederick inherited the travel yen from his namesake uncle, Frederick Walter, and travelled to Sydney where his subsequent career there has not been unearthed. He appeared back at

Troughton & Simms about 1865 when he took over from his Uncle Henry in the firm's new factory at Charlton as its correspondent. In the meantime he is said to have 'travelled widely' though whether this indicates destinations other than Sydney has not yet come to light. It would be likely that if his Australian venture failed, he would visit his elder brother, William Henry (1820) in Ceylon. There is also a mention of a Frederick Simms, watchmaker, at 45 Great Dover Street, Borough, in the Post Office directory of 1855, though no other evidence that this was he, and perhaps unlikely in view of his youth.

The main astronomical instrument completed by William in 1853 seems to have been a transit circle for the Cape Observatory.[354] Following the successful establishment of his instrument at Greenwich the previous year, similar models were constantly replacing earlier transit telescopes and mural circles at a number of national observatories, and continued to be made by William's own son James after his death, including notably the one at Cambridge, England in 1870. Surviving correspondence with Challis in 1853, however, was of the more mundane but important subject of his experiments for casting iron, for which Challis had invented a new method of building a trough.[355] Designs were sent to Challis in April, but a week later William wrote again to say the trough was not up to expectations, because although the foreman had 'adhered in all aspects to (Challis') instructions, but that when the iron bevels were moved they were too deeply embedded in the wood frame',[356] and had to be cut to extract them. Such practical problems in this precise work continually raised their heads although the skilled results are taken for granted. They were also time-consuming. This is reflected in the cost as in the preparation of lenses, an example of which comes in correspondence with Airy this year.[357] An 8-inch object glass of 'very good' quality which William had prepared was priced at £250-0s-0d, and a 9-inch one at £350-0s-0d, huge amounts at that time.

The household at Bramble Haw was now predominantly female, despite the departure of Elizabeth Ann to Croydon. Still at home were Sarah, now aged twenty-seven, Mary and Caroline aged seventeen and fourteen, and the four year old Lorina Maria. James sometimes came out to Surrey for the night but when more convenient would remain at Fleet Street even though the railway now extended to Epsom since 1847, the present station of Wallington having been originally named Carshalton. One also is reminded by Dickens how far the Victorians were prepared to walk without turning a hair, as for instance David Copperfield who thought nothing of 'tramping out to Putney and back of an evening to see Dora after a day's work – a distance about half that to Carshalton.

In October 1853 the twelfth and last of William's children was born to Emma, a longed-for boy to ease the pain of little Walter's death. Once again she determined the name of her first husband, Henry Hennell, should be

229

commemorated in the second christian name of this new little Simms. For his first name she revived her memories of last November and called him Arthur, showing once more her propensity for popular fashion. The boy, Arthur Hennell, is an interesting character as he became the exception to the long Simms tradition of following a career in precision instrument or jewellery making or surveying. A very intelligent child, his life was greatly affected by the death of his father when he was only seven, from which time his ambitious but graceful mother guided him away from a scientific future. That he was doubtless pampered by her and his six older sisters must have been inevitable, and his education followed that which was now in vogue for well-to-do youngsters, namely that of the public school.[358]

Gossip in the London of 1853 was increasingly jingoistic. During the Great Exhibition attitudes had been pacifist in the extreme; all countries would work together, war would be no more, everyone would be happy, and so on. The fact was that by the early 1850s one had to be at least forty-five years old to remember the unpleasant side of war, the killings and maimings, the loss of loved ones, the shortages of materials and the increased taxes. In 1853 only the glory and excitement of war was recalled, and Wellington's recent death brought back to mind his victories in Spain and France, as well as those of Nelson at Aboukir Bay and Trafalgar. Even when almost all Europe had been in a state of revolution in 1848, Britain had remained at peace. She had, however, had her collective fury aroused by some of the incidents across the water, especially those caused by the 'Holy Alliance' of Austria, Prussia and Russia in their treatment of Poland. Later, Britain resented very much the cruel way that Russia stamped out Hungarian liberties, and the brutal oppression with which Austria clamped down on Italy. Now Russia was threatening Turkey, the excuse being a religious combat to free Christians in the Balkans and the Holy Land, but it was seen as purely Russian expansionism towards control of the Mediterranean. Russia was a major power, and totally mistrusted by Britain. Moreover, an alliance against the Tsar was an insurance against war with France, who in any case desired continuing peace in order to be able to afford improvements in her inland facilities such as roads and canals.

By October 1853, Turkey was at war with Russia, and indeed fired the first shot at the on-coming armies as they invaded Moldavia and Wallachia. During that winter the Russians without mercy sank the Turkish fleet off Synope in the Black Sea, and London was in transports of anger over such bullying. By March 1854 a great armada of British, French and Turkish ships gathered together around the port of Varna at the western end of the Black Sea, spreading eastwards in an effort to prevent Russian invasion of Bulgaria and from her having free use of the sea. Britain was now in the thick of the conflict, and declared war on 27th March, to the echo of cheers back home where pride in her army and navy was revived to its previous level during the French wars. This, however, was a war without sufficient justification, and when the crack troops which were first sent out from England were massacred in the Crimea because of indecisive command, poor communication and abysmal supplies, untrained soldiers followed, coinciding with the Russian winter, frost-bite, and cholera. The suffering was beyond belief.

William Simms remained on the side-line in this conflict, surrounded by nationalistic enthusiasm, and with the sudden task of providing small-scale instruments to the army and navy for use in the field or at sea. It was a pity that such a gifted nation did not think of laying a railway in the Balkans and Crimea to provide an efficient supply line, but such was never contemplated. In fact the even tenor of civilian life in England continued mainly unaffected by reports from the Crimea, the newspapers flooding the country with articles now the stamp duty on journals was rescinded, soon to be followed by the first-ever authentic photographs of warfare. More, almost, than anything else to affect the general public were the habits which soldiers returning home passed on to them, notably smoking which came back into favour after eighty years, since it had been excluded from polite society during the tobacco 'famine' caused by the American War of Independence. The other remarkable legacy of the war was the growing of beards which had been adopted by the soldiers as a method of keeping warm in the arctic conditions of the Crimea, and after this date hirsute gentlemen became common, and indeed beards continued in great abundance up to the First World War.

In general the optical world was unruffled by the Crimean troubles, and William's correspondence shows little reference to it. This year he was engaged in checking the Standard Measures for the island of Guernsey, comparing their old-fashioned names of bushel, denere, pot, quint and pint to cubic inches.[359] About the same time he was preparing Standard Lengths for New Brunswick[360] in one of his frequent departures into metrology, a close relation to optics for which he normally provided the instruments for ascertaining the accuracy of the fine micrometers involved. During the spring he received his usual visit from the Norfolk parson, the Reverend Samuel King, a man of broad scientific interests, who was now expanding his knowledge to include astronomy. Later, Challis visited William regarding some business, but there was a delay in carrying out the work as William Simms junior was on holiday and William himself also was absent from Fleet Street, probably due to illness. However, by 10th October he was able to provide a sketch for Challis' proposed new mounting, to replace that for two object glasses which was unsteady. Always practical in his approach to such matters, he even suggested that Challis laid the tracing on a sheet of white paper in order the better to see it.[361]

William's premises in Fleet Street, and indeed Bramble Haw too, constantly were the focus of attention for his widening circle of acquaintances, and his clients usually became his life-long friends.[362] He was therefore all the more concerned when in October news of the Crimean battle of Alma arrived in England, closely followed up by the intelligence of the death of an old client and friend, John Lloyd, whom he had first known during the latter's investigation into the difference of levels in the Thames between London Bridge and the sea. Lloyd had later visited William Henry (1820) in Ceylon about 1849, and William's own acquaintance with him had been reinforced during the Great Exhibition with which he had been involved in amassing industrial products. An FRS, he was on the Council of the Institution of Civil Engineers, and was gathering survey information at Therapia when he died of the all-too-prevalent cholera which swept through the Crimea.

Cholera also was raising its ugly head in the counties about London, killing 10,000 people that year, though only 211 of these deaths occurred in the City. Proper drainage was still a problem, and wherever a backyard was devoid of efficient sewage disposal, sooner or later would follow a focus of infection. This implied the absolute necessity of a good supply of clean water. Infection happened in all the large towns where there was gross inadequacy of water provision, and rubbish was discarded in the streets and yards. It was not for another twelve years that further outbreaks of disease led to legislation which forced the authorities to appoint sanitary inspectors and provide proper water supplies, sewers, and refuse disposal.

With his thoughts intermittently on the Crimea, William was absorbed with the packing of another transit circle for America[363] in one direction, and an 18-inch altazimuth for Melbourne,[364] Australia, in the other. In between these important preoccupations, the usual niggling little events occurred to ruffle his sang froid. The carrier reappears in disgrace, having this time lost through negligence (breakage?) ten pounds of mercury costing £1-15s-0d.[365] Not very much is heard from Airy this year, due to his prolonged sojourn near South Shields where, down the Harton colliery at a depth of 1,260 feet he designed and carried out a series of highly technical pendulum experiments to determine the ratio of increase of gravity with descent. His earlier work with Sheepshanks at the Cornish mine of Dolcoath in 1826 where he had examined the same problem, had been unsuccessful because of flash floods, but on this occasion, though he completed his readings, his results were later found to be inaccurate.

As William travelled home to Carshalton this year, on the hill to his left the impressive mass of Paxton's great Crystal Palace rose again, removed from the Exhibition site at Hyde Park which now returned to its normal green tranquility, to its permanent home near the old spa village of Sydenham. Coincidentally its rail link with London Bridge was built to provide easy access for the Londoners to enjoy the green heights of Sydenham Hill in their leisure hours. On 10th June the Queen and Prince

Albert once again visited this remarkable building in its new surroundings and now with its added water towers 282-feet high, to declare it open for public entertainment and pleasure, exhibitions and concerts or just perambulation amidst the potted palms, and a meal in one of the many restaurants. The acres of surrounding green slopes were now easily reached by townsfolk and became a place for picnics and play away from the smokey prosperity of London, as a southern counterbalance to Hampstead Heath for a family day out.

For those whose pleasure was in academia and the arts, there began to emerge plans for the rebuilding of Old Burlington House in Piccadilly as a home for the Royal Academy. The Government had in 1854 purchased the great mansion altered by Colin Campbell in 1695-1743 for Richard Lord Burlington, for the sum of £140,000 including its gardens, and on these to the south of the main building were to be erected wings to enclose the present arched gateway. These Italianate extensions were to house various Learned Societies including the Royal Astronomical, whose rooms were to be at the south end of the western range. The main architects were to be Charles Barry and R. R. Banks, but work did not commence for another twelve years, and the RAS did not move into its new abode from Somerset House until autumn 1874. Here, rent-free, it found itself in possession of a splendidly imposing pile, with elegant rooms, impressively grand staircase, and a most beautiful galleried library from the windows of which the members could look down on the motley company crossing the forecourt.

At the time of the Government's first involvement with Old Burlington House, it required the whole of Somerset House for its own offices, and therefore had also to rehouse the Royal Society, which from 1857 therefore occupied the main central block of Colin Campbell's grand old mansion, sharing it on the first floor with the Linnean and Chemical Societies. The collonaded wings on the east side of the forecourt which curved elegantly south from the house were used by the offices of London University, and the western counterpart as a meeting room for the Royal Society. Subsequently after Barry's rebuilding, the Royal Society was housed in the new eastern range, but if William Simms ever managed to attend meetings towards the end of his life, it was at the main front entrance in the plainer Palladian facade that his carriage must have drawn up, with the view of Piccadilly unobstructed by Barry's monumental southern gateway.

Simms family opticians/Lee

James
1792-1857

William
1793-1860

William
1817-1907

William
Henry
1820-1875

James
1828-1915

Elizabeth Ann   m.   Henry Lee
1824-1881   1852

Henry

Elizabeth
Louise

William
Simms

Mary Matilda
1857-1858

CHAPTER 20

1855-1858

THE NEWS FROM THE CRIMEA continued to be dreary. The battles of Balaclava and Inkerman had produced success, and so did Alma, but at a terrible cost in illness and suffering. In October 1854 Sebastopol had been surrounded by the Allies, but no rapid fall was envisaged. The cost of the war in monetary terms had in 1854 led to an increase in income tax to 1s-2d, an unprecedented level which was maintained until after the Indian Mutiny three years later. The horrifying stories of the cold, the vermin, the sickness, the hunger and thirst of troops fed on nothing but salt pork, continued to appear in the reports from the war front, followed eventually by hints of the appalling lack of organisation of the army, and then the harrowing descriptions which confirmed the suspicions of complete mismanagement.

This January of 1855, in a year marked by the publication of the Bonn Durchmusterang, that memorable star atlas known affectionately to astronomers ever since as 'the BD', William was re-elected to the Council of the Royal Astronomical Society for his third period of tenure. Professor Airy was in the Chair, although in June he was unable to be present at the monthly meeting, his place being taken by the President, Mr I. Johnson.[366] William attended Council meetings assiduously this year, only absenting himself in December, and was re-elected for the next three years up to the end of 1858. He was an active member, perhaps more confident than in earlier years, and as usual spoke only when he had something of substance to say. Never one to waste words, his colleagues had learned that if William Simms chose to express an opinion, it was well worth their while to listen and take note. His obituary in the RAS Monthly Notices[367] particularly emphasises his 'sound judgement'. One suspects also his unpretentious sense of humour was appreciated when proceedings became too fraught, or heavily personal, or indeed tangential to the point under discussion.

Sadly, William's old friend, Bryan Donkin, was not on the Council with him this time. In February this remarkable man of many parts and great humanity, died at his home at 6 The Paragon, the beautiful curved terrace overlooking the Heath and the distant walls of Greenwich Park. William first met him in his early days at the Society of Arts. Donkin had later been closely involved with Troughton & Simms during the Sir John South fiasco, and had provided some of the larger parts for that famous telescope, such as the tube, from his own factory in 1829. Subsequently he became one of the witnesses for William Simms in his successful law-suit against South. After a varied career of invention and mechanics, he became President of the Institute of Civil Engineers. One of the original members of the Astronomical Society, he was in the Chair when it received its Charter in 1831. In 1838 he became an FRS, and later sponsored William for the same honour, remaining a good friend ever since, although of a generation older.

In June William completed 'apparatus' for Sir John Lubbock, Bart, the astronomer and mathematician, and first Vice-Chancellor of London University but was unable through illness to be present when Sir John visited Fleet Street to inspect it on Saturday 9th June. James (1828) did the honours instead, and as his father admitted, was more expert than he himself at 'finding objects'. James would also, if required, accompany Sir John to Lord Hardinge to discuss matters,[368] though the nature of the 'apparatus' is not revealed. It does, however, indicate how much confidence William already had in this steady son who eventually became the most eminent of all his children. The connection also is of interest as Lord Hardinge had been Governor General in India when James' uncle Frederick Walter arrived in Bengal in 1845. He had had several appointments since then, and was at present involved in supplying the needs of the army in the Crimea, the want of preparation for which he was widely blamed. Nevertheless he was to be promoted to Field-Marshall that October, perhaps in recognition for his previous service with Wellington and Sir John Moore in Spain and in view of his imminent retirement. In fact he died the following September. As Sir John Lubbock's primary interest was in metrology, it seems probable that whatever he ordered from William was connected with that science, possibly a theodolite and micrometers, or measuring rods.

Since 1841, William's other friend of long-standing, Richard Sheepshanks, had been living in Reading, moving out to the country no doubt for the usual reason amongst star-watchers. His observatory at his house at Woburn Place became affected by the fogs of London, and in Reading this wealthy man built yet another one for himself, travelling in to Somerset House frequently to pursue his vast project to produce the Standard Lengths. His last extant letter to William, dated 1st April 1852, is, suitably enough, on the subject of the effect of temperature on the length of different metals.[369] His work, officially taken over from Francis Baily in 1844, had now been completed, involving nearly 90,000 micrometrical readings using thermometers of his own design,[370] and with help over the eleven years from various men of science including William who provided some, if not all, of the instruments. The results of this magnum opus were laid before

Parliament in 1854. On 29th July 1855 came the news of the severe stroke which Sheepshanks had sustained and which laid him low. The very next day his Standards received the Royal Assent, both for the main items and for some official copies, though whether he ever knew of this success is not recorded. Two days later, William, writing to Challis on the matter of his account with Cambridge Observatory – 'not that I desire immediate payment, for I am willing to wait any length of time', (compare with today's attitude) – ends with mention of 'the sudden and dangerous illness of our Excellent friend'. Sheepshanks had indeed been a good friend and mentor to William, and it is ironical that the two men who were so generous with support and wise counselling in the South affair, should die within six months of each other. Although said by some to be a 'rogue', Sheepshanks was unsparing in his kindness if he felt it was deserved, though gratingly sarcastic if otherwise. Highly intelligent, he was better a friend than a foe. To William he was uncompromisingly generous in his attitudes.

Four days after William's letter, Sheepshanks died at Reading, much lamented by William to whose house at Carshalton he had been a frequent visitor. As at Fleet Street he was often unannounced at Bramble Haw, and came to see how things were progressing.

By coincidence, that very month Airy demanded a workman 'as early as maybe' to put the clockwork of the Sheepshanks equatorial at the Royal Observatory in order. He avowed that he would not tolerate William's workman named Burry being let loose on the instrument again, as last time he had made a complete hash of it, since when it had been 'absolutely useless'[371] Airy's exasperation with 'the stupid fellow' can readily be discerned, and his ascerbic remarks almost scratch holes in the thin tracing paper which he habitually used for scrawling his orders. William's reply was, as far as one knows, to send another man, and that correspondence is closed, but within a month another demand comes from Airy for a quotation for dismantling the Schuckburgh equatorial at the Observatory which William had previously divided in the autumn of 1838.[372] William replied fully in writing by including the price for re-dividing the hour circle, remounting the equatorial, and supplying two micrometer microscopes for it, the total cost of which would be £90-0s-0d.[373] He also discussed with Airy the question of object glasses, a matter now of intense concern to the Astronomer Royal as he completed his plans for a great new equatorial for Greenwich. It is interesting to consider how long these large pieces of crown or flint glass were under working. One of 15 inches which William may have obtained from Merz originally, had been first worked in 1848, seven years previously. This particular piece was crown glass, and was the fifth he had worked, all the former ones being faulty. This one passed muster, and he had promised first refusal of it to Mr Whitbread. He was still busy with it a year later,[374] presumably the same piece, or possibly the Merz glass destined for the Great Equatorial at Greenwich.

237

The so-called 'working' of a glass disc for use as an object lens was a highly technical affair, outside the province of this book. It was the basis of the success or failure of an optical instrument – its most important component. Not only had the required convexity to be formed entirely correctly in symmetrical fashion in the two planes, but the surface of the glass had to be smooth and without even the most minute irregularities. Flaws within the glass or in its cut edge had to be erased by fine burnishing, and where possible veining and cloudiness produced in the manufacture either avoided in choice of a disc, or gently polished away. In addition the two parts of the lens, the flint component and the crown, had to fit exactly into each other. Carried out in haphazard fashion, the working of a lens could all too easily damage what had already been achieved, and it was only by testing within an optical system that it could finally be passed as satisfactory for the use intended, whether 'star-gazing' or transit observations. The whole process involved immense patience and skill over many hours of intense concentration, only in some cases to find that some part of it was not perfect and must be returned to the work-bench for further improvement.

No wonder then that the price of the finished lens constituted a major portion of the cost of the instrument, both in time and money, or that the damage inflicted during transport was so upsetting to the maker, even of small items. When in September 1858, Troughton & Simms received a letter of complaint from the Observatory at Harvard regarding poor packaging of 'several Barometers, self-registering thermometers, Daniels hygrometers, and the last Fox Dip Circle, totally or nearly destroyed', 'and the transit circle for Dartmouth (Professor Young) much injured' there was much concern. The added sting was in the tail of the complaint, namely that German instruments always arrived intact, and 'may be rolled from New York to Boston without injury'.[375] As a welcome boost to Simms pride, however, came some good results from the Harvard Transit Circle observations.

On 9th September, Sebastopol fell to the Allies after nearly a year's seige, and at the cost of one-and-a-half million shells and the digging of seventy miles of trenches. The victory was not really so much Britain's, as due to the French storming of the Malakoff Fort, but it did mean that the end of this useless war was in sight. William had plenty of orders from other sources, so his pleasure in the news was for the country rather than concern for himself. Perhaps income tax would now be reduced. After a minor request for a trammel for Mr Howlett, a huge list of surveying requirements arrived from the Honourable East India Company, at a time when the completion and publication of the Principal Triangulation of the United Kingdom was occurring. A large number of theodolites of varying sizes from 12-inch (six) to 5-inch (fifty) were ordered, also object glasses of various focal lengths, double convex lenses, artificial horizons for hilly or forested country, protractors, Gunter scales and standard scales.[376] The metrology side of the business was given an order by the Topographical Department in Buenos Aires to construct and standardise the vara – which William noted, is equal to 8.66 French millimeters.[377] Finally he corresponds with Challis about a telescope object glass which the latter had undertaken to test for him, taking a particular star (which he does not specify in his letter) as the object, but having problems with the radiation experienced through the lens. Relieved by Challis' kindly advice, he will 'set out to work again with renewed vigour in the hope of lessening its amount'.[378]

Was this in fact the object glass he had in mind for Airy's great new reflecting equatorial, whispers of which had been circulating for the last year or two in astronomical circles? At last in 1855, Airy officially placed before the Royal Observatory Visitors his ideas. He passionately believed that the Observatory's primary function was basic physical astronomy, and to that end he aimed to see it fully equipped with the best and most up-to-date instruments. He had already extracted from his committee funds for the new altazimuth in 1847, and the reflex zenith telescope and the great transit circle, both in 1851. Now he aimed to complete the basic needs of the Observatory with the fundamental telescope for studying the discs of the planets, their positioning and course. He already had the two smaller equatorials, the Schuckburgh and the Sheepshanks, both of which were under William's care this autumn for repair. Sir George Schuckburgh's had been completed by Ramsden in 1793, and was at the time the largest of its kind in existence. In 1811 it was presented to the Royal Observatory by the future Lord Liverpool. The equatorial which Sheepshanks presented to the Observatory in 1838 had an object glass by Cauchoix, of 6¾-inches, and had in fact probably been under-used. Interest in Airy's new project grew, and after much thought and discussion, he received the Visitors' permission to go ahead.

The whole series of events leading up to the decision to make the Great Equatorial sheds an extraordinary light on the Astronomer Royal's ability to contend with problems great and small all at the same time. Moreover it demonstrates his enormous capacity for absorbing facts to the extent that he was able to deal with matters of great complexity and the highly qualified and respected members of his management committee, and yet he had his finger in every little pie however trivial in the Observatory larder. His assistants could have dealt with the 'tradesmen', to spare him, but he preferred to keep everything in his own hands, whether it concerned the plumbers, the builders, or the observatory odd-job man. When a consignment of quicksilver from Troughton & Simms was 'lost', and could not be accounted for when the bill came to be paid, he himself wrote to complain.[379] He had the most remarkable mental energy.

William, who could already be considered to have scored a hat-trick with his three capital instruments at the Royal Observatory, now had in prospect a fourth, and what was to be his last major creation.

★　　　★　　　★　　　★

The war in the Crimea was at stalemate after the horrific encounter of the Light Brigade at Balaclava when 700 British horsemen had charged down the Valley of Death but only 195 had returned. Palmerston, now in power, goaded on the country into wanting to turn the action into decisive victories but the new-style war correspondent in the person of William Russell of *The Times* opened peoples eyes to the realities of the situation including the incompetence of the higher command. Moreover, Napoleon III, who now badly wanted peace, insisted that further military action would jeopardise the liberation of Poland, an outcome which even Palmerston did not relish. The Peace of Paris in March 1856 therefore brought to an end this untimely conflict which had cost Britain 26,000 men, including many of her best troops. The terms of the treaty concerned mainly the freeing of the Danube and the Black Sea to all navigation, and Turkey to the Sultan's Christian subjects. In effect all its measures were of a temporary nature, and merely gave Turkey a new lease of life for a limited period. It did, however, for ever change the face of war, as it was the last time that British generals in the battlefied were not under telegraphic orders from London. It also altered the whole organisation of the army, making equipment and supply an all-important ingredient. Public opinion had never been so vocal, either in the press or in open meetings, in its condemnation of political issues, and it was impossible for anyone to be unaware of the need for improvement in the prime care of the troops, and in the professional management of warfare by the top ranks. It was the first time, in fact, that the British public through its collective opinion radically altered military organisation, though no real reform occurred for a dozen years.

Socially the Crimean War had significant personal effects on everyone in Britain. The work of Florence Nightingale brought into prominence the appalling medical conditions of hospitals of the time, particularly of course the military. The radical improvements she wrought in the ghastly state of the hospital at Scutari, very largely in commonsense matters of cleanliness, orderliness, and adequate space and ventilation, set the tone for nursing as a highly professional activity, to be carried out by thoroughly trained and supervised nurses. The realisation that such nurses must come from acceptable backgrounds and be blessed with intelligence and integrity, gave the impulse for well-to-do women to have proper careers. It was really the beginning of woman suffrage, from which female education blossomed into improvements in girl's schools and the institution of women's colleges in a

240

range of subjects. From now on girls were gradually accepted into professions which had previously been thought unsuitable, but in which they could show themselves to excell. From this time also, the sick had the right to expect proper care by trained nurses, through a gradually developing revolution over a period of several years. The casualties and suffering of the war in the end saved many more lives in the future, though public awareness of the remedies and medical advances in antisepsis, anaesthetics, and nursing skills followed hand-in-hand with improved standards of public hygiene.

One feels from the small amount of correspondence between William Simms and his main clients that the middle years of the decade were a time of consolidation from which grew the capping achievement of his life, the Great Equatorial at Greenwich. Certainly he was much concerned with the object glass, upon which he was working throughout 1856. He was also busy with a telescope for Professor Challis, who had drawn designs to give it equatorial motion which William thought 'very good'.[380] In addition he was absorbed with problems of metrology which James (1828) was examining in connection with the length of bronze bars, of which he submitted to Airy his sketches.[381] The transit circle at Paramatta, Australia, was home for repair in May, for which he calculated an estimate, and work was required on the axis of the altitude circle of the Greenwich altazimuth instrument. Meanwhile the object glass for the Great Equatorial continued to fail the standard of perfection which William demanded of it. He took it to Carshalton and mounted it there, intermittently working improvements on it, but warned Airy it was not yet worth his while to visit Bramble Haw to inspect it.[382]

In February he noted details of a theodolite invented by Mr Metford, showing a photograph of the completed instrument,[383] an example of the increasing use of this medium for practical purposes as well as social niceties at a time when it was also being experimented with by astronomers, and for which Airy planned to use the Great Equatorial in pioneering work. Light had always fascinated him as his famous lectures early in his career at Cambridge showed, and in May 1856 William Simms supplied him with apparatus for his experiments upon polarization. The decade was a transitional period when new methods and modes of research were developing in general physics and in tools such as spectrum analysis, which came to fruition in the 1860s and 1870s. William worked at the beginning of this exciting period of advance, and was often only to see the infancy of new facets in astronomical investigation. It would be his son, James, who would follow through in the second half of the century.

In August Airy came up with a further proposition. Why not use a diamond point for 'turning'. William, however, already had experimented with the use of diamond for finishing the pivots of transit instruments in previous years, and had found them unreliable as they were constantly breaking. He discontinued the practice as he believed that well-hardened cast steel did the job quite as well,[384] and now he advised the Astronomer Royal accordingly.

That autumn was plagued by illness at Troughton & Simms. James (1828) is never mentioned in this connection, being young and diligent. His cousin William Simms junior (1817) was less reliable, and once more was having time off work 'in the country'. Since he eventually lived to almost ninety, one is a little sceptical about the cause of all this disease, although he genuinely did have trouble with his eyes later in life, but at a very much delayed date. William Simms (1793) himself however, was certainly experiencing the effects of his developing chronic nephritic illness, and in September was again in the hands of the doctor, and worrying about the resulting arrears in his work.[385] He again warns Airy not to visit Bramble Haw yet as things are so much behind. Henry is having to write letters which he himself would normally have seen to.[386]

However, one ray of sunshine was the return to England of his eldest son, William Henry (1820), from Ceylon, though the pleasure of having him back in this country was somewhat tempered by some clash in their relationship. William Henry was now quite a formidable mathematician, and probably also at least a competent astronomer. On 12th December,[387] he presented a paper to the Royal Astronomical Society, containing a whole range of formulae for deducting the latitude of an observatory from the observations of stars with a transit instrument in the Prime Vertical, from which he calculated the latitude of Liverpool Observatory in combination with results reported by Mr Hartnup. He had previously been in contact with this gentleman in correspondence from Colombo, but now introduced the effect of an error of collimation on the results, which he therefore modified.[388] He also presented a further paper about the same time on the corrections of sextant observation, again exhibiting a facility for mathematics. One relevant practical issue is his advice to darken the image by a shade placed before the eye-piece of the telescope, a precaution later neglected by his cousin, William (1817), and used by him as an explanation for his subsequent blindness.[389] Other practical matters are attended to, but in no way does his emulate the quiet competantly practical style of his father's prose. It is the intellectual out-pouring of an extremely gifted operator. There is no evidence that he co-operated with his father or his brother, James in their work, or had any connection with his cousin, William. When the occultation of Jupiter occurred on 2nd January in the New Year, William reported on the appearance of the moon's limbs from Carshalton, whilst James (1828) and William junior (1817) observed from two different telescopes at Fleet Street[390] of the same phenomenon. There is no mention of William Henry having taken part in their combined observation, though he was now living at Gravesend.

James' (1828) name now appears more and more frequently in the archival correspondence. Partly this was due to his father's increasingly frequent bouts of indisposition, but quite as much it was that he was gradually taking over responsibility for the firm which he would ultimately inherit from William. His formal apprenticeship was completed in 1849, though he did not take up the Freedom of the Goldsmith's Company as his father had done at the same age. Indeed, methods of commercial organisation had so changed that by the mid-19th century there was no practical reason for doing so as far as his working life was concerned. To become a Freeman of a Company or of the City of London was now more of an honour in a social dimension rather than a necessity, and it cost a fee which father and son saw no point in spending needlessly. James' spare time was spent in other matters, as will become plain. Meanwhile, William was now sixty-three, and as in the normal course of events James was gradually taking his father's place in Troughton & Simms, although in this particular firm it was a tripartite arrangement, whereby William Simms junior was also being schooled for ownership, though on a lesser rung of the ladder.

It was in March 1857 that James (1828) was elected as a Fellow of the Royal Astronomical Society at the age of twenty-nine, a recognition of his quality that must greatly have pleased his father. Pleasure in this event occurred simultaneously with the first circulation of rumours in London of trouble in India with some of the Sepoy regiments in British pay. There was an air of discontent in the central provinces of the upper Ganges valley, particularly that Europisation was proceeding too rapidly, and that the coming of the railways and telegraphs, changes in sanitation, education and general expectations were altering life at an unacceptable rate. The Governor General, Lord Dalhousie, precipitated events by annexing the state of Oudh, and the well-known occasion when Indian troops were ordered to bite the ends off their cartridges which were covered with the fat of the Hindu's sacred cow or the Moslem's unclean pig, was merely the squib which set the revolt alight. The Mutiny of the Bengal Army began at Meerut in May with much bloody loss of life and destruction, soon followed by the fall of Delhi to the mutineers, then by Cawnpore with appalling ferocity, and then Lucknow. Civilians for the most part, did not join in the fighting, and by the summer the British troops together with loyal Indian soldiers were gaining control which was soon complete, from which a lengthy period of wise and humane government resulted.

The personal relevance to emerge from the melée for William Simms were the reports coming through from Lieutenant J. F. Tennant, then a young officer with the Survey of India and an FRAS, who entered Lucknow at its relief by the British troops. The observatory which had been founded there by the King of Oudh in 1841 and largely equipped with instruments made by Troughton & Simms, had been abolished as a working concern in 1848 when 'the new toy ceased to amuse'. No one had known what had become of the contents, but now Tennant was able to confirm that all the instruments had disappeared, no doubt by dishonest means sold, and he discovered the powdery remains of the records which had all been destroyed by white ants.[391]

William was engaging in a correspondence in April and May with Challis about the graduating of the Cambridge equatorial, and how detailed this should be. Would one minute be fine enough?[392] Following further directions from Challis, the dividing was completed promptly, and a fortnight later, 'will be in your hands'.[393] Sure enough, on 5th May William reported that the equatorial was 'sent off today in two packing cases', with an accompanying notice from James regarding the adjustment of the circle and the declination verniers.[394] May normally is the best time in England for testing optical instruments. The weather is calm, the equinoctial gales of the spring have subsided, and dust and fog are at a minimum now the coal fires of winter are suspended for the summer months. Moreover temperatures are not usually high enough to cause severe convection currents, and visibility is habitually clear. If he possibly could test his lenses at this time of the year, William did so, and most years some remark is passed in his correspondence to this effect. This year, he wanted to have the 8-inch object glass back from Airy to see if it could be improved. After further work on it, a month later he duly returned it in the care of a workman, together with its eye-piece. He was also busy with a transit circle for the East India Company for Madras, with Richard Carrington appointed by the Surveyor, Captain Jacobs, to supervise the work. Carrington was not satisfied with the object glass. It was therefore, in May, undergoing tests, without resolution of the problem. As so often in the reciprocal relationship between Airy and William Simms, where one of them would beg advice from the other when difficulties arose, this time it was William's turn to request help – 'can you oblige by undertaking to look through it (the lens). I dare not press it however, for I know you have enough on your hands at all times'. How true. However, Airy agreed to have the object glass up to Greenwich to examine it, and William Simms junior was duly despatched in charge of the glass and eye-piece to the Observatory.

The unequivocal answer from Airy arrived five days later. 'The green glass was much the better, and showed the star very well indeed.' It would be satisfactory on condition it underwent further adjustment by William (1793) – 'it is abominably in want of centering – I am not at all surprised at Mr Carrington rejecting it', said Airy without mincing his words, 'I should probably have done so myself'. Moreover, he added, however well adjusted, it would still not do for a graduated instrument such as a transit circle, but only 'as an efficient gazing telescope'.[395]

William's letter of thanks duly came back next day – it was only five lines in all, including the introductory and concluding phrases – 'I thank you for assisting me with your judgement',[396] he humbly writes.

Annoying gaps appear this year in the correspondence between William Simms and his main clients, but the Great Equatorial for Greenwich was in hand, about which more gradually appears. It is probable that, at this vital stage in its creation, personal contact between William and Airy and the iron founders, Ransome & May, were a common occurrence, either at the Observatory or at Fleet Street, or possibly often at Bramble Haw, with James (1828) frequently in attendance, but sadly, no record of these meetings remain. Meanwhile, family events coincided with professional developments in the autumn, when it became apparent that William's elder brother, James (1792), was mortally ill with probably what is now known as a type of motor neurone disease. In mid-October, James (1792) had his Will executed, and witnessed by his three children, William Simms junior, Sarah (still unmarried) and Emma, whose married surname was Jones. A fourth witness was Robert Hood, whose background is unknown, but may have been a servant or the solicitors clerk. When James died in December, William (1793) was called in to sign an affadavit to the Will, as James' wife, Catherine Pruday, was the sole executrix, and a female must be vouched for, especially as to her were left all James' worldly goods. Probate was granted to Catherine on 24th December.

This coincided within forty-eight hours with the birth of a fourth baby to Elizabeth Ann and Henry Lee. They already had had, in quick succession, a son, Henry, a daughter, Elizabeth Louise (called after the baby's paternal Aunt Louise), and another son, William Simms. It appears typical that Elizabeth Ann should complete her family tidily with a second girl, Mary Matilda, presumably called after Elizabeth's sister and mother-in-law. Christmas was thus blessed with a new member of the family for William to dandle on his knee, enjoying as he did so much, the presence of children.

On the 14th and 15th March 1858, there occurred an annular eclipse of the sun visible from England, not a very frequent event, and very awe-inspiring. William Simms junior (1817) submitted a report to the Royal Astronomical Society.[397] The eerieness of this phenomenon is extraordinary. In broad daylight the moon gradually passes over the face of the sun, first biting an ellipse from its side, then completely blocking it altogether as sun and moon coincide in the path from the earth. At that moment the black disc of the moon appears to be surrounded by a bright halo of sunlight coming from behind it, and as this develops, the shadow of the moon falls upon the earth, making it dark as night. There is a chill in the air, and a weird silence, and then gradually as the shadow passes away, the sun's disc reappears and daylight returns to earth, accompanied by a sort of dawn chorus as the birds realise that it is not night-time after all. The whole episode presents an atmosphere of foreboding as if events of mysterious moment are about to occur.

245

These thoughts must have been in Elizabeth Ann's mind as she watched the 1858 eclipse from Croydon. Next day, 16th March, tragedy struck. Her baby was found in her cot quite dead. Mary Matilda was only 2½ months old, and she died without warning. It was a 19th century 'cot death' from no known cause.

The devastation caused by such a shattering incident can be imagined, not only to the stricken parents, but to the whole family, including the baby's grandfather. The coroner's inquest was held at 76 Blackfriars Lane, and his verdict was 'Accidental asphyxia in Bed'. The little girl was subsequently buried on 20th March in the big grave on the top of the hill in Norwood Cemetery, with Walter Hennell and the two Ann's, one of them her maternal grandmother.

That January, 1858, William had been re-elected for the last time to the Council of the Royal Astronomical Society. He attended the January meeting, and in February was at the first of the afternoon meetings, held at 2.00 pm to avoid the members travelling home in the insalubrious conditions of the London evenings with their attendant hazards of fog, pick-pocketing and attack. In March he was, not surprisingly, absent, but he sent in a communication (No. 674) on the subject of sextant observation. In April he was present to give weight to nephew William Simms' (1817) communication (No. 782) on the solar eclipse, but in May he was again absent. June 1858 the meeting at 3.00 pm was William's very last attendance at Somerset House, and in December it was all too obvious that he was too ill to be on the Council any more, and he was not re-elected. The following year he did not attend any of the meetings of the Society.[398]

Towards the end of June 1858, reports came through from Florence of the appearance of a new comet, seen at first telescopically by the astronomer, Giambattista Donati. As this object travelled towards Earth and reached its perihelion, it became more and more remarkable for its beautiful long curved main tail, on each side of which were two shorter tails. For three months Donati's comet could be seen in England that summer with the naked eye, and into the New Year by telescope. Astronomers such as William were fascinated by the huge apparition, particularly the disturbance apparent in its tail, reporting circular pockets billowing from its nucleus down the tail in masses of brilliant clouds. Donati was later, in 1864, to perform the first ever spectroscopy on his comet to show the presence of unsuspected gases, but in William's day it was only tentatively suggested what the nature of the spectacle might be as it sped away again into space. Although the comet, as usual with celestial phenomenon, caused a good deal of superstitious attention, scientists found its appearance a spur to their studies. The widespread interest was shared by William, who doubtless was to see the first photograph ever taken of any comet, which was produced by Mr Usherwood of Walton Common with a stationary camera,[399] and noted in the History of the Royal Astronomical Society. Spectrum analysis, though discovered by Stokes in 1853, was not applied to the atmosphere until the next decade, and it seems remarkable now that the Astronomer Royal did not even allude to it in his suggestions for study of the solar eclipse in 1860.[400]

★   ★   ★   ★

The Indian Mutiny was over by 1858, and the continent was settling down into well-governed peace. The East India Company, which had started out as its reigning power due to its control on commerce and trade before General Clive's day, gradually took over the entire regulation of public amenities, and in effect ruled a large part of the country, leaving the Rajas mainly responsible for their own states. Back in 1813 the monopoly by the Company for trade between India and Britain was abolished, and in 1833 trade with China also was freed from the Company's control. The Honourable East India Company did however, maintain its powers in some activities, as in the areas with which Frederick Walter had been connected in the 1840s, though technically authority was invested in the British Crown. In 1833 Lord Bentinck's Charter laid down that Indians, or indeed any native, should not be debarred from office or position because of his colour or background, and in general there was good will between the British administrators and the very few other British who lived and worked in India, and the Indians themselves. Britain was four months away until the Overland Route started in 1845, and even then forty-six days until the Suez Canal opened in 1869 when it was reduced still further. Thus the majority of Indians had absolutely no idea of European ways or culture, and there was a great longing to learn English and to study English customs, science and thought. It was not that British education was forced on India so much as the yearning of Indians to become familiar with Western ways, including their government, justice and police. Frederick Walter's sojourn in India came towards the end of East India Company rule, and in 1858 when it was formerly abolished by the India Act, very little actually changed, except that entry to the civil service was to be by very stiff examination rather than by patronage. From 1858 the London end of the chain of government of India was managed from India House in Leadenhall Street. This continued (in different buildings) up to Independence after the Second World War. Even now, the archives are kept in an unlovely office block called India House in Blackfriars Road. Connection with Troughton & Simms was maintained throughout the pre-Independence years, particularly during the First World War when William's great grandson was seconded from the firm to serve in the India Office in London.

During 1858 William's main professional concern was his Great Equatorial for Greenwich. In February James (1828) and William Simms junior (1817) proceeded to Ipswich where the circles had been thoroughly examined by Airy, and where they were to mark them out ready for dividing.[401] Ransome & May, the iron founders for this project had works at Ipswich as well as their main foundry at St George Street, Westminster, so could easily be called in by Airy to discuss it. By April the circles were back in Fleet Street, and they were busy with the hour circle, but finding that the engraving was 'awkward work', and 'will occupy at least a fortnight'.[402] By October they were proceeding with the object and eye ends, but there had been delays from illness. Moreover they had been engaged in completing the transit circle for Sydney, Australia, which was finally tested in the mid-summer months, and after adjustment was packed and despatched in mid-August.[403] It would arrive in Sydney in the middle of their best season there, January or February 1859.

That summer, Airy produced his plan for mounting Standards of Length at the entrance to the Royal Observatory, where the public could use them but also, one feels, as a memorial to the huge amount of work over many years which had gone, unseen, into this achievement. In August William was living at Bramble Haw, and after studying Airy's letter about the Standards, James took it over to Carshalton for his father's opinion and advice. By October the work was in hand, and the base plate was at the founders.[404] By the last day of the year the whole thing was due to be finished, and Airy sent along precise instructions for the fixing. He described the Observatory wall ranging to the east of the entrance door, where it is 'perfectly straight for some distance and then begins to curve. The place of fixing the Standards is at the furthest part of the straight wall, before it begins to curve. The height of the highest Standard may be about 4-ft 5-inches above the ground'. He had ordered the builder, Mr Green, to position a slate roof above as a protection for the Standards, to be 5-ft long and 8-inches broad, with front drip, and 5-ft 9-inches above the ground. Unfortunately, such were the new industrial requirements just come into use, that the workmen had to be given a holiday at Christmas which delayed the work, and nothing Airy might decree could alter this fact. However, all was fixed and finished by 4th January 1859, and the same Standards can be inspected to this day[405] beneath the Gate Clock erected in 1851 – one of the earliest electricity-driven public clocks in existence.

Repairs and alterations were carried out this year for Cambridge Observatory, notably in October for the eye-piece, probably of the 6-inch equatorial, which required modification, and was sent back from London by the 'Rail-Way'. An account also was sent to the University for the equatorial. However, the most exciting news from Cambridge this year, apart from reports of sightings of Donati's comet, were of a more practical nature, when Miss Anne Sheepshanks, sister of the late Richard, gave £10,000 to the University specifically for the promotion of research at the Observatory. Five years older than her brother, she had housekept for him

248

Standard Lengths on the wall of the Royal Observatory at Greenwich.
BY PERMISSION OF NATIONAL MARITIME MUSEUM, LONDON

ever since he left college, and on his death inherited his not inconsiderable wealth. The present bequest was also to include the funding of an exhibition in astronomy to be called after her brother, and Challis rejoiced that she had seen fit to underwrite the work of the Observatory rather than add new buildings or land, by ordaining that the income from the endowment was to be used, whilst the capital was to be preserved in perpetuity, as it still is.[406] She had already in 1851 presented her brother's large collection of instruments to the Royal Astronomical Society, and there were whispers of yet more money to come.

The only Simms publication this year was a book by William Henry on *The Sextant and its applications*. It was printed by Taylor and Francis of Red Lion Court, Fleet Street, (a firm which exists there to this day), and published by Troughton & Simms, so that he must have made recent contact with his father. He now lived at Gravesend, but what work exactly he was pursuing is unclear. There is something oddly unreliable about him, and he never became an FRAS or produced any further reports for the RAS, but this book as usual is a mass of mathematics and tables,[407] which had taken a great deal of labour to assemble. As no later professional sighting of him has been brought to light, it is possible he inherited sufficient funds by marriage to enable him to become a dilettante.

249

William Simms' family beneficiaries
June 1860

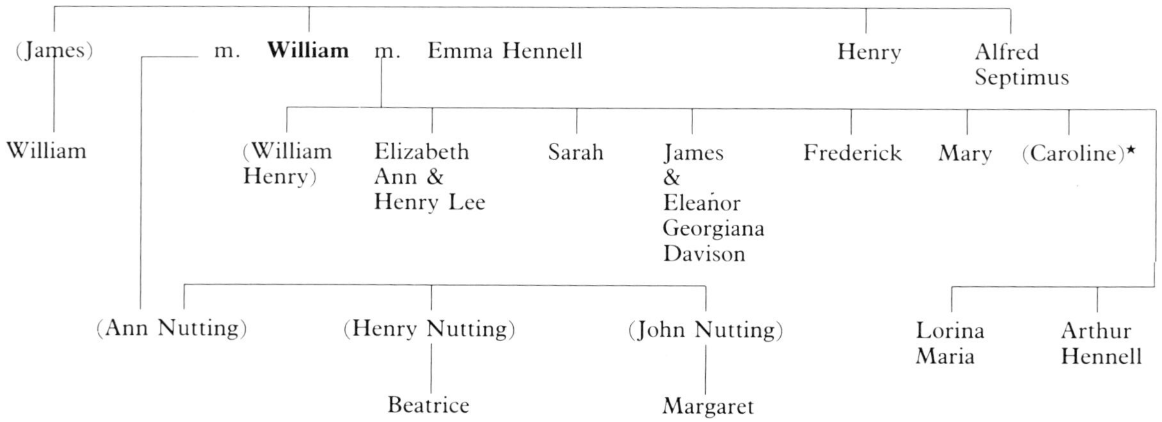

(James)

William

m.

(Ann Nutting)

William

m.

Emma Hennell

(William Henry)

Elizabeth Ann & Henry Lee

(Henry Nutting)

Beatrice

Sarah

James & Eleanor Georgiana Davison

(John Nutting)

Margaret

Henry

Alfred Septimus

Frederick

Mary (Caroline)★

Lorina Maria

Arthur Hennell

★Caroline later claimed her share

250

CHAPTER 21
1859-1860

AN ACCOUNT BOOK BELONGING TO William Simms[408] gives some idea of his financial state at this juncture. As well as his Fleet Street premises he also owned Gothic Cottage in Campden Town, and had at some point also bought an estate in West Kent consisting of two farms 'let as one, containing together about 138 acres'. They were called Portlands and Parsonage Farms, the former in the parish of Knockholt, the latter next door in Cusham. The dwelling house and farm buildings were all within Knockholt parish.[409] All the properties mentioned were leasehold, as was usual at this period, and so also was Bramble Haw. Thus by now, William had become a very considerable property owner, and a very rich man when one recalls that he started with nothing in his Broad Way days.

In February 1858 William noted in the account book his acquisition of £18,600 worth of 3% shares which would supply interest of £543-0s-0d per year after income tax had been deducted.[410] He had also bought Consolidated £3% annuities that year, £8,000 at 97½% in February, followed by £2,000 at 98% in May. The dividends for the year from these amounted to £462-13s-3d, a comfortable income which was reinvested.[411] These large sums may have some relevance when we find that in January 1859 he made two cash loans amounting to £877-6s-11d to an unknown recipient, and a further loan of £1,000 at 3½% to Henry Lee,[412] Elizabeth Ann's husband. Next month he repeated this last with £600, and in May another £400, all of which were for Lee's business as a Skinner. Thus the total amount owed to him by Henry Lee was £2,000, not counting interest. What exactly this vast sum was actually for can only be surmised, and it is reflected in William's Will executed in the autumn, in which the loan is mentioned regarding Elizabeth Ann's share of his bequest, which he directs must not be lessened even if Henry has not yet repaid the money at his demise.

Money matters were much to the fore of his mind just now. Not only was he an ailing and elderly man, but his son, James, was to be married in June 1859. He thus was carefully considering his financial position, the future of his business, and provision for his wife and family, particularly his six year

251

old son and his five daughters, only one of whom (Elizabeth Ann) was so far married. His thoughts were briefly side-tracked in early May when brother George died at Greville Street, leaving a bequest of plate to his brothers, other items to his nephews, Frederick Simms, surgeon, and Arthur George Simms, artist, and all his household goods to Jane, wife of Richard Goulding, his brother-in-law from his brief second marriage. He also provided £1,000 in Trust for Henry – as did all the brothers in turn.

Rumour had it that James (1828) had been contemplating marriage for some time, but, being a careful soul and with his work becoming an increasing responsibility as his father's health failed, he had procrastinated to the point that the lady in question attempted to force his hand in an unseemly fashion, and received the rebuff she deserved.[413] James quite quickly rebounded to another lady whom he knew to be more prudent, and although nine years his senior, was suitable in every way. She was Eleanor Georgiana Davison, whose father was a merchant, Thomas Robinson Davison, living in Stockwell. William's approval of this match is acknowledged by the nominal bequest he made to Eleanor in his Will.

James meanwhile had bought a house, Westbourne Lodge, in Charlton, very close to Greenwich Park. It must have been in his mind that this was the obvious area to which Troughton & Simms should be removed, away from the fog and dust of Fleet Street, and within easy distance of the Royal Observatory. The house was stone-built, classical, square, good quality, and remarkably like Bramble Haw. James and Eleanor moved in after their marriage on 3rd June 1859, and lived there for the rest of their lives, he until 1915, and here their three children were born.[414]

Their wedding had been performed by licence, at the Stockwell 'district' church of St Michaels, near the bride's home at Montague Place off Clapham Road. The reason for the licence may have been to avoid the publicity of banns, which in view of the brides' age and the illness of the bridegroom's father would have been preferable. However, although marriages were not now required to be held in an Anglican church since the Act of 1754 in this case it was so done. But it may well be that James did not regularly attend an Established church, so that it was inappropriate for his banns to be called at All Saints, Carshalton. From the first days of his marriage, he attended the Congregational church in Blackheath, then newly built, and within ten years he had opened his own Nonconformist chapel at Charlton attached to the factory, and known later as the Simms Mission Hall. The Anglican church in England had gone through great upheavals in the last several decades with an increasing sense of the need for reform of its services and its clergy, so many of whom in the 18th century had ceased to care for their flocks, instead living idle indulgent lives, or so often completely absent from their parishes. Early in the 19th century the well-heeled aristocratic bishop and his wife ceased to exist, and were replaced by the working bishop we know today. The ordinary parson began to take his work seriously, and no more was he the absentee cleric of yesteryear. Moreover, the vast difference in income between the wealthy incumbent of parsonage and palace, and the curate pale with hardly two pennies to rub together, received adjustment by Peel's Ecclesiastical Commission. The Dissenting parishioners of the late 18th century who, especially in industrial areas, returned to sincere Bible-based religion with Sunday church-going as sacrosanct as daily family prayers, spread their influence upwards through the middle classes to the upper classes and aristocracy, until by Victoria's reign England was a staunchly Protestant country of Sunday observers and Bible-readers. However, the practices in the Church of England were slack and in places almost heretical; and it was the religious revival stimulated by the Tractarians in the 1830s and 1840s and the resulting Oxford Movement which pulled the Church back into the study of the Thirty-Nine Articles, replacing the free interpretation of traditional religion by a strict regime of ceremonial incorporating the Book of Common Prayer. The Evangelical Protestants for their part preached that the soul was more important than the building or the ritual of the Church. Between these two extremes came the Christian Socialists led by Rev Charles Kingsley and Frederick Denison Maurice who held that loving co-operation between man and man must form the basis of successful industry. They were unsuccessful in their attempts at social reform because they had no notion of business management of social organisation. They did, however, open the door to genuine concern within the Church for the poor and needy, to complement its strictly religious activities. It was the so-called Broad Churchmen who combined their churchmanship with social care for others. Some of these remained within the Established Church. Others joined the Nonconformists. They came from all classes, but many were middle-class merchants and manufacturers, or upper class men of means. In their lives they lived out their convictions, and formed all sorts of organisations financed from their own purses and encouraged by personal participation, to alleviate want and ignorance.

There is little evidence to ascertain the attitude of William Simms to these activities except a few odd remarks in his correspondence regarding his workmen's welfare. The fact that his eldest son was admitted to Cambridge University confirms that he was, in fact, an Anglican. He was probably typical of his type and age, a hardworking conscientious employer of high integrity, a benevolent church-going family man, with politics which were mildly Liberal. The best indication of his views is from the career of his son, James, about whom far more is known on a personal level. At Charlton James made the welfare of his workmen and their families an integral part of his responsibility. From this he spread his protecting wing to the impoverished streets surrounding his new factory and to the wharves and docks of Woolwich. The London City Mission had come into being in

1835 in a cottage at Hoxton to care for the poor, both body and soul, and although James was only a child at that date, it is likely he took an interest in its activities from his earliest adulthood. Like the Salvation Army which came a little later, it believed that food for a man's soul must be accompanied by food for his body, and by endowing the London City Mission locally in Charlton, and organising a band of helpers, James ministered as far as he was able to the needs of his families.[415]

James' application to Doctors Commons for a marriage licence was therefore probably due to his affinity to a Nonconformist church, whether or not Eleanor normally attended St Michael's at Stockwell, or it was obtained merely as was commonly done by the well-to-do. Eleanor's elder sister, Margaret, was one of her witnesses at the ceremony, and her father the other. William Simms was unwell and unable to be present, but most probably was represented by his daughters, Sarah and Mary. Elizabeth Ann was still in mourning for her baby, and Caroline had left home. William and James had a good understanding between them and it is therefore to Bramble Haw that James and Eleanor most certainly drove after the ceremony for William to give them his blessing before they set off on their honeymoon, which, judging by James' later travels, may well have been abroad.

This decade of transition in the world of science came to an end in 1859 with a tremendous explosion as Charles Darwin presented his paper on the Origin of Species to the Linnean Society, now established in the east wing of Burlington House. The idea that evolution of the lower animals occurred over many millions of years to produce man, was entirely against all previous thought, and there was the question of man's soul. Such nonsense was contrary to the teaching of the sanctity of human beings. The 'monkey to man' concept was unpleasant for sensitive gentlefolk to accept. This was the start of a great battle of minds which never would have occurred had the theologians and the scientists kept to their own fields, and admitted that neither had the complete answer to man's origins. For astronomers there was no problem in acknowledging that the Creation occupied a great length of time, as their own speculations had suggested as much. For the Evangelicals and some Dissidents it was sinful beyond belief to negate the verbal inspiration of the Bible. For the Broad Churchmen science was a tool which they welcomed as an aid to understanding the truths of religion, but declared that the Bible was no authority on non-religious subjects. Without this acceptance of the relation between religious and science, the Church seriously damaged its own credibility.

One can only speculate on William's attitude to the furore as he found himself with increasing time for thought during 1859. His own future was now in increasing doubt, and his mind, that of a mathematician and scientist must have turned to such unknowns. It is likely that he belonged to the Broad Church faction as he was unable to jettison the clear facts placed before him in Darwin's hypothesis of creation. The survival of the fittest was to him, faced with his own mortality, a truth, and from it Darwin's arguments fell into place.

At the beginning of the year his letters to Airy are headed as from Fleet Street, and a bill for £249-15s-4d for work completed on the Great Equatorial which Airy asked to be broken down into sections likely to be more appetising to his committee members, was dealt with by Henry.[416] As usual it was difficult to persuade the Visitors that work on their instruments cost money, and so often the final account appeared to them to be out of scale, and they jibbed at the expense.

More frequently now William mentions James or William junior in his notes – 'my son intends to fix the level to the altazimuth on Monday next';[417] 'my nephew will be at the Observatory with the declination microscopes tomorrow'.[418] To Challis he writes 'my brother informs me – – –'. It is as if he is at the directors' desk, and now delegates all the physical labour. However, he has a finger in all the firm's pies, including the payment of bills, and he remarks to Challis that his account for the 6-inch equatorial for Cambridge has been discharged by the Vice-Chancellor.[419]

During the summer the Great Equatorial was transferred to Greenwich for final fixing, adjustment and testing. James, who was now more or less in charge, accompanied the great packing cases on their journey, and had no small cause to complain to Airy about the conduct of the Greenwich carrier[420] who was careless and clumsy. What damage was sustained by the delicate load is not revealed, and Airy's reply must have been verbal as there is no record of it. Nor is there any record of whether William was able to visit his precious instrument in its new home, though every effort will have been made for him to do so, and perhaps for the last time look down from the terrace of the Observatory over the Queen's House, the naval hospital and the river, and the broad panorama over his own smokey City of London. Behind him was the Meridian Building with his transit circle visible through the opened shutters aligned on the new Greenwich meridian, and to the south-east the recently completed octagonal observatory with its drum-shaped dome summounted by the distinctive scalloped sky-line, now containing his Great Equatorial. To the south-west was the dome in which his wonderfully successful altazimuth instrument had been hard at work for twelve years. Just without the gateway to the terrace were the Standard Lengths which James had recently fixed to the wall, and at the opposite end of the terrace was the home of the Astronomer Royal in Flamstead House, where he had spent so many invigorating – and usually convivial – hours with George Airy and his family, discussing, arguing, rationalising, analysing, stipulating, and (usually) agreeing a plan of campaign. Above was the Octagon Room where he had so often

255

Flamstead House.   BY PERMISSION OF NATIONAL MARITIME MUSEUM, LONDON

submitted his opinions to the committee, and met the Visitors for their annual Visiting Day banquet. The Royal Observatory was an integral part of his life, and its energetic Astronomer an endless source of colour.

Of all William's acquaintances, one of the most irresistible after Airy, must have been Isambard Brunel, whose career had so often surfaced to coincide with his own interests. Brunel's *Great Eastern* was the last of his magnificent ships, and was probably his reaction to railway mania. Financial difficulties had dogged his plans for three years up to 1856, but by June 1857 it had been ready for launching. Built in the docks beside the Thames, it was to be launched sideways because of its enormous length, a most hazardous enterprise, and one for which Airy, amongst others, was called in to advise. Widespread publicity preceded the project, and all London travelled down to the ceremony, much of it anticipating chaos, only to find the invited guests were admitted but no one else. A near riot ensued, but in the end there was a great anticlimax as the vast ship refused to budge when the chocks were removed, and the procedure was delayed repeatedly until belatedly it reached the water and was taken for fitting. By 1858 the worry of the *Great Eastern* and the constant soakings Brunel sustained in the terrible winter visits to the ship, resulted in a severe dose of nephritis – Bright's disease – with which William was only too familiar. Brunel spent the winter of 1858 in Egypt – perhaps that is where William Simms should have been instead of struggling on with his Great Equatorial in London. In May 1859 Brunel returned to England, but all July and August he was ill, though insisting on 5th September in boarding the *Great Eastern* when she left on her trials. No sooner was anchor raised, than he sustained a most severe stroke, and was so badly affected that it was doubtful whether he ever knew as he lay paralysed on Canvey Island, of the disastrous steam explosion on board. On 15th September he died, a series of events only too real in the mind of the patient at Bramble Haw. Less spectacular than Brunel's career, William's own had followed in a similar pattern right up to this final act.

Perhaps Brunel's death brought home to William once again his own mortality, and for the next few weeks he was figuring out how he should divide his assets. By November he was ready to discuss his Will with his lawyer, Frederick West, who came up to Carshalton from his office in Charlotte Row near the Mansion House to see him. Later, West returned to the City and gave instructions to his clerk, James Wicks, who wrote out the text of the Will, and sent it up to Bramble Haw for William to study before signing it in the presence of his coachman, James Driver, and a maid, Eliza Childs, on 9th November.

As one would expect, the document was concise and without frills. The business at 138 Fleet Street and Peterborough Court and all their secondary buildings and contents were to go to his son, James, who also was to receive

£1,000. Emma was to inherit the contents of Bramble Haw. All his other three sons were each to receive £3,000, that for Arthur Hennell to remain in Trust pending his 21st birthday. His eldest son, William Henry, in addition was to inherit his valuable chronometer made by Ferdinand Berthoud, one of the most eminent of the 18th century French clockmakers. £1,000 was to be invested for the support of his brother Alfred Septimus, and £10,000 for Emma. For his five daughters, whether they married or not, £30,000 was to be invested, and they were specifically to sign for the income each time they received their share. Smaller amounts of £60 would go to his niece Beatrice, daughter of his beloved Ann's brother, Henry Nutting, and to Margaret, orphaned daughter of Ann's other brother, John Nutting. Henry Lee again appears, being bequeathed £100 and William's copy of the Edinburgh Encyclopaedia; and old Sarah Newall was to receive a well-earned £100. All his books on science were to go to James, and the rest of his library to Elizabeth Ann. His pictures and prints from 138 Fleet Street to Sarah, all of which must have comprised a fascinating collection. The whole family were each to receive individually £50 for their mourning apparel, and this included Eleanor Georgiana whom William evidently treated as a daughter. £50 seems a disproportionate amount until the extended length of the Victorian period of mourning is considered; the money was not just for one occasion but for at least six months. With thought for the feelings of Emma and his daughters still at home, he directed that they should be permitted to remain at Bramble Haw for a year after his demise, the ground rent, taxes, and repairs being paid by the Trustees, together with the wages of the groom and gardener for a twelve month period.

There were other minor items, but this in essence was all.

Christmas 1859 must have been a weary time. On 3rd January James, in a letter to Professor Challis regarding the repair of a barometer ('making it as new') added that 'My father has been very ill for several months and is still so'.[421] All the main correspondence of the firm was now James' responsibility, with Henry still dealing with the day-to-day accounts and minor matters, and William junior occasionally providing his bit.

Somehow William went on living, in great pain and almost certainly undergoing frequent and agonising surgical procedures for his enlarged prostate which was leading to kidney failure. His children gathered round, all except for the eldest and the youngest of his first family, William Henry and Caroline. In vain was every endeavour made to find them, but without success. It may be that William Henry had recently travelled abroad once more, and yet no evidence for this has emerged, and it is odd that James could not locate him. Caroline, it turned out, was only in Hampstead, though with whom she stayed or worked for was kept a secret, certainly from her dying father. If she knew of his suffering, she must indeed have been hard-hearted to find herself unable to bury her antipathy to her step-mother in such circumstances.

258

Having given up hope of contact with the two, and knowing that the end was not far off, in May William sadly once again sent for Frederick West, the solicitor, in order to add a codicil to his Will in which he bequeathed small sums to his whole domestic staff at Bramble Haw, three maids, a groom and a gardener, presumably in recognition of their faithful service during his long illness. He directed that a further £500 should be placed in trust for Emma, and with a heavy heart revoked the legacies to William Henry and Caroline 'unless they appear personally before the trustees within five years'. As a last thought he appointed Emma as guardian of Lorina Maria and Arthur Hennell, and, having done all his sums to his satisfaction, signed the codicil on 5th May 1860. It was one of the greatest sorrows of his life that this revocation should have been necessary.

His mind was still clear, trying desperately to check and recheck whether all his affairs were in good order, and four days later a further codicil was signed by him in the presence of Jesse Richardson and Thomas Dawson, to direct that brother Henry should be allowed to remain at his home at 14 Camden Cottages for the rest of his ground lease, which in effect would provide him with a home for life. £3,000 worth of Bank £3% Consolidated annuities should be set aside for him, to return to William's residuary estate on his death. This codicil, dated 9th May was his final effort to tidy up the remaining loose ends of his property.

William lingered on another six weeks, sinking into unconsciousness from his sick body at long last, to die at the age of sixty-six on the evening of midsummer day, 21st June 1860. A week later the last of the five Simms funeral corteges to do so, climbed the hill at Norwood Cemetery, and gently let down the coffin into the great dark grave, where he lay with his beloved Ann, with two of his children, and his baby granddaughter, Mary Matilda. The grave was never used again.

Next day Henry wrote on black-edged notepaper to inform the Astronomer Royal of the death of 'Mr Simms'.[422] On the 23rd Henry reverted to his usual duties, writing again on black-edged paper to present 'his respectful compliments to the Astronomer Royal, and sends the second eye-piece and the feet plates for the stand'.[423] Work cannot be allowed to mark time, and faithful Henry continues to play his part.

At his home, Flamstead House at Greenwich Observatory, Airy wrote to James a remarkable tribute in reply:[424]

Dear Sir,

With great sorrow I received yesterday the report of the decease of your excellent father. It is about thirty-seven years since I first saw him, and for more than thirty years I knew him very well. No person with whom I transact business so completely commanded my confidence. I esteemed him as a man of talent and integrity, an honourable man in every transaction, and in the best sense of the word a gentleman.

I am dear Sir,

Yours truly,

G. B. Airy.

The Simms family vault at West Norwood.   BY PERMISSION OF PETER MENNIM

CHAPTER 22

Epilogue

THOUGH LONG EXPECTED, AND THANKFULLY endured for the close it brought to his suffering, the loss of William could not but affect almost every member of his near family. Over were the days of the typical Victorian master of the house – though in William's case the most tolerant – with servants, coach and horses, and a large garden tended by a resident gardener. Gone were the family attendances at Sunday worship at Carshalton Parish Church, with pleasant intercourse afterwards with other local families, and a run round the village pond for the two little ones to wake them up from the torpor of the long sermon. Only a memory now were the family outings to the Crystal Palace, to Greenwich Park, trips down the river to Gravesend, or by train to the seaside at Brighton or Dover, Hastings or the Isle of Wight.

England now was at the zenith of her long period of peace, and so of her unrivalled prosperity. She was learning to care for her poor and unfortunate, for their health, their housing, and even their education. There was a gaity in the air due to the self-confidence born of success in industry and all things British, and especially of her Empire of which she was justifiably proud. Very soon, at the end of 1861, came the unforeseen drama of the death of the Prince Consort, and for a time the country was bowed by the Queen's sorrow. But the British were a cheerfully optimistic nation, and mourning could not for them continue long. The jollity of the costermongers and street traders, in spite of their often shocking home circumstances, burst out in the fairs at Greenwich and Smithfield, in a hilarity which nothing could dampen, to the echo of the Cockney songs, and no amount of misfortune could dampen this native joie de vivre.

William had lived at a time of great opportunity. Born during,the years of the French Revolution, he could remember Trafalgar, and in spite of Britain's domination of the seas, the fear of French invasion. He was a young adult at the time of Waterloo, and he witnessed the unemployment and destitution that followed, then of the mass emigration fuelled by the horrors of the Irish famine, and the anti Corn Law mobs. Just now tales of unrest which were leading to civil war, filtered in from the crews of ships

John Simms' family

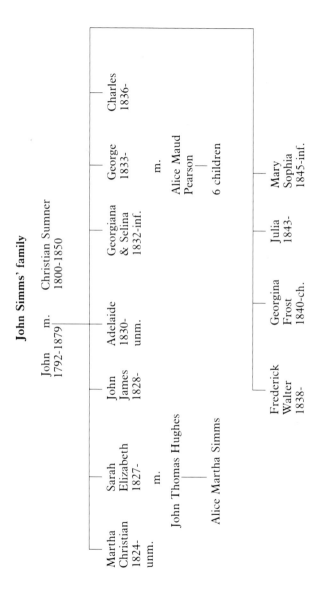

John   m.   Christian Sumner
1792-1879   1800-1850

Martha Christian 1824- unm.

Sarah Elizabeth 1827-
m.
John Thomas Hughes
Alice Martha Simms

John James 1828-

Adelaide 1830- unm.

Georgiana & Selina 1832-inf.

George 1833-
m.
Alice Maud Pearson
6 children

Charles 1836-

Frederick Walter 1838-

Georgina Frost 1840-ch.

Julia 1843-

Mary Sophia 1845-inf.

Henry Simms' family

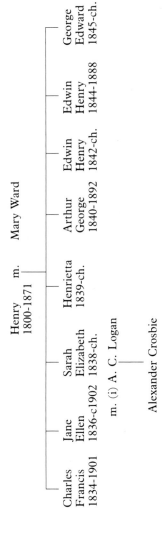
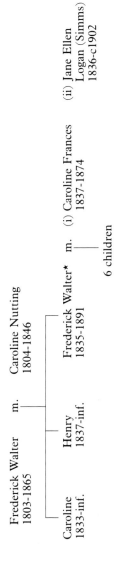

Henry 1800-1871   m.   Mary Ward

Charles Francis 1834-1901 · Jane Ellen 1836-c1902 · Sarah Elizabeth 1838-ch. · Henrietta 1839-ch. · Arthur George 1840-1892 · Edwin Henry 1842-ch. · Edwin Henry 1844-1888 · George Edward 1845-ch.

m. (i) A. C. Logan

Alexander Crosbie

(ii) Frederick Simms*

Frederick Walter Simms' family

Frederick Walter 1803-1865   m.   Caroline Nutting 1804-1846

Caroline 1833-inf. · Frederick Walter* 1835-1891 · Henry 1837-inf.

Frederick Walter*   m.   (i) Caroline Frances 1837-1874

6 children

(ii) Jane Ellen Logan (Simms) 1836-c1902

returning to the Pool of London from the United States. But William's world was broader, and embraced the countries of the world which were opening up their lands, and to do so needed his instruments. He was fortunate to live at a period of unqualified expansion combined with financial security and unerring drive and skill.

In the Royal Observatory at Greenwich, there was now a full range of Troughton & Simms' instruments, which would be engaged in consolidating and broadening previous work in preparation for the great developments of magnetic observations, astronomical photography, and spectrum analysis which were to come in the 1860s. The staff would enlarge and diversify. Robert Main, who had fulfilled with solemn efficiency the position of Chief Assistant for twenty-five years ever since Airy was first appointed Astronomer Royal in 1835, left at about the time of William's death to become Radcliffe Observer at Oxford. He was also in his second year as President of the Royal Astronomical Society, still in its old rooms at Somerset House until its move to Burlington House in 1874. As the news of William's demise came through, Airy was preparing to journey to Spain with a large international group of astronomers, for which the Admiralty supplied the troopship, *Himalaya*, to convey them to Bilbao and Santander in order to observe an eclipse of the sun on 18th July. Many of the participants of this expedition were known to William though some of his long-standing friends were becoming too old for such junketings. Airy, however, was still active and energetic and had many travels, achievements, and honours yet to come. He resigned at last from the office of Astronomer Royal in 1881, thereafter living with his two unmarried daughters at his beloved White House at Playford until his death after a fall in 1892 at the great age of ninety-one.

At Cambridge too, there were inevitably changes. The year after William's death, Professor Challis, that kindly ally, retired, to be replaced by John Couch Adams, mathematician, and joint discoverer of Uranus, who became Lowndean Professor of Astronomy at the University. Miss Anne Sheepshanks once again presented the University with a generous gift, this time £2,000 expressly for the provision of a transit circle at the Observatory. This enabled Professor Adams to purchase an instrument of the highest quality, and James Simms, William's son, to maintain his association with Cambridge where his father had spent so many hours of fascinating work. The old Dolland transit instrument of 1824 was dismounted from its original stone piers in July 1869, and the new circle mounted in its place on the same piers. It continued in active work until 1919, after which it continued to be used for teaching purposes until about 1945, when it was dismantled and its useful parts were given to the optics group at Imperial College, South Kensington.[425]

Some of William's friends and colleagues were now long since dead – Edward Troughton, John Pond, Francis Baily. Others, who had been true

264

champions in times of need, such as Bryan Donkin, Richard Sheepshanks, and old Thomas Jones who had given William his first encouragement back in 1816, had died more recently. Numerous men who were both friends and clients, still held his instruments in their private observatories – the names are legion – Sir John Wrottesley, Reverend Samuel King, Professor Charles Pritchard, Sir John Lubbock, William Dawes, John Lee, Sir John Herschel, and Richard Carrington. Others became friends through the Learned Societies, notably William Parsons, Third Earl of Rosse of Birr Castle, and Edward Cooper of Markree, both of whom it is likely, though never proved conclusively, that William Simms visited to inspect their observatories in Ireland. Old colleagues such as Sir George Everest, William Yolland and Sir William Cubitt, were still active in their various fields. Generals Sabine and Smythe were still surveying with instruments designed in personal collaboration at Fleet Street, by William. Even that old adversary – the only individual who ever took up arms against him – Sir James South, was still alive but much subdued, and thinking of donating his precious Chaucoix glass which had caused William so much trouble, to Armagh Observatory.

After 1860, William's family all went their own ways. The heart had gone out of the family. Emma was still only forty-six, widowed for the second time, and with two surviving children, Lorina Maria, eleven years old the week her father died, and Arthur only six-and-a-half. Immediately William's Will was read out by Frederick West to the assembled family gathered round the table in the exquisite dining-room at Bramble Haw, she knew she could breath easily for the time being as she would not have to leave their home within the year. Next mid-summer, just before the year was up, she removed to 4 Reigate Villas at nearby Sutton, still within range of her friends at Carshalton, but from where Arthur could be sent daily to school at Kings College in the Strand. From there he later matriculated to Trinity College, Cambridge with a small bursary in the Michaelmas term, 1872. Lorina may have attended a local girl's school in Sutton, or, being the last child left at home, had a governess. She may, however, have been taught by her mother, cementing an affinity between the two, which resulted in her remaining unmarried, as a companion to Emma in the true Victorian fashion, for the rest of her short life. When Arthur firmly set his face away from the optical world of his forefathers, and became ordained deacon at Exeter Cathedral in 1878, and priest the following year, Lorina accompanied her mother to live with Arthur in his new position as curate of Lifton in Devon. By now she had already been ill for two years, and it was here at Lifton in 1880 at the age of only thirty that Lorina died from tuberculosis, that scourge of the 19th century. Arthur moved on to Clifton, taking his mother with him, and then obtained the living of Kingsbridge in the south of the county, and whilst he was here, Emma, who was now seventy-seven[426] died of a profound dose of 'flu' on 23rd May 1888. Shortly

265

afterwards Arthur transferred to Newton Abbot where, in 1896, he married a local woman named Jennie Marks, and accepted the living of St Michael's, Cambridge. Then followed benefices at Holy Trinity, Ely, and St Luke's, Torquay where he became Archdeacon of Totnes in 1910, and finally Canon Residentiary of Exeter for the last year of his life, dying in 1921 after a distinguished clerical career. Of him, his great-niece reported, after a childhood visit during the First World War, 'he was very holy'. Arthur was perhaps a confirmed bachelor before he married, and never really changed, so different from his avuncular father. He and Jennie never had any children. He was an academic as well as a parish priest, and married relatively late in life, for companionship.

Of William Simms' other sons, William Henry was somewhat of a disappointment. Starting life with great promise and of high intellect, he apparently never achieved the heights of which he was capable. There are no known publications by him after his book on the Sextant in 1858, nor any records of affiliation to the Learned Societies. He may have travelled abroad again about the time of William's death, and dates and locations of the births of four of his children remain obscure. His own eldest son, William Henry, however, fathered twins, Alexander and Lucy, at Shalford, Surrey, in 1879, and it was this boy who became an assistant astronomer at the Cape of Good Hope and was later drowned at sea in 1918.[427] Whether William Henry (1820) fulfilled the conditions of his father's Will, enabling him to inherit his share of the bequest, is not known. He himself died suddenly of a heart attack at his home at East Greenwich in 1875. He was a widower and intestate, and his daughter Katie Janet was granted Administration of his estate – just £400.

The next son, James, however, was what William must have considered a great success. He carried on his father's work with all the integrity, application and intelligence of the elder Simms. In addition there is ample written evidence of his benevolent care of his work people in the great traditions of Liberal Nonconformism. He continued the respected name of Troughton & Simms, his optical instruments travelling to all corners of the globe, and became a distinguished metrologist, winning in the 1890s the signal personal recognition of the Tsar of Russia in the shape of a beautiful cloisonné tea set. James and Eleanor Davison produced three children. The first, William, arrived the autumn after his grandfather, the great William Simms, died. Two years later James Simms junior was born, and then in 1864 a talented daughter, Eleanor Elizabeth, arrived, who was destined to die at the early age of thirty-six from cancer. This youngest William and James never aspired to the talents of their father and grandfather, but the son of Eleanor Elizabeth, another James, was similarly gifted, though in very much less favourable world conditions. He, however, carried on the family tradition until retirement in 1956, a man very similar in character and appearance to his great grandfather, William.[428] Eleanor Georgiana

266

James Simms and Eleanor, 1866.

Davison was thirty-eight when she married James, and twenty-three years later she succumbed to consumption whilst wintering in Madeira. James outlived her by thirty-three years.[429]

The third son of William Simms and Ann, Frederick, after some years abroad, returned to England, but never seems to have made his mark as a civil engineer, nor as far as is known did he ever marry. Later in life, perhaps about 1870, he joined his brother, James, at Charlton, taking over the mantle of old Henry, and becoming accountant, clerk, and general factotum at the works. He died at 67 Church Lane, Charlton in October 1900 at the age of seventy, leaving his effects, worth £1,201-10s, to his sole executor, Frederick Jacoby of the Dentsche Bank, Lombard Street.

Of William's five surviving daughters, one, Elizabeth Ann, was already married when their father died in 1860. Some time after this, the business belonging to her husband, Henry Lee, that of a skinner, must have failed, in spite of the £2,000 which William had lent him in 1859. At any rate he is said to have become an assistant at the Brighton aquarium in later life, which caused the family a good deal of hilarity. However, when Elizabeth Ann died in 1881 of some sort of neurological disease of several years' duration, she was living with her son Henry (also a furrier) at Ethelburt House, Fort

267

Crescent, Margate, so may already have been widowed. Their sojourn at Brighton, if it occurred, must have therefore been prior to this date.

William's other three daughters by Ann Nutting all married within three years of his death and within fifteen months of each other. Caroline was the first to do so, in March 1862. It seems likely that she had been in touch with her Uncle Frederick Walter – possibly it was him who was financing her – and through him his son Frederick had introduced other medical students to his cousin Mary Simms and through her to Caroline. The exact train of events is uncertain, but both girls eventually married 'Barts' doctors. A further connection was a result of Frederick Walter's long-standing friendship with William Froude, an engineer, since the days when they both worked for Henry Robinson Palmer in building the South-East Railway. William Froude's father was Archdeacon of Totnes, and his paternal aunt had married a Langworthy. South Devon was full of Froudes and Langworthys, all inter-related, and it was John Bartlet Moysey Langworthy whom Caroline married at St John's Church, Hampstead in 1862. She had contacted the Trustees of her father's Will shortly after his death, and received her share of the Trust twice a year thereafter, but she never returned home. After her wedding, witnessed by her sister, Mary, (and not, significantly, by her elder brother James) she and John returned to live at Malborough, near Salcombe, where he, his father, and his brother (both called William Froude Langworthy) practised medicine from Brooke House, Modbury, a large stone house which still serves as a nursing-home.

John and Caroline then, in quick succession, produced four little girls; twins Ethelind Marion and Gertrude Hellen in December 1862, Lillian Mildred Caroline Simms in March 1864, and Hester Douglas (her paternal grandmother's full name) in June 1865. Significantly three of the four babies were not named after the Simms side of the family, only the third after her mother, and none after her sisters. It was as if Caroline had cut herself off from Carshalton, but it seems probable that she visited her elder sister, Sarah, at Wesbury, near Bristol. Sarah had married James Walton, a merchant and general broker of Bristol, at Sutton Parish Church in June 1863, but must very soon afterwards have begun to show signs of consumption from which she died only twenty months later. Caroline developed overt symptoms of the same disease in the autumn of 1866, from which she died at Malborough in May 1867, exactly five years after her marriage to John Langworthy. Apparently starting with the illness of John Nutting who coughed his life away at Fleet Street in 1837, a remorseless chain of cases attacked the Simms family, in the end squeezing the breath from at least eight of them, a vivid example of the terrible hold which tuberculosis had over the Victorian family. John Nutting's sister Ann probably did not succumb to it, but her daughter, Ann, did so at ten years of age in 1843. Then followed little Walter Simms in 1848 at three-and-a-half; possibly baby Mary Matilda of an overwhelming infection in 1858, Sarah at thirty-nine in 1865, Caroline at twenty-eight in 1867, Lorina at thirty in 1880, and finally, Eleanor Georgiana at sixty-one in 1882. It was a terrible legacy, but typical of the time. Once Robert Koch discovered the bacillus responsible, (ironically the year Eleanor died), the methods of infection began to be understood, and the beginnings of control to appear.

A third young doctor, also trained at Barts and qualified in 1852, belonged to Caroline's group of friends. This was Robert Storrs, who represented the third generation of a family of surgeons working in Doncaster. Either through Frederick Simms or Caroline and John, he had come to know Mary Simms, and was married to her at Sutton Parish Church a month after Caroline's wedding on 24th April 1862. Their witnesses were their respective brothers, James Simms and Charles Edward Storrs. Thereafter he and Mary returned to 7 Hallgate, Doncaster where for the rest of his days he carried on with his medical work. They had a happy life together, blessed with nine children, one of whom continued the family name and profession. After Robert's death in October 1889, Mary went to live with her two unmarried daughters, Winifred and Hilda, at Beverley in the East Riding, where she died in 1917 at the age of eighty-one.

Of William Simms' brothers, James and George and young Francis had already died by 1860. Henry had recently become a widower, and as his four surviving children dispersed, only one, Jane Ellen Logan to marry, he remained at Camden Cottage by virtue of the codicil in William's Will. When Jane's surgeon husband died, she came back to live with her father, and some time after his death in 1871, she married her cousin Frederick (son of Frederick Walter) as his second wife following the death in childbirth of Caroline Frances in 1874. After Frederick's death she lived near her bachelor brother, Charles Francis at Brighton. Henry had never shone at anything, but all his life he seems to have been dependable, serious and kindly. He certainly was most industrious in his position as clerk at Troughton & Simms, even if he did sometimes make mistakes which had to be rectified by William. He remained with the firm until about the time they moved to Charlton, when his age of sixty-five prejudiced his ability to make the long journey from Camden each day. When he died in January 1871, he left less than £3,000 in spite of his rent-free house and emoluments from William. Everything about his life seems to have been impoverished, even his sole grandchild. Of the eight children which Mary Ward bore him, four died in childhood. To each of his surviving three sons, Charles, Francis, Arthur George and Edwin Henry, he left £100, and the residue of his goods to his only executrix, Jane Ellen Logan in whom he evidently had more confidence than in his sons. 14 Camden Cottages remained empty for several years after Henry's death, and was then pulled down to make space for the big St Pancras Way. Henry was buried with his wife, Mary, and their four predeceased children at Highgate Cemetery.

The future of Charles Francis and Edwin Henry is obscure, the former dying in rather reduced circumstances at North Sudeley Terrace, Brighton in 1901 probably well subsidised by his sister, Jane Ellen who lived at No. 4, and the latter (unmarried) in 1888. Arthur George was an artist, although so far little has been discovered about him. He was a bachelor, and suffered from chronic heart disease. He was appointed in 1860 by Frederick Walter to be his executor, but a later codicil rescinded this in favour of another nephew (in-law), John Lloyd, but does not give a reason. He lived latterly at 41 Townshead Road, St John's Wood, but died at 25 Devonshire Street, Marylebone in January 1892, like his cousin William Henry, intestate. The Administration was granted to his sister, Jane Ellen for his pitiful estate of £53-15s-8d. Only now in 1892 was it evidently realised that William Henry also had died intestate, and his daughter, Katie Janet was encouraged to apply for Administration of his small estate seventeen years after his death. Arthur George should not be confused with George, son of John, who probably identifies with the watercolourist, who worked in London, Kent and Italy in the 1870s,[430] and died at Berne. As well as being a man of means himself, he inherited considerable property from his father in 1879 and was therefore in a position to do this.

Two years older than Henry was John, that cheerful character, who with his much loved wife Christian Sumner, had probably been the brother closest to William. John and Christian had happily procreated almost every other year between 1824 and 1845, losing only one pair of twins from a brood of twelve children, and followed by Christian's own lamented death in December 1850. John remained at Wine Office Court until about 1870, and then moved to 29 Warwick Gardens, Kensington with his unmarried son, Charles, and three spinster daughters. Georgina Frost and Maria Sophia had died in youth, and a son, John James, had emigrated to Valparaiso in 1860 with financial help from his father. One daughter, Sarah Elizabeth, had had a single child called Alice Martha Simms from an unhappy marriage, and had since been deserted by her husband, John Thomas Hughes. John Simms had provided Sarah with furniture and household goods, and doubtless financial help too, leaving her £4,000 in Trust in his Will. The three unmarried daughters, Martha Christian, Adelaide, and Julia inherited the Warwick Gardens House, together with £4,000 each. His son, George, who was his kindred spirit and with whom he had gone into partnership in the hardware/warehouse business tucked away in the warrens behind the north side of Fleet Street, married in 1864, and continued to live at No. 141, where he flourished happily, later moving to Windsor about 1870. John senior and this George bought a considerable amount of property that year, perhaps as a speculation, some freehold, some leasehold, in the vicinity of 141, and earlier John alone had bought freehold property in and near the Broad Way, Ludgate Hill. The latter he left to George, with the option on the former. When he died in 1879, John's estate amounted to what his nephew, William Simms (1817), described as 'a fortune', and was nearly £40,000. By 1871 no one was living at 141, which was noted as a warehouse in the census of that year. Further down Wine Office Court the Press Association, formed in 1868, had taken up its abode.

The next brother was Frederick Walter, of whom a great deal is known. After William's death he removed himself to Devonshire to an 'isolated residence' where he lived 'almost alone'. For want of occupation in the following winter he wrote his fascinating book *From London to Calcutta by the Overland Route*. The reasons for this move right away from London are uncertain, but there is a good deal of evidence that after his return from India he never was the same man as of earlier years, and depression was certainly a major factor. This may have accompanied debilitation due to recurring tropical disease, or was fuelled by the loss of his wife, Caroline, and all but one of their children. The surviving son, Frederick, the young doctor, had recently married Caroline Frances Wyon, daughter of William Wyon, Chief Engraver at the Royal Mint, a Royal Academicean, and a long-standing family friend from the Birmingham days. Frederick and Caroline Frances were to live and work in the London area for the rest of their lives, so it is strange that Frederick Walter chose to distance himself from his only child. The causes may have been two-fold. In Devon he had his old friend William Froude (of South-Eastern Railway days), and a whole group of Froude's relations into whose midst his niece Caroline was soon to marry. One of the Langworthy uncles, a number of whom were doctors, specialised in the treatment of mental illness, and indeed was the proprietor of Plympton House Lunatic Asylum. It may be that Frederick Walter placed himself in the capable hands of Dr Richard Langworthy when the mental strains of his life became overwhelming. Later he returned to live with Frederick and Caroline Frances at their home at Heath Lane, Twickenham, and the last few months of his life he stayed at 50 Torrington Square in west-central London where he could be nursed properly. Eighteen months before he died, he was elected a Director of the East India Railway Company, but it was something of a consolation prize for all his labour and anxiety in India. He died in February 1865 from 'disease of the heart' – of about 3½ years duration – in fact dating from shortly after the Devonshire episode, and probably the reason why he returned to live with his son. Ironically, disease of the heart was indeed his complaint. A highly intelligent man, but without his brother, William's happy disposition, his life was dogged by misfortune, some of his own making, and his venture in India was doomed to failure by his incompatibility with the pundits with whom he had to deal. His Will, dated December 1860, stipulated that any shares or funds whatsoever still possessed by him in India should be sold, as if he wished to wash his hands of the country to which he owed nothing but tears and sorrow – and a small plot of ground in a Calcutta cemetery.

Lastly there was old Alfred Septimus, the seventh of the eight Simms brothers, who for about the previous thirty years had been in the care of Mrs Fish first at Margate and then at 1 Shakespeare Terrace in the St Lawrence district of Ramsgate. In November 1875 he died from 'paralysis', though the duration of the malady was not noted on the certificate. The final payment from his brother William's trustees was passed to Mrs Fish in March 1876.[431] Alfred was said by his nephew, William Simms (1817), to have been of unsound mind, though whether this meant low mental calibre or some neurological illness such as epilepsy, is not clear. That there was a hereditary tendency to instability in the family is evident from such a study as this, a trait showing itself as much in the highly gifted members as in the less well endowed. The cousins, William Henry (1820) (eldest son of William, subject of this book) and William (1817) (son of James) were both bright, but were under-achievers, and lacked perseverence. Frederick Walter was unable to cope with the exigencies of India, and the turmoil later in the building of the South-East Railway. Caroline, William's daughter, absented herself from her father and step-mother when she was still under-age, a most unusual thing for a young woman without means and yet from a well-to-do family to do, and in the next generation, James Simms' son William (born 1860) was generally thought of in the family as a buffoon, whose three sons all had tendencies towards eccentricity as well as (at least two of them) high intellect.

Happily, William Simms (1793) quite clearly had a philosophical temperament and only rarely do his letters betray irritation. The archives all underline his quiet kindness, and a certain humility, reliability and pragmatism. One suspects that he inherited his serenity from his mother, Sarah Thompson, whilst the more unreliable members of the family took after old William, whom we are told 'was, during the latter years of his life reduced by adverse speculation'.[432]

For several years before his father's death, James Simms had been gradually taking over the reins of Troughton & Simms, though the main decision-making had remained with William. For the last nine months the latter was usually too ill to partake in day-to-day management of affairs and James was in effect in control, assisted by cousin William in a rather subsiduary role. The business is usually said to have been left by William (1793) jointly to his son, James and his nephew, William (1817), in the ratio of 2 : 1. This is in fact not so. All the buildings, equipment and tools were specifically bequeathed to James in his father's Will dated 9th November 1859 and in two later codicils just before he died. However, the stock-in-trade which must have amounted to a pretty sum, was left to the three trustees, who were these two cousins and in addition, William's brother John, with the proviso that James should be given the option to buy up the shares of the other two trustees if he so desired, even to the extent of borrowing the required cash. What seems to have occurred, although the

272

relevant papers have not survived, is that William Simms junior retained his share, to become a one-third partner with James, and that James himself acquired his Uncle John's share, thus owning two-thirds of the business. Thereafter the firm was carried on jointly by James and William junior in an agreement due to last for fourteen years. The two cousins were, however, of very different moulds, and many references point to a lack of sustainable drive in the latter. William junior never seems to have cultivated the commitment to the work which James inherited from his father, and which made the latter so successful with his clients. William junior was certainly talented, but there was a lack of perseverance in his dealings. There is some evidence that his visits to Wymondham, where Charlotte Needham's family still lived, continued, and possible that he was the creator of several watercolour paintings of the district still in the possession of local people. It may be that this artistic tendency detracted in time and concentration from the work at the factory. At any rate, he retired from his contract with James, signed in the autumn of 1860, three years before the specified time of fourteen years, one source stating that this was due to illness, another to poor eyesight, and still another due to dissatisfaction with the remuneration. It appears much more likely that the real reason was an incompatibility of personalities between the two cousins.

William Simms junior moved several times after leaving Troughton & Simms. He seems to have been rather a discontented man, blaming others for his own shortcomings, and the photograph in the Royal Astronomical Society Archives bears this out, as does the accompanying letter from his daughter, Catherine McLachlan, who evidently inherited the same chip on her shoulder. After several addresses, William and Charlotte finally retired to the Isle of Wight where they lived first at Ryde and then at Albert Lodge, Shanklin. Here the two old people received attention from Queen Victoria in her last year, and she in fact granted to William a small pension in recognition of his blindness 'caused by devotion to science'. He died in January 1907 in his eighty-ninth year, and Charlotte, also blind, outlived him by only six months to die at ninety-six.

By 1860 it was already apparent that Fleet Street was quite inappropriate for the manufacture of optical instruments. Moreover, the huge amount of orders coming in simply could not be accommodated in the factory behind 138. James, who now lived at Charlton, began to look around for a site on which to build new premises, shortly afterwards purchasing land to the south of Woolwich Road, which was within a short distance of Greenwich Observatory, the railway, and the docks. He now set to work to design his factory exactly as requirements demanded, with plenty of light and air, surrounded by garden in which to test instruments, and at the east end a chapel. By the autumn of 1865 all was completed, and men, benches, lathes and tools were brought down to the new building in a series of cartloads from Fleet Street, and local workmen from Woolwich were engaged to swell the numbers of those from the old factory. By 1871 there were one hundred men working at Charlton, probably more than twice the number employed at 138. The business continued to flourish until the slump after the First World War. Happily James never saw the development of this tragedy as he died in 1915 following nine months of complete incapacity due to a stroke, and several years of total blindness.[433]

Once the move to Charlton had been effected, Fleet Street was for the first time for eighty-three years without a Troughton or a Simms. The ground lease of 138 would not conclude until Christmas 1921, and until that date James retained the house for the use of his staff, the first of whom was a young journeyman instrument maker named John Valentine, and his wife and growing family, and for the ground-floor front to continue as his shop. The factory buildings at the back were sub-let to the *Birmingham Daily Post*, most likely via a Simms relative in that city, until 1902 when the *Liverpool Daily Post* obtained the lease at a rental of £300 per annum. Meanwhile the *Daily Telegraph* bought up the house and land belonging to 136, including Peterborough Court where their printer, J. M. Levy had his business. Ever since the stamp duty on newspapers had been rescinded in November 1854, the newspaper business had vastly expanded, and the many small printers and booksellers in and around Fleet Street became involved in their production. The *Daily Telegraph*, formed in 1855, was foremost amongst the dailies, and at first housed its Advertisement Manager, Thomas Newcome, and their fireman James Fleming, in the house at 136, using William's old workshops at the back as printing rooms, upper floors as composing rooms, and his old shop looking onto Fleet Street as their own sales outlet. Thereafter the *Daily Telegraph* bought up No. 135, a large triple-bayed house to the east, and here, in 1881, began to build a large new office block, its rather flamboyant facade a mixture of classical and decorative typical of Victorian commercial edifices of the period, facing onto Fleet Street. Its architects were Arding, Bond and Buzzard.[434] Since the work of producing a newspaper had to continue during the re-building of 135, the back premises were not altered until 1912, when they were transformed into modern machine shops. The front block, by contrast, was extremely advanced in its style and the lavishness of its space, especially in its 'Pillar Hall' and its huge clock cantilevered over Fleet Street. Later the paper bought up further buildings to the east, and in 1929 built the huge contemporary pile familiar to City workers today, erasing thereby the last vestige of William's premises at 136 which were swallowed up in the new design, now under new ownership.

138, however remained, though altered after Troughton & Simms ceased to own it at the end of 1921. Wine Office Court also survives, with John's house in place over the archway from Fleet Street. The Cheshire Cheese continues to thrive, and a few yards east of it, the name of Peterborough Court is to be seen in a 20th century entrance to the *Daily*

Telegraph basement. The great Wren gateway to the City of London, Temple Bar, was removed to a temporary site on the Isle of Dogs in 1878, and re-erected at Theobalds Park, Waltham Cross in 1888, thus denuding Fleet Street of the cosy effect of enclosure, but retaining the hubbub of constant traffic every weekday. To the east, the view of St Paul's was intruded upon by the building of the viaduct of the London, Chatham and Dover Railway across Ludgate Hill in 1864, when instead of the grand sweep of the street rising to the great western portico of the cathedral, the astonishing sight of a train in its green and brown livery crossing over the traffic to Farringdon Station, brought the idyllic to the level of the mundane. The Bridewell was demolished in 1864, and the new Blackfriars Bridge was built by William Cubitt in 1869, the same year as the great swathe of the Queen Victoria Street was cut through remorselessly to the Mansion House, sweeping everything away in its vanguard, including the graves of old William and Sarah lying before St Andrew-by-the-Wardrobe, and the Doctor's Commons where all the Simms bridegrooms had acquired their marriage licences. To the north of Fleet Street appeared the monstrosity of Holborn Viaduct, dwarfing the tower of St Andrew's Church which had served as meridian mark for Troughton's 'little gazebo', soon to be darkened by the grime exuding from the new station of London's first 'underground' railway, the Metropolitan, at Farringdon Street.

And Bramble Haw? What of that gem of a house? After Emma finally closed its fine front door behind her in March 1862, and looked her last westwards to William's forest trees over the top of which she could just see the tip of the church tower, and in the foreground his monkey-puzzle tree, with the little River Wandle meandering its way down to the mill to the north, the great lawns and the happy memories, Bramble Haw had a series of different owners. At the turn of the century it suffered the indignity of crude additions on the north side, which ruined its symmetry and simplicity, and yet seemed needless, and as if to add insult to injury, the name was altered to Bramblehaw. Heavy plasterwork was added to the dining-room ceiling, 'William and Mary' oak panels incongruously to the walls; fussy decorative additions were appended to the panels in the drawing-room, and the front door fanlight was over-painted.[435] After the First World War, no one wanted Bramblehaw and it stood empty and unloved. Finally in 1929 it was pulled down, and the whole estate except for the coach house, the barn and the neighbouring staff house, was covered in a maze of little semi-detached houses typical of the period, with small front gardens facing the entire lengths of Acre Lane (widened at the same time into a main road) and Westercroft Road. The Wandle disappeared under concrete and tarmac. The church where two Simms baptisms, one wedding, and two funerals had taken place was enormously extended by the architect, Reginald Blomfield, and the old mediaeval nave now forms the south aisle. Carshalton Place was never built except for its grotto, and

Carshalton House was transformed into a convent. Other large houses eventually became the property of the local authority with inevitable loss of affectionate warmth. Only the ponds and the few remaining ancient cottages continue essentially unchanged, except for the dust of perpetual traffic passing through the erstwhile country village.

Troughton & Simms continued under James' wise control to supply astronomical instruments to major observatories throughout the world, and Troughton & Simms surveying instruments maintained their predominance throughout the life of the firm long after the Survey of England and Scotland was completed in 1862. However, in the appalling industrial conditions following the First World War, it became financially impossible to make single instruments for individual customers, and the wealthy private client had all but ceased to exist. The astronomical business was forced to become either wholesale or government-sponsored for the few major telescopes now needed or viable in the world, neither option suiting the firm as it then was. The last astronomical instrument to be undertaken by a Simms was designed by the then Astronomer Royal, Sir Frank Dyson, for the Royal Greenwich Observatory, and completed in 1936 by James Simms Wilson, William's great grandson. Appropriately, it was a Transit Circle.

List of instruments mentioned in text

Instruments by William Simms as mentioned in various archives. 1826-c1831 in conjunction with Troughton. See Preface.

Protractor design	1816
Theodolites etc for Survey of England – Col. Colby	c1817 foll.
Instruments for Survey in India – Hon. East India Co.	before 1826
Altazimuth for India – Surveyor General at Calcutta	1824-25
Theodolites for Colonel Everest, India	1830
Theodolites for Revenue surveys of India	c1830
Instruments for Survey of Ireland – Col. Colby	1825 foll.
Instruments for Survey of Ireland – Col. Colby	1826
Geodesic theodolite – Col. Colby	1827
Ordnance Standards	1826-1827
Troughton's pillar sextants	1826 foll.
Troughton's reflecting circle	1826 foll.
Transit for Cracow	1828
Telescope for Mr James South	1829
Zenith Sector for Profs Schumacher and Gauss	1829
Altazimuths for India – HEIC	1830
Equipment for Colonel Everest	1830
Altazimuth for Edinburgh Observatory	1830
Mural circle for Madras Observatory	1830
Mural circle for Cracow Observatory	1830
Large transit for Markree	1830
Levelling instrument for J. A. Lloyd	1830
Mural circle for Cambridge Observatory	1832
Instruments for Survey of Ireland	1832 foll.
Theodolites for Colonel Hodgson, India	1832
Theodolites for Messrs Jopp and Shortrede	1832
Pillar sextants – Colonel Everest	1832
Reverbatory lamps – Colonel Everest	1832
Altazimuth for Lucknow	1832
2 astronomical circles for Calcutta – made 1829	arrived 1832
Mural circle for Edinburgh	1834

Equatorial for Brussels	1834
Mural circle for Brussels	1835
Equatorial for Liverpool	1837
Rain gauge for Cambridge	1838
Anemometer for Cambridge	1838
Various for India	1838
Equatorial for Cambridge	1839
Mural circle for Lucknow	1839
Achromatic telescope for Edinburgh	1839
Transit instrument for Mayor of Louth	1839
Northumberland telescope for Cambridge	1839
Gravitt's Dumpy Level	1840
7-inch sextant for Prof Schumacher	1840
Magnetic theodolite for Major Sabine	1840
Telescopes for Ordnance Survey signal stations	1840
Protractor for Royal Marines, Portsmouth	1840
Dipping needle for Mr Heron, Glasgow	1840
Rain gauge for Mr Heron, Glasgow	1840
Artificial horizon for Rev Sheepshanks	1840
Levels for RMA, Woolwich	1840
Equatorial for Sir John Wrottesley	1842
5-inch mural circle for Washington Observatory	1843
5-inch mural circle for West Point Observatory	1843
Transit instrument for Oxford Observatory	1843
Standard chains for Admiralty	1843
Measuring calipers for Woolwich Arsenal	1843
Double microscope for Jones' equatorial at Greenwich	1843
Double microscope for Troughton's zenith sector at Greenwich	1843
Self-acting dividing engine	1843
Equatorial for Liverpool Observatory	1845
Transit instrument for Prof Bache, US Coastal Survey	1846
4-inch transit circle for Harvard College, Boston, Mass	1846
Mural circle for Harvard College, Boston, Mass	1846
Theodolites for India Survey	1846
Altazimuth for Royal Observatory, Greenwich	1847
Transit and zenith and equal altitude instruments, and others for Prof Bache, US Coastal Survey	1847
Telescope for Mr Bonditch, Cambridge, Mass	1847
Equatorial for Harvard College, Boston, Mass	1847
2-feet transit circle for William Dawes	1847
Compound microscope for Rev Samuel King	1850
Compound microscope for Mr Ewbanks	1850
Equatorial for Sir W. K. Murray	1850

Calculating machine for Prof Challis	1850
Transit circle for Royal Observatory, Greenwich	1851
Zenith instrument for Royal Observatory, Greenwich	1851
Levelling instruments, Y levels, telescopes for India	1851
Equatorial for India	1851
'Philosophical apparatus' for Senior Don S. Montago	1851
Equatorial for Colonel Sabine's magnetic experiments, Woolwich	1851
Transit circle for Colonel Pritchard	1851
Compound microscope for Smith Eldon	1852
'Philosophical apparatus' for Senior Don S. Montago	1852
Equatorial and transit circle for Mr Collingwood	1852
Transit circle for Richard Carrington	1852
Equatorial for Richard Carrington	1852
Transit circle for the Cape Observatory	1852
Standard Measures for Guernsey	1854
Standard Lengths for New Brunswick	1854
Transit circle for America	1854
Altazimuth for America	1854
Altazimuth for Melbourne, Australia	1854
'Apparatus' for Sir John Lubbock	1855
Standard Lengths for British Parliament	1855
Large list of surveying requirements for HEIC	1855
Standardisation of Lengths for Buenos Aires	1855
Equatorial for Prof Challis	1856
Apparatus for Prof Airy's experiments on polarization	1856
Transit circle for HEIC for Madras	1857
Transit circle for Sydney, Australia (Paramatta)	1858
Great Equatorial for Royal Observatory, Greenwich	1859

This list is by no means complete: for instance it includes few of the smaller instruments. It merely contains all those items referred to in archival material and which I have mentioned in my text. Full sales catalogues can be found as an appendix to F. W. Simms book on Mathematical Instruments, or in several Collections.

Selected bibliography

Portrait of an Age – Victorian England	G. M. Younge
History of England	G. M Trevelyan
English Social History	G. M. Trevelyan
History of Europe	H. A. L. Fisher
Life and Times of Queen Victoria – Vols. I and II	Robert Wilson
Victoria R.L.	Elizabeth Longford
English Saga	Arthur Bryant
Short History of our Religion	D. C. Somervell
Moore's Poetical Works	
Dictionary of National Biography	
Encyclopaedia Britannica	
England in the Eighteenth Century	J. A. Plumb
England in the Nineteenth Century	David Thompson
The Life and Times of William IV	Anne Somerset
Blue Guide to London	
Baedeckers London 1898	
The City of London	Mary Cathcart Borer
A History of London	Robert Gray
King's England (London north of the Thames)	Arthur Mee
London Life in the Eighteenth Century	M. Dorothy George
Guide to London Churches	Merveyn Blatch
Preserving London	Kathleen Denbigh
Georgian London	John Summerson
The Story of Islington	Sonia Roberts
Portrait of Birmingham	Vivien Bird
Birmingham Heritage	Joan Zuckerman and Geoffrey Eley
Shell Guide to Leicestershire	W. G. Hoskins
Shell Guide to Rutland	W. G. Hoskins

Shell Book of English Villages

Surrey – Batsford   Maxwell Fraser

The Year is 1851   Patrick Howarth

Dombey and Son   Hard Times   Charles Dickens

David Copperfield Bleak House   Charles Dickens

Barnaby Rudge   Our Mutual Friend   Charles Dickens

Great Expectations   Charles Dickens

Oliver Twist   Charles Dickens

Charles Dickens   Una Pope Hennessy

The Royal Greenwich Observatory   W. H. McCrea

History of the Cambridge Observatory   J. W. Clark

At the Sign of the Orrery   J. S. Wilson and
                                                Wilfred Taylor

History of the Ordnance Survey. Ed W. A. Seymour

Vulgar and Mechanick   J. E. Burnett and
                                                A. D. Morrison-Low

Historical Records of the Survey of India,
    Vols. 3 and 4   Col. R. H. Phillimore

Mathematical Instrument Makers in the Grocers
    Company   Joyce Brown

The Compleat Surveyor   J. A. Bennett and
                                                Olivia Brown

Science at the Great Exhibition   J. A. Bennett

History of the Royal Astronomical Society   J. L. E. Dreyer et al

History of the Society of Arts   Hudson & Luckhurst

Edward Troughton – monograph (Royal Society)   Joyce Brown and
                                                A. W. Skempton

Blue Guide to Ireland

The Reason Why   Cecil Woodham Smith

The Great Eastern Railway   Cecil J. Allen

The South East & Chatham Railway   O. S. Nock

Isambard Kingdom Brunel   L. T. C. Rolt

Quakers in Science and Industry   Arthur Raistrick

Guide to Comets   Patrick Moore

Nagels Ceylon

Observatories in London & vicinity   John Weale

The Universal Provider – the story of
    William Whiteley   R. S. Lambert

The Penny Post	Frank Staff
Farewell to Fleet Street. English Heritage	Susie Benson and Andrew Saint
The Achromatic Telescope	William Simms
Treatise on Mathematical Instruments	F. W. Simms
Practical Tunnelling	F. W. Simms
From London to Calcutta by the Overland Route	F. W. Simms
The Sextant and its applications	W. H. Simms
Memorials of our Family (1885)	W. Simms
Reid's Heirs – Biography of James Simms Wilson	Eleanor Mennim
Dictionary of Watercolour Artists	
The Story of Astronomy in Edinburgh	Hermann A. Bruck
European Costume	Doreen Yarwood
Costume Reference, 5 and 6	Marion Sichet
What the Judge thought. London 1922	E. A. Parry
Modern English Biography	Frederic Boase
British Watercolour Artists, Vol. I	H. L. Mallalieu
London Goldsmiths – 1697-1837	Arthur G. Grimwade

Notes

[1] *The Streets and Inhabitants of Birmingham in 1770.* Sketchley & Adams.

[2] He later returned to England and eventually died on 2nd January 1863 at Spohr Lodge, Upper Tulse Hall.

[3] The various Williams and James of the different generations are confusing, and where it may be unclear the date of birth is added to the name.

[4] Now held at the Borthwick Institute, University of York.

[5] *Dombey and Son*, Chapter IV.

[6] When visited in 1989 most of these old gravestones had worn so that their inscriptions were lost.

[7] There were at least five others: Elizabeth 1792 (died in infancy), Henry 1794 (died in infancy), twins Harriet (died in infancy) and Henry 1796, and Elizabeth Harriett (1797).

[8] V.I.A., 1.2.2.

[9] Ibid.

[10] R.S.A., LA F1/177.

[11] Ibid.

[12] Min. Proc. ICE., Vol. 20, 1860-61.

[13] R.A.S., Mem. i. 135.

[14] R.A.S., Vol. XXI Obit.

[15] R.A.S., M.N., Vol. III, p150, p154.

[16] R.S. 1973, Vol. 27.

[17] R.A.S., M.N., Vol. III, p154.

[18] R.A.S., M.N., Vol. III, p150.

[19] Gentleman's Magazine 4, p15-16 (1835).

[20] R.G.O. 6/718, 923, 925.

[21] R.G.O. 6/166, 205.

[22] Phillimore. Vol. III, p461.

[23] V.I.A., p30.

[24] Phillimore. Vol. III, p216.

[25] Dreyer. Chap. 1.

[26] R.A.S. Council Archives.

[27] R.S., 1973, Vol. 27, p235.

[28] *David Copperfield*. Chap. XXIII.

[29] At this date 'optician' denoted craftsman working with lenses, often an optical instrument maker.

[30] 'The Achromatic Telescope' by William Simms, 1852. London 1852.

[31] V.I.A., Lease Indenture 1825.

[32] Phillimore. Vol. II, p191, p223.

[33] Phillimore. Vol. II, p252.
[34] Phillimore. Vol. III, p216.
[35] Phillimore. Vol. IV, p140.
[36] Phillimore. Vol. IV, p140.
[37] Phillimore. Vol. IV, p144.
[38] Phillimore. Vol. IV, p144.
[39] R.S., 1973, Vol. 27, Skempton & Brown.
[40] Yolland 1847.
[41] H.O.S., Ed. A. Seymour, p81 foll.
[42] V.I.A. Workbook.
[43] H.O.S., Ed. A. Seymour, p83.
[44] H.O.S., Ed. A. Seymour, p83.
[45] R.A.S., M.N., 1836, Vol. III, p153-155.
[46] C.O.A. Stratton.
[47] V.I.A.
[48] R.A.S. Dreyer, Chap. 1, p16.
[49] Ibid., p21.
[50] Ibid., Chap. II.
[51] A.R.O.E., 325
[52] Ibid.
[53] M.E.A.I., Vol. 1, p185.
[54] Ibid., p175-177, p181.
[55] Ibid., p201.
[56] Ibid., p201, p203.
[57] V.I.A., W.S. 1833.
[58] Minutes Proc. Vol. 20, 1860-61.
[59] Royal Society of Arts. IIs Subscription Book.
[60] V.I.A., W.S. 1833.
[61] Ibid.
[62] Ibid.
[63] Ibid.
[64] Ibid.
[65] M.E.A.I., Vol. 2, p290.
[66] Ibid., p292.
[67] Ibid., p294.
[68] Ibid., p299.
[69] M.E.A.I., Vol. 2, p72.
[70] Ibid., p3.
[71] Yolland. 1847.
[72] R.A.S., Vol. III, p152.
[73] Proc. I.C.E. Vol. 25.
[74] R.A.S. Proc. Vol. 12, 1830.
[75] History of R.A.S., p50-52.
[76] Ibid., p55.
[77] V.I.A., W.S. 1833.
[78] History of R.A.S., p53.
[79] Ibid.
[80] R.A.S. Monthly Notices, Vol. II, No. 13.

[81] Ibid.
[82] G. M. Trevelyn, *History of England*, Book VI, Chap. II.
[83] R.G.O., 6/157, 281.
[84] H.O.S., p821.
[85] Phillimore, p216.
[86] Ibid., p217.
[87] Ibid., p197.
[88] Ibid., p88.
[89] Ibid., p124.
[90] Ibid., p115.
[91] Ibid., p131.
[92] C.O.A., 184, 3.1.
[93] C.O.A., 1832, 1.
[94] C.O.A., 1830, 6.
[95] C.O.A., 1832, 1.
[96] C.O.A., 1832, 2.
[97] R.A.S., M.N., XI, p104.
[98] V.I.A., 1833 notebook.
[99] Ibid.
[100] History of the R.A.S.
[101] V.I.A., 1833 notebook, p41.
[102] Ibid., p44.
[103] Ibid., cont.
[104] M.E.A.I., Vol. 2, p90.
[105] Proc. I.C.E., Vol. 20, 1860-61.
[106] V.I.A., W.S. Tech., p9.
[107] Ibid., p62.
[108] Ibid., p27.
[109] Ibid., p69.
[110] Proc. I.C.E., Vol. 25, 1845-66.
[111] *A Treatise on Mathematical Instruments* by F. W. Simms, 1836.
[112] Gentleman's Magazine 4, p15-16 (1835).
[113] R.A.S. Monthly Notices, Vol. III, 1836, p149.
[114] Airy's Autobiography, 1896, p109 and p128.
[115] V.I.A. Tech. 1835, see note also at end of chapter.
[116] Phillimore. Vol. IV, p149.
[117] M.E.A.I., Vol. 12, p136.
[118] V.I.A., W.S. Tech., p61.
[119] Ibid., p62.
[120] Ibid., p64.
[121] Ibid., p65.
[122] R.G.O. 6/157, No. 335.
[123] R.G.O. 6/716, Sect. 15, No. 237.
[124] R.G.O. 6/716, 237.
[125] Ibid., 241.
[126] R.G.O. 6/157, 258 and also note at end of chapter.
[127] Ibid., 246.
[128] Ibid., 274.

[129] R.G.O. 6/716, 250 and 251.
[130] The microscope for reading off the results of the zenith instrument.
[131] R.G.O. 6/157, 258.
[132] Ibid., 260.
[133] Ibid., 262.
[134] Ibid., 281.
[135] R.G.O. 6/716, 264.
[136] Ibid., 269.
[137] Ibid., 265.
[138] C.O.A., 1837, 9.
[139] R.G.O. 6/157, 288.
[140] Ibid., 295.
[141] C.O.A., 1838, 2, 3.
[142] Phillimore IV, p138 and p149.
[143] R.A.S. Council Minutes, 1838.
[144] History of the R.A.S., p81.
[145] C.O.A., 1838, 15.
[146] Ibid., 17.
[147] Ibid., 18.
[148] C.O.A., 1838, 20.
[149] Ibid., 21.
[150] Ibid., 23.
[151] Ibid., 23.
[152] Ibid., 25.
[153] Ibid.
[154] R.G.O. 6/157, 316.
[155] Ibid., 319.
[156] C.O.A., 1839, 11.
[157] Ibid., 11.
[158] Ibid., 7.
[159] R.A.S. Council Minutes.
[160] V.I.A. Design Book.
[161] M.E.A.I., Vol. 2, p146.
[162] R.G.O. 6/157, 324.
[163] Ibid., 327.
[164] C.O.A., 1839, 9.
[165] R.A.S. Mem., Vol. XI, 840.
[166] Ibid.
[167] R.G.O. 6/151, 330.
[168] C.O.A., 1839, 22.
[169] Ibid.
[170] R.G.O. 6/716, 350.
[171] Ibid., 353.
[172] Ibid., 351.
[173] Ibid., 351.
[174] Ibid., 365.
[175] C.O.A., 1839, 30.
[176] R.S., S., 206.

[177] McCrea, p16.
[178] R.G.O. 6/716, 590.
[179] V.I.A. Design Book.
[180] Ibid.
[181] D.N.B.
[182] C.O.A., 1840, 7.
[183] Ibid.
[184] C.O.A., 1840, 14.
[185] Ibid., 51.
[186] R.G.O. 6/716, 786.
[187] C.O.A., 1841, 16 and 29.
[188] V.I.A. Workbook, p34.
[189] Ibid., p42.
[190] V.I.A. Workbook, p41.
[191] Ibid., p41.
[192] Ibid., p39.
[193] V.I.A. Workbook, p15 and others.
[194] C.O.A., 1842, 1.
[195] Ibid., 2.
[196] Ibid., 7.
[197] R.G.O. 6/718, 813.
[198] V.I.A. Workbook, p149.
[199] C.O.A., 1842, 15.
[200] Ibid., 20.
[201] Ibid., 20.
[202] Ibid., 22.
[203] R.G.O. 6/159, 100.
[204] Ibid., 102.
[205] C.O.A., 1843, 3.
[206] R.G.O. 6/718, 840.
[207] R.A.S. Memoirs, Vol. XV, p19 foll.
[208] C.O.A., 1843.
[209] Ibid., 3.
[210] V.I.A. Workbook, p66.
[211] U.A.V. 630, 1843, 31st May.
[212] U.A.V., 1845, 2nd January.
[213] V.I.A. Workbook, p44.
[214] Ibid., p45.
[215] Ibid., p52.
[216] Ibid., p55, p58, p59.
[217] *Reids Heirs*, Eleanor Mennim 1990.
[218] C.O.A., 1843, 5.
[219] Ibid., 5
[220] Ibid., 20.
[221] R.G.O. 6/718, 884.
[222] R.A.S. Memoirs, Vol. XV, 1846.
[223] *From London to Calcutta*, 1878.
[224] V.I.A. Workbook, 64.

[225] R.G.O. 6/718, 889.

[226] Ibid., 890.

[227] Ibid., 891.

[228] R.G.O. 6/718, 901.

[229] C.O.A., 1844, 16.

[230] Ibid.

[231] R.G.O. 6/718, 910.

[232] Ibid., 923.

[233] Ibid.

[234] U.A.V. 630.2.

[235] R.G.O. 6/158, 300.

[236] Ibid., 301.

[237] Ibid., 302.

[238] R.G.O. 6/720, 180.

[239] Ibid., 202.

[240] Ibid., 205.

[241] R.A.S. M.N., Vol. VI, 1845.

[242] S.A. M.S. 8207.

[243] S.A. M.S. 8206.

[244] Emma's death certificate in May 1888 stated her age as 74 years, which would have made her only 16 when she first married. However, the International Geneological Index of the Mormons gives her date of birth as 4th September 1811, confirming the Parish Register of Lambeth St Mary. This would make her 18 in July 1830, which seems more likely. The 1851 census states her age as 39, the 1861 as 48. It appears that the death certificate is in error, which in this case is surprising as her son was so punctilious, though in general it is not unusual.

[245] S.A. M.S. 8223.

[246] Personal communication, Major Charles O'Leary.

[247] S.A. M.S. 8223.

[248] Ibid.

[249] Never built, though the grounds were partially set out, including a grotto.

[250] Description taken partly from photographs in possession of London Borough of Sutton Heritage Department and the Peatling Papers.

[251] R.G.O. 6/720, 220.

[252] C.O.A., 1846, 14.

[253] Ibid., 19.

[254] Ibid., 22.

[255] Ibid., 23.

[256] R.A.S. History, p108.

[257] U.A.V. 630, 2.

[258] R.G.O. 7/720, 229.

[259] Ibid., 230.

[260] V.I.A. Workbook, 93.

[261] Ibid., 94.

[262] U.A.I. 50, 8 V.T., Vol. VII.

[263] V.I.A. Workbook, 96.

[264] R.A.S. Minutes of Council, Vol. V.

[265] R.A.S. Obit. Monthly Notices, Vol. XXI, 1861.

[266] R.G.O. 6/720, 253.
[267] Ibid., 6/159, 375.
[268] Ibid., 6/720, 259.
[269] Ibid., 269.
[270] Ibid., 271.
[271] R.G.O. 6/164, 30-33.
[272] *Victoria RI*, Chapter XIV.
[273] V.I.A. Workbook, 99.
[274] Ibid., 100.
[275] Ibid., 102.
[276] Ibid, 98.
[277] R.G.O. 6/721, 829.
[278] Ibid., 833.
[279] Ibid., 834.
[280] Ibid., 837.
[281] R.G.O. 6/721, 836.
[282] Ibid., 828.
[283] R.A.S. Memoirs, XVI.
[284] V.I.A. Workbook, p109.
[285] Ibid., p110.
[286] R.G.O. 6/160, 62.
[287] Ibid.
[288] R.A.S. History, p108 foll.
[289] R.A.S. Memoirs, IX, 147.
[290] U.A.V. 630, 2.
[291] Ibid.
[292] Ibid.
[293] Ibid.
[294] Ibid.
[295] Ibid.
[296] Ibid.
[297] Ibid., July 1849.
[298] Ibid.
[299] Ibid.
[300] R.G.O. 6/721.
[301] G. M. Young, Portrait of an Age.
[302] Ibid.
[303] R.G.O. 6/722, 730.
[304] Ibid., 752.
[305] Ibid., 741.
[306] V.I.A. Workbook, p128.
[307] Ibid., p137, p139.
[308] A telescope able to view a broad belt of the heavens extending at least eight degrees each side of the apparent path of the sun.
[309] London Borough of Sutton Heritage Department.
[310] C.O.A., 1850, 18.
[311] Ibid., 10.
[312] Ibid., 12.

[313] Ibid., 17.
[314] Ibid., 19.
[315] Ibid., 23.
[316] Ibid., 25.
[317] Ibid., 26.
[318] R.G.O. 6/163, 106.
[319] Ibid., 108.
[320] R.G.O. 6/722, 774.
[321] Ibid., 779.
[322] Ibid., 784.
[323] Ibid., 790.
[324] C.O.A., 1850, 63.
[325] R.G.O. 6/723, 682.
[326] Ibid., 681.
[327] V.I.A. Workbook, p144.
[328] Ibid., p149.
[329] Ibid., p149.
[330] Ibid., p147.
[331] Great Exhibition lectures.
[332] R.G.O. 6/164, 29.
[333] Lecture 401, Great Exhibition and *Science of the Great Exhibition*, J. A. Bennett.
[334] R.G.O. 6/723, 708.
[335] Ibid., 715.
[336] Great Exhibition Lectures, 399-401 and J. A. Bennett.
[337] R.G.O. 6/723, 715.
[338] Ibid., 719.
[339] See *Reid's Heirs*, Eleanor Mennim 1990.
[340] R.G.O. 6/723, 733.
[341] I.C.E. Obit.
[342] R.G.O. 6/723, 749.
[343] Ibid., 751.
[344] V.I.A., p108, p128.
[345] V.I.A. Workbook, p151-153, p154.
[346] Ibid.
[347] C.O.A., 1853, 3.
[348] V.I.A. Workbook, p154-157.
[349] R.S. Archives.
[350] V.I.A.
[351] C.O.A., 1853, 3.
[352] Personal communication, Dr D. Dewhirst.
[353] C.O.A., 1953, 3.
[354] V.I.A. Workbook, p159.
[355] C.O.A., 1803, 13.
[356] Ibid., 19.
[357] R.G.O. 6/166, 165 and 169.
[358] See Epilogue.
[359] V.I.A. Workbook, p162.
[360] Ibid., p163.

[361] C.O.A., 1854, 47.
[362] R.A.S., M.N., Vol. XXI, p106.
[363] V.I.A. Workbook, p167, p168.
[364] Ibid.
[365] R.G.O. 6/729, 808.
[366] R.A.S., Minutes of Council, Vol. V.
[367] R.A.S., M.N., Vol. XXV, p106.
[368] R.S. L.U.B., 3, 138.
[369] R.A.S. M.S.S., Add 24, 5.
[370] R.S., Phil. Trans., CX/vii, 646.
[371] R.G.O. 6/729, 825.
[372] V.I.A. Workbook, p69.
[373] R.G.O. 6/166, 34.
[374] Ibid., 68.
[375] U.A.V. 630, 2, 1858, 20th September.
[376] V.I.A. Workbook, p183.
[377] Ibid., p187.
[378] C.O.A., 1855, 26.
[379] R.G.O. 6/729, 812.
[380] C.O.A., 1856, 10.
[381] R.G.O. 6/731, 352.
[382] Ibid., 68.
[383] C.O.A. Workbook, 1856.
[384] R.G.O. 6/731, 363.
[385] Ibid., 371.
[386] Ibid., 365.
[387] R.A.S., Memoirs, Vol. XXV.
[388] R.A.S., M.N., Vol. XVII, p27, p28.
[389] See Epilogue.
[390] R.A.S., M.N., 17, 1857, p80-81.
[391] History of R.A.S., p118, p119.
[392] C.O.A., 1857, 12.
[393] Ibid., 14.
[394] Ibid., 21.
[395] R.G.O. 6/169, 208 foll.
[396] Ibid., 213.
[397] R.A.S., M.N., XVIII, p189.
[398] R.A.S., Minutes of Council, Vol. V.
[399] R.A.S. History, p113.
[400] Ibid., p114.
[401] R.G.O. 6/733, 286.
[402] Ibid., 293.
[403] Ibid., 308.
[404] Ibid., 308.
[405] R.G.O. 6/737, 321.
[406] J. W. Clark (1904) – *Endowments of the University of Cambridge*, p134.
[407] R.A.S. Library.
[408] V.I.A.

[409] Ibid., p21.
[410] Ibid., p27.
[411] Ibid., p31.
[412] Ibid., p38.
[413] *Reids Heirs*, Eleanor Mennim 1990, Chapter II.
[414] Ibid.
[415] See *Reids Heirs*, Eleanor Mennim 1990.
[416] R.G.O. 6/737, 327, 328.
[417] Ibid., 340.
[418] Ibid., 380.
[419] C.O.A., 1859, 5.
[420] R.G.O. 6/737, 405.
[421] C.O.A., 1860, 1.
[422] R.G.O. 6/738, 796.
[423] Ibid., 799.
[424] Ibid., 798.
[425] Dr D. W. Dewhirst, Personal Communication.
[426] See discussion in Chapter 16.
[427] *Reids Heirs*, Eleanor Mennim 1990, p122.
[428] Ibid.
[429] Ibid.
[430] Dictionary of British Watercolour Artists.
[431] V.I.A. Account Book.
[432] Mins. Proc., I.C.E., Vol. 25, 1865-66.
[433] *Reids Heirs*, Eleanor Mennim 1990.
[434] *A Farewell to Fleet Street*.
[435] Peatling Papers, London Borough of Sutton Heritage Department.

Index

Brunel, Isambard Kingdom, vii, 56, 79, 101, 115, 116, 130, 138, 168, 180, 226, 257
Brunel, Marc, 79
Brussels, 114, 126
Buenos Aires, 239
Building Acts, 64, 65
Butchers, Worshipful Company of, 16, 18, 27, 33
Buxton, Fowell, 118

CALCUTTA, 55, 67, 68, 101, 102, 179, 194, 195, 203, 214, 220, 271
Caldwell, William, 18
Cambridge
    Observatory, 71, 73, 92, 98, 102, 103-107, [104], 109, 114, 127, 128, 133, 137, 139-141, 143, 145, 149, 150, 156, 157, 159, 161, 162, 164, 166, 192, 213, 220, 228, 229, 241, 244, 248, 255
    Pembrooke College, 139-141, 143, 145, 152
    Town/University, 56, 57, 71, 73, 93, 105, 106, 109, 177, 241, 248, 253, 265
Cambridge, Massachusetts (see Bonditch), 157
Camden ('Gothic') Cottages, 60, 251, 259, 269
Camden Hill Observatory, 56, 85, 86, 92, 96, 97, 109, 111, 114, 141, 162
Camden Town, 60, 123, 203, 251, 259
Canals (see also Regent Canal), 7, 11, 18
Cape of Good Hope, 71, 92, 218, 229, 266
Carrington, Richard, 225, 244, 265
Carshalton (see also Bramble Haw), 187-191, 194, 195, 199, 206, 220, 229, 241, 242, 248, 252, 261, 265, 276
Cauchoix, Robert Aglaé, 85, 109, 239, 265
Ceylon, 102, 174, 180, 194, 215, 229, 242
Challis, Mrs, 111, 140, 152, 160, 161

Challis, Professor, 111, 127, 133, 137, 139, 140, 143, 152, 153, 157, 160, 161, 163, 166, 192, 213, 215, 223, 228, 229, 231, 239, 241, 244, 255, 258, 264
Chance Bros, 20, 145, 204
Chantry, Sir Francis, 124
Chapman, William, 18
Charlotte, Princess, 81
Charlton, 135, 156, 229, 252-254, 267, 269, 273, 274
Chartists, 159, 197, 202
Cholera, 98, 130, 202, 207, 208, 232
Cranch, Joseph, 157, 164
Christian Socialists, 101, 253
Christie, Sir William, 201
Christmas, 163, 169, 170, 258
Church of England (Anglican), 1, 2, 8, 13, 19, 23, 93, 94, 252, 253
Clothing, 43, 44, 61, 186, 187, 209
Clothworkers' Company, 32, 98, 111, 129
Cloudesley Estate, 59, 80, [81], 89
Coaching Inns, 28, 45, 79, 105, 160, 161
Coach travel, 6, 7, 18, 58, 79, 105, 132, 139, 140, 141, 157, 160, 161
Coffee houses, 16, 48, 51
Colby, Thomas, 49, 50, 51, 55, 68-70, 77, 100, 115, 137, 174, 176, 218, 226
Cole, Benjamin, 63, 123
Colebrook, Henry Thomas, 67
Collingwood, Mr, 223, 228
Collins, Samuel, 14
Comet, Donati's, 246, 248
Commons Preservation Society, 178
Constables, 82, 94
Cooper, Edward, 88, 107, 108, 265
Corn Laws, 41, 156, 159, 183, 197, 198, 261
Coronation – Queen Victoria, 139
Cracow, 70, 88, 92, 109, 115
Crimean War, 230-232, 235, 238, 240
Crystal Palace, 148, 210, 216, 228, 232, 233, 261
Cubitt, Lewis, 131

294

Morpeth family, 184, 185
Mudge, General William, 49, 50
Munich, 192, 193, 194, 202, 204, 228
Murray, Sir William Keith, 210

NAPOLEON, 21, 23, 27, 34
Napoleonic Wars, 19, 21, 27, 28, 34,
    40-42, 94, 159
Nelson, 23, 28, 136, 230
Newall, Sarah, 140, 145, 147, 148,
    163, 183, 206, 218, 228, 258
Newton, Sir Isaac, 63
New York, 138, 180, 181, 207
Nightingale, Florence, 240
Nonconformists, 8, 13, 93, 253, 266
Northumberland
    Duke of, 109, 150
    Telescope, 109, 127, 128, 133,
        140, 141, 143, 145, 149,
        160-162, 171
Norwood (South Metropolitan)
    Cemetery, 84, 148, 149, 163, 215,
        246, 259, [260]
Nutting, Beatrice, 258
Nutting, Henry, 43, 99, 184
Nutting, John, 43, 67, 109, 111, 119,
    124, 135, 141, 163, 184, 258, 268
Nutting, Margaret, 135, 258

OLD Bailey, 17, 82
Omnibus – Mr Shillibeer, 60, 129
Ordnance Survey, 49, 55, 69, 158,
    175, 207, 225
Orrery, 63
Orwell, SS, 171
Osbourne House, 202
Overland Route to India, 102, 179,
    247, 271
Oxford
    Movement, 93, 94, 253
    Observatory, 164, 210

PALMER, Henry Robinson, 116, 268
Paramatta (Sydney), 92, 241, 248
Paris, 116, 168, 169, 193, 201, 202,
    204
    Royal Observatory, 55, 71, 85

Parsons, William, 3rd Earl of Rosse,
    73, 74, 146, 163, 180, 223, 265
Pasley, Major General Sir Charles, 178
Pearson, Dr William, 75, 88
Peel, Sir Robert, 95, 159, 168, 253
Penny Cyclopaedia, 102, 212
Penstone, Thomas, 29, 30
Penton, Henry, 59, 93
Pentonville, 43, 99, 124, 175
Photography, 226, 227, 231, 241, 246
Playfair, William, 77, 87
Playford, 56, 146, 169, 171, 192, 195,
    201, 213, 248, 264
Police force, 17, 82, 95, 117, 159
Pond, John, 51, 53, 56, 88, 89, 109,
    112, 124, 126, 129, 139, 217, 218,
    264
Poor Law, 96, 117
Postal Service, 152, 153, 160
Priestley, Joseph, 5, 19, 23
Pritchard, Professor Charles, 265
Public Health Act, 208

QUAKERS – see Society of Friends

RAILWAY
    Brighton, 187
    Bristol and Exeter, 157
    Cambridge, 171, 173, 177, 192,
        213
    East India Company, 178, 194,
        195, 203, 214, 271
    General, 79, 115, 116, 123, 130,
        131, 157, 168, 169, 171-173,
        177, 178, 187, 193, 229, 248
    Great Western, 101, 115, 130, 168
    Greenwich, 131
    Mid-Kent (London, Chatham
        and Dover), 220, 275
    South-eastern, 116, 130, 169,
        173, 174, 177, 178, 226, 268,
        272
    Stockton and Darlington, 79
    Time, 218
Ramsden, Jesse, 30, 31, 33, 48, 53, 69,
    136, 157, 167, 239
Ransome and May, 245, 248

298

Emma (1829), 111, 245
Emma Victoria (1838), 136, 148
Francis Octavius (1808), 27, 45
Frederick (1831), 89, 99, 147,
168, 183, 228, 229, 267
Frederick Walter (1803), 27, 47,
48, 69, 88, 97, 98, 111,
114-117, 129, 130, 132, 141,
157, 161, 168-170, 173, 174,
177-179, 193-195, 199, 203,
214, 215, 218-220, [221], 228,
236, 247, 268, 270, 271, 272
Frederick Walter (1835), 116,
179, 195, 214, 215, 220, 252,
269, 271
George (1799), 26, 32, 46, 83,
111, 112, 114, 148, 154, 180,
213, 252
George (1833), 270
Georgina and Selina (1832), 112
Hannah Ann (Collins), 14, 24,
112
Henry, 26, 32, 42, 45, 60, 84,
111, 114, 135, 141, 148, 149,
152, 157, 170, 180, 199, 203,
229, 242, 252, 255, 258, 259,
267, 269
James (1710), 14, 16, 23, 24, 26,
112
James (1755), 16
James (1779), 23
James (1792), 23, 32, 33, 36, 42,
44-46, 58, 82, 83, 111, 112,
114, 129, 130, 170, 180, 213,
245, 272
James and Catherine (1822), 46
James (1828), 80, 98, 99, 131,
147, 151, 156, 165, 183, 191,
201, 213, 228, 229, 241-244,
247, 251-255, 257, 258, 264,
266, [267], 269, 272-274, 276
James (1862), 266
Jane (1751), 16, 18
Jane (1795), 24
Jane Ellen (1836), 269, 270
John (1761), 16
John (1798), 26, 32, 42, 45, 62,
83, 84, 99, 111, 114, 147, 154,
161, 170, 180, 270, 272, 273

Lorina Maria, 206, 215, 229, 259,
265, 269
Mary (1757), 16, 18
Mary (1836), 128, 145, 147, 168,
183, 191, 229, 254, 268, 269
Mary Ann (Ward), 111, 148, 170,
180, 269
Mary Matilda (1847), 245, 246,
259, 268
Mary Sophia (1845), 180
Sarah (1759), 16, 18, 23, 119
Sarah (Thompson 1767), 19, 24,
26, 46, 82-84, 112, 191
Sarah (1795), 24
Sarah (1819), 44, 111, 148, 245
Sarah (1826), 80, 98, 99, 147,
168, 183, 191, 229, 254, 258,
268, 269
Sophia (Davy), 83, 111, 136, 148,
180
Walter Hennell (1847), 125, 194,
199, 202, 215, 268
William (1640), 1, 13
William (1670), 1, 13
William (1715), 1, 14, 16, 18
William (1763), 1, 16-20, 23, 24,
26, 28, 30, 32, 33, 44-46, 50,
51, 78, 82-84, 112, 129, 272
William (1793) – see separate
list at end of main index
William (1817) 'Junior', 42, 44,
45, 78, 83, 89, 98, 111,
129-131, 146, 148, 152, 154,
161, 174, 176, 192, 199, 203,
213, 217, 223, 242, 245, 246,
255, 258, 271-273
William (1860), 266, 272
William Henry (1820), 44, 45, 82,
98, 99, 119, 128, 129, 139, 140,
143, 145-147, 152, 174, 180,
194, 215, 229, 242, 249, 258,
259, 266, 272
Smythe, General W. H., 90, [91], 194,
265
Society of Apothecaries, 184-186
Society for Diffusion of Useful
Knowledge, 75, 162, 212
Society of Friends ('Quakers'), 8, 14,
19, 24

William Simms (1793)